THE
YEATS READER

REVISED EDITION

A Portable Compendium
of Poetry, Drama, and Prose

EDITED BY Richard J. Finneran

Scribner Poetry

NEW YORK   LONDON   TORONTO   SYDNEY

SCRIBNER POETRY
SCRIBNER
1230 Avenue of the Americas
New York, NY 10020

SCRIBNER POETRY and design are trademarks of Macmillan Library Reference USA, Inc.,
used under license by Simon & Schuster, the publisher of this work.

For information about special discounts for bulk purchases,
please contact Simon & Schuster Special Sales:
1-800-465-6798 or business@simonandschuster.com

Designed by Jenny Dossin

Text set in Sabon

Manufactured in the United States of America

3   5   7   9   10   8   6   4   2

Library of Congress Cataloging-in-Publication Data
Yeats, W. B. (William Butler), 1865–1939
[Selections. 2002]
The Yeats reader : a portable compendium of poetry, drama, and prose /
edited by Richard J. Finneran.—Rev. ed.
p.   cm.
1. Ireland—Literary collections. I. Title
PR5902.F56 2002
821'.8—dc21   2002070670

ISBN 0-7432-3315-8
0-7432-2798-0 (Pbk)

ACKNOWLEDGMENTS

THIS REVISED EDITION includes fifty-seven additional poems and corrects some texts to accord with recently published volumes in the Scribner/Palgrave Collected Edition of the Works of W. B. Yeats. In addition, an Appendix offers the original versions of several poems, so that a reader can gain a sense of Yeats's constant process of revision (and not only of his early poetry). I am again indebted to Professor George Bornstein for his suggestions and to Sarah McGrath of Scribner for her support of the project.

Wildwood, Missouri   R.J.F.
15 March 2002

CONTENTS

Plays

[Dates and order follow *The Plays* (2001)]

Autobiographical Writings

Critical Writings

Prose Fiction

Appendix

Notes

PREFACE

THE REPUTATION of William Butler Yeats as one of the major writers in English of the twentieth century of course rests primarily on his poetry. But while it was the most central, poetry was only one of the many genres in which Yeats worked. The purpose of *The Yeats Reader* is to present a selection of his poems accompanied by a sampling of his other work. This material is not only a useful adjunct to an understanding of the poetry but also often a substantial achievement on its own terms.

Had Yeats not been first and foremost a poet, he doubtless would have been a dramatist. Indeed, in 1917 he confessed that "I need a theatre; I believe myself to be a dramatist; I desire to show events and not merely tell of them; . . . two of my best friends were won for me by my plays, and I seem to myself most alive at the moment when a room full of people share the one lofty emotion."[1] Likewise, in his speech accepting the Nobel Prize for Literature in 1923, Yeats suggested that "perhaps the English committees would never have sent you my name if I had written no plays, no dramatic criticism, if my lyric poetry had not a quality of speech practised upon the stage . . ."[2] In fact, from the end of the century forward, Yeats was very much a practicing dramatist, and many of his plays were significantly strengthened as a result of their first production, often at the Abbey Theatre in Dublin. The selection included here ranges from the early nationalistic *Cathleen ni Houlihan*, a collaboration with Lady Gregory which Yeats would point to when criticized for being insufficiently committed to the struggle against English rule in Ireland; to *At the Hawk's Well*, the first play showing the influence of the Japanese Noh drama to which he was introduced by Ezra Pound; to *The Words upon the Window-pane*, which closely follows the conventions of the drawing-room drama, only to undercut them by the introduction of the supernatural.

[1]Preface to *At the Hawk's Well* (1917), in *The Plays*, ed. David R. Clark and Rosalind E. Clark (New York: Scribner, 2001), p. 690. The friends were Lady Gregory and John Millington Synge.
[2]*The Bounty of Sweden* (1924), in *Autobiographies*, ed. William H. O'Donnell and Douglas N. Archibald (New York: Scribner, 1999), p. 410.

Both Yeats's poetry and plays were often derived from events in his personal life, the most famous being his nearly ceaseless pursuit of Maud Gonne for almost thirty years, from their encounter in London on 30 January 1889 to shortly before his marriage on 20 October 1917 to Bertha Georgie Hyde-Lees. He began to compose his autobiography proper shortly before he began his fiftieth year, and he continued it sporadically for the next two decades. Not wanting to compromise the privacy of those still living, he ends his narrative just after the start of the new century;[1] but some diaries and his account of the Nobel Prize offer glimpses of the later years. Moreover, a comparison of *Memoirs*, a draft of part of his autobiography, with the published version discloses what he chose not to disclose, as well as demonstrating that even in this supposedly most personal of genres, Yeats was at least as interested in the artistry of his work as in its factual accuracy.

Yeats also tried his hand at prose fiction. His third separate publication, *John Sherman and Dhoya* (1891), consisted of a realistic novelette and an heroic Irish tale, and the latter would provide the model for most of his later endeavors in the genre. His work ranges from fairy and folk tales, often collected with the assistance of Lady Gregory, to occult and esoteric stories such as "The Adoration of the Magi." Although Yeats's work in prose fiction was essentially completed in the early years of the century, he would resurrect some of its characters for both his poetry and his philosophical prose in his later years.

Indeed, there is a continual interchange between Yeats's creative work and his critical writings. In the early years he produced a considerable body of reviews and journalistic writings. By the turn of the century, however, his critical writings took on a more substantial form, with essays on such subjects as William Blake (one of his masters), "The Symbolism of Poetry," or the contemporary condition of the English and Irish stage. In 1918 he published *Per Amica Silentia Lunae,* a summary of his thinking to date on the relationship between the Self and the Anti-Self and between the Self and the World, particularly the archetypal repository of images on which

---

[1] As Yeats noted in the Preface to *The Trembling of the Veil,* "Except in one or two trivial details, where I have the warrant of old friendship, I have not, without permission, quoted conversation or described occurrence from the private life of named or recognizable living persons" (*Autobiographies,* p. 111).

the artist draws. But even before *Per Amica* was in print, his wife had begun the automatic writing and related psychical activities which provided the basis for *A Vision*, first published in 1925 and revised in 1937, Yeats's fundamental statement on such topics as the nature of human personality, the fate of the soul between lives, and the cyclical basis of history. In 1937 he composed three prefaces for the Scribner Edition, an unpublished seven-volume edition of his essential canon: of these, the Introduction to the first volume is a seminal statement of his objectives as a writer.

Whether within or across the various genres which Yeats essayed, arguably a fundamental characteristic is the refusal to be satisfied with what had been accomplished. Any published text was always available to be revised for its next printing, and often was. If a particular kind of writing had been—as he wrote in "What Then?"—"to perfection brought," such was only the occasion to search for a new style, a new consummation (it was not for want of a better title that the volume of poetry published a month before his seventy-third birthday was called simply *New Poems*). For much of his life Yeats was haunted by the specter of "Wordsworth withering into eighty years, honoured and empty-witted" (see page 408). Yeats would not reach eighty, but neither would his wits nor his imaginative powers diminish. Rather, his astonishing achievement may cause us to think that, as he wrote of the figure of the poet in the Introduction to the Scribner Edition, William Butler Yeats "has been re-born as an idea, something intended, complete. . . . He is part of his own phantasmagoria and we adore him because nature has grown intelligible, and by so doing a part of our creative power" (see page 422).

CHRONOLOGY

1865   William Butler Yeats born at Georgeville, Sandymount Avenue, Dublin, the first child of John Butler Yeats (JBY) and Susan Mary Pollexfen Yeats.

1866   JBY called to the Irish bar. Susan Mary Yeats (Lily) born.

1867   JBY gives up the law and moves to London to study art.

1868   Elizabeth Corbet Yeats (Lollie) born. Summer in Sligo.

1869   In Sligo from summer through December.

1870   Robert Corbet (Bobbie) Yeats born. Summer in Sligo.

1871   John Butler (Jack) Yeats born. Short holiday in Sligo in September.

1872   Family moves to Sligo in July.

1873   Robert Corbet Yeats dies.

1874   Family returns to London in October.

1875   Jane Grace Yeats born.

1876   Jane Grace Yeats dies. Summer in Sligo. Yeats joins his father in England in the autumn.

1877   Family moves to London. Yeats enters the Godolphin School, Hammersmith.

1881   Yeats leaves Godolphin School. Family moves to Dublin. Yeats enters the Erasmus Smith High School.

1883   Hears Oscar Wilde lecture in Dublin. Leaves Erasmus Smith High School.

1884   Attends the Metropolitan School of Art. Meets the writer George W. Russell, whose pen name was A.E.

1885   First poems published in the March issue of the *Dublin University Review*. First meeting of Dublin Hermetic Society. Meets Katharine Tynan.

1886   Leaves the Metropolitan School of Art. Attends lecture by and meets William Morris. *Mosada,* previously published in the *Dublin University Review,* issued as a pamphlet, Yeats's first separate publication.

1887   Family moves to London. Yeats meets Ernest Rhys, May Morris, Madame Blavatsky. Stays with his uncle George Pollexfen in Sligo August to November, thence to Dublin.

1888   Returns to London late January. Meets George Bernard Shaw and Lady Wilde. *Fairy and Folk Tales of the Irish Peasantry.* Joins Esoteric Section of Madame Blavatsky's Theosophical Society.

1889   *The Wanderings of Oisin and Other Poems.* Meets Maud Gonne on 30 January.

1890   Helps to found the Rhymers' Club. Joins the Order of the Golden Dawn, 7 March. Asked to resign from the Esoteric Section of the Theosophical Society.

1891   *Representative Irish Tales.* First of many marriage proposals to Maud Gonne, 3 August. *John Sherman and Dhoya.*

1892   *Irish Fairy Tales. The Countess Kathleen and Various Legends and Lyrics.*

1893   *The Works of William Blake,* co-edited with Edwin Ellis. *The Celtic Twilight.*

1894   *The Land of Heart's Desire* produced in London, March–April. Meets Olivia Shakespear and Lady Gregory.

1895   *A Book of Irish Verse. Poems.* Takes rooms with Arthur Symons in Fountain Court, the Temple.

1896   Moves to 18 Woburn Buildings in London. Liaison with Olivia Shakespear. Visits Aran Islands, summer. Meets John Millington Synge in Paris, December.

1897   End of liaison with Olivia Shakespear. *The Secret Rose. The Tables of the Law and The Adoration of the Magi.* To Coole Park to stay with Lady Gregory, July–November.

1899   *The Wind Among the Reeds. The Countess Cathleen* produced in Dublin, 8 May, the opening of the Irish Literary Theatre.

1900   Susan Pollexfen Yeats dies, 3 January.

1901   Visits Stratford, April. *Diarmuid and Grania,* a collaboration with George Moore, produced in Dublin, 21–23 October.

1902   Meets James Joyce. Dun Emer (later Cuala) Press established.

1903   Maud Gonne marries Major John MacBride, 21 February. *Ideas of Good and Evil. In the Seven Woods.* Leaves on American lecture tour, 4 November.

1904   Returns to London, March. *Where There Is Nothing* produced in London, 26–29 June. *On Baile's Strand* produced at the opening of the Abbey Theatre, Dublin, 27 December.

1905   Maud Gonne granted a separation from Major John MacBride. Abbey company on tour in England, November.

1906   Edits *The Poems of Spenser. Poems 1899–1905.*

1907   Disturbances over Synge's *The Playboy of the Western World,* January. To Italy with Lady Gregory and her son, Robert, May. JBY leaves for an Irish exhibition in New York, never to return, 21 December.

1908 Liaison with Mabel Dickinson. *Collected Works in Verse and Prose,* eight volumes.

1909 Death of Synge, 24 March.

1910 Granted Civil List pension of £150 per annum. *The Green Helmet and Other Poems.*

1911 Meets Ezra Pound. Accompanies the Abbey Players in America, September–October.

1912 Meets Rabindranath Tagore. *The Cutting of an Agate.*

1913 *Poems Written in Discouragement.* Rents Stone Cottage in Sussex, with Pound as secretary, November–January.

1914 American lecture tour, January–April. *Responsibilities: Poems and a Play.*

1915 At Stone Cottage with Ezra and Dorothy Pound, January–February. Hugh Lane drowned on the *Lusitania,* May. Refuses a knighthood, December.

1916 At Stone Cottage with Ezra and Dorothy Pound, January–March. *Reveries Over Childhood and Youth.* Private performance of *At the Hawk's Well,* 4 April. Easter Rebellion in Dublin, 24 April. Major John MacBride among leaders executed by the British, 3–12 May. Visits Maud Gonne in Normandy and for the last time proposes marriage, July–August.

1917 Purchases and names Thoor Ballylee, a Norman tower near Gort, County Galway, March. Visits Maud Gonne in Normandy; proposes to her daughter, Iseult, but is rejected, August. Proposes to Bertha Georgie Hyde-Lees and is accepted, September. Marries, 20 October; shortly thereafter George Yeats begins the automatic writing that will be the basis for *A Vision. The Wild Swans at Coole.*

1918 *Per Amica Silentia Lunae.* Moves to Oxford. Robert Gregory killed in action in Italy. Thoor Ballylee restored and used thereafter as a summer residence.

1919 *Two Plays for Dancers.* Anne Yeats born, 26 February. *The Player Queen* produced in London. Gives up 18 Woburn Buildings.

1920 American lecture tour, January–May.

1921 *Michael Robartes and the Dancer.* Michael Yeats born, 22 August. *Four Plays for Dancers. Four Years.*

1922 JBY dies in New York, 3 February. Returns to Dublin and becomes a Senator in the Irish Free State. *The Trembling of the Veil. Later Poems. Plays in Prose and Verse.*

1923 Wins Nobel Prize for Literature, November. *Plays and Contro-versies.*

1924 *Essays. The Cat and the Moon.*

1925 Visit to Sicily and Rome, January–February. *The Bounty of Swe-den. Early Poems and Stories. A Vision* (issued to subscribers 15 January 1926).

1926 *Estrangement. Autobiographies.*

1927 *October Blast.* To Algeciras, Seville, and Cannes, November.

1928 *The Tower. Sophocles' King Oedipus. The Death of Synge.* Resigns from Senate. To Rapallo for the winter, November.

1929 *A Packet for Ezra Pound. The Winding Stair.* Dangerously ill in Rapallo with Malta Fever, December to early 1930.

1930 Meets Walter de la Mare and Virginia Woolf.

1931 Honorary degree at Oxford. Arranges with Macmillan, London, for an Edition de Luxe.

1932 *Stories of Michael Robartes and His Friends.* Death of Lady Greg-ory, 22 May. Moves to Riversdale, Rathfarnam, Dublin. *Words for Music Perhaps.* American lecture tour, October–January 1933.

1933 *The Winding Stair and Other Poems. Collected Poems.*

1934 *Letters to the New Island.* Steinach rejuvenation operation in London, April. *Wheels and Butterflies. Collected Plays. The King of the Great Clock Tower.*

1935 Seventieth birthday celebrations, 13 June. Death of George W. Russell, A.E., 17 July. *A Full Moon in March. Dramatis Personae.* Arranges with Charles Scribner's Sons, New York, for the Dublin Edition.

1936 Seriously ill in Majorca, January. Edits *Oxford Book of Modern Verse.*

1937 Revised version of *A Vision. Essays, 1931–1936.* Writes Intro-ductions for the Scribner Edition.

1938 *The Herne's Egg. New Poems. Purgatory* produced at the Abbey Theatre, Dublin, 10 August. Death of Olivia Shakespear.

1939 Dies in the South of France, 28 January. *Last Poems and Two Plays. On the Boiler.*

1940 *Last Poems & Plays.*

1948 Body reinterred at Drumcliff, County Sligo, 17 September.

Poems

FROM Crossways

(1889)

The Song of the Happy Shepherd

The woods of Arcady are dead,
And over is their antique joy;
Of old the world on dreaming fed;
Grey Truth is now her painted toy;
Yet still she turns her restless head:
But O, sick children of the world,
Of all the many changing things
In dreary dancing past us whirled,
To the cracked tune that Chronos sings,
Words alone are certain good.   10
Where are now the warring kings,
Word be-mockers?—By the Rood
Where are now the warring kings?
An idle word is now their glory,
By the stammering schoolboy said,
Reading some entangled story:
The kings of the old time are dead;
The wandering earth herself may be
Only a sudden flaming word,
In clanging space a moment heard,   20
Troubling the endless reverie.

Then nowise worship dusty deeds,
Nor seek, for this is also sooth,
To hunger fiercely after truth,
Lest all thy toiling only breeds
New dreams, new dreams; there is no truth
Saving in thine own heart. Seek, then,
No learning from the starry men,

Who follow with the optic glass
30 The whirling ways of stars that pass—
Seek, then, for this is also sooth,
No word of theirs—the cold star-bane
Has cloven and rent their hearts in twain,
And dead is all their human truth.
Go gather by the humming sea
Some twisted, echo-harbouring shell,
And to its lips thy story tell,
And they thy comforters will be,
Rewarding in melodious guile
40 Thy fretful words a little while,
Till they shall singing fade in ruth
And die a pearly brotherhood;
For words alone are certain good:
Sing, then, for this is also sooth.

I must be gone: there is a grave
Where daffodil and lily wave,
And I would please the hapless faun,
Buried under the sleepy ground,
With mirthful songs before the dawn.
50 His shouting days with mirth were crowned;
And still I dream he treads the lawn,
Walking ghostly in the dew,
Pierced by my glad singing through,
My songs of old earth's dreamy youth:
But ah! she dreams not now; dream thou!
For fair are poppies on the brow:
Dream, dream, for this is also sooth.

The Sad Shepherd

There was a man whom Sorrow named his friend,
And he, of his high comrade Sorrow dreaming,
Went walking with slow steps along the gleaming
And humming sands, where windy surges wend:
And he called loudly to the stars to bend

From their pale thrones and comfort him, but they
Among themselves laugh on and sing alway:
And then the man whom Sorrow named his friend
Cried out, *Dim sea, hear my most piteous story!*
The sea swept on and cried her old cry still,　　　　10
Rolling along in dreams from hill to hill.
He fled the persecution of her glory
And, in a far-off, gentle valley stopping,
Cried all his story to the dewdrops glistening.
But naught they heard, for they are always listening,
The dewdrops, for the sound of their own dropping.
And then the man whom Sorrow named his friend
Sought once again the shore, and found a shell,
And thought, *I will my heavy story tell*
Till my own words, re-echoing, shall send　　　　20
Their sadness through a hollow, pearly heart;
And my own tale again for me shall sing,
And my own whispering words be comforting,
And lo! my ancient burden may depart.
Then he sang softly nigh the pearly rim;
But the sad dweller by the sea-ways lone
Changed all he sang to inarticulate moan
Among her wildering whirls, forgetting him.

The Cloak, the Boat, and the Shoes

'What do you make so fair and bright?'

'I make the cloak of Sorrow:
O lovely to see in all men's sight
Shall be the cloak of Sorrow,
In all men's sight.'

'What do you build with sails for flight?'

'I build a boat for Sorrow:
O swift on the seas all day and night
Saileth the rover Sorrow,
All day and night.'　　　　10

'What do you weave with wool so white?'

'I weave the shoes of Sorrow:
Soundless shall be the footfall light
In all men's ears of Sorrow,
Sudden and light.'

The Indian to his Love

The island dreams under the dawn
And great boughs drop tranquillity;
The peahens dance on a smooth lawn,
A parrot sways upon a tree,
Raging at his own image in the enamelled sea.

Here we will moor our lonely ship
And wander ever with woven hands,
Murmuring softly lip to lip,
Along the grass, along the sands,
10 Murmuring how far away are the unquiet lands:

How we alone of mortals are
Hid under quiet boughs apart,
While our love grows an Indian star,
A meteor of the burning heart,
One with the tide that gleams, the wings that gleam and dart,

The heavy boughs, the burnished dove
That moans and sighs a hundred days:
How when we die our shades will rove,
When eve has hushed the feathered ways,
20 With vapoury footsole by the water's drowsy blaze.

The Falling of the Leaves

Autumn is over the long leaves that love us,
And over the mice in the barley sheaves;
Yellow the leaves of the rowan above us,
And yellow the wet wild-strawberry leaves.

The hour of the waning of love has beset us,
And weary and worn are our sad souls now;
Let us part, ere the season of passion forget us,
With a kiss and a tear on thy drooping brow.

Ephemera

'Your eyes that once were never weary of mine
Are bowed in sorrow under pendulous lids,
Because our love is waning.'
　　　　　　　　　　And then she:
'Although our love is waning, let us stand
By the lone border of the lake once more,
Together in that hour of gentleness
When the poor tired child, Passion, falls asleep:
How far away the stars seem, and how far
Is our first kiss, and ah, how old my heart!'

Pensive they paced along the faded leaves,　　　　　10
While slowly he whose hand held hers replied:
'Passion has often worn our wandering hearts.'

The woods were round them, and the yellow leaves
Fell like faint meteors in the gloom, and once
A rabbit old and lame limped down the path;
Autumn was over him: and now they stood
On the lone border of the lake once more:
Turning, he saw that she had thrust dead leaves
Gathered in silence, dewy as her eyes,
In bosom and hair.　　　　　　　　　　　　　20
　　　　　　　　　'Ah, do not mourn,' he said,
'That we are tired, for other loves await us;
Hate on and love through unrepining hours.
Before us lies eternity; our souls
Are love, and a continual farewell.'

The Stolen Child

Where dips the rocky highland
Of Sleuth Wood in the lake,
There lies a leafy island
Where flapping herons wake
The drowsy water-rats;
There we've hid our faery vats,
Full of berries
And of reddest stolen cherries.
Come away, O human child!
To the waters and the wild
With a faery, hand in hand,
For the world's more full of weeping
than you can understand.

Where the wave of moonlight glosses
The dim grey sands with light,
Far off by furthest Rosses
We foot it all the night,
Weaving olden dances,
Mingling hands and mingling glances
Till the moon has taken flight;
To and fro we leap
And chase the frothy bubbles,
While the world is full of troubles
And is anxious in its sleep.
Come away, O human child!
To the waters and the wild
With a faery, hand in hand,
For the world's more full of weeping
than you can understand.

Where the wandering water gushes
From the hills above Glen-Car,
In pools among the rushes
That scarce could bathe a star,
We seek for slumbering trout
And whispering in their ears

Give them unquiet dreams;
Leaning softly out
From ferns that drop their tears
Over the young streams.
Come away, O human child!
To the waters and the wild
With a faery, hand in hand,   40
For the world's more full of weeping
  than you can understand.

Away with us he's going,
The solemn-eyed:
He'll hear no more the lowing
Of the calves on the warm hillside
Or the kettle on the hob
Sing peace into his breast,
Or see the brown mice bob
Round and round the oatmeal-chest.
For he comes, the human child,   50
To the waters and the wild
With a faery, hand in hand,
From a world more full of weeping
  than he can understand.

To an Isle in the Water

Shy one, shy one,
Shy one of my heart,
She moves in the firelight
Pensively apart.

She carries in the dishes,
And lays them in a row.
To an isle in the water
With her would I go.

She carries in the candles,
And lights the curtained room,   10
Shy in the doorway
And shy in the gloom;

And shy as a rabbit,
Helpful and shy.
To an isle in the water
With her would I fly.

Down by the Salley Gardens

Down by the salley gardens my love and I did meet;
She passed the salley gardens with little snow-white feet.
She bid me take love easy, as the leaves grow on the tree;
But I, being young and foolish, with her would not agree.

In a field by the river my love and I did stand,
And on my leaning shoulder she laid her snow-white hand.
She bid me take life easy, as the grass grows on the weirs;
But I was young and foolish, and now am full of tears.

The Meditation of the Old Fisherman

You waves, though you dance by my feet like children at play,
Though you glow and you glance, though you purr and you dart;
In the Junes that were warmer than these are, the waves were
    more gay,
When I was a boy with never a crack in my heart.

The herring are not in the tides as they were of old;
My sorrow! for many a creak gave the creel in the cart
That carried the take to Sligo town to be sold,
When I was a boy with never a crack in my heart.

And ah, you proud maiden, you are not so fair when his oar
Is heard on the water, as they were, the proud and apart,
Who paced in the eve by the nets on the pebbly shore,
When I was a boy with never a crack in my heart.

10

To the Rose upon the Rood of Time

Red Rose, proud Rose, sad Rose of all my days!
Come near me, while I sing the ancient ways:
Cuchulain battling with the bitter tide;
The Druid, grey, wood-nurtured, quiet-eyed,
Who cast round Fergus dreams, and ruin untold;
And thine own sadness, whereof stars, grown old
In dancing silver-sandalled on the sea,
Sing in their high and lonely melody.
Come near, that no more blinded by man's fate,
I find under the boughs of love and hate,   10
In all poor foolish things that live a day,
Eternal beauty wandering on her way.

Come near, come near, come near—Ah, leave me still
A little space for the rose-breath to fill!
Lest I no more hear common things that crave;
The weak worm hiding down in its small cave,
The field-mouse running by me in the grass,
And heavy mortal hopes that toil and pass;
But seek alone to hear the strange things said
By God to the bright hearts of those long dead,   20
And learn to chaunt a tongue men do not know.
Come near; I would, before my time to go,
Sing of old Eire and the ancient ways:
Red Rose, proud Rose, sad Rose of all my days.

Fergus and the Druid

Fergus. This whole day have I followed in the rocks,
    And you have changed and flowed from shape to shape,
    First as a raven on whose ancient wings
    Scarcely a feather lingered, then you seemed
    A weasel moving on from stone to stone,
    And now at last you wear a human shape,
    A thin grey man half lost in gathering night.

Druid. What would you, king of the proud Red Branch kings?

Fergus. This would I say, most wise of living souls:
10   Young subtle Conchubar sat close by me
    When I gave judgment, and his words were wise,
    And what to me was burden without end,
    To him seemed easy, so I laid the crown
    Upon his head to cast away my sorrow.

Druid. What would you, king of the proud Red Branch kings?

Fergus. A king and proud! and that is my despair.
    I feast amid my people on the hill,
    And pace the woods, and drive my chariot-wheels
    In the white border of the murmuring sea;
20   And still I feel the crown upon my head.

Druid. What would you, Fergus?

Fergus.   Be no more a king
    But learn the dreaming wisdom that is yours.

Druid. Look on my thin grey hair and hollow cheeks
    And on these hands that may not lift the sword,
    This body trembling like a wind-blown reed.
    No woman's loved me, no man sought my help.

Fergus. A king is but a foolish labourer
    Who wastes his blood to be another's dream.

Druid. Take, if you must, this little bag of dreams;
30   Unloose the cord, and they will wrap you round.

Fergus. I see my life go drifting like a river
    From change to change; I have been many things—
    A green drop in the surge, a gleam of light
    Upon a sword, a fir-tree on a hill,
    An old slave grinding at a heavy quern,
    A king sitting upon a chair of gold—
    And all these things were wonderful and great;
    But now I have grown nothing, knowing all.
    Ah! Druid, Druid, how great webs of sorrow
    Lay hidden in the small slate-coloured thing!   40

The Rose of the World

Who dreamed that beauty passes like a dream?
For these red lips, with all their mournful pride,
Mournful that no new wonder may betide,
Troy passed away in one high funeral gleam,
And Usna's children died.

We and the labouring world are passing by:
Amid men's souls, that waver and give place
Like the pale waters in their wintry race,
Under the passing stars, foam of the sky,
Lives on this lonely face.   10

Bow down, archangels, in your dim abode:
Before you were, or any hearts to beat,
Weary and kind one lingered by His seat;
He made the world to be a grassy road
Before her wandering feet.

The Lake Isle of Innisfree

I will arise and go now, and go to Innisfree,
And a small cabin build there, of clay and wattles made:
Nine bean-rows will I have there, a hive for the honey-bee,
And live alone in the bee-loud glade.

And I shall have some peace there, for peace comes dropping slow,
Dropping from the veils of the morning to where the cricket sings;
There midnight's all a glimmer, and noon a purple glow,
And evening full of the linnet's wings.

I will arise and go now, for always night and day
10   I hear lake water lapping with low sounds by the shore;
While I stand on the roadway, or on the pavements grey,
I hear it in the deep heart's core.

The Pity of Love

A pity beyond all telling
Is hid in the heart of love:
The folk who are buying and selling,
The clouds on their journey above,
The cold wet winds ever blowing,
And the shadowy hazel grove
Where mouse-grey waters are flowing,
Threaten the head that I love.

The Sorrow of Love

The brawling of a sparrow in the eaves,
The brilliant moon and all the milky sky,
And all that famous harmony of leaves,
Had blotted out man's image and his cry.

A girl arose that had red mournful lips
And seemed the greatness of the world in tears,
Doomed like Odysseus and the labouring ships
And proud as Priam murdered with his peers;

Arose, and on the instant clamorous eaves,
10   A climbing moon upon an empty sky,
And all that lamentation of the leaves,
Could but compose man's image and his cry.

When You are Old

When you are old and grey and full of sleep,
And nodding by the fire, take down this book,
And slowly read, and dream of the soft look
Your eyes had once, and of their shadows deep;

How many loved your moments of glad grace,
And loved your beauty with love false or true,
But one man loved the pilgrim soul in you,
And loved the sorrows of your changing face;

And bending down beside the glowing bars,
Murmur, a little sadly, how Love fled   10
And paced upon the mountains overhead
And hid his face amid a crowd of stars.

The White Birds

I would that we were, my beloved, white birds on the foam of the
    sea!
We tire of the flame of the meteor, before it can fade and flee;
And the flame of the blue star of twilight, hung low on the rim of
    the sky,
Has awaked in our hearts, my beloved, a sadness that may not
    die.

A weariness comes from those dreamers, dew-dabbled, the lily and
    rose;
Ah, dream not of them, my beloved, the flame of the meteor that
    goes,
Or the flame of the blue star that lingers hung low in the fall of
    the dew:
For I would we were changed to white birds on the wandering
    foam: I and you!

I am haunted by numberless islands, and many a Danaan shore,
Where Time would surely forget us, and Sorrow come near us no   10
    more;

Soon far from the rose and the lily and fret of the flames would we
  be,
Were we only white birds, my beloved, buoyed out on the foam of
  the sea!

Who goes with Fergus?

Who will go drive with Fergus now,
And pierce the deep wood's woven shade,
And dance upon the level shore?
Young man, lift up your russet brow,
And lift your tender eyelids, maid,
And brood on hopes and fear no more.

And no more turn aside and brood
Upon love's bitter mystery;
For Fergus rules the brazen cars,
10   And rules the shadows of the wood,
And the white breast of the dim sea
And all dishevelled wandering stars.

The Man who dreamed of Faeryland

He stood among a crowd at Drumahair;
His heart hung all upon a silken dress,
And he had known at last some tenderness,
Before earth took him to her stony care;
But when a man poured fish into a pile,
It seemed they raised their little silver heads,
And sang what gold morning or evening sheds
Upon a woven world-forgotten isle
Where people love beside the ravelled seas;
10   That Time can never mar a lover's vows
Under that woven changeless roof of boughs:
The singing shook him out of his new ease.

He wandered by the sands of Lissadell;
His mind ran all on money cares and fears,
And he had known at last some prudent years
Before they heaped his grave under the hill;
But while he passed before a plashy place,
A lug-worm with its grey and muddy mouth
Sang that somewhere to north or west or south
There dwelt a gay, exulting, gentle race   20
Under the golden or the silver skies;
That if a dancer stayed his hungry foot
It seemed the sun and moon were in the fruit:
And at that singing he was no more wise.

He mused beside the well of Scanavin,
He mused upon his mockers: without fail
His sudden vengeance were a country tale,
When earthy night had drunk his body in;
But one small knot-grass growing by the pool
Sang where—unnecessary cruel voice—   30
Old silence bids its chosen race rejoice,
Whatever ravelled waters rise and fall
Or stormy silver fret the gold of day,
And midnight there enfold them like a fleece
And lover there by lover be at peace.
The tale drove his fine angry mood away.

He slept under the hill of Lugnagall;
And might have known at last unhaunted sleep
Under that cold and vapour-turbaned steep,
Now that the earth had taken man and all: 40
Did not the worms that spired about his bones
Proclaim with that unwearied, reedy cry
That God has laid His fingers on the sky,
That from those fingers glittering summer runs
Upon the dancer by the dreamless wave.
Why should those lovers that no lovers miss
Dream, until God burn Nature with a kiss?
The man has found no comfort in the grave.

The Dedication to a Book of Stories selected from the Irish Novelists

There was a green branch hung with many a bell
When her own people ruled this tragic Eire;
And from its murmuring greenness, calm of Faery,
A Druid kindness, on all hearers fell.

It charmed away the merchant from his guile,
And turned the farmer's memory from his cattle,
And hushed in sleep the roaring ranks of battle:
And all grew friendly for a little while.

Ah, Exiles wandering over lands and seas,
And planning, plotting always that some morrow
May set a stone upon ancestral Sorrow!
I also bear a bell-branch full of ease.

I tore it from green boughs winds tore and tossed
Until the sap of summer had grown weary!
I tore it from the barren boughs of Eire,
That country where a man can be so crossed;

Can be so battered, badgered and destroyed
That he's a loveless man: gay bells bring laughter
That shakes a mouldering cobweb from the rafter;
And yet the saddest chimes are best enjoyed.

Gay bells or sad, they bring you memories
Of half-forgotten innocent old places:
We and our bitterness have left no traces
On Munster grass and Connemara skies.

The Lamentation of the Old Pensioner

Although I shelter from the rain
Under a broken tree,
My chair was nearest to the fire
In every company

That talked of love or politics,
Ere Time transfigured me.

Though lads are making pikes again
For some conspiracy,
And crazy rascals rage their fill
At human tyranny;   10
My contemplations are of Time
That has transfigured me.

There's not a woman turns her face
Upon a broken tree,
And yet the beauties that I loved
Are in my memory;
I spit into the face of Time
That has transfigured me.

The Two Trees

Beloved, gaze in thine own heart,
The holy tree is growing there;
From joy the holy branches start,
And all the trembling flowers they bear.
The changing colours of its fruit
Have dowered the stars with merry light;
The surety of its hidden root
Has planted quiet in the night;
The shaking of its leafy head
Has given the waves their melody,   10
And made my lips and music wed,
Murmuring a wizard song for thee.
There the Loves a circle go,
The flaming circle of our days,
Gyring, spiring to and fro
In those great ignorant leafy ways;
Remembering all that shaken hair
And how the wingèd sandals dart,
Thine eyes grow full of tender care:
Beloved, gaze in thine own heart.   20

Gaze no more in the bitter glass
The demons, with their subtle guile,
Lift up before us when they pass,
Or only gaze a little while;
For there a fatal image grows
That the stormy night receives,
Roots half hidden under snows,
Broken boughs and blackened leaves.
For all things turn to barrenness
In the dim glass the demons hold,
The glass of outer weariness,
Made when God slept in times of old.
There, through the broken branches, go
The ravens of unresting thought;
Flying, crying, to and fro,
Cruel claw and hungry throat,
Or else they stand and sniff the wind,
And shake their ragged wings; alas!
Thy tender eyes grow all unkind:
Gaze no more in the bitter glass.

To Ireland in the Coming Times

Know, that I would accounted be
True brother of a company
That sang, to sweeten Ireland's wrong,
Ballad and story, rann and song;
Nor be I any less of them,
Because the red-rose-bordered hem
Of her, whose history began
Before God made the angelic clan,
Trails all about the written page.
When Time began to rant and rage
The measure of her flying feet
Made Ireland's heart begin to beat;
And Time bade all his candles flare
To light a measure here and there;

And may the thoughts of Ireland brood
Upon a measured quietude.

Nor may I less be counted one
With Davis, Mangan, Ferguson,
Because, to him who ponders well,
My rhymes more than their rhyming tell   20
Of things discovered in the deep,
Where only body's laid asleep.
For the elemental creatures go
About my table to and fro,
That hurry from unmeasured mind
To rant and rage in flood and wind;
Yet he who treads in measured ways
May surely barter gaze for gaze.
Man ever journeys on with them
After the red-rose-bordered hem.   30
Ah, faeries, dancing under the moon,
A Druid land, a Druid tune!

While still I may, I write for you
The love I lived, the dream I knew.
From our birthday, until we die,
Is but the winking of an eye;
And we, our singing and our love,
What measurer Time has lit above,
And all benighted things that go
About my table to and fro,   40
Are passing on to where may be,
In truth's consuming ecstasy,
No place for love and dream at all;
For God goes by with white footfall.
I cast my heart into my rhymes,
That you, in the dim coming times,
May know how my heart went with them
After the red-rose-bordered hem.

FROM The Wind Among the Reeds

(1899)

The Hosting of the Sidhe

The host is riding from Knocknarea
And over the grave of Clooth-na-Bare;
Caoilte tossing his burning hair,
And Niamh calling *Away, come away:*
Empty your heart of its mortal dream.
The winds awaken, the leaves whirl round,
Our cheeks are pale, our hair is unbound,
Our breasts are heaving, our eyes are agleam,
Our arms are waving, our lips are apart;
And if any gaze on our rushing band,
We come between him and the deed of his hand,
We come between him and the hope of his heart.
The host is rushing 'twixt night and day,
And where is there hope or deed as fair?
Caoilte tossing his burning hair,
And Niamh calling *Away, come away.*

10

The Lover tells of the Rose in his Heart

All things uncomely and broken, all things worn out and old,
The cry of a child by the roadway, the creak of a lumbering cart,
The heavy steps of the ploughman, splashing the wintry mould,
Are wronging your image that blossoms a rose in the deeps of my
    heart.

The wrong of unshapely things is a wrong too great to be told;
I hunger to build them anew and sit on a green knoll apart,
With the earth and the sky and the water, re-made, like a casket of
    gold
For my dreams of your image that blossoms a rose in the deeps of
    my heart.

The Fish

Although you hide in the ebb and flow
Of the pale tide when the moon has set,
The people of coming days will know
About the casting out of my net,
And how you have leaped times out of mind
Over the little silver cords,
And think that you were hard and unkind,
And blame you with many bitter words.

The Song of Wandering Aengus

I went out to the hazel wood,
Because a fire was in my head,
And cut and peeled a hazel wand,
And hooked a berry to a thread;
And when white moths were on the wing,
And moth-like stars were flickering out,
I dropped the berry in a stream
And caught a little silver trout.

When I had laid it on the floor
I went to blow the fire aflame,
But something rustled on the floor,
And some one called me by my name:
It had become a glimmering girl
With apple blossom in her hair
Who called me by my name and ran
And faded through the brightening air.

10

Though I am old with wandering
Through hollow lands and hilly lands,
I will find out where she has gone,
20   And kiss her lips and take her hands;
And walk among long dappled grass,
And pluck till time and times are done
The silver apples of the moon,
The golden apples of the sun.

The Lover mourns for the Loss of Love

Pale brows, still hands and dim hair,
I had a beautiful friend
And dreamed that the old despair
Would end in love in the end:
She looked in my heart one day
And saw your image was there;
She has gone weeping away.

He reproves the Curlew

O curlew, cry no more in the air,
Or only to the water in the West;
Because your crying brings to my mind
Passion-dimmed eyes and long heavy hair
That was shaken out over my breast:
There is enough evil in the crying of wind.

He remembers forgotten Beauty

When my arms wrap you round I press
My heart upon the loveliness
That has long faded from the world;
The jewelled crowns that kings have hurled
In shadowy pools, when armies fled;
The love-tales wrought with silken thread

By dreaming ladies upon cloth
That has made fat the murderous moth;
The roses that of old time were
Woven by ladies in their hair,   10
The dew-cold lilies ladies bore
Through many a sacred corridor
Where such grey clouds of incense rose
That only God's eyes did not close:
For that pale breast and lingering hand
Come from a more dream-heavy land,
A more dream-heavy hour than this;
And when you sigh from kiss to kiss
I hear white Beauty sighing, too,
For hours when all must fade like dew,   20
But flame on flame, and deep on deep,
Throne over throne where in half sleep,
Their swords upon their iron knees,
Brood her high lonely mysteries.

A Poet to his Beloved

I bring you with reverent hands
The books of my numberless dreams,
White woman that passion has worn
As the tide wears the dove-grey sands,
And with heart more old than the horn
That is brimmed from the pale fire of time:
White woman with numberless dreams,
I bring you my passionate rhyme.

He gives his Beloved certain Rhymes

Fasten your hair with a golden pin,
And bind up every wandering tress;
I bade my heart build these poor rhymes:
It worked at them, day out, day in,
Building a sorrowful loveliness
Out of the battles of old times.

You need but lift a pearl-pale hand,
And bind up your long hair and sigh;
And all men's hearts must burn and beat;
10   And candle-like foam on the dim sand,
And stars climbing the dew-dropping sky,
Live but to light your passing feet.

To his Heart, bidding it have no Fear

Be you still, be you still, trembling heart;
Remember the wisdom out of the old days:
Him who trembles before the flame and the flood,
And the winds that blow through the starry ways,
Let the starry winds and the flame and the flood
Cover over and hide, for he has no part
With the lonely, majestical multitude.

The Cap and Bells

The jester walked in the garden:
The garden had fallen still;
He bade his soul rise upward
And stand on her window-sill.

It rose in a straight blue garment,
When owls began to call:
It had grown wise-tongued by thinking
Of a quiet and light footfall;

But the young queen would not listen;
10   She rose in her pale night-gown;
She drew in the heavy casement
And pushed the latches down.

He bade his heart go to her,
When the owls called out no more;
In a red and quivering garment
It sang to her through the door.

It had grown sweet-tongued by dreaming
Of a flutter of flower-like hair;
But she took up her fan from the table
And waved it off on the air.　　　　　　　　20

'I have cap and bells,' he pondered,
'I will send them to her and die';
And when the morning whitened
He left them where she went by.

She laid them upon her bosom,
Under a cloud of her hair,
And her red lips sang them a love-song
Till stars grew out of the air.

She opened her door and her window,
And the heart and the soul came through,　　　30
To her right hand came the red one,
To her left hand came the blue.

They set up a noise like crickets,
A chattering wise and sweet,
And her hair was a folded flower
And the quiet of love in her feet.

He hears the Cry of the Sedge

I wander by the edge
Of this desolate lake
Where wind cries in the sedge:
Until the axle break
That keeps the stars in their round,
And hands hurl in the deep
The banners of East and West,
And the girdle of light is unbound,
Your breast will not lie by the breast
Of your beloved in sleep.　　　　　　　　10

He thinks of Those who have spoken Evil of his Beloved

Half close your eyelids, loosen your hair,
And dream about the great and their pride;
They have spoken against you everywhere,
But weigh this song with the great and their pride;
I made it out of a mouthful of air,
Their children's children shall say they have lied.

The Lover pleads with his Friend for Old Friends

Though you are in your shining days,
Voices among the crowd
And new friends busy with your praise,
Be not unkind or proud,
But think about old friends the most:
Time's bitter flood will rise,
Your beauty perish and be lost
For all eyes but these eyes.

He wishes his Beloved were Dead

Were you but lying cold and dead,
And lights were paling out of the West,
You would come hither, and bend your head,
And I would lay my head on your breast;
And you would murmur tender words,
Forgiving me, because you were dead:
Nor would you rise and hasten away,
Though you have the will of the wild birds,
But know your hair was bound and wound
About the stars and moon and sun:
O would, beloved, that you lay

10

Under the dock-leaves in the ground,
While lights were paling one by one.

He wishes for the Cloths of Heaven

Had I the heavens' embroidered cloths,
Enwrought with golden and silver light,
The blue and the dim and the dark cloths
Of night and light and the half-light,
I would spread the cloths under your feet:
But I, being poor, have only my dreams;
I have spread my dreams under your feet;
Tread softly because you tread on my dreams.

FROM In the Seven Woods

(1903)

In the Seven Woods

I have heard the pigeons of the Seven Woods
Make their faint thunder, and the garden bees
Hum in the lime-tree flowers; and put away
The unavailing outcries and the old bitterness
That empty the heart. I have forgot awhile
Tara uprooted, and new commonness
Upon the throne and crying about the streets
And hanging its paper flowers from post to post,
Because it is alone of all things happy.
10   I am contented, for I know that Quiet
Wanders laughing and eating her wild heart
Among pigeons and bees, while that Great Archer,
Who but awaits His hour to shoot, still hangs
A cloudy quiver over Pairc-na-lee.

August 1902

The Arrow

I thought of your beauty, and this arrow,
Made out of a wild thought, is in my marrow.
There's no man may look upon her, no man,
As when newly grown to be a woman,
Tall and noble but with face and bosom
Delicate in colour as apple blossom.
This beauty's kinder, yet for a reason
I could weep that the old is out of season.

The Folly of being Comforted

One that is ever kind said yesterday:
'Your well-belovèd's hair has threads of grey,
And little shadows come about her eyes;
Time can but make it easier to be wise
Though now it seems impossible, and so
All that you need is patience.'
                              Heart cries, 'No,
I have not a crumb of comfort, not a grain.
Time can but make her beauty over again:
Because of that great nobleness of hers
The fire that stirs about her, when she stirs,   10
Burns but more clearly. O she had not these ways
When all the wild summer was in her gaze.'

O heart! O heart! if she'd but turn her head,
You'd know the folly of being comforted.

Never give all the Heart

Never give all the heart, for love
Will hardly seem worth thinking of
To passionate women if it seem
Certain, and they never dream
That it fades out from kiss to kiss;
For everything that's lovely is
But a brief, dreamy, kind delight.
O never give the heart outright,
For they, for all smooth lips can say,
Have given their hearts up to the play.   20
And who could play it well enough
If deaf and dumb and blind with love?
He that made this knows all the cost,
For he gave all his heart and lost.

Adam's Curse

We sat together at one summer's end,
That beautiful mild woman, your close friend,
And you and I, and talked of poetry.
I said, 'A line will take us hours maybe;
Yet if it does not seem a moment's thought,
Our stitching and unstitching has been naught.
Better go down upon your marrow-bones
And scrub a kitchen pavement, or break stones
Like an old pauper, in all kinds of weather;
For to articulate sweet sounds together
Is to work harder than all these, and yet
Be thought an idler by the noisy set
Of bankers, schoolmasters, and clergymen
The martyrs call the world.'

                              And thereupon
That beautiful mild woman for whose sake
There's many a one shall find out all heartache
On finding that her voice is sweet and low
Replied, 'To be born woman is to know—
Although they do not talk of it at school—
That we must labour to be beautiful.'

I said, 'It's certain there is no fine thing
Since Adam's fall but needs much labouring.
There have been lovers who thought love should be
So much compounded of high courtesy
That they would sigh and quote with learned looks
Precedents out of beautiful old books;
Yet now it seems an idle trade enough.'

We sat grown quiet at the name of love;
We saw the last embers of daylight die,
And in the trembling blue-green of the sky
A moon, worn as if it had been a shell
Washed by time's waters as they rose and fell
About the stars and broke in days and years.

I had a thought for no one's but your ears:
That you were beautiful, and that I strove
To love you in the old high way of love;
That it had all seemed happy, and yet we'd grown
As weary-hearted as that hollow moon.

Red Hanrahan's Song about Ireland

The old brown thorn-trees break in two high over Cummen Strand,
Under a bitter black wind that blows from the left hand;
Our courage breaks like an old tree in a black wind and dies,
But we have hidden in our hearts the flame out of the eyes
Of Cathleen, the daughter of Houlihan.

The wind has bundled up the clouds high over Knocknarea,
And thrown the thunder on the stones for all that Maeve can say.
Angers that are like noisy clouds have set our hearts abeat;
But we have all bent low and low and kissed the quiet feet
Of Cathleen, the daughter of Houlihan.   10

The yellow pool has overflowed high up on Clooth-na-Bare,
For the wet winds are blowing out of the clinging air;
Like heavy flooded waters our bodies and our blood;
But purer than a tall candle before the Holy Rood
Is Cathleen, the daughter of Houlihan.

The Old Men admiring Themselves in the Water

I heard the old, old men say,
'Everything alters,
And one by one we drop away.'
They had hands like claws, and their knees
Were twisted like the old thorn-trees
By the waters.
I heard the old, old men say,
'All that's beautiful drifts away
Like the waters.'

O do not Love Too Long

Sweetheart, do not love too long:
I loved long and long,
And grew to be out of fashion
Like an old song.

All through the years of our youth
Neither could have known
Their own thought from the other's,
We were so much at one.

But O, in a minute she changed—
O do not love too long,
Or you will grow out of fashion
Like an old song.

His Dream

I swayed upon the gaudy stern
The butt-end of a steering-oar,
And saw wherever I could turn
A crowd upon a shore.

And though I would have hushed the crowd,
There was no mother's son but said,
'What is the figure in a shroud
Upon a gaudy bed?'

And after running at the brim
Cried out upon that thing beneath   10
—It had such dignity of limb—
By the sweet name of Death.

Though I'd my finger on my lip,
What could I but take up the song?
And running crowd and gaudy ship
Cried out the whole night long,

Crying amid the glittering sea,
Naming it with ecstatic breath,
Because it had such dignity,
By the sweet name of Death.   20

A Woman Homer sung

If any man drew near
When I was young,
I thought, 'He holds her dear,'
And shook with hate and fear.
But O! 'twas bitter wrong
If he could pass her by
With an indifferent eye.

Whereon I wrote and wrought,
And now, being grey,
10   I dream that I have brought
To such a pitch my thought
That coming time can say,
'He shadowed in a glass
What thing her body was.'

For she had fiery blood
When I was young,
And trod so sweetly proud
As 'twere upon a cloud,
A woman Homer sung,
20   That life and letters seem
But an heroic dream.

Words

I had this thought a while ago,
'My darling cannot understand
What I have done, or what would do
In this blind bitter land.'

And I grew weary of the sun
Until my thoughts cleared up again,
Remembering that the best I have done
Was done to make it plain;

That every year I have cried, 'At length
10   My darling understands it all,

Because I have come into my strength,
And words obey my call';

That had she done so who can say
What would have shaken from the sieve?
I might have thrown poor words away
And been content to live.

No Second Troy

Why should I blame her that she filled my days
With misery, or that she would of late
Have taught to ignorant men most violent ways,
Or hurled the little streets upon the great,
Had they but courage equal to desire?
What could have made her peaceful with a mind
That nobleness made simple as a fire,
With beauty like a tightened bow, a kind
That is not natural in an age like this,
Being high and solitary and most stern?   10
Why, what could she have done, being what she is?
Was there another Troy for her to burn?

Reconciliation

Some may have blamed you that you took away
The verses that could move them on the day
When, the ears being deafened, the sight of the eyes blind
With lightning, you went from me, and I could find
Nothing to make a song about but kings,
Helmets, and swords, and half-forgotten things
That were like memories of you—but now
We'll out, for the world lives as long ago;
And while we're in our laughing, weeping fit,
Hurl helmets, crowns, and swords into the pit.   10
But, dear, cling close to me; since you were gone,
My barren thoughts have chilled me to the bone.

The Fascination of What's Difficult

The fascination of what's difficult
Has dried the sap out of my veins, and rent
Spontaneous joy and natural content
Out of my heart. There's something ails our colt
That must, as if it had not holy blood
Nor on Olympus leaped from cloud to cloud,
Shiver under the lash, strain, sweat and jolt
As though it dragged road metal. My curse on plays
That have to be set up in fifty ways,
On the day's war with every knave and dolt,
Theatre business, management of men.
I swear before the dawn comes round again
I'll find the stable and pull out the bolt.

10

A Drinking Song

Wine comes in at the mouth
And love comes in at the eye;
That's all we shall know for truth
Before we grow old and die.
I lift the glass to my mouth,
I look at you, and I sigh.

The Coming of Wisdom with Time

Though leaves are many, the root is one;
Through all the lying days of my youth
I swayed my leaves and flowers in the sun;
Now I may wither into the truth.

On hearing that the Students of our New University have joined the Agitation against Immoral Literature

Where, where but here have Pride and Truth,
That long to give themselves for wage,
To shake their wicked sides at youth
Restraining reckless middle-age?

To a Poet, who would have me Praise certain Bad Poets, Imitators of His and Mine

You say, as I have often given tongue
In praise of what another's said or sung,
'Twere politic to do the like by these;
But was there ever dog that praised his fleas?

The Mask

'Put off that mask of burning gold
With emerald eyes.'
'O no, my dear, you make so bold
To find if hearts be wild and wise,
And yet not cold.'

'I would but find what's there to find,
Love or deceit.'
'It was the mask engaged your mind,
And after set your heart to beat,
Not what's behind.'

'But lest you are my enemy,
I must enquire.'
'O no, my dear, let all that be;
What matter, so there is but fire
In you, in me?'

Upon a House shaken by the Land Agitation

How should the world be luckier if this house,
Where passion and precision have been one
Time out of mind, became too ruinous
To breed the lidless eye that loves the sun?
And the sweet laughing eagle thoughts that grow
Where wings have memory of wings, and all
That comes of the best knit to the best? Although
Mean roof-trees were the sturdier for its fall,
How should their luck run high enough to reach
10   The gifts that govern men, and after these
To gradual Time's last gift, a written speech
Wrought of high laughter, loveliness and ease?

All Things can tempt Me

All things can tempt me from this craft of verse:
One time it was a woman's face, or worse—
The seeming needs of my fool-driven land;
Now nothing but comes readier to the hand
Than this accustomed toil. When I was young,
I had not given a penny for a song
Did not the poet sing it with such airs
That one believed he had a sword upstairs;
Yet would be now, could I but have my wish,
10   Colder and dumber and deafer than a fish.

Brown Penny

I whispered, 'I am too young,'
And then, 'I am old enough';
Wherefore I threw a penny
To find out if I might love.
'Go and love, go and love, young man,
If the lady be young and fair.'

Ah, penny, brown penny, brown penny,
I am looped in the loops of her hair.

And the penny sang up in my face,
'There is nobody wise enough
To find out all that is in it,
For he would be thinking of love
That is looped in the loops of her hair,
Till the loops of time had run.'
Ah, penny, brown penny, brown penny.
One cannot begin it too soon.

[Introductory Rhymes]

Pardon, old fathers, if you still remain
Somewhere in ear-shot for the story's end,
Old Dublin merchant 'free of the ten and four'
Or trading out of Galway into Spain;
Old country scholar, Robert Emmet's friend,
A hundred-year-old memory to the poor;
Merchant and scholar who have left me blood
That has not passed through any huckster's loin,
Soldiers that gave, whatever die was cast:
10 *A Butler or an Armstrong that withstood*
Beside the brackish waters of the Boyne
James and his Irish when the Dutchman crossed;
Old merchant skipper that leaped overboard
After a ragged hat in Biscay Bay;
You most of all, silent and fierce old man,
Because the daily spectacle that stirred
My fancy, and set my boyish lips to say,
'Only the wasteful virtues earn the sun';
Pardon that for a barren passion's sake,
20 *Although I have come close on forty-nine,*
I have no child, I have nothing but a book,
Nothing but that to prove your blood and mine.

January 1914

To a Wealthy Man who promised a second Subscription to the Dublin Municipal Gallery if it were proved the People wanted Pictures

You gave, but will not give again
Until enough of Paudeen's pence
By Biddy's halfpennies have lain
To be 'some sort of evidence,'
Before you'll put your guineas down,
That things it were a pride to give
Are what the blind and ignorant town
Imagines best to make it thrive.
What cared Duke Ercole, that bid
His mummers to the market-place,   10
What th' onion-sellers thought or did
So that his Plautus set the pace
For the Italian comedies?
And Guidobaldo, when he made
That grammar school of courtesies
Where wit and beauty learned their trade
Upon Urbino's windy hill,
Had sent no runners to and fro
That he might learn the shepherds' will.
And when they drove out Cosimo,   20
Indifferent how the rancour ran,
He gave the hours they had set free
To Michelozzo's latest plan
For the San Marco Library,
Whence turbulent Italy should draw
Delight in Art whose end is peace,
In logic and in natural law
By sucking at the dugs of Greece.

Your open hand but shows our loss,
For he knew better how to live.   30
Let Paudeens play at pitch and toss,
Look up in the sun's eye and give

What the exultant heart calls good
That some new day may breed the best
Because you gave, not what they would,
But the right twigs for an eagle's nest!

December 1912

September 1913

What need you, being come to sense,
But fumble in a greasy till
And add the halfpence to the pence
And prayer to shivering prayer, until
You have dried the marrow from the bone;
For men were born to pray and save:
Romantic Ireland's dead and gone,
It's with O'Leary in the grave.

Yet they were of a different kind,
The names that stilled your childish play,
They have gone about the world like wind,
But little time had they to pray
For whom the hangman's rope was spun,
And what, God help us, could they save?
Romantic Ireland's dead and gone,
It's with O'Leary in the grave.

Was it for this the wild geese spread
The grey wing upon every tide;
For this that all that blood was shed,
For this Edward Fitzgerald died,
And Robert Emmet and Wolfe Tone,
All that delirium of the brave?
Romantic Ireland's dead and gone,
It's with O'Leary in the grave.

Yet could we turn the years again,
And call those exiles as they were
In all their loneliness and pain,
You'd cry, 'Some woman's yellow hair

Has maddened every mother's son':
They weighed so lightly what they gave. 30
But let them be, they're dead and gone,
They're with O'Leary in the grave.

To a Friend whose Work has come to Nothing

Now all the truth is out,
Be secret and take defeat
From any brazen throat,
For how can you compete,
Being honour bred, with one
Who, were it proved he lies,
Were neither shamed in his own
Nor in his neighbours' eyes?
Bred to a harder thing
Than Triumph, turn away 10
And like a laughing string
Whereon mad fingers play
Amid a place of stone,
Be secret and exult,
Because of all things known
That is most difficult.

Paudeen

Indignant at the fumbling wits, the obscure spite
Of our old Paudeen in his shop, I stumbled blind
Among the stones and thorn-trees, under morning light;
Until a curlew cried and in the luminous wind
A curlew answered; and suddenly thereupon I thought
That on the lonely height where all are in God's eye,
There cannot be, confusion of our sound forgot,
A single soul that lacks a sweet crystalline cry.

When Helen lived

We have cried in our despair
That men desert,
For some trivial affair
Or noisy, insolent sport,
Beauty that we have won
From bitterest hours;
Yet we, had we walked within
Those topless towers
Where Helen walked with her boy,
Had given but as the rest
Of the men and women of Troy,
A word and a jest.

10

On Those that hated
'The Playboy of the Western World,' 1907

Once, when midnight smote the air,
Eunuchs ran through Hell and met
On every crowded street to stare
Upon great Juan riding by:
Even like these to rail and sweat
Staring upon his sinewy thigh.

The Three Beggars

'Though to my feathers in the wet,
I have stood here from break of day,
I have not found a thing to eat,
For only rubbish comes my way.
Am I to live on lebeen-lone?'
Muttered the old crane of Gort.
'For all my pains on lebeen-lone?'

King Guaire walked amid his court
The palace-yard and river-side
And there to three old beggars said,   10
'You that have wandered far and wide
Can ravel out what's in my head.
Do men who least desire get most,
Or get the most who most desire?'
A beggar said, 'They get the most
Whom man or devil cannot tire,
And what could make their muscles taut
Unless desire had made them so?'
But Guaire laughed with secret thought,
'If that be true as it seems true,   20
One of you three is a rich man,
For he shall have a thousand pounds
Who is first asleep, if but he can
Sleep before the third noon sounds.'
And thereon, merry as a bird
With his old thoughts, King Guaire went
From river-side and palace-yard
And left them to their argument.
'And if I win,' one beggar said,
'Though I am old I shall persuade   30
A pretty girl to share my bed';
The second: 'I shall learn a trade';
The third: 'I'll hurry to the course
Among the other gentlemen,
And lay it all upon a horse';
The second: 'I have thought again:
A farmer has more dignity.'
One to another sighed and cried:
The exorbitant dreams of beggary,
That idleness had borne to pride,   40
Sang through their teeth from noon to noon;
And when the second twilight brought
The frenzy of the beggars' moon
None closed his blood-shot eyes but sought
To keep his fellows from their sleep;

All shouted till their anger grew
And they were whirling in a heap.

They mauled and bit the whole night through;
They mauled and bit till the day shone;
50   They mauled and bit through all that day
And till another night had gone,
Or if they made a moment's stay
They sat upon their heels to rail,
And when old Guaire came and stood
Before the three to end this tale,
They were commingling lice and blood.
'Time's up,' he cried, and all the three
With blood-shot eyes upon him stared.
'Time's up,' he cried, and all the three
60   Fell down upon the dust and snored.

'Maybe I shall be lucky yet,
Now they are silent,' said the crane.
'Though to my feathers in the wet
I've stood as I were made of stone
And seen the rubbish run about,
It's certain there are trout somewhere
And maybe I shall take a trout
If but I do not seem to care.'

Beggar to Beggar cried

'Time to put off the world and go somewhere
And find my health again in the sea air,'
Beggar to beggar cried, being frenzy-struck,
'And make my soul before my pate is bare.'

'And get a comfortable wife and house
To rid me of the devil in my shoes,'
Beggar to beggar cried, being frenzy-struck,
'And the worse devil that is between my thighs.'

'And though I'd marry with a comely lass,
10   She need not be too comely—let it pass,'

Beggar to beggar cried, being frenzy-struck,
'But there's a devil in a looking-glass.'

'Nor should she be too rich, because the rich
Are driven by wealth as beggars by the itch,'
Beggar to beggar cried, being frenzy-struck,
'And cannot have a humorous happy speech.'

'And there I'll grow respected at my ease,
And hear amid the garden's nightly peace,'
Beggar to beggar cried, being frenzy-struck,
'The wind-blown clamour of the barnacle-geese.' 20

I. The Witch

Toil and grow rich,
What's that but to lie
With a foul witch
And after, drained dry,
To be brought
To the chamber where
Lies one long sought
With despair?

II. The Peacock

What's riches to him
That has made a great peacock
With the pride of his eye?
The wind-beaten, stone-grey,
And desolate Three Rock
Would nourish his whim.
Live he or die
Amid wet rocks and heather,
His ghost will be gay
Adding feather to feather 10
For the pride of his eye.

I. To a Child dancing in the Wind

Dance there upon the shore;
What need have you to care
For wind or water's roar?
And tumble out your hair
That the salt drops have wet;
Being young you have not known
The fool's triumph, nor yet
Love lost as soon as won,
Nor the best labourer dead
10   And all the sheaves to bind.
What need have you to dread
The monstrous crying of wind?

II. Two Years Later

Has no one said those daring
Kind eyes should be more learn'd?
Or warned you how despairing
The moths are when they are burned?
I could have warned you; but you are young,
So we speak a different tongue.

O you will take whatever's offered
And dream that all the world's a friend,
Suffer as your mother suffered,
10   Be as broken in the end.
But I am old and you are young,
And I speak a barbarous tongue.

A Memory of Youth

The moments passed as at a play;
I had the wisdom love brings forth;
I had my share of mother-wit,
And yet for all that I could say,
And though I had her praise for it,
A cloud blown from the cut-throat north
Suddenly hid Love's moon away.

Believing every word I said,
I praised her body and her mind
Till pride had made her eyes grow bright,   10
And pleasure made her cheeks grow red,
And vanity her footfall light,
Yet we, for all that praise, could find
Nothing but darkness overhead.

We sat as silent as a stone,
We knew, though she'd not said a word,
That even the best of love must die,
And had been savagely undone
Were it not that Love upon the cry
Of a most ridiculous little bird   20
Tore from the clouds his marvellous moon.

Fallen Majesty

Although crowds gathered once if she but showed her face,
And even old men's eyes grew dim, this hand alone,
Like some last courtier at a gypsy camping-place
Babbling of fallen majesty, records what's gone.

The lineaments, a heart that laughter has made sweet,
These, these remain, but I record what's gone. A crowd
Will gather, and not know it walks the very street
Whereon a thing once walked that seemed a burning cloud.

Friends

Now must I these three praise—
Three women that have wrought
What joy is in my days:
One because no thought,
Nor those unpassing cares,
No, not in these fifteen
Many-times-troubled years,
Could ever come between
Mind and delighted mind;
And one because her hand
Had strength that could unbind
What none can understand,
What none can have and thrive,
Youth's dreamy load, till she
So changed me that I live
Labouring in ecstasy.
And what of her that took
All till my youth was gone
With scarce a pitying look?
How could I praise that one?
When day begins to break
I count my good and bad,
Being wakeful for her sake,
Remembering what she had,
What eagle look still shows,
While up from my heart's root
So great a sweetness flows
I shake from head to foot.

The Cold Heaven

Suddenly I saw the cold and rook-delighting heaven
That seemed as though ice burned and was but the more ice,
And thereupon imagination and heart were driven
So wild that every casual thought of that and this

Vanished, and left but memories, that should be out of season
With the hot blood of youth, of love crossed long ago;
And I took all the blame out of all sense and reason,
Until I cried and trembled and rocked to and fro,
Riddled with light. Ah! when the ghost begins to quicken,
Confusion of the death-bed over, is it sent   10
Out naked on the roads, as the books say, and stricken
By the injustice of the skies for punishment?

That the Night come

She lived in storm and strife,
Her soul had such desire
For what proud death may bring
That it could not endure
The common good of life,
But lived as 'twere a king
That packed his marriage day
With banneret and pennon,
Trumpet and kettledrum,
And the outrageous cannon,   10
To bundle time away
That the night come.

The Magi

Now as at all times I can see in the mind's eye,
In their stiff, painted clothes, the pale unsatisfied ones
Appear and disappear in the blue depth of the sky
With all their ancient faces like rain-beaten stones,
And all their helms of silver hovering side by side,
And all their eyes still fixed, hoping to find once more,
Being by Calvary's turbulence unsatisfied,
The uncontrollable mystery on the bestial floor.

The Dolls

A doll in the doll-maker's house
Looks at the cradle and bawls:
'That is an insult to us.'
But the oldest of all the dolls,
Who had seen, being kept for show,
Generations of his sort,
Out-screams the whole shelf: 'Although
There's not a man can report
Evil of this place,
10   The man and the woman bring
Hither, to our disgrace,
A noisy and filthy thing.'
Hearing him groan and stretch
The doll-maker's wife is aware
Her husband has heard the wretch,
And crouched by the arm of his chair,
She murmurs into his ear,
Head upon shoulder leant:
'My dear, my dear, O dear,
20   It was an accident.'

A Coat

I made my song a coat
Covered with embroideries
Out of old mythologies
From heel to throat;
But the fools caught it,
Wore it in the world's eyes
As though they'd wrought it.
Song, let them take it,
For there's more enterprise
10   In walking naked.

[Closing Rhyme]

While I, from that reed-throated whisperer
Who comes at need, although not now as once
A clear articulation in the air,
But inwardly, surmise companions
Beyond the fling of the dull ass's hoof,
—Ben Jonson's phrase—and find when June is come
At Kyle-na-no under that ancient roof
A sterner conscience and a friendlier home,
I can forgive even that wrong of wrongs,
Those undreamt accidents that have made me   10
—Seeing that Fame has perished this long while,
Being but a part of ancient ceremony—
Notorious, till all my priceless things
Are but a post the passing dogs defile.

FROM *The Wild Swans at Coole*

(1917)

The Wild Swans at Coole

The trees are in their autumn beauty,
The woodland paths are dry,
Under the October twilight the water
Mirrors a still sky;
Upon the brimming water among the stones
Are nine-and-fifty swans.

The nineteenth autumn has come upon me
Since I first made my count;
I saw, before I had well finished,
All suddenly mount
And scatter wheeling in great broken rings
Upon their clamorous wings.

I have looked upon those brilliant creatures,
And now my heart is sore.
All's changed since I, hearing at twilight,
The first time on this shore,
The bell-beat of their wings above my head,
Trod with a lighter tread.

Unwearied still, lover by lover,
They paddle in the cold
Companionable streams or climb the air;
Their hearts have not grown old;
Passion or conquest, wander where they will,
Attend upon them still.

But now they drift on the still water,
Mysterious, beautiful;
Among what rushes will they build,
By what lake's edge or pool
Delight men's eyes when I awake some day
To find they have flown away?   30

In Memory of Major Robert Gregory

I

Now that we're almost settled in our house
I'll name the friends that cannot sup with us
Beside a fire of turf in th' ancient tower,
And having talked to some late hour
Climb up the narrow winding stair to bed:
Discoverers of forgotten truth
Or mere companions of my youth,
All, all are in my thoughts to-night being dead.

II

Always we'd have the new friend meet the old
And we are hurt if either friend seem cold,   10
And there is salt to lengthen out the smart
In the affections of our heart,
And quarrels are blown up upon that head;
But not a friend that I would bring
This night can set us quarrelling,
For all that come into my mind are dead.

III

Lionel Johnson comes the first to mind,
That loved his learning better than mankind,
Though courteous to the worst; much falling he
Brooded upon sanctity   20
Till all his Greek and Latin learning seemed
A long blast upon the horn that brought
A little nearer to his thought
A measureless consummation that he dreamed.

IV

And that enquiring man John Synge comes next,
That dying chose the living world for text
And never could have rested in the tomb
But that, long travelling, he had come
Towards nightfall upon certain set apart
30   In a most desolate stony place,
Towards nightfall upon a race
Passionate and simple like his heart.

V

And then I think of old George Pollexfen,
In muscular youth well known to Mayo men
For horsemanship at meets or at racecourses,
That could have shown how pure-bred horses
And solid men, for all their passion, live
But as the outrageous stars incline
By opposition, square and trine;
40   Having grown sluggish and contemplative.

VI

They were my close companions many a year,
A portion of my mind and life, as it were,
And now their breathless faces seem to look
Out of some old picture-book;
I am accustomed to their lack of breath,
But not that my dear friend's dear son,
Our Sidney and our perfect man,
Could share in that discourtesy of death.

VII

For all things the delighted eye now sees
50   Were loved by him; the old storm-broken trees
That cast their shadows upon road and bridge;
The tower set on the stream's edge;
The ford where drinking cattle make a stir
Nightly, and startled by that sound

The water-hen must change her ground;
He might have been your heartiest welcomer.

VIII

When with the Galway foxhounds he would ride
From Castle Taylor to the Roxborough side
Or Esserkelly plain, few kept his pace;
At Mooneen he had leaped a place   60
So perilous that half the astonished meet
Had shut their eyes; and where was it
He rode a race without a bit?
And yet his mind outran the horses' feet.

IX

We dreamed that a great painter had been born
To cold Clare rock and Galway rock and thorn,
To that stern colour and that delicate line
That are our secret discipline
Wherein the gazing heart doubles her might.
Soldier, scholar, horseman, he,   70
And yet he had the intensity
To have published all to be a world's delight.

X

What other could so well have counselled us
In all lovely intricacies of a house
As he that practised or that understood
All work in metal or in wood,
In moulded plaster or in carven stone?
Soldier, scholar, horseman, he,
And all he did done perfectly
As though he had but that one trade alone.   80

XI

Some burn damp faggots, others may consume
The entire combustible world in one small room
As though dried straw, and if we turn about

The bare chimney is gone black out
Because the work had finished in that flare.
Soldier, scholar, horseman, he,
As 'twere all life's epitome.
What made us dream that he could comb grey hair?

XII

I had thought, seeing how bitter is that wind
90   That shakes the shutter, to have brought to mind
All those that manhood tried, or childhood loved
Or boyish intellect approved,
With some appropriate commentary on each;
Until imagination brought
A fitter welcome; but a thought
Of that late death took all my heart for speech.

An Irish Airman foresees his Death

I know that I shall meet my fate
Somewhere among the clouds above;
Those that I fight I do not hate,
Those that I guard I do not love;
My country is Kiltartan Cross,
My countrymen Kiltartan's poor,
No likely end could bring them loss
Or leave them happier than before.
Nor law, nor duty bade me fight,
10   Nor public men, nor cheering crowds,
A lonely impulse of delight
Drove to this tumult in the clouds;
I balanced all, brought all to mind,
The years to come seemed waste of breath,
A waste of breath the years behind
In balance with this life, this death.

Men improve with the Years

I am worn out with dreams;
A weather-worn, marble triton
Among the streams;
And all day long I look
Upon this lady's beauty
As though I had found in a book
A pictured beauty,
Pleased to have filled the eyes
Or the discerning ears,
Delighted to be but wise,   10
For men improve with the years;
And yet, and yet,
Is this my dream, or the truth?
O would that we had met
When I had my burning youth!
But I grow old among dreams,
A weather-worn, marble triton
Among the streams.

The Living Beauty

I bade, because the wick and oil are spent
And frozen are the channels of the blood,
My discontented heart to draw content
From beauty that is cast out of a mould
In bronze, or that in dazzling marble appears,
Appears, but when we have gone is gone again,
Being more indifferent to our solitude
Than 'twere an apparition. O heart, we are old;
The living beauty is for younger men:
We cannot pay its tribute of wild tears.   10

A Song

I thought no more was needed
Youth to prolong
Than dumb-bell and foil
To keep the body young.
*O who could have foretold
That the heart grows old?*

Though I have many words,
What woman's satisfied,
I am no longer faint
Because at her side?
*O who could have foretold
That the heart grows old?*

I have not lost desire
But the heart that I had;
I thought 'twould burn my body
Laid on the death-bed,
*For who could have foretold
That the heart grows old?*

The Scholars

Bald heads forgetful of their sins,
Old, learned, respectable bald heads
Edit and annotate the lines
That young men, tossing on their beds,
Rhymed out in love's despair
To flatter beauty's ignorant ear.

All shuffle there; all cough in ink;
All wear the carpet with their shoes;
All think what other people think;
All know the man their neighbour knows.
Lord, what would they say
Did their Catullus walk that way?

Lines written in Dejection

When have I last looked on
The round green eyes and the long wavering bodies
Of the dark leopards of the moon?
All the wild witches, those most noble ladies,
For all their broom-sticks and their tears,
Their angry tears, are gone.
The holy centaurs of the hills are vanished;
I have nothing but the embittered sun;
Banished heroic mother moon and vanished,
And now that I have come to fifty years   10
I must endure the timid sun.

On Woman

May God be praised for woman
That gives up all her mind,
A man may find in no man
A friendship of her kind
That covers all he has brought
As with her flesh and bone,
Nor quarrels with a thought
Because it is not her own.

Though pedantry denies,
It's plain the Bible means   10
That Solomon grew wise
While talking with his queens,
Yet never could, although
They say he counted grass,
Count all the praises due
When Sheba was his lass,
When she the iron wrought, or
When from the smithy fire
It shuddered in the water:
Harshness of their desire   20
That made them stretch and yawn,

Pleasure that comes with sleep,
Shudder that made them one.
What else He give or keep
God grant me—no, not here,
For I am not so bold
To hope a thing so dear
Now I am growing old,
But when, if the tale's true,
30   The Pestle of the moon
That pounds up all anew
Brings me to birth again—
To find what once I had
And know what once I have known,
Until I am driven mad,
Sleep driven from my bed,
By tenderness and care,
Pity, an aching head,
Gnashing of teeth, despair;
40   And all because of some one
Perverse creature of chance,
And live like Solomon
That Sheba led a dance.

The Fisherman

Although I can see him still,
The freckled man who goes
To a grey place on a hill
In grey Connemara clothes
At dawn to cast his flies,
It's long since I began
To call up to the eyes
This wise and simple man.
All day I'd looked in the face
10   What I had hoped 'twould be
To write for my own race
And the reality;
The living men that I hate,

The dead man that I loved,
The craven man in his seat,
The insolent unreproved,
And no knave brought to book
Who has won a drunken cheer,
The witty man and his joke
Aimed at the commonest ear,   20
The clever man who cries
The catch-cries of the clown,
The beating down of the wise
And great Art beaten down.

Maybe a twelvemonth since
Suddenly I began,
In scorn of this audience,
Imagining a man,
And his sun-freckled face,
And grey Connemara cloth,   30
Climbing up to a place
Where stone is dark under froth,
And the down-turn of his wrist
When the flies drop in the stream;
A man who does not exist,
A man who is but a dream;
And cried, 'Before I am old
I shall have written him one
Poem maybe as cold
And passionate as the dawn.'   40

Memory

One had a lovely face,
And two or three had charm,
But charm and face were in vain
Because the mountain grass
Cannot but keep the form
Where the mountain hare has lain.

The People

'What have I earned for all that work,' I said,
'For all that I have done at my own charge?
The daily spite of this unmannerly town,
Where who has served the most is most defamed,
The reputation of his lifetime lost
Between the night and morning. I might have lived,
And you know well how great the longing has been,
Where every day my footfall should have lit
In the green shadow of Ferrara wall;
Or climbed among the images of the past—
The unperturbed and courtly images—
Evening and morning, the steep street of Urbino
To where the duchess and her people talked
The stately midnight through until they stood
In their great window looking at the dawn;
I might have had no friend that could not mix
Courtesy and passion into one like those
That saw the wicks grow yellow in the dawn;
I might have used the one substantial right
My trade allows: chosen my company,
And chosen what scenery had pleased me best.'
Thereon my phoenix answered in reproof,
'The drunkards, pilferers of public funds,
All the dishonest crowd I had driven away,
When my luck changed and they dared meet my face,
Crawled from obscurity, and set upon me
Those I had served and some that I had fed;
Yet never have I, now nor any time,
Complained of the people.'

                                    All I could reply
Was: 'You, that have not lived in thought but deed,
Can have the purity of a natural force,
But I, whose virtues are the definitions
Of the analytic mind, can neither close
The eye of the mind nor keep my tongue from speech.'

And yet, because my heart leaped at her words,
I was abashed, and now they come to mind
After nine years, I sink my head abashed.

Broken Dreams

There is grey in your hair.
Young men no longer suddenly catch their breath
When you are passing;
But maybe some old gaffer mutters a blessing
Because it was your prayer
Recovered him upon the bed of death.
For your sole sake—that all heart's ache have known,
And given to others all heart's ache,
From meagre girlhood's putting on
Burdensome beauty—for your sole sake   10
Heaven has put away the stroke of her doom,
So great her portion in that peace you make
By merely walking in a room.

Your beauty can but leave among us
Vague memories, nothing but memories.
A young man when the old men are done talking
Will say to an old man, 'Tell me of that lady
The poet stubborn with his passion sang us
When age might well have chilled his blood.'

Vague memories, nothing but memories,   20
But in the grave all, all, shall be renewed.
The certainty that I shall see that lady
Leaning or standing or walking
In the first loveliness of womanhood,
And with the fervour of my youthful eyes,
Has set me muttering like a fool.

You are more beautiful than any one,
And yet your body had a flaw:
Your small hands were not beautiful,
And I am afraid that you will run   30

And paddle to the wrist
In that mysterious, always brimming lake
Where those that have obeyed the holy law
Paddle and are perfect. Leave unchanged
The hands that I have kissed,
For old sake's sake.

The last stroke of midnight dies.
All day in the one chair
From dream to dream and rhyme to rhyme I have ranged
In rambling talk with an image of air:
Vague memories, nothing but memories.

40

A Deep-sworn Vow

Others because you did not keep
That deep-sworn vow have been friends of mine;
Yet always when I look death in the face,
When I clamber to the heights of sleep,
Or when I grow excited with wine,
Suddenly I meet your face.

The Balloon of the Mind

Hands, do what you're bid:
Bring the balloon of the mind
That bellies and drags in the wind
Into its narrow shed.

On being asked for a War Poem

I think it better that in times like these
A poet's mouth be silent, for in truth
We have no gift to set a statesman right;
He has had enough of meddling who can please
A young girl in the indolence of her youth,
Or an old man upon a winter's night.

Ego Dominus Tuus

Hic. On the grey sand beside the shallow stream
   Under your old wind-beaten tower, where still
   A lamp burns on beside the open book
   That Michael Robartes left, you walk in the moon
   And though you have passed the best of life still trace,
   Enthralled by the unconquerable delusion,
   Magical shapes.

Ille.   By the help of an image
   I call to my own opposite, summon all
   That I have handled least, least looked upon.

Hic. And I would find myself and not an image.   10

Ille. That is our modern hope and by its light
   We have lit upon the gentle, sensitive mind
   And lost the old nonchalance of the hand;
   Whether we have chosen chisel, pen or brush,
   We are but critics, or but half create,
   Timid, entangled, empty and abashed,
   Lacking the countenance of our friends.

Hic.   And yet
   The chief imagination of Christendom,
   Dante Alighieri, so utterly found himself
   That he has made that hollow face of his   20
   More plain to the mind's eye than any face
   But that of Christ.

Ille.   And did he find himself
   Or was the hunger that had made it hollow
   A hunger for the apple on the bough
   Most out of reach? and is that spectral image
   The man that Lapo and that Guido knew?
   I think he fashioned from his opposite
   An image that might have been a stony face
   Staring upon a Bedouin's horse-hair roof
   From doored and windowed cliff, or half upturned   30

Among the coarse grass and the camel-dung.
He set his chisel to the hardest stone.
Being mocked by Guido for his lecherous life,
Derided and deriding, driven out
To climb that stair and eat that bitter bread,
He found the unpersuadable justice, he found
The most exalted lady loved by a man.

Hic. Yet surely there are men who have made their art
    Out of no tragic war, lovers of life,
40   Impulsive men that look for happiness
    And sing when they have found it.

    Ille.   No, not sing,
    For those that love the world serve it in action,
    Grow rich, popular and full of influence,
    And should they paint or write, still it is action:
    The struggle of the fly in marmalade.
    The rhetorician would deceive his neighbours,
    The sentimentalist himself; while art
    Is but a vision of reality.
    What portion in the world can the artist have
50   Who has awakened from the common dream
    But dissipation and despair?

Hic.   And yet
    No one denies to Keats love of the world;
    Remember his deliberate happiness.

Ille. His art is happy, but who knows his mind?
    I see a schoolboy when I think of him,
    With face and nose pressed to a sweet-shop window,
    For certainly he sank into his grave
    His senses and his heart unsatisfied,
    And made—being poor, ailing and ignorant,
60   Shut out from all the luxury of the world,
    The coarse-bred son of a livery-stable keeper—
    Luxuriant song.

Hic.   Why should you leave the lamp
    Burning alone beside an open book,

And trace these characters upon the sands?
A style is found by sedentary toil
And by the imitation of great masters.

Ille. Because I seek an image, not a book.
 Those men that in their writings are most wise
 Own nothing but their blind, stupefied hearts.
 I call to the mysterious one who yet   70
 Shall walk the wet sands by the edge of the stream
 And look most like me, being indeed my double,
 And prove of all imaginable things
 The most unlike, being my anti-self,
 And standing by these characters disclose
 All that I seek; and whisper it as though
 He were afraid the birds, who cry aloud
 Their momentary cries before it is dawn,
 Would carry it away to blasphemous men.

The Double Vision of Michael Robartes

I

On the grey rock of Cashel the mind's eye
Has called up the cold spirits that are born
When the old moon is vanished from the sky
And the new still hides her horn.

Under blank eyes and fingers never still
The particular is pounded till it is man.
When had I my own will?
O not since life began.

Constrained, arraigned, baffled, bent and unbent
By these wire-jointed jaws and limbs of wood,   10
Themselves obedient,
Knowing not evil and good;

Obedient to some hidden magical breath.
They do not even feel, so abstract are they,
So dead beyond our death,
Triumph that we obey.

II

On the grey rock of Cashel I suddenly saw
A Sphinx with woman breast and lion paw,
A Buddha, hand at rest,
20   Hand lifted up that blest;

And right between these two a girl at play
That, it may be, had danced her life away,
For now being dead it seemed
That she of dancing dreamed.

Although I saw it all in the mind's eye
There can be nothing solider till I die;
I saw by the moon's light
Now at its fifteenth night.

One lashed her tail; her eyes lit by the moon
30   Gazed upon all things known, all things unknown,
In triumph of intellect
With motionless head erect.

That other's moonlit eyeballs never moved,
Being fixed on all things loved, all things unloved,
Yet little peace he had,
For those that love are sad.

O little did they care who danced between,
And little she by whom her dance was seen
So she had outdanced thought.
40   Body perfection brought,

For what but eye and ear silence the mind
With the minute particulars of mankind?
Mind moved yet seemed to stop
As 'twere a spinning-top.

In contemplation had those three so wrought
Upon a moment, and so stretched it out
That they, time overthrown,
Were dead yet flesh and bone.

III

I knew that I had seen, had seen at last
That girl my unremembering nights hold fast 50
Or else my dreams that fly
If I should rub an eye,

And yet in flying fling into my meat
A crazy juice that makes the pulses beat
As though I had been undone
By Homer's Paragon

Who never gave the burning town a thought;
To such a pitch of folly I am brought,
Being caught between the pull
Of the dark moon and the full, 60

The commonness of thought and images
That have the frenzy of our western seas.
Thereon I made my moan,
And after kissed a stone,

And after that arranged it in a song
Seeing that I, ignorant for so long,
Had been rewarded thus
In Cormac's ruined house.

Michael Robartes and the Dancer

(1921)

Michael Robartes and the Dancer

He. Opinion is not worth a rush;
   In this altar-piece the knight,
   Who grips his long spear so to push
   That dragon through the fading light,
   Loved the lady; and it's plain
   The half-dead dragon was her thought,
   That every morning rose again
   And dug its claws and shrieked and fought.
   Could the impossible come to pass
10   She would have time to turn her eyes,
   Her lover thought, upon the glass
   And on the instant would grow wise.

She. You mean they argued.

He.   Put it so;
   But bear in mind your lover's wage
   Is what your looking-glass can show,
   And that he will turn green with rage
   At all that is not pictured there.

She. May I not put myself to college?

He. Go pluck Athena by the hair;
20   For what mere book can grant a knowledge
   With an impassioned gravity
   Appropriate to that beating breast,

That vigorous thigh, that dreaming eye?
And may the devil take the rest.

She. And must no beautiful woman be
Learned like a man?

He.   Paul Veronese
And all his sacred company
Imagined bodies all their days
By the lagoon you love so much,
For proud, soft, ceremonious proof   30
That all must come to sight and touch;
While Michael Angelo's Sistine roof,
His 'Morning' and his 'Night' disclose
How sinew that has been pulled tight,
Or it may be loosened in repose,
Can rule by supernatural right
Yet be but sinew.

She.   I have heard said
There is great danger in the body.

He. Did God in portioning wine and bread
Give man His thought or His mere body?   40

She. My wretched dragon is perplexed.

He. I have principles to prove me right.
It follows from this Latin text
That blest souls are not composite,
And that all beautiful women may
Live in uncomposite blessedness,
And lead us to the like—if they
Will banish every thought, unless
The lineaments that please their view
When the long looking-glass is full,   50
Even from the foot-sole think it too.

She. They say such different things at school.

Easter, 1916

I have met them at close of day
Coming with vivid faces
From counter or desk among grey
Eighteenth-century houses.
I have passed with a nod of the head
Or polite meaningless words,
Or have lingered awhile and said
Polite meaningless words,
And thought before I had done
Of a mocking tale or a gibe
To please a companion
Around the fire at the club,
Being certain that they and I
But lived where motley is worn:
All changed, changed utterly:
A terrible beauty is born.

That woman's days were spent
In ignorant good-will,
Her nights in argument
Until her voice grew shrill.
What voice more sweet than hers
When, young and beautiful,
She rode to harriers?
This man had kept a school
And rode our wingèd horse;
This other his helper and friend
Was coming into his force;
He might have won fame in the end,
So sensitive his nature seemed,
So daring and sweet his thought.
This other man I had dreamed
A drunken, vainglorious lout.
He had done most bitter wrong
To some who are near my heart,
Yet I number him in the song;

He, too, has resigned his part
In the casual comedy;
He, too, has been changed in his turn,
Transformed utterly:
A terrible beauty is born.   40

Hearts with one purpose alone
Through summer and winter seem
Enchanted to a stone
To trouble the living stream.
The horse that comes from the road,
The rider, the birds that range
From cloud to tumbling cloud,
Minute by minute they change;
A shadow of cloud on the stream
Changes minute by minute;   50
A horse-hoof slides on the brim,
And a horse plashes within it;
The long-legged moor-hens dive,
And hens to moor-cocks call;
Minute by minute they live:
The stone's in the midst of all.

Too long a sacrifice
Can make a stone of the heart.
O when may it suffice?
That is Heaven's part, our part   60
To murmur name upon name,
As a mother names her child
When sleep at last has come
On limbs that had run wild.
What is it but nightfall?
No, no, not night but death;
Was it needless death after all?
For England may keep faith
For all that is done and said.
We know their dream; enough   70
To know they dreamed and are dead;
And what if excess of love
Bewildered them till they died?

I write it out in a verse—
MacDonagh and MacBride
And Connolly and Pearse
Now and in time to be,
Wherever green is worn,
Are changed, changed utterly:
80   A terrible beauty is born.

September 25, 1916

Sixteen Dead Men

O but we talked at large before
The sixteen men were shot,
But who can talk of give and take,
What should be and what not
While those dead men are loitering there
To stir the boiling pot?

You say that we should still the land
Till Germany's overcome;
But who is there to argue that
10   Now Pearse is deaf and dumb?
And is their logic to outweigh
MacDonagh's bony thumb?

How could you dream they'd listen
That have an ear alone
For those new comrades they have found,
Lord Edward and Wolfe Tone,
Or meddle with our give and take
That converse bone to bone?

The Rose Tree

'O words are lightly spoken,'
Said Pearse to Connolly,
'Maybe a breath of politic words
Has withered our Rose Tree;
Or maybe but a wind that blows
Across the bitter sea.'

'It needs to be but watered,'
James Connolly replied,
'To make the green come out again
And spread on every side,   10
And shake the blossom from the bud
To be the garden's pride.'

'But where can we draw water,'
Said Pearse to Connolly,
'When all the wells are parched away?
O plain as plain can be
There's nothing but our own red blood
Can make a right Rose Tree.'

On a Political Prisoner

She that but little patience knew,
From childhood on, had now so much
A grey gull lost its fear and flew
Down to her cell and there alit,
And there endured her fingers' touch
And from her fingers ate its bit.

Did she in touching that lone wing
Recall the years before her mind
Became a bitter, an abstract thing,
Her thought some popular enmity: 10
Blind and leader of the blind
Drinking the foul ditch where they lie?

When long ago I saw her ride
Under Ben Bulben to the meet,
The beauty of her country-side
With all youth's lonely wildness stirred,
She seemed to have grown clean and sweet
Like any rock-bred, sea-borne bird:

Sea-borne, or balanced on the air
When first it sprang out of the nest
Upon some lofty rock to stare
Upon the cloudy canopy,
While under its storm-beaten breast
Cried out the hollows of the sea.

The Second Coming

Turning and turning in the widening gyre
The falcon cannot hear the falconer;
Things fall apart; the centre cannot hold;
Mere anarchy is loosed upon the world,
The blood-dimmed tide is loosed, and everywhere
The ceremony of innocence is drowned;
The best lack all conviction, while the worst
Are full of passionate intensity.

Surely some revelation is at hand;
Surely the Second Coming is at hand.
The Second Coming! Hardly are those words out
When a vast image out of *Spiritus Mundi*
Troubles my sight: somewhere in sands of the desert
A shape with lion body and the head of a man,
A gaze blank and pitiless as the sun,
Is moving its slow thighs, while all about it
Reel shadows of the indignant desert birds.
The darkness drops again; but now I know
That twenty centuries of stony sleep
Were vexed to nightmare by a rocking cradle,
And what rough beast, its hour come round at last,
Slouches towards Bethlehem to be born?

A Prayer for my Daughter

Once more the storm is howling, and half hid
Under this cradle-hood and coverlid
My child sleeps on. There is no obstacle
But Gregory's wood and one bare hill
Whereby the haystack- and roof-levelling wind,
Bred on the Atlantic, can be stayed;
And for an hour I have walked and prayed
Because of the great gloom that is in my mind.

I have walked and prayed for this young child an hour
And heard the sea-wind scream upon the tower,   10
And under the arches of the bridge, and scream
In the elms above the flooded stream;
Imagining in excited reverie
That the future years had come,
Dancing to a frenzied drum,
Out of the murderous innocence of the sea.

May she be granted beauty and yet not
Beauty to make a stranger's eye distraught,
Or hers before a looking-glass, for such,
Being made beautiful overmuch,   20
Consider beauty a sufficient end,
Lose natural kindness and maybe
The heart-revealing intimacy
That chooses right, and never find a friend.

Helen being chosen found life flat and dull
And later had much trouble from a fool,
While that great Queen, that rose out of the spray,
Being fatherless could have her way
Yet chose a bandy-leggèd smith for man.
It's certain that fine women eat   30
A crazy salad with their meat
Whereby the Horn of Plenty is undone.

In courtesy I'd have her chiefly learned;
Hearts are not had as a gift but hearts are earned
By those that are not entirely beautiful;
Yet many, that have played the fool
For beauty's very self, has charm made wise,
And many a poor man that has roved,
Loved and thought himself beloved,
40   From a glad kindness cannot take his eyes.

May she become a flourishing hidden tree
That all her thoughts may like the linnet be,
And have no business but dispensing round
Their magnanimities of sound,
Nor but in merriment begin a chase,
Nor but in merriment a quarrel.
O may she live like some green laurel
Rooted in one dear perpetual place.

My mind, because the minds that I have loved,
50   The sort of beauty that I have approved,
Prosper but little, has dried up of late,
Yet knows that to be choked with hate
May well be of all evil chances chief.
If there's no hatred in a mind
Assault and battery of the wind
Can never tear the linnet from the leaf.

An intellectual hatred is the worst,
So let her think opinions are accursed.
Have I not seen the loveliest woman born
60   Out of the mouth of Plenty's horn,
Because of her opinionated mind
Barter that horn and every good
By quiet natures understood
For an old bellows full of angry wind?

Considering that, all hatred driven hence,
The soul recovers radical innocence
And learns at last that it is self-delighting,
Self-appeasing, self-affrighting,
And that its own sweet will is Heaven's will;
She can, though every face should scowl　　　70
And every windy quarter howl
Or every bellows burst, be happy still.

And may her bridegroom bring her to a house
Where all's accustomed, ceremonious;
For arrogance and hatred are the wares
Peddled in the thoroughfares.
How but in custom and in ceremony
Are innocence and beauty born?
Ceremony's a name for the rich horn,
And custom for the spreading laurel tree.　　　80

June 1919

To be carved on a Stone at Thoor Ballylee

I, the poet William Yeats,
With old mill boards and sea-green slates,
And smithy work from the Gort forge,
Restored this tower for my wife George;
And may these characters remain
When all is ruin once again.

The Tower

(1928)

Sailing to Byzantium

I

That is no country for old men. The young
In one another's arms, birds in the trees,
—Those dying generations—at their song,
The salmon-falls, the mackerel-crowded seas,
Fish, flesh, or fowl, commend all summer long
Whatever is begotten, born, and dies.
Caught in that sensual music all neglect
Monuments of unageing intellect.

II

An aged man is but a paltry thing,
A tattered coat upon a stick, unless
Soul clap its hands and sing, and louder sing
For every tatter in its mortal dress,
Nor is there singing school but studying
Monuments of its own magnificence;
And therefore I have sailed the seas and come
To the holy city of Byzantium.

III

O sages standing in God's holy fire
As in the gold mosaic of a wall,
Come from the holy fire, perne in a gyre,
And be the singing-masters of my soul.
Consume my heart away; sick with desire

And fastened to a dying animal
It knows not what it is; and gather me
Into the artifice of eternity.

IV

Once out of nature I shall never take
My bodily form from any natural thing,
But such a form as Grecian goldsmiths make
Of hammered gold and gold enamelling
To keep a drowsy Emperor awake;
Or set upon a golden bough to sing   30
To lords and ladies of Byzantium
Of what is past, or passing, or to come.

1927

The Tower

I

What shall I do with this absurdity—
O heart, O troubled heart—this caricature,
Decrepit age that has been tied to me
As to a dog's tail?
                    Never had I more
Excited, passionate, fantastical
Imagination, nor an ear and eye
That more expected the impossible—
No, not in boyhood when with rod and fly,
Or the humbler worm, I climbed Ben Bulben's back
And had the livelong summer day to spend.   10
It seems that I must bid the Muse go pack,
Choose Plato and Plotinus for a friend
Until imagination, ear and eye,
Can be content with argument and deal
In abstract things; or be derided by
A sort of battered kettle at the heel.

II

I pace upon the battlements and stare
On the foundations of a house, or where
Tree, like a sooty finger, starts from the earth;
20   And send imagination forth
Under the day's declining beam, and call
Images and memories
From ruin or from ancient trees,
For I would ask a question of them all.

Beyond that ridge lived Mrs. French, and once
When every silver candlestick or sconce
Lit up the dark mahogany and the wine,
A serving-man, that could divine
That most respected lady's every wish,
30   Ran and with the garden shears
Clipped an insolent farmer's ears
And brought them in a little covered dish.

Some few remembered still when I was young
A peasant girl commended by a song,
Who'd lived somewhere upon that rocky place,
And praised the colour of her face,
And had the greater joy in praising her,
Remembering that, if walked she there,
Farmers jostled at the fair
40   So great a glory did the song confer.

And certain men, being maddened by those rhymes,
Or else by toasting her a score of times,
Rose from the table and declared it right
To test their fancy by their sight;
But they mistook the brightness of the moon
For the prosaic light of day—
Music had driven their wits astray—
And one was drowned in the great bog of Cloone.

Strange, but the man who made the song was blind;
50   Yet, now I have considered it, I find
That nothing strange; the tragedy began

With Homer that was a blind man,
And Helen has all living hearts betrayed.
O may the moon and sunlight seem
One inextricable beam,
For if I triumph I must make men mad.

And I myself created Hanrahan
And drove him drunk or sober through the dawn
From somewhere in the neighbouring cottages.
Caught by an old man's juggleries   60
He stumbled, tumbled, fumbled to and fro
And had but broken knees for hire
And horrible splendour of desire;
I thought it all out twenty years ago:

Good fellows shuffled cards in an old bawn;
And when that ancient ruffian's turn was on
He so bewitched the cards under his thumb
That all but the one card became
A pack of hounds and not a pack of cards,
And that he changed into a hare.   70
Hanrahan rose in frenzy there
And followed up those baying creatures towards—

O towards I have forgotten what—enough!
I must recall a man that neither love
Nor music nor an enemy's clipped ear
Could, he was so harried, cheer;
A figure that has grown so fabulous
There's not a neighbour left to say
When he finished his dog's day:
An ancient bankrupt master of this house.   80

Before that ruin came, for centuries,
Rough men-at-arms, cross-gartered to the knees
Or shod in iron, climbed the narrow stairs,
And certain men-at-arms there were
Whose images, in the Great Memory stored,
Come with loud cry and panting breast
To break upon a sleeper's rest
While their great wooden dice beat on the board.

As I would question all, come all who can;
Come old, necessitous, half-mounted man;
And bring beauty's blind rambling celebrant;
The red man the juggler sent
Through God-forsaken meadows; Mrs. French,
Gifted with so fine an ear;
The man drowned in a bog's mire,
When mocking muses chose the country wench.

Did all old men and women, rich and poor,
Who trod upon these rocks or passed this door,
Whether in public or in secret rage
As I do now against old age?
But I have found an answer in those eyes
That are impatient to be gone;
Go therefore; but leave Hanrahan,
For I need all his mighty memories.

Old lecher with a love on every wind,
Bring up out of that deep considering mind
All that you have discovered in the grave,
For it is certain that you have
Reckoned up every unforeknown, unseeing
Plunge, lured by a softening eye,
Or by a touch or a sigh,
Into the labyrinth of another's being;

Does the imagination dwell the most
Upon a woman won or woman lost?
If on the lost, admit you turned aside
From a great labyrinth out of pride,
Cowardice, some silly over-subtle thought
Or anything called conscience once;
And that if memory recur, the sun's
Under eclipse and the day blotted out.

III

It is time that I wrote my will;
I choose upstanding men
That climb the streams until

The fountain leap, and at dawn
Drop their cast at the side
Of dripping stone; I declare
They shall inherit my pride,
The pride of people that were
Bound neither to Cause nor to State,
Neither to slaves that were spat on,   130
Nor to the tyrants that spat,
The people of Burke and of Grattan
That gave, though free to refuse—
Pride, like that of the morn,
When the headlong light is loose,
Or that of the fabulous horn,
Or that of the sudden shower
When all streams are dry,
Or that of the hour
When the swan must fix his eye   140
Upon a fading gleam,
Float out upon a long
Last reach of glittering stream
And there sing his last song.
And I declare my faith:
I mock Plotinus' thought
And cry in Plato's teeth,
Death and life were not
Till man made up the whole,
Made lock, stock and barrel   150
Out of his bitter soul,
Aye, sun and moon and star, all,
And further add to that
That, being dead, we rise,
Dream and so create
Translunar Paradise.
I have prepared my peace
With learned Italian things
And the proud stones of Greece,
Poet's imaginings   160
And memories of love,
Memories of the words of women,

All those things whereof
Man makes a superhuman
Mirror-resembling dream.

As at the loophole there
The daws chatter and scream,
And drop twigs layer upon layer.
When they have mounted up,
170   The mother bird will rest
On their hollow top,
And so warm her wild nest.

I leave both faith and pride
To young upstanding men
Climbing the mountain side,
That under bursting dawn
They may drop a fly;
Being of that metal made
Till it was broken by
180   This sedentary trade.

Now shall I make my soul,
Compelling it to study
In a learned school
Till the wreck of body,
Slow decay of blood,
Testy delirium
Or dull decrepitude,
Or what worse evil come—
The death of friends, or death
190   Of every brilliant eye
That made a catch in the breath—
Seem but the clouds of the sky
When the horizon fades;
Or a bird's sleepy cry
Among the deepening shades.

1926

Meditations in Time of Civil War

I. *Ancestral Houses*

Surely among a rich man's flowering lawns,
Amid the rustle of his planted hills,
Life overflows without ambitious pains;
And rains down life until the basin spills,
And mounts more dizzy high the more it rains
As though to choose whatever shape it wills
And never stoop to a mechanical
Or servile shape, at others' beck and call.

Mere dreams, mere dreams! Yet Homer had not sung
Had he not found it certain beyond dreams   10
That out of life's own self-delight had sprung
The abounding glittering jet; though now it seems
As if some marvellous empty sea-shell flung
Out of the obscure dark of the rich streams,
And not a fountain, were the symbol which
Shadows the inherited glory of the rich.

Some violent bitter man, some powerful man
Called architect and artist in, that they,
Bitter and violent men, might rear in stone
The sweetness that all longed for night and day,   20
The gentleness none there had ever known;
But when the master's buried mice can play,
And maybe the great-grandson of that house,
For all its bronze and marble, 's but a mouse.

O what if gardens where the peacock strays
With delicate feet upon old terraces,
Or else all Juno from an urn displays
Before the indifferent garden deities;
O what if levelled lawns and gravelled ways
Where slippered Contemplation finds his ease   30
And Childhood a delight for every sense,
But take our greatness with our violence?

What if the glory of escutcheoned doors,
And buildings that a haughtier age designed,
The pacing to and fro on polished floors
Amid great chambers and long galleries, lined
With famous portraits of our ancestors;
What if those things the greatest of mankind
Consider most to magnify, or to bless,
40   But take our greatness with our bitterness?

II. My House

An ancient bridge, and a more ancient tower,
A farmhouse that is sheltered by its wall,
An acre of stony ground,
Where the symbolic rose can break in flower,
Old ragged elms, old thorns innumerable,
The sound of the rain or sound
Of every wind that blows;
The stilted water-hen
Crossing stream again
10   Scared by the splashing of a dozen cows;

A winding stair, a chamber arched with stone,
A grey stone fireplace with an open hearth,
A candle and written page.
Il Penseroso's Platonist toiled on
In some like chamber, shadowing forth
How the daemonic rage
Imagined everything.
Benighted travellers
From markets and from fairs
20   Have seen his midnight candle glimmering.

Two men have founded here. A man-at-arms
Gathered a score of horse and spent his days
In this tumultuous spot,
Where through long wars and sudden night alarms
His dwindling score and he seemed castaways
Forgetting and forgot;
And I, that after me

My bodily heirs may find,
To exalt a lonely mind,
Befitting emblems of adversity.   30

III. My Table

Two heavy trestles, and a board
Where Sato's gift, a changeless sword,
By pen and paper lies,
That it may moralise
My days out of their aimlessness.
A bit of an embroidered dress
Covers its wooden sheath.
Chaucer had not drawn breath
When it was forged. In Sato's house,
Curved like new moon, moon-luminous,   10
It lay five hundred years.
Yet if no change appears
No moon; only an aching heart
Conceives a changeless work of art.
Our learned men have urged
That when and where 'twas forged
A marvellous accomplishment,
In painting or in pottery, went
From father unto son
And through the centuries ran   20
And seemed unchanging like the sword.
Soul's beauty being most adored,
Men and their business took
The soul's unchanging look;
For the most rich inheritor,
Knowing that none could pass Heaven's door
That loved inferior art,
Had such an aching heart
That he, although a country's talk
For silken clothes and stately walk,   30
Had waking wits; it seemed
Juno's peacock screamed.

IV. My Descendants

Having inherited a vigorous mind
From my old fathers, I must nourish dreams
And leave a woman and a man behind
As vigorous of mind, and yet it seems
Life scarce can cast a fragrance on the wind,
Scarce spread a glory to the morning beams,
But the torn petals strew the garden plot;
And there's but common greenness after that.

And what if my descendants lose the flower
10 Through natural declension of the soul,
Through too much business with the passing hour,
Through too much play, or marriage with a fool?
May this laborious stair and this stark tower
Become a roofless ruin that the owl
May build in the cracked masonry and cry
Her desolation to the desolate sky.

The Primum Mobile that fashioned us
Has made the very owls in circles move;
And I, that count myself most prosperous,
20 Seeing that love and friendship are enough,
For an old neighbour's friendship chose the house
And decked and altered it for a girl's love,
And know whatever flourish and decline
These stones remain their monument and mine.

V. The Road at My Door

An affable Irregular,
A heavily-built Falstaffian man,
Comes cracking jokes of civil war
As though to die by gunshot were
The finest play under the sun.

A brown Lieutenant and his men,
Half dressed in national uniform,
Stand at my door, and I complain
Of the foul weather, hail and rain,
A pear tree broken by the storm.   10

I count those feathered balls of soot
The moor-hen guides upon the stream,
To silence the envy in my thought;
And turn towards my chamber, caught
In the cold snows of a dream.

VI.   The Stare's Nest by My Window

The bees build in the crevices
Of loosening masonry, and there
The mother birds bring grubs and flies.
My wall is loosening; honey-bees,
Come build in the empty house of the stare.

We are closed in, and the key is turned
On our uncertainty; somewhere
A man is killed, or a house burned,
Yet no clear fact to be discerned:
Come build in the empty house of the stare.   10

A barricade of stone or of wood;
Some fourteen days of civil war;
Last night they trundled down the road
That dead young soldier in his blood:
Come build in the empty house of the stare.

We had fed the heart on fantasies,
The heart's grown brutal from the fare;
More substance in our enmities
Than in our love; O honey-bees,
Come build in the empty house of the stare.   20

VII. I see Phantoms of Hatred and of the Heart's Fullness and of the Coming Emptiness

I climb to the tower-top and lean upon broken stone,
A mist that is like blown snow is sweeping over all,
Valley, river, and elms, under the light of a moon
That seems unlike itself, that seems unchangeable,
A glittering sword out of the east. A puff of wind
And those white glimmering fragments of the mist sweep by.
Frenzies bewilder, reveries perturb the mind;
Monstrous familiar images swim to the mind's eye.

'Vengeance upon the murderers,' the cry goes up,
10 'Vengeance for Jacques Molay.' In cloud-pale rags, or in lace,
The rage-driven, rage-tormented, and rage-hungry troop,
Trooper belabouring trooper, biting at arm or at face,
Plunges towards nothing, arms and fingers spreading wide
For the embrace of nothing; and I, my wits astray
Because of all that senseless tumult, all but cried
For vengeance on the murderers of Jacques Molay.

Their legs long, delicate and slender, aquamarine their eyes,
Magical unicorns bear ladies on their backs.
The ladies close their musing eyes. No prophecies,
20 Remembered out of Babylonian almanacs,
Have closed the ladies' eyes, their minds are but a pool
Where even longing drowns under its own excess;
Nothing but stillness can remain when hearts are full
Of their own sweetness, bodies of their loveliness.

The cloud-pale unicorns, the eyes of aquamarine,
The quivering half-closed eyelids, the rags of cloud or of lace,
Or eyes that rage has brightened, arms it has made lean,
Give place to an indifferent multitude, give place
To brazen hawks. Nor self-delighting reverie,
30 Nor hate of what's to come, nor pity for what's gone,
Nothing but grip of claw, and the eye's complacency,
The innumerable clanging wings that have put out the moon.

I turn away and shut the door, and on the stair
Wonder how many times I could have proved my worth
In something that all others understand or share;
But O! ambitious heart, had such a proof drawn forth
A company of friends, a conscience set at ease,
It had but made us pine the more. The abstract joy,
The half-read wisdom of daemonic images,
Suffice the ageing man as once the growing boy.   40

1923

Nineteen Hundred and Nineteen

I

Many ingenious lovely things are gone
That seemed sheer miracle to the multitude,
Protected from the circle of the moon
That pitches common things about. There stood
Amid the ornamental bronze and stone
An ancient image made of olive wood—
And gone are Phidias' famous ivories
And all the golden grasshoppers and bees.

We too had many pretty toys when young;
A law indifferent to blame or praise,   10
To bribe or threat; habits that made old wrong
Melt down, as it were wax in the sun's rays;
Public opinion ripening for so long
We thought it would outlive all future days.
O what fine thought we had because we thought
That the worst rogues and rascals had died out.

All teeth were drawn, all ancient tricks unlearned,
And a great army but a showy thing;
What matter that no cannon had been turned
Into a ploughshare? Parliament and king   20
Thought that unless a little powder burned
The trumpeters might burst with trumpeting
And yet it lack all glory; and perchance
The guardsmen's drowsy chargers would not prance.

Now days are dragon-ridden, the nightmare
Rides upon sleep: a drunken soldiery
Can leave the mother, murdered at her door,
To crawl in her own blood, and go scot-free;
The night can sweat with terror as before
30   We pieced our thoughts into philosophy,
And planned to bring the world under a rule,
Who are but weasels fighting in a hole.

He who can read the signs nor sink unmanned
Into the half-deceit of some intoxicant
From shallow wits; who knows no work can stand,
Whether health, wealth or peace of mind were spent
On master-work of intellect or hand,
No honour leave its mighty monument,
Has but one comfort left: all triumph would
40   But break upon his ghostly solitude.

But is there any comfort to be found?
Man is in love and loves what vanishes,
What more is there to say? That country round
None dared admit, if such a thought were his,
Incendiary or bigot could be found
To burn that stump on the Acropolis,
Or break in bits the famous ivories
Or traffic in the grasshoppers or bees.

II

When Loie Fuller's Chinese dancers enwound
50   A shining web, a floating ribbon of cloth,
It seemed that a dragon of air
Had fallen among dancers, had whirled them round
Or hurried them off on its own furious path;
So the Platonic Year
Whirls out new right and wrong,
Whirls in the old instead;
All men are dancers and their tread
Goes to the barbarous clangour of a gong.

III

Some moralist or mythological poet
Compares the solitary soul to a swan;   60
I am satisfied with that,
Satisfied if a troubled mirror show it,
Before that brief gleam of its life be gone,
An image of its state;
The wings half spread for flight,
The breast thrust out in pride
Whether to play, or to ride
Those winds that clamour of approaching night.

A man in his own secret meditation
Is lost amid the labyrinth that he has made   70
In art or politics;
Some Platonist affirms that in the station
Where we should cast off body and trade
The ancient habit sticks,
And that if our works could
But vanish with our breath
That were a lucky death,
For triumph can but mar our solitude.

The swan has leaped into the desolate heaven:
That image can bring wildness, bring a rage   80
To end all things, to end
What my laborious life imagined, even
The half-imagined, the half-written page;
O but we dreamed to mend
Whatever mischief seemed
To afflict mankind, but now
That winds of winter blow
Learn that we were crack-pated when we dreamed.

IV

We, who seven years ago
Talked of honour and of truth,   90
Shriek with pleasure if we show
The weasel's twist, the weasel's tooth.

V

Come let us mock at the great
That had such burdens on the mind
And toiled so hard and late
To leave some monument behind,
Nor thought of the levelling wind.

Come let us mock at the wise;
With all those calendars whereon
They fixed old aching eyes,
They never saw how seasons run,
And now but gape at the sun.

Come let us mock at the good
That fancied goodness might be gay,
And sick of solitude
Might proclaim a holiday:
Wind shrieked—and where are they?

Mock mockers after that
That would not lift a hand maybe
To help good, wise or great
To bar that foul storm out, for we
Traffic in mockery.

VI

Violence upon the roads: violence of horses;
Some few have handsome riders, are garlanded
On delicate sensitive ear or tossing mane,
But wearied running round and round in their courses
All break and vanish, and evil gathers head:
Herodias' daughters have returned again,
A sudden blast of dusty wind and after
Thunder of feet, tumult of images,
Their purpose in the labyrinth of the wind;
And should some crazy hand dare touch a daughter
All turn with amorous cries, or angry cries,
According to the wind, for all are blind.
But now wind drops, dust settles; thereupon

There lurches past, his great eyes without thought
Under the shadow of stupid straw-pale locks,
That insolent fiend Robert Artisson
To whom the love-lorn Lady Kyteler brought
Bronzed peacock feathers, red combs of her cocks.   130

1919

A Prayer for my Son

Bid a strong ghost stand at the head
That my Michael may sleep sound,
Nor cry, nor turn in the bed
Till his morning meal come round;
And may departing twilight keep
All dread afar till morning's back,
That his mother may not lack
Her fill of sleep.

Bid the ghost have sword in fist:
Some there are, for I avow   10
Such devilish things exist,
Who have planned his murder, for they know
Of some most haughty deed or thought
That waits upon his future days,
And would through hatred of the bays
Bring that to nought.

Though You can fashion everything
From nothing every day, and teach
The morning stars to sing,
You have lacked articulate speech   20
To tell Your simplest want, and known,
Wailing upon a woman's knee,
All of that worst ignominy
Of flesh and bone;

And when through all the town there ran
The servants of Your enemy,
A woman and a man,

Unless the Holy Writings lie,
Hurried through the smooth and rough
30   And through the fertile and waste,
Protecting, till the danger past,
With human love.

Fragments

I

Locke sank into a swoon;
The Garden died;
God took the spinning-jenny
Out of his side.

II

Where got I that truth?
Out of a medium's mouth,
Out of nothing it came,
Out of the forest loam,
Out of dark night where lay
The crowns of Nineveh.

Leda and the Swan

A sudden blow: the great wings beating still
Above the staggering girl, her thighs caressed
By the dark webs, her nape caught in his bill,
He holds her helpless breast upon his breast.

How can those terrified vague fingers push
The feathered glory from her loosening thighs?
And how can body, laid in that white rush,
But feel the strange heart beating where it lies?

A shudder in the loins engenders there
10   The broken wall, the burning roof and tower
And Agamemnon dead.

Being so caught up,
So mastered by the brute blood of the air,
Did she put on his knowledge with his power
Before the indifferent beak could let her drop?

1923

Among School Children

I

I walk through the long schoolroom questioning;
A kind old nun in a white hood replies;
The children learn to cipher and to sing,
To study reading-books and history,
To cut and sew, be neat in everything
In the best modern way—the children's eyes
In momentary wonder stare upon
A sixty-year-old smiling public man.

II

I dream of a Ledaean body, bent
Above a sinking fire, a tale that she   10
Told of a harsh reproof, or trivial event
That changed some childish day to tragedy—
Told, and it seemed that our two natures blent
Into a sphere from youthful sympathy,
Or else, to alter Plato's parable,
Into the yolk and white of the one shell.

III

And thinking of that fit of grief or rage
I look upon one child or t'other there
And wonder if she stood so at that age—
For even daughters of the swan can share   20
Something of every paddler's heritage—
And had that colour upon cheek or hair,
And thereupon my heart is driven wild:
She stands before me as a living child.

IV

Her present image floats into the mind—
Did Quattrocento finger fashion it
Hollow of cheek as though it drank the wind
And took a mess of shadows for its meat?
And I though never of Ledaean kind
30   Had pretty plumage once—enough of that,
Better to smile on all that smile, and show
There is a comfortable kind of old scarecrow.

V

What youthful mother, a shape upon her lap
Honey of generation had betrayed,
And that must sleep, shriek, struggle to escape
As recollection or the drug decide,
Would think her son, did she but see that shape
With sixty or more winters on its head,
A compensation for the pang of his birth,
40   Or the uncertainty of his setting forth?

VI

Plato thought nature but a spume that plays
Upon a ghostly paradigm of things;
Solider Aristotle played the taws
Upon the bottom of a king of kings;
World-famous golden-thighed Pythagoras
Fingered upon a fiddle-stick or strings
What a star sang and careless Muses heard:
Old clothes upon old sticks to scare a bird.

VII

Both nuns and mothers worship images,
50   But those the candles light are not as those
That animate a mother's reveries,
But keep a marble or a bronze repose.
And yet they too break hearts—O Presences
That passion, piety or affection knows,

And that all heavenly glory symbolise—
O self-born mockers of man's enterprise;

VIII

Labour is blossoming or dancing where
The body is not bruised to pleasure soul,
Nor beauty born out of its own despair,
Nor blear-eyed wisdom out of midnight oil.
O chestnut tree, great rooted blossomer,
Are you the leaf, the blossom or the bole?
O body swayed to music, O brightening glance,
How can we know the dancer from the dance?

60

From 'Oedipus at Colonus'

Endure what life God gives and ask no longer span;
Cease to remember the delights of youth, travel-wearied aged man;
Delight becomes death-longing if all longing else be vain.

Even from that delight memory treasures so,
Death, despair, division of families, all entanglements of mankind grow,
As that old wandering beggar and these God-hated children know.

In the long echoing street the laughing dancers throng,
The bride is carried to the bridegroom's chamber through
    torchlight and tumultuous song;
I celebrate the silent kiss that ends short life or long.

Never to have lived is best, ancient writers say;
Never to have drawn the breath of life, never to have looked into
    the eye of day;
The second best's a gay goodnight and quickly turn away.

10

All Souls' Night

Epilogue to 'A Vision'

Midnight has come and the great Christ Church bell
And many a lesser bell sound through the room;
And it is All Souls' Night.
And two long glasses brimmed with muscatel
Bubble upon the table. A ghost may come;
For it is a ghost's right,
His element is so fine
Being sharpened by his death,
To drink from the wine-breath
10   While our gross palates drink from the whole wine.

I need some mind that, if the cannon sound
From every quarter of the world, can stay
Wound in mind's pondering,
As mummies in the mummy-cloth are wound;
Because I have a marvellous thing to say,
A certain marvellous thing
None but the living mock,
Though not for sober ear;
It may be all that hear
20   Should laugh and weep an hour upon the clock.

Horton's the first I call. He loved strange thought
And knew that sweet extremity of pride
That's called platonic love,
And that to such a pitch of passion wrought
Nothing could bring him, when his lady died,
Anodyne for his love.
Words were but wasted breath;
One dear hope had he:
The inclemency
30   Of that or the next winter would be death.

Two thoughts were so mixed up I could not tell
Whether of her or God he thought the most,
But think that his mind's eye,

When upward turned, on one sole image fell;
And that a slight companionable ghost,
Wild with divinity,
Had so lit up the whole
Immense miraculous house
The Bible promised us,
It seemed a gold-fish swimming in a bowl.   40

On Florence Emery I call the next,
Who finding the first wrinkles on a face
Admired and beautiful,
And by foreknowledge of the future vexed;
Diminished beauty, multiplied commonplace;
Preferred to teach a school
Away from neighbour or friend,
Among dark skins, and there
Permit foul years to wear
Hidden from eyesight to the unnoticed end.   50

Before that end much had she ravelled out
From a discourse in figurative speech
By some learned Indian
On the soul's journey. How it is whirled about
Wherever the orbit of the moon can reach,
Until it plunge into the sun;
And there, free and yet fast,
Being both Chance and Choice,
Forget its broken toys
And sink into its own delight at last.   60

I call MacGregor Mathers from his grave,
For in my first hard spring-time we were friends,
Although of late estranged.
I thought him half a lunatic, half knave,
And told him so, but friendship never ends;
And what if mind seem changed,
And it seem changed with the mind,
When thoughts rise up unbid
On generous things that he did
And I grow half contented to be blind!   70

He had much industry at setting out,
Much boisterous courage, before loneliness
Had driven him crazed;
For meditations upon unknown thought
Make human intercourse grow less and less;
They are neither paid nor praised.
But he'd object to the host,
The glass because my glass;
A ghost-lover he was
80   And may have grown more arrogant being a ghost.

But names are nothing. What matter who it be,
So that his elements have grown so fine
The fume of muscatel
Can give his sharpened palate ecstasy
No living man can drink from the whole wine.
I have mummy truths to tell
Whereat the living mock,
Though not for sober ear,
For maybe all that hear
90   Should laugh and weep an hour upon the clock.

Such thought—such thought have I that hold it tight
Till meditation master all its parts,
Nothing can stay my glance
Until that glance run in the world's despite
To where the damned have howled away their hearts,
And where the blessed dance;
Such thought, that in it bound
I need no other thing,
Wound in mind's wandering
100   As mummies in the mummy-cloth are wound.

Oxford, Autumn 1920

FROM The Winding Stair and Other Poems

(1933)

In Memory of Eva Gore-Booth and Con Markiewicz

The light of evening, Lissadell,
Great windows open to the south,
Two girls in silk kimonos, both
Beautiful, one a gazelle.
But a raving autumn shears
Blossom from the summer's wreath;
The older is condemned to death,
Pardoned, drags out lonely years
Conspiring among the ignorant.
I know not what the younger dreams—   10
Some vague Utopia—and she seems,
When withered old and skeleton-gaunt,
An image of such politics.
Many a time I think to seek
One or the other out and speak
Of that old Georgian mansion, mix
Pictures of the mind, recall
That table and the talk of youth,
Two girls in silk kimonos, both
Beautiful, one a gazelle.   20

Dear shadows, now you know it all,
All the folly of a fight
With a common wrong or right.

The innocent and the beautiful
Have no enemy but time;
Arise and bid me strike a match
And strike another till time catch;
Should the conflagration climb,
Run till all the sages know.
30   We the great gazebo built,
They convicted us of guilt;
Bid me strike a match and blow.

October 1927

A Dialogue
of Self and Soul

I

My Soul. I summon to the winding ancient stair;
Set all your mind upon the steep ascent,
Upon the broken, crumbling battlement,
Upon the breathless starlit air,
Upon the star that marks the hidden pole;
Fix every wandering thought upon
That quarter where all thought is done:
Who can distinguish darkness from the soul?

My Self. The consecrated blade upon my knees
10   Is Sato's ancient blade, still as it was,
Still razor-keen, still like a looking-glass
Unspotted by the centuries;
That flowering, silken, old embroidery, torn
From some court-lady's dress and round
The wooden scabbard bound and wound,
Can, tattered, still protect, faded adorn.

My Soul. Why should the imagination of a man
Long past his prime remember things that are
Emblematical of love and war?
20   Think of ancestral night that can,
If but imagination scorn the earth

And intellect its wandering
To this and that and t'other thing,
Deliver from the crime of death and birth.

My Self. Montashigi, third of his family, fashioned it
   Five hundred years ago, about it lie
   Flowers from I know not what embroidery—
   Heart's purple—and all these I set
   For emblems of the day against the tower
   Emblematical of the night,   30
   And claim as by a soldier's right
   A charter to commit the crime once more.

My Soul. Such fullness in that quarter overflows
   And falls into the basin of the mind
   That man is stricken deaf and dumb and blind,
   For intellect no longer knows
   Is from the *Ought,* or *Knower* from the *Known*—
   That is to say, ascends to Heaven;
   Only the dead can be forgiven;
   But when I think of that my tongue's a stone.   40

II

My Self. A living man is blind and drinks his drop.
   What matter if the ditches are impure?
   What matter if I live it all once more?
   Endure that toil of growing up;
   The ignominy of boyhood; the distress
   Of boyhood changing into man;
   The unfinished man and his pain
   Brought face to face with his own clumsiness;

   The finished man among his enemies?—
   How in the name of Heaven can he escape   50
   That defiling and disfigured shape
   The mirror of malicious eyes
   Casts upon his eyes until at last
   He thinks that shape must be his shape?
   And what's the good of an escape
   If honour find him in the wintry blast?

I am content to live it all again
And yet again, if it be life to pitch
Into the frog-spawn of a blind man's ditch,
60   A blind man battering blind men;
Or into that most fecund ditch of all,
The folly that man does
Or must suffer, if he woos
A proud woman not kindred of his soul.

I am content to follow to its source
Every event in action or in thought;
Measure the lot; forgive myself the lot!
When such as I cast out remorse
So great a sweetness flows into the breast
70   We must laugh and we must sing,
We are blest by everything,
Everything we look upon is blest.

Coole Park, 1929

I meditate upon a swallow's flight,
Upon an aged woman and her house,
A sycamore and lime tree lost in night
Although that western cloud is luminous,
Great works constructed there in nature's spite
For scholars and for poets after us,
Thoughts long knitted into a single thought,
A dance-like glory that those walls begot.

There Hyde before he had beaten into prose
10   That noble blade the Muses buckled on,
There one that ruffled in a manly pose
For all his timid heart, there that slow man,
That meditative man, John Synge, and those
Impetuous men, Shawe-Taylor and Hugh Lane,
Found pride established in humility,
A scene well set and excellent company.

They came like swallows and like swallows went,
And yet a woman's powerful character
Could keep a swallow to its first intent;
And half a dozen in formation there, 20
That seemed to whirl upon a compass-point,
Found certainty upon the dreaming air,
The intellectual sweetness of those lines
That cut through time or cross it withershins.

Here, traveller, scholar, poet, take your stand
When all those rooms and passages are gone,
When nettles wave upon a shapeless mound
And saplings root among the broken stone,
And dedicate—eyes bent upon the ground,
Back turned upon the brightness of the sun 30
And all the sensuality of the shade—
A moment's memory to that laurelled head.

Coole and Ballylee, 1931

Under my window-ledge the waters race,
Otters below and moor-hens on the top,
Run for a mile undimmed in Heaven's face
Then darkening through 'dark' Raftery's 'cellar' drop,
Run underground, rise in a rocky place
In Coole demesne, and there to finish up
Spread to a lake and drop into a hole.
What's water but the generated soul?

Upon the border of that lake's a wood
Now all dry sticks under a wintry sun, 10
And in a copse of beeches there I stood,
For Nature's pulled her tragic buskin on
And all the rant's a mirror of my mood:
At sudden thunder of the mounting swan
I turned about and looked where branches break
The glittering reaches of the flooded lake.

Another emblem there! That stormy white
But seems a concentration of the sky;
And, like the soul, it sails into the sight
20   And in the morning's gone, no man knows why;
And is so lovely that it sets to right
What knowledge or its lack had set awry,
So arrogantly pure, a child might think
It can be murdered with a spot of ink.

Sound of a stick upon the floor, a sound
From somebody that toils from chair to chair;
Beloved books that famous hands have bound,
Old marble heads, old pictures everywhere;
Great rooms where travelled men and children found
30   Content or joy; a last inheritor
Where none has reigned that lacked a name and fame
Or out of folly into folly came.

A spot whereon the founders lived and died
Seemed once more dear than life; ancestral trees
Or gardens rich in memory glorified
Marriages, alliances and families,
And every bride's ambition satisfied.
Where fashion or mere fantasy decrees
Man shifts about—all that great glory spent—
40   Like some poor Arab tribesman and his tent.

We were the last romantics—chose for theme
Traditional sanctity and loveliness;
Whatever's written in what poets name
The book of the people; whatever most can bless
The mind of man or elevate a rhyme;
But all is changed, that high horse riderless,
Though mounted in that saddle Homer rode
Where the swan drifts upon a darkening flood.

The Choice

The intellect of man is forced to choose
Perfection of the life, or of the work,
And if it take the second must refuse
A heavenly mansion, raging in the dark.
When all that story's finished, what's the news?
In luck or out the toil has left its mark:
That old perplexity an empty purse,
Or the day's vanity, the night's remorse.

Mohini Chatterjee

I asked if I should pray,
But the Brahmin said,
'Pray for nothing, say
Every night in bed,
"I have been a king,
I have been a slave,
Nor is there anything,
Fool, rascal, knave,
That I have not been,
And yet upon my breast   10
A myriad heads have lain." '

That he might set at rest
A boy's turbulent days
Mohini Chatterjee
Spoke these, or words like these.
I add in commentary,
'Old lovers yet may have
All that time denied—
Grave is heaped on grave
That they be satisfied—   20
Over the blackened earth
The old troops parade,
Birth is heaped on birth
That such cannonade

May thunder time away,
Birth-hour and death-hour meet,
Or, as great sages say,
Men dance on deathless feet.'

1928

Byzantium

The unpurged images of day recede;
The Emperor's drunken soldiery are abed;
Night resonance recedes, night-walkers' song
After great cathedral gong;
A starlit or a moonlit dome disdains
All that man is,
All mere complexities,
The fury and the mire of human veins.

Before me floats an image, man or shade,
10   Shade more than man, more image than a shade;
For Hades' bobbin bound in mummy-cloth
May unwind the winding path;
A mouth that has no moisture and no breath
Breathless mouths may summon;
I hail the superhuman;
I call it death-in-life and life-in-death.

Miracle, bird or golden handiwork,
More miracle than bird or handiwork,
Planted on the starlit golden bough,
20   Can like the cocks of Hades crow,
Or, by the moon embittered, scorn aloud
In glory of changeless metal
Common bird or petal
And all complexities of mire or blood.

At midnight on the Emperor's pavement flit
Flames that no faggot feeds, nor steel has lit,
Nor storm disturbs, flames begotten of flame,
Where blood-begotten spirits come

And all complexities of fury leave,
Dying into a dance,   30
An agony of trance,
An agony of flame that cannot singe a sleeve.

Astraddle on the dolphin's mire and blood,
Spirit after spirit! The smithies break the flood,
The golden smithies of the Emperor!
Marbles of the dancing floor
Break bitter furies of complexity,
Those images that yet
Fresh images beget,
That dolphin-torn, that gong-tormented sea.   40

1930

Vacillation

I

Between extremities
Man runs his course;
A brand, or flaming breath,
Comes to destroy
All those antinomies
Of day and night;
The body calls it death,
The heart remorse.
But if these be right
What is joy?   10

II

A tree there is that from its topmost bough
Is half all glittering flame and half all green
Abounding foliage moistened with the dew;
And half is half and yet is all the scene;
And half and half consume what they renew,
And he that Attis' image hangs between
That staring fury and the blind lush leaf
May know not what he knows, but knows not grief.

III

Get all the gold and silver that you can,
Satisfy ambition, or animate
The trivial days and ram them with the sun,
And yet upon these maxims meditate:
All women dote upon an idle man
Although their children need a rich estate;
No man has ever lived that had enough
Of children's gratitude or woman's love.

No longer in Lethean foliage caught
Begin the preparation for your death
And from the fortieth winter by that thought
Test every work of intellect or faith
And everything that your own hands have wrought,
And call those works extravagance of breath
That are not suited for such men as come
Proud, open-eyed and laughing to the tomb.

IV

My fiftieth year had come and gone,
I sat, a solitary man,
In a crowded London shop,
An open book and empty cup
On the marble table-top.

While on the shop and street I gazed
My body of a sudden blazed;
And twenty minutes more or less
It seemed, so great my happiness,
That I was blessèd and could bless.

V

Although the summer sunlight gild
Cloudy leafage of the sky,
Or wintry moonlight sink the field
In storm-scattered intricacy,
I cannot look thereon,
Responsibility so weighs me down.

Things said or done long years ago,
Or things I did not do or say
But thought that I might say or do,
Weigh me down, and not a day
But something is recalled,
My conscience or my vanity appalled.

VI

A rivery field spread out below,
An odour of the new-mown hay
In his nostrils, the great lord of Chou
Cried, casting off the mountain snow,   60
'Let all things pass away.'

Wheels by milk-white asses drawn
Where Babylon or Nineveh
Rose; some conqueror drew rein
And cried to battle-weary men,
'Let all things pass away.'

From man's blood-sodden heart are sprung
Those branches of the night and day
Where the gaudy moon is hung.
What's the meaning of all song?   70
'Let all things pass away.'

VII

The Soul. Seek out reality, leave things that seem.
The Heart. What, be a singer born and lack a theme?
The Soul. Isaiah's coal, what more can man desire?
The Heart. Struck dumb in the simplicity of fire!
The Soul. Look on that fire, salvation walks within.
The Heart. What theme had Homer but original sin?

VIII

Must we part, Von Hügel, though much alike, for we
Accept the miracles of the saints and honour sanctity?
The body of Saint Teresa lies undecayed in tomb,   80
Bathed in miraculous oil, sweet odours from it come,

Healing from its lettered slab. Those self-same hands perchance
Eternalised the body of a modern saint that once
Had scooped out Pharaoh's mummy. I—though heart might find
   relief
Did I become a Christian man and choose for my belief
What seems most welcome in the tomb—play a predestined part.
Homer is my example and his unchristened heart.
The lion and the honeycomb, what has Scripture said?
So get you gone, Von Hügel, though with blessings on your head.

                                                            1932

Crazy Jane and the Bishop

Bring me to the blasted oak
That I, midnight upon the stroke,
(All find safety in the tomb.)
May call down curses on his head
Because of my dear Jack that's dead.
Coxcomb was the least he said:
The solid man and the coxcomb.

Nor was he Bishop when his ban
Banished Jack the Journeyman,
(All find safety in the tomb.)
Nor so much as parish priest,
Yet he, an old book in his fist,
Cried that we lived like beast and beast:
The solid man and the coxcomb.

The Bishop has a skin, God knows,
Wrinkled like the foot of a goose,
(All find safety in the tomb.)
Nor can he hide in holy black
The heron's hunch upon his back,
But a birch-tree stood my Jack:
The solid man and the coxcomb.

Jack had my virginity,
And bids me to the oak, for he
(All find safety in the tomb.)

Wanders out into the night
And there is shelter under it,
But should that other come, I spit:
The solid man and the coxcomb.

Crazy Jane Talks with the Bishop

I met the Bishop on the road
And much said he and I.
'Those breasts are flat and fallen now
Those veins must soon be dry;
Live in a heavenly mansion,
Not in some foul sty.'

'Fair and foul are near of kin,
And fair needs foul,' I cried.
'My friends are gone, but that's a truth
Nor grave nor bed denied,
Learned in bodily lowliness
And in the heart's pride.

10

'A woman can be proud and stiff
When on love intent;
But Love has pitched his mansion in
The place of excrement;
For nothing can be sole or whole
That has not been rent.'

Her Anxiety

Earth in beauty dressed
Awaits returning spring.
All true love must die,
Alter at the best
Into some lesser thing.
Prove that I lie.

Such body lovers have,
Such exacting breath,

That they touch or sigh.
10   Every touch they give,
Love is nearer death.
Prove that I lie.

Lullaby

Beloved, may your sleep be sound
That have found it where you fed.
What were all the world's alarms
To mighty Paris when he found
Sleep upon a golden bed
That first dawn in Helen's arms?

Sleep, beloved, such a sleep
As did that wild Tristram know
When, the potion's work being done,
10   Roe could run or doe could leap
Under oak and beechen bough,
Roe could leap or doe could run;

Such a sleep and sound as fell
Upon Eurotas' grassy bank
When the holy bird, that there
Accomplished his predestined will,
From the limbs of Leda sank
But not from her protecting care.

After Long Silence

Speech after long silence; it is right,
All other lovers being estranged or dead,
Unfriendly lamplight hid under its shade,
The curtains drawn upon unfriendly night,
That we descant and yet again descant
Upon the supreme theme of Art and Song:
Bodily decrepitude is wisdom; young
We loved each other and were ignorant.

Father and Child

She hears me strike the board and say
That she is under ban
Of all good men and women,
Being mentioned with a man
That has the worst of all bad names;
And thereupon replies
That his hair is beautiful,
Cold as the March wind his eyes.

Parting

He. Dear, I must be gone
    While night shuts the eyes
    Of the household spies;
    That song announces dawn.

She. No, night's bird and love's
    Bids all true lovers rest,
    While his loud song reproves
    The murderous stealth of day.

He. Daylight already flies
    From mountain crest to crest.   10

She. That light is from the moon.

He. That bird . . .

She.   Let him sing on,
    I offer to love's play
    My dark declivities.

Her Vision in the Wood

Dry timber under that rich foliage,
At wine-dark midnight in the sacred wood,
Too old for a man's love I stood in rage
Imagining men. Imagining that I could
A greater with a lesser pang assuage
Or but to find if withered vein ran blood,
I tore my body that its wine might cover
Whatever could recall the lip of lover.

And after that I held my fingers up,
10   Stared at the wine-dark nail, or dark that ran
Down every withered finger from the top;
But the dark changed to red, and torches shone,
And deafening music shook the leaves; a troop
Shouldered a litter with a wounded man,
Or smote upon the string and to the sound
Sang of the beast that gave the fatal wound.

All stately women moving to a song
With loosened hair or foreheads grief-distraught,
It seemed a Quattrocento painter's throng,
20   A thoughtless image of Mantegna's thought—
Why should they think that are for ever young?
Till suddenly in grief's contagion caught,
I stared upon his blood-bedabbled breast
And sang my malediction with the rest.

That thing all blood and mire, that beast-torn wreck,
Half turned and fixed a glazing eye on mine,
And, though love's bitter-sweet had all come back,
Those bodies from a picture or a coin
Nor saw my body fall nor heard it shriek,
30   Nor knew, drunken with singing as with wine,
That they had brought no fabulous symbol there
But my heart's victim and its torturer.

A Last Confession

What lively lad most pleasured me
Of all that with me lay?
I answer that I gave my soul
And loved in misery,
But had great pleasure with a lad
That I loved bodily.

Flinging from his arms I laughed
To think his passion such
He fancied that I gave a soul
Did but our bodies touch,   10
And laughed upon his breast to think
Beast gave beast as much.

I gave what other women gave
That stepped out of their clothes,
But when this soul, its body off,
Naked to naked goes,
He it has found shall find therein
What none other knows,

And give his own and take his own
And rule in his own right;   20
And though it loved in misery
Close and cling so tight,
There's not a bird of day that dare
Extinguish that delight.

From the 'Antigone'

Overcome—O bitter sweetness,
Inhabitant of the soft cheek of a girl—
The rich man and his affairs,
The fat flocks and the fields' fatness,
Mariners, rough harvesters;
Overcome Gods upon Parnassus;

Overcome the Empyrean; hurl
Heaven and Earth out of their places,
That in the same calamity
Brother and brother, friend and friend,
Family and family,
City and city may contend,
By that great glory driven wild.

Pray I will and sing I must,
And yet I weep—Oedipus' child
Descends into the loveless dust.

Parnell's Funeral and Other Poems

(1935)

Parnell's Funeral

I

Under the Great Comedian's tomb the crowd.
A bundle of tempestuous cloud is blown
About the sky; where that is clear of cloud
Brightness remains; a brighter star shoots down;
What shudders run through all that animal blood?
What is this sacrifice? Can someone there
Recall the Cretan barb that pierced a star?

Rich foliage that the starlight glittered through,
A frenzied crowd, and where the branches sprang
A beautiful seated boy; a sacred bow;   10
A woman, and an arrow on a string;
A pierced boy, image of a star laid low.
That woman, the Great Mother imaging,
Cut out his heart. Some master of design
Stamped boy and tree upon Sicilian coin.

An age is the reversal of an age:
When strangers murdered Emmet, Fitzgerald, Tone,
We lived like men that watch a painted stage.
What matter for the scene, the scene once gone:
It had not touched our lives. But popular rage,
Hysterica passio dragged this quarry down.   20
None shared our guilt; nor did we play a part
Upon a painted stage when we devoured his heart.

Come, fix upon me that accusing eye.
I thirst for accusation. All that was sung,
All that was said in Ireland is a lie
Bred out of the contagion of the throng,
Saving the rhyme rats hear before they die.
Leave nothing but the nothings that belong
30   To this bare soul, let all men judge that can
Whether it be an animal or a man.

II

The rest I pass, one sentence I unsay.
Had de Valera eaten Parnell's heart
No loose-lipped demagogue had won the day,
No civil rancour torn the land apart.

Had Cosgrave eaten Parnell's heart, the land's
Imagination had been satisfied,
Or lacking that, government in such hands,
O'Higgins its sole statesman had not died.

Had even O'Duffy—but I name no more—
40   Their school a crowd, his master solitude;
Through Jonathan Swift's dark grove he passed, and there
Plucked bitter wisdom that enriched his blood.

A Prayer for Old Age

God guard me from those thoughts men think
In the mind alone;
He that sings a lasting song
Thinks in a marrow-bone;

From all that makes a wise old man
That can be praised of all;
O what am I that I should not seem
For the song's sake a fool?

I pray—for fashion's word is out
10   And prayer comes round again—

That I may seem, though I die old,
A foolish, passionate man.

Ribh at the Tomb
of Baile and Aillinn

Because you have found me in the pitch-dark night
With open book you ask me what I do.
Mark and digest my tale, carry it afar
To those that never saw this tonsured head
Nor heard this voice that ninety years have cracked.
Of Baile and Aillinn you need not speak,
All know their tale, all know what leaf and twig,
What juncture of the apple and the yew,
Surmount their bones; but speak what none have heard.

The miracle that gave them such a death   10
Transfigured to pure substance what had once
Been bone and sinew; when such bodies join
There is no touching here, nor touching there,
Nor straining joy, but whole is joined to whole;
For the intercourse of angels is a light
Where for its moment both seem lost, consumed.

Here in the pitch-dark atmosphere above
The trembling of the apple and the yew,
Here on the anniversary of their death,   20
The anniversary of their first embrace,
Those lovers, purified by tragedy,
Hurry into each other's arms; these eyes,
By water, herb and solitary prayer
Made aquiline, are open to that light.
Though somewhat broken by the leaves, that light
Lies in a circle on the grass; therein
I turn the pages of my holy book.

The Four Ages of Man

He with body waged a fight,
But body won; it walks upright.

Then he struggled with the heart;
Innocence and peace depart.

Then he struggled with the mind;
His proud heart he left behind.

Now his wars on God begin;
At stroke of midnight God shall win.

Meru

Civilisation is hooped together, brought
Under a rule, under the semblance of peace
By manifold illusion; but man's life is thought,
And he, despite his terror, cannot cease
Ravening through century after century,
Ravening, raging, and uprooting that he may come
Into the desolation of reality:
Egypt and Greece good-bye, and good-bye, Rome!
Hermits upon Mount Meru or Everest,
Caverned in night under the drifted snow,
Or where that snow and winter's dreadful blast
Beat down upon their naked bodies, know
That day brings round the night, that before dawn
His glory and his monuments are gone.

The Gyres

The gyres! the gyres! Old Rocky Face look forth;
Things thought too long can be no longer thought
For beauty dies of beauty, worth of worth,
And ancient lineaments are blotted out.
Irrational streams of blood are staining earth;
Empedocles has thrown all things about;
Hector is dead and there's a light in Troy;
We that look on but laugh in tragic joy.

What matter though numb nightmare ride on top
And blood and mire the sensitive body stain?   10
What matter? Heave no sigh, let no tear drop,
A greater, a more gracious time has gone;
For painted forms or boxes of make-up
In ancient tombs I sighed, but not again;
What matter? Out of Cavern comes a voice
And all it knows is that one word 'Rejoice.'

Conduct and work grow coarse, and coarse the soul,
What matter! Those that Rocky Face holds dear,
Lovers of horses and of women, shall
From marble of a broken sepulchre   20
Or dark betwixt the polecat and the owl,
Or any rich, dark nothing disinter
The workman, noble and saint, and all things run
On that unfashionable gyre again.

Lapis Lazuli
(For Harry Clifton)

I have heard that hysterical women say
They are sick of the palette and fiddle-bow,
Of poets that are always gay,
For everybody knows or else should know
That if nothing drastic is done
Aeroplane and Zeppelin will come out,
Pitch like King Billy bomb-balls in
Until the town lie beaten flat.

All perform their tragic play,
There struts Hamlet, there is Lear,
That's Ophelia, that Cordelia;
Yet they, should the last scene be there,
The great stage curtain about to drop,
If worthy their prominent part in the play,
Do not break up their lines to weep.
They know that Hamlet and Lear are gay;
Gaiety transfiguring all that dread.
All men have aimed at, found and lost;
Black out; Heaven blazing into the head:
Tragedy wrought to its uttermost.
Though Hamlet rambles and Lear rages,
And all the drop scenes drop at once
Upon a hundred thousand stages,
It cannot grow by an inch or an ounce.

On their own feet they came, or on shipboard,
Camel-back, horse-back, ass-back, mule-back,
Old civilisations put to the sword.
Then they and their wisdom went to rack:
No handiwork of Callimachus
Who handled marble as if it were bronze,
Made draperies that seemed to rise
When sea-wind swept the corner, stands;
His long lamp chimney shaped like the stem

Of a slender palm, stood but a day;
All things fall and are built again
And those that build them again are gay.

Two Chinamen, behind them a third,
Are carved in Lapis Lazuli,
Over them flies a long-legged bird
A symbol of longevity;   40
The third, doubtless a serving-man,
Carries a musical instrument.
Every discolouration of the stone,
Every accidental crack or dent
Seems a water-course or an avalanche,
Or lofty slope where it still snows
Though doubtless plum or cherry-branch
Sweetens the little half-way house
Those Chinamen climb towards, and I
Delight to imagine them seated there;   50
There, on the mountain and the sky,
On all the tragic scene they stare.
One asks for mournful melodies;
Accomplished fingers begin to play.
Their eyes mid many wrinkles, their eyes,
Their ancient, glittering eyes, are gay.

Imitated from the Japanese

A most astonishing thing
Seventy years have I lived;

(Hurrah for the flowers of Spring
For Spring is here again.)

Seventy years have I lived
No ragged beggar man,
Seventy years have I lived,
Seventy years man and boy,
And never have I danced for joy.

An Acre of Grass

Picture and book remain,
An acre of green grass
For air and exercise,
Now strength of body goes;
Midnight an old house
Where nothing stirs but a mouse.

My temptation is quiet.
Here at life's end
Neither loose imagination,
Nor the mill of the mind
Consuming its rag and bone,
Can make the truth known.

Grant me an old man's frenzy.
Myself must I remake
Till I am Timon and Lear
Or that William Blake
Who beat upon the wall
Till truth obeyed his call;

A mind Michael Angelo knew
That can pierce the clouds
Or inspired by frenzy
Shake the dead in their shrouds;
Forgotten else by mankind
An old man's eagle mind.

What Then?

His chosen comrades thought at school
He must grow a famous man;
He thought the same and lived by rule,
All his twenties crammed with toil;
'What then?' sang Plato's ghost, 'what then?'

Everything he wrote was read,
After certain years he won
Sufficient money for his need,
Friends that have been friends indeed;
'What then?' sang Plato's ghost, 'what then?'   10

All his happier dreams came true—
A small old house, wife, daughter, son,
Grounds where plum and cabbage grew,
Poets and Wits about him drew;
'What then?' sang Plato's ghost, 'what then?'

'The work is done,' grown old he thought,
'According to my boyish plan;
Let the fools rage, I swerved in nought,
Something to perfection brought;'
But louder sang that ghost 'What then?'   20

Beautiful Lofty Things

Beautiful lofty things; O'Leary's noble head;
My father upon the Abbey stage, before him a raging crowd.
'This Land of Saints,' and then as the applause died out,
'Of plaster Saints;' his beautiful mischievous head thrown back.
Standish O'Grady supporting himself between the tables
Speaking to a drunken audience high nonsensical words;
Augusta Gregory seated at her great ormolu table
Her eightieth winter approaching; 'Yesterday he threatened my life,
I told him that nightly from six to seven I sat at this table
The blinds drawn up;' Maud Gonne at Howth station waiting a   10
    train,
Pallas Athena in that straight back and arrogant head:
All the Olympians; a thing never known again.

Come Gather
Round Me Parnellites

Come gather round me Parnellites
And praise our chosen man,
Stand upright on your legs awhile,
Stand upright while you can,
For soon we lie where he is laid
And he is underground;
Come fill up all those glasses
And pass the bottle round.

And here's a cogent reason
And I have many more,
He fought the might of England
And saved the Irish poor,
Whatever good a farmer's got
He brought it all to pass;
And here's another reason,
That Parnell loved a lass.

And here's a final reason,
He was of such a kind
Every man that sings a song
Keeps Parnell in his mind
For Parnell was a proud man,
No prouder trod the ground,
And a proud man's a lovely man
So pass the bottle round.

The Bishops and the Party
That tragic story made,
A husband that had sold his wife
And after that betrayed;
But stories that live longest
Are sung above the glass,
And Parnell loved his country
And Parnell loved his lass.

The Great Day

Hurrah for revolution and more cannon shot;
A beggar upon horseback lashes a beggar upon foot;
Hurrah for revolution and cannon come again,
The beggars have changed places but the lash goes on.

Parnell

Parnell came down the road, he said to a cheering man;
'Ireland shall get her freedom and you still break stone.'

The Spur

You think it horrible that lust and rage
Should dance attendance upon my old age;
They were not such a plague when I was young;
What else have I to spur me into song?

The Municipal Gallery Re-visited

I

Around me the images of thirty years;
An ambush; pilgrims at the water-side;
Casement upon trial, half hidden by the bars,
Guarded; Griffith staring in hysterical pride;
Kevin O'Higgins' countenance that wears
A gentle questioning look that cannot hide
A soul incapable of remorse or rest;
A revolutionary soldier kneeling to be blessed.

II

An Abbot or Archbishop with an upraised hand
Blessing the Tricolour. 'This is not' I say
'The dead Ireland of my youth, but an Ireland
The poets have imagined, terrible and gay.'
Before a woman's portrait suddenly I stand;
Beautiful and gentle in her Venetian way.
I met her all but fifty years ago
For twenty minutes in some studio.

III

Heart smitten with emotion I sink down
My heart recovering with covered eyes;
Wherever I had looked I had looked upon
My permanent or impermanent images;
Augusta Gregory's son; her sister's son,
Hugh Lane, 'onlie begetter' of all these;
Hazel Lavery living and dying, that tale
As though some ballad singer had sung it all.

IV

Mancini's portrait of Augusta Gregory,
'Greatest since Rembrandt,' according to John Synge;
A great ebullient portrait certainly;
But where is the brush that could show anything
Of all that pride and that humility,
And I am in despair that time may bring
Approved patterns of women or of men
But not that selfsame excellence again.

V

My mediaeval knees lack health until they bend,
But in that woman, in that household where
Honour had lived so long, all lacking found.
Childless I thought 'my children may find here
Deep-rooted things,' but never foresaw its end,
And now that end has come I have not wept;
No fox can foul the lair the badger swept.

VI

(An image out of Spenser and the common tongue.) 40
John Synge, I and Augusta Gregory, thought
All that we did, all that we said or sang
Must come from contact with the soil, from that
Contact everything Antaeus-like grew strong.
We three alone in modern times had brought
Everything down to that sole test again,
Dream of the noble and the beggarman.

VII

And here's John Synge himself, that rooted man
'Forgetting human words,' a grave deep face.
You that would judge me do not judge alone 50
This book or that, come to this hallowed place
Where my friends' portraits hang and look thereon;
Ireland's history in their lineaments trace;
Think where man's glory most begins and ends
And say my glory was I had such friends.

Are You Content

I call on those that call me son,
Grandson, or great-grandson,
On uncles, aunts, great-uncles or great-aunts
To judge what I have done.
Have I, that put it into words,
Spoilt what old loins have sent?
Eyes spiritualised by death can judge,
I cannot, but I am not content.

He that in Sligo at Drumcliff
Set up the old stone Cross,
That red-headed rector in County Down 10
A good man on a horse,
Sandymount Corbets, that notable man
Old William Pollexfen,

The smuggler Middleton, Butlers far back,
Half legendary men.

Infirm and aged I might stay
In some good company,
I who have always hated work,
Smiling at the sea,
Or demonstrate in my own life
What Robert Browning meant
By an old hunter talking with Gods;
But I am not content.

[Last Poems, 1938–39]

Under Ben Bulben

I

Swear by what the Sages spoke
Round the Mareotic Lake
That the Witch of Atlas knew,
Spoke and set the cocks a-crow.

Swear by those horsemen, by those women,
Complexion and form prove superhuman,
That pale, long visaged company
That airs an immortality
Completeness of their passions won;
Now they ride the wintry dawn   10
Where Ben Bulben sets the scene.

Here's the gist of what they mean.

II

Many times man lives and dies
Between his two eternities,
That of race and that of soul,
And ancient Ireland knew it all.
Whether man dies in his bed
Or the rifle knocks him dead,
A brief parting from those dear
Is the worst man has to fear.   20
Though grave-diggers' toil is long,
Sharp their spades, their muscle strong,

They but thrust their buried men
Back in the human mind again.

III

You that Mitchel's prayer have heard
'Send war in our time, O Lord!'
Know that when all words are said
And a man is fighting mad,
Something drops from eyes long blind
30   He completes his partial mind,
For an instant stands at ease,
Laughs aloud, his heart at peace,
Even the wisest man grows tense
With some sort of violence
Before he can accomplish fate
Know his work or choose his mate.

IV

Poet and sculptor do the work
Nor let the modish painter shirk
What his great forefathers did,
40   Bring the soul of man to God,
Make him fill the cradles right.

Measurement began our might:
Forms a stark Egyptian thought,
Forms that gentler Phidias wrought.

Michael Angelo left a proof
On the Sistine Chapel roof,
Where but half-awakened Adam
Can disturb globe-trotting Madam
Till her bowels are in heat,
50   Proof that there's a purpose set
Before the secret working mind:
Profane perfection of mankind.

Quattrocento put in paint,
On backgrounds for a God or Saint,
Gardens where a soul's at ease;

Where everything that meets the eye
Flowers and grass and cloudless sky
Resemble forms that are, or seem
When sleepers wake and yet still dream,
And when it's vanished still declare,   60
With only bed and bedstead there,
That Heavens had opened.

                   Gyres run on;
When that greater dream had gone
Calvert and Wilson, Blake and Claude
Prepared a rest for the people of God,
Palmer's phrase, but after that
Confusion fell upon our thought.

V

Irish poets learn your trade
Sing whatever is well made,
Scorn the sort now growing up   70
All out of shape from toe to top,
Their unremembering hearts and heads
Base-born products of base beds.
Sing the peasantry, and then
Hard-riding country gentlemen,
The holiness of monks, and after
Porter-drinkers' randy laughter;
Sing the lords and ladies gay
That were beaten into the clay
Through seven heroic centuries;   80
Cast your mind on other days
That we in coming days may be
Still the indomitable Irishry.

VI

Under bare Ben Bulben's head
In Drumcliff churchyard Yeats is laid,
An ancestor was rector there
Long years ago; a church stands near,
By the road an ancient Cross.

No marble, no conventional phrase,
90   On limestone quarried near the spot
By his command these words are cut:

     Cast a cold eye
     On life, on death.
     Horseman, pass by!

The Black Tower

Say that the men of the old black tower
Though they but feed as the goatherd feeds
Their money spent, their wine gone sour,
Lack nothing that a soldier needs,
That all are oath-bound men
Those banners come not in.

There in the tomb stand the dead upright
But winds come up from the shore
They shake when the winds roar
10   *Old bones upon the mountain shake.*

Those banners come to bribe or threaten
Or whisper that a man's a fool
Who when his own right king's forgotten
Cares what king sets up his rule.
If he died long ago
Why do you dread us so?

There in the tomb drops the faint moonlight
But wind comes up from the shore
They shake when the winds roar
20   *Old bones upon the mountain shake.*

The tower's old cook that must climb and clamber
Catching small birds in the dew of the morn
When we hale men lie stretched in slumber
Swears that he hears the king's great horn.
But he's a lying hound;
Stand we on guard oath-bound.

There in the tomb the dark grows blacker
But wind comes up from the shore
They shake when the winds roar
Old bones upon the mountain shake. 30

Cuchulain Comforted

A man that had six mortal wounds, a man
Violent and famous, strode among the dead;
Eyes stared out of the branches and were gone.

Then certain Shrouds that muttered head to head
Came and were gone. He leant upon a tree
As though to meditate on wounds and blood.

A Shroud that seemed to have authority
Among those bird-like things came, and let fall
A bundle of linen. Shrouds by two and three

Came creeping up because the man was still. 10
And thereupon that linen-carrier said
'Your life can grow much sweeter if you will

'Obey our ancient rule and make a shroud;
Mainly because of what we only know
The rattle of those arms makes us afraid.

'We thread the needles' eyes and all we do
All must together do.' That done, the man
Took up the nearest and began to sew.

'Now we shall sing and sing the best we can
But first you must be told our character: 20
Convicted cowards all by kindred slain

'Or driven from home and left to die in fear.'
They sang but had nor human notes nor words,
Though all was done in common as before,

They had changed their throats and had the throats of birds.

The Statues

Pythagoras planned it. Why did the people stare?
His numbers, though they moved or seemed to move
In marble or in bronze, lacked character.
But boys and girls, pale from the imagined love
Of solitary beds, knew what they were,
That passion could bring character enough,
And pressed at midnight in some public place
Live lips upon a plummet-measured face.

No! Greater than Pythagoras, for the men
That with a mallet or a chisel modelled these
Calculations that look but casual flesh, put down
All Asiatic vague immensities,
And not the banks of oars that swam upon
The many-headed foam at Salamis.
Europe put off that foam when Phidias
Gave women dreams and dreams their looking glass.

One image crossed the many-headed, sat
Under the tropic shade, grew round and slow,
No Hamlet thin from eating flies, a fat
Dreamer of the Middle-Ages. Empty eye-balls knew
That knowledge increases unreality, that
Mirror on mirror mirrored is all the show.
When gong and conch declare the hour to bless,
Grimalkin crawls to Buddha's emptiness.

When Pearse summoned Cuchulain to his side
What stalked through the Post Office? What intellect,
What calculation, number, measurement, replied?
We Irish, born into that ancient sect
But thrown upon this filthy modern tide
And by its formless, spawning, fury wrecked
Climb to our proper dark, that we may trace
The lineaments of a plummet-measured face.

10

20

30

Long-legged Fly

That civilisation may not sink
Its great battle lost,
Quiet the dog, tether the pony
To a distant post.
Our master Caesar is in the tent
Where the maps are spread,
His eyes fixed upon nothing,
A hand under his head.

Like a long-legged fly upon the stream
His mind moves upon silence.   10

That the topless towers be burnt
And men recall that face,
Move most gently if move you must
In this lonely place.
She thinks, part woman, three parts a child,
That nobody looks; her feet
Practise a tinker shuffle
Picked up on the street.

Like a long-legged fly upon the stream
Her mind moves upon silence.   20

That girls at puberty may find
The first Adam in their thought,
Shut the door of the Pope's chapel,
Keep those children out.
There on that scaffolding reclines
Michael Angelo.
With no more sound than the mice make
His hand moves to and fro.

Like a long-legged fly upon the stream
His mind moves upon silence.   30

High Talk

Processions that lack high stilts have nothing that catches the eye.
What if my great-granddad had a pair that were twenty foot high,
And mine were but fifteen foot, no modern stalks upon higher,
Some rogue of the world stole them to patch up a fence or a fire.

Because piebald ponies, led bears, caged lions, make but poor shows,
Because children demand Daddy-long-legs upon his timber toes,
Because women in the upper stories demand a face at the pane
That patching old heels they may shriek, I take to chisel and plane.

Malachi Stilt-Jack am I, whatever I learned has run wild,
10   From collar to collar, from stilt to stilt, from father to child.

All metaphor, Malachi, stilts and all. A barnacle goose
Far up in the stretches of night; night splits and the dawn breaks
    loose;
I, through the terrible novelty of light, stalk on, stalk on;
Those great sea-horses bare their teeth and laugh at the dawn.

Man and the Echo

Man. In a cleft that's christened Alt
    Under broken stone I halt
    At the bottom of a pit
    That broad noon has never lit,
    And shout a secret to the stone.
    All that I have said and done,
    Now that I am old and ill,
    Turns into a question till
    I lie awake night after night
10   And never get the answers right.
    Did that play of mine send out
    Certain men the English shot?
    Did words of mine put too great strain
    On that woman's reeling brain?
    Could my spoken words have checked

That whereby a house lay wrecked?
And all seems evil until I
Sleepless would lie down and die.

Echo. Lie down and die.

Man.   That were to shirk
    The spiritual intellect's great work   20
    And shirk it in vain. There is no release
    In a bodkin or disease,
    Nor can there be a work so great
    As that which cleans man's dirty slate.
    While man can still his body keep
    Wine or love drug him to sleep,
    Waking he thanks the Lord that he
    Has body and its stupidity,
    But body gone he sleeps no more
    And till his intellect grows sure   30
    That all's arranged in one clear view
    Pursues the thoughts that I pursue,
    Then stands in judgment on his soul,
    And, all work done, dismisses all
    Out of intellect and sight
    And sinks at last into the night.

Echo. Into the night.

Man.   O rocky voice
    Shall we in that great night rejoice?
    What do we know but that we face
    One another in this place?   40
    But hush, for I have lost the theme
    Its joy or night seem but a dream;
    Up there some hawk or owl has struck
    Dropping out of sky or rock,
    A stricken rabbit is crying out
    And its cry distracts my thought.

The Circus Animals' Desertion

I

I sought a theme and sought for it in vain,
I sought it daily for six weeks or so.
Maybe at last being but a broken man
I must be satisfied with my heart, although
Winter and summer till old age began
My circus animals were all on show,
Those stilted boys, that burnished chariot,
Lion and woman and the Lord knows what.

II

What can I but enumerate old themes,
First that sea-rider Oisin led by the nose
Through three enchanted islands, allegorical dreams,
Vain gaiety, vain battle, vain repose,
Themes of the embittered heart, or so it seems,
That might adorn old songs or courtly shows;
But what cared I that set him on to ride,
I, starved for the bosom of his fairy bride.

And then a counter-truth filled out its play,
'The Countess Cathleen' was the name I gave it,
She, pity-crazed, had given her soul away
But masterful Heaven had intervened to save it.
I thought my dear must her own soul destroy
So did fanaticism and hate enslave it,
And this brought forth a dream and soon enough
This dream itself had all my thought and love.

And when the Fool and Blind Man stole the bread
Cuchulain fought the ungovernable sea;
Heart mysteries there, and yet when all is said
It was the dream itself enchanted me:
Character isolated by a deed
To engross the present and dominate memory.
Players and painted stage took all my love
And not those things that they were emblems of.

III

Those masterful images because complete
Grew in pure mind but out of what began?
A mound of refuse or the sweepings of a street,
Old kettles, old bottles, and a broken can,
Old iron, old bones, old rags, that raving slut
Who keeps the till. Now that my ladder's gone
I must lie down where all the ladders start
In the foul rag and bone shop of the heart.   40

Politics

*'In our time the destiny of man
presents its meanings in political terms.'*
THOMAS MANN.

How can I, that girl standing there,
My attention fix
On Roman or on Russian
Or on Spanish politics,
Yet here's a travelled man that knows
What he talks about,
And there's a politician
That has both read and thought,
And maybe what they say is true
Of war and war's alarms,   10
But O that I were young again
And held her in my arms.

Plays

Cathleen ni Houlihan

(1902)

Persons in the Play

Peter Gillane

Michael Gillane, *his son, going to be married*

Patrick Gillane, *a lad of twelve, Michael's brother*

Bridget Gillane, *Peter's wife*

Delia Cahel, *engaged to Michael*

The Poor Old Woman

Neighbours

Interior of a cottage close to Killala, in 1798. Bridget is standing at a table undoing a parcel. Peter is sitting at one side of the fire, Patrick at the other.

Peter. What is that sound I hear?

Patrick. I don't hear anything. [*He listens.*] I hear it now. It's like cheering. [*He goes to the window and looks out.*] I wonder what they are cheering about. I don't see anybody.

Peter. It might be a hurling.

Patrick. There's no hurling to-day. It must be down in the town the cheering is.

Bridget. I suppose the boys must be having some sport of their own. Come over here, Peter, and look at Michael's wedding clothes.

Peter [*shifts his chair to table*]. Those are grand clothes, indeed.

Bridget. You hadn't clothes like that when you married me, and no coat to put on of a Sunday more than any other day.

Peter. That is true, indeed. We never thought a son of our own would be wearing a suit of that sort for his wedding, or have so good a place to bring a wife to.

Patrick [*who is still at the window*]. There's an old woman coming down the road. I don't know is it here she is coming.

Bridget. It will be a neighbour coming to hear about Michael's wedding. Can you see who it is?

Patrick. I think it is a stranger, but she's not coming to the house. She's turned into the gap that goes down where Maurteen and his sons are shearing sheep. [*He turns towards Bridget.*] Do you remember what Winny of the Cross-Roads was saying the other night about the strange woman that goes through the country whatever time there's war or trouble coming?

Bridget. Don't be bothering us about Winny's talk, but go and open the door for your brother. I hear him coming up the path.

Peter. I hope he has brought Delia's fortune with him safe, for fear the people might go back on the bargain and I after making it. Trouble enough I had making it.

> [*Patrick opens the door and Michael comes in.*

Bridget. What kept you, Michael? We were looking out for you this long time.

Michael. I went round by the priest's house to bid him be ready to marry us to-morrow.

Bridget. Did he say anything?

Michael. He said it was a very nice match, and that he was never better pleased to marry any two in his parish than myself and Delia Cahel.

Peter. Have you got the fortune, Michael?

Michael. Here it is.

> [*Michael puts bag on table and goes over and leans against chimney-jamb. Bridget, who has been all this time examining the clothes, pulling the seams and trying the lining of the pockets, etc., puts the clothes on the dresser.*

Peter [*getting up and taking the bag in his hand and turning out the money*]. Yes, I made the bargain well for you, Michael. Old John Cahel would sooner have kept a share of this a while longer. 'Let me keep the half of it until the first boy is born,' says he. 'You will not,' says I. 'Whether there is or is not a boy, the whole hundred pounds must be in Michael's hands before he brings your daughter to the house.' The wife spoke to him then, and he gave in at the end.

Bridget. You seem well pleased to be handling the money, Peter.

Peter. Indeed, I wish I had had the luck to get a hundred pounds, or twenty pounds itself, with the wife I married.

Bridget. Well, if I didn't bring much I didn't get much. What had you the day I married you but a flock of hens and you feeding them, and a few lambs and you driving them to the market at Ballina? [*She is vexed and bangs a jug on the dresser.*] If I brought no fortune I worked it out in my bones, laying down the baby, Michael that is standing there now, on a stook of straw, while I dug the potatoes, and never asking big dresses or anything but to be working.

Peter. That is true, indeed. [*He pats her arm.*

Bridget. Leave me alone now till I ready the house for the woman that is to come into it.

Peter. You are the best woman in Ireland, but money is good, too. [*He begins handling the money again and sits down.*] I never thought to see so much money within my four walls. We can do great things now we have it. We can take the ten acres of land we have the chance of since Jamsie Dempsey died, and stock it. We will go to the fair at Ballina to buy the stock. Did Delia ask any of the money for her own use, Michael?

Michael. She did not, indeed. She did not seem to take much notice of it, or to look at it at all.

Bridget. That's no wonder. Why would she look at it when she had yourself to look at, a fine, strong young man? It is proud she must be to get you; a good steady boy that will make use of the money, and not be running through it or spending it on drink like another.

Peter. It's likely Michael himself was not thinking much of the fortune either, but of what sort the girl was to look at.

Michael [*coming over towards the table*]. Well, you would like a nice comely girl to be beside you, and to go walking with you. The fortune only lasts for a while, but the woman will be there always.

Patrick [*turning round from the window*]. They are cheering again down in the town. Maybe they are landing horses from Enniscrone. They do be cheering when the horses take the water well.

Michael. There are no horses in it. Where would they be going and no fair at hand? Go down to the town, Patrick, and see what is going on.

Patrick [*opens the door to go out, but stops for a moment on the threshold*]. Will Delia remember, do you think, to bring the greyhound pup she promised me when she would be coming to the house?

Michael. She will surely.

[*Patrick goes out, leaving the door open.*

Peter. It will be Patrick's turn next to be looking for a fortune, but he won't find it so easy to get it and he with no place of his own.

Bridget. I do be thinking sometimes, now things are going so well with us, and the Cahels such a good back to us in the district, and Delia's own uncle a priest, we might be put in the way of making Patrick a priest some day, and he so good at his books.

Peter. Time enough, time enough. You have always your head full of plans, Bridget.

Bridget. We will be well able to give him learning, and not to send him tramping the country like a poor scholar that lives on charity.

Michael. They're not done cheering yet.

[*He goes over to the door and stands there for a moment, putting up his hand to shade his eyes.*

Bridget. Do you see anything?

Michael. I see an old woman coming up the path.

Bridget. Who is it, I wonder? It must be the strange woman
Patrick saw a while ago.

Michael. I don't think it's one of the neighbours anyway, but she
has her cloak over her face.

Bridget. It might be some poor woman heard we were making
ready for the wedding and came to look for her share.

Peter. I may as well put the money out of sight. There is no use
leaving it out for every stranger to look at.
[*He goes over to a large box in the corner, opens it and puts
the bag in and fumbles at the lock.*

Michael. There she is, father! [*An Old Woman passes the window
slowly. She looks at Michael as she passes.*] I'd sooner a
stranger not to come to the house the night before my wedding.

Bridget. Open the door, Michael; don't keep the poor woman
waiting.
[*The Old Woman comes in. Michael stands aside to make way
for her.*

Old Woman. God save all here!

Peter. God save you kindly!

Old Woman. You have good shelter here.

Peter. You are welcome to whatever shelter we have.

Bridget. Sit down there by the fire and welcome.

Old Woman [*warming her hands*]. There is a hard wind outside.
[*Michael watches her curiously from the door. Peter comes
over to the table.*

Peter. Have you travelled far to-day?

Old Woman. I have travelled far, very far; there are few have
travelled so far as myself, and there's many a one that doesn't
make me welcome. There was one that had strong sons I
thought were friends of mine, but they were shearing their
sheep, and they wouldn't listen to me.

Peter. It's a pity indeed for any person to have no place of their own.

Old Woman. That's true for you indeed, and it's long I'm on the roads since I first went wandering.

Bridget. It is a wonder you are not worn out with so much wandering.

Old Woman. Sometimes my feet are tired and my hands are quiet, but there is no quiet in my heart. When the people see me quiet, they think old age has come on me and that all the stir has gone out of me. But when the trouble is on me I must be talking to my friends.

Bridget. What was it put you wandering?

Old Woman. Too many strangers in the house.

Bridget. Indeed you look as if you'd had your share of trouble.

Old Woman. I have had trouble indeed.

Bridget. What was it put the trouble on you?

Old Woman. My land that was taken from me.

Peter. Was it much land they took from you?

Old Woman. My four beautiful green fields.

Peter [*aside to Bridget*]. Do you think could she be the widow Casey that was put out of her holding at Kilglass a while ago?

Bridget. She is not. I saw the widow Casey one time at the market in Ballina, a stout fresh woman.

Peter [*to Old Woman*]. Did you hear a noise of cheering, and you coming up the hill?

Old Woman. I thought I heard the noise I used to hear when my friends came to visit me.
[*She begins singing half to herself.*
  I will go cry with the woman,
  For yellow-haired Donough is dead,
  With a hempen rope for a neckcloth,
  And a white cloth on his head,—

Michael [*coming from the door*]. What is it that you are singing, ma'am?

Old Woman. Singing I am about a man I knew one time, yellow-haired Donough that was hanged in Galway.

> [*She goes on singing, much louder.*]
> I am come to cry with you, woman,
> My hair is unwound and unbound;
> I remember him ploughing his field,
> Turning up the red side of the ground,
> And building his barn on the hill
> With the good mortared stone;
> O! we'd have pulled down the gallows
> Had it happened in Enniscrone!

Michael. What was it brought him to his death?

Old Woman. He died for love of me: many a man has died for love of me.

Peter [*aside to Bridget*]. Her trouble has put her wits astray.

Michael. Is it long since that song was made? Is it long since he got his death?

Old Woman. Not long, not long. But there were others that died for love of me a long time ago.

Michael. Were they neighbours of your own, ma'am?

Old Woman. Come here beside me and I'll tell you about them. [*Michael sits down beside her on the hearth.*] There was a red man of the O'Donnells from the north, and a man of the O'Sullivans from the south, and there was one Brian that lost his life at Clontarf by the sea, and there were a great many in the west, some that died hundreds of years ago, and there are some that will die to-morrow.

Michael. Is it in the west that men will die to-morrow?

Old Woman. Come nearer, nearer to me.

Bridget. Is she right, do you think? Or is she a woman from beyond the world?

Peter. She doesn't know well what she's talking about, with the want and the trouble she has gone through.

Bridget. The poor thing, we should treat her well.

Peter. Give her a drink of milk and a bit of the oaten cake.

Bridget. Maybe we should give her something along with that, to bring her on her way. A few pence or a shilling itself, and we with so much money in the house.

Peter. Indeed I'd not begrudge it to her if we had it to spare, but if we go running through what we have, we'll soon have to break the hundred pounds, and that would be a pity.

Bridget. Shame on you, Peter. Give her the shilling and your blessing with it, or our own luck will go from us.
> [*Peter goes to the box and takes out a shilling.*

Bridget [*to the Old Woman*]. Will you have a drink of milk, ma'am?

Old Woman. It is not food or drink that I want.

Peter [*offering the shilling*]. Here is something for you.

Old Woman. This is not what I want. It is not silver I want.

Peter. What is it you would be asking for?

Old Woman. If any one would give me help he must give me himself, he must give me all.
> [*Peter goes over to the table staring at the shilling in his hand in a bewildered way, and stands whispering to Bridget.*

Michael. Have you no one to care you in your age, ma'am?

Old Woman. I have not. With all the lovers that brought me their love I never set out the bed for any.

Michael. Are you lonely going the roads, ma'am?

Old Woman. I have my thoughts and I have my hopes.

Michael. What hopes have you to hold to?

Old Woman. The hope of getting my beautiful fields back again; the hope of putting the strangers out of my house.

Michael. What way will you do that, ma'am?

Old Woman. I have good friends that will help me. They are
gathering to help me now. I am not afraid. If they are put down
to-day they will get the upper hand to-morrow. [*She gets up.*] I
must be going to meet my friends. They are coming to help me
and I must be there to welcome them. I must call the
neighbours together to welcome them.

Michael. I will go with you.

Bridget. It is not her friends you have to go and welcome,
Michael; it is the girl coming into the house you have to
welcome. You have plenty to do; it is food and drink you have
to bring to the house. The woman that is coming home is not
coming with empty hands; you would not have an empty house
before her. [*To the Old Woman.*] Maybe you don't know,
ma'am, that my son is going to be married to-morrow.

Old Woman. It is not a man going to his marriage that I look to
for help.

Peter [*to Bridget*]. Who is she, do you think, at all?

Bridget. You did not tell us your name yet, ma'am.

Old Woman. Some call me the Poor Old Woman, and there are
some that call me Cathleen, the daughter of Houlihan.

Peter. I think I knew some one of that name, once. Who was it, I
wonder? It must have been some one I knew when I was a boy.
No, no; I remember, I heard it in a song.

Old Woman [*who is standing in the doorway*]. They are
wondering that there were songs made for me; there have been
many songs made for me. I heard one on the wind this morning.
                          [*Sings*]
     Do not make a great keening
     When the graves have been dug to-morrow.
     Do not call the white-scarfed riders
     To the burying that shall be to-morrow.

     Do not spread food to call strangers
     To the wakes that shall be to-morrow;

Do not give money for prayers
For the dead that shall die to-morrow. . . .

They will have no need of prayers, they will have no need of
prayers.

Michael. I do not know what that song means, but tell me
something I can do for you.

Peter. Come over to me, Michael.

Michael. Hush, father, listen to her.

Old Woman. It is a hard service they take that help me. Many that
are red-cheeked now will be pale-cheeked; many that have been
free to walk the hills and the bogs and the rushes will be sent to
walk hard streets in far countries; many a good plan will be
broken; many that have gathered money will not stay to spend it;
many a child will be born and there will be no father at its
christening to give it a name. They that have red cheeks will have
pale cheeks for my sake, and for all that, they will think they are
well paid.   [*She goes out; her voice is heard outside singing.*
They shall be remembered for ever,
They shall be alive for ever,
They shall be speaking for ever,
The people shall hear them for ever.

Bridget [*to Peter*]. Look at him, Peter; he has the look of a man
that has got the touch. [*Raising her voice.*] Look here, Michael,
at the wedding clothes. Such grand clothes as these are! You
have a right to fit them on now; it would be a pity to-morrow if
they did not fit. The boys would be laughing at you. Take them,
Michael, and go into the room and fit them on.
                                    [*She puts them on his arm.*

Michael. What wedding are you talking of? What clothes will I be
wearing to-morrow?

Bridget. These are the clothes you are going to wear when you
marry Delia Cahel to-morrow.

Michael. I had forgotten that.
        [*He looks at the clothes and turns towards the inner room,
        but stops at the sound of cheering outside.*

Peter. There is the shouting come to our own door. What is it has happened?

[*Neighbours come crowding in, Patrick and Delia with them.*

Patrick. There are ships in the Bay; the French are landing at Killala!

[*Peter takes his pipe from his mouth and his hat off, and stands up. The clothes slip from Michael's arm.*

Delia. Michael! [*He takes no notice.*] Michael! [*He turns towards her.*] Why do you look at me like a stranger?

[*She drops his arm. Bridget goes over towards her.*

Patrick. The boys are all hurrying down the hillside to join the French.

Delia. Michael won't be going to join the French.

Bridget [*to Peter*]. Tell him not to go, Peter.

Peter. It's no use. He doesn't hear a word we're saying.

Bridget. Try and coax him over to the fire.

Delia. Michael, Michael! You won't leave me! You won't join the French, and we going to be married!

[*She puts her arms about him, he turns towards her as if about to yield.*

Old Woman's voice outside.

> They shall be speaking for ever,
> The people shall hear them for ever.

[*Michael breaks away from Delia, stands for a second at the door, then rushes out, following the Old Woman's voice. Bridget takes Delia, who is crying silently, into her arms.*

Peter [*to Patrick, laying a hand on his arm*]. Did you see an old woman going down the path?

Patrick. I did not, but I saw a young girl, and she had the walk of a queen.

On Baile's Strand

(1904)

TO

WILLIAM FAY

BECAUSE OF THE BEAUTIFUL FANTASY OF HIS
PLAYING IN THE CHARACTER OF THE FOOL

Persons in the Play

A Fool

A Blind Man

Cuchulain, *King of Muirthemne*

Conchubar, *High King of Ulad*

A Young Man, son of *Cuchulain*

Kings and Singing Women

A great hall at Dundealgan, not 'Cuchulain's great ancient house' but an assembly-house nearer to the sea. A big door at the back, and through the door misty light as of sea-mist. There are many chairs and one long bench. One of these chairs, which is towards the front of the stage, is bigger than the others. Somewhere at the back there is a table with flagons of ale upon it and drinking-horns. There is a small door at one side of the hall. A Fool and Blind Man, both ragged, and their features made grotesque and extravagant by masks, come in through the door at the back. The Blind Man leans upon a staff.

Fool. What a clever man you are though you are blind! There's nobody with two eyes in his head that is as clever as you are. Who but you could have thought that the henwife sleeps every day a little at noon? I would never be able to steal anything if you didn't tell me where to look for it. And what a good cook you are! You take the fowl out of my hands after I have stolen it and plucked it, and you put it into the big pot at the fire

there, and I can go out and run races with the witches at the
edge of the waves and get an appetite, and when I've got it,
there's the hen waiting inside for me, done to the turn.

Blind Man [*who is feeling about with his stick*]. Done to the turn.

Fool [*putting his arm round Blind Man's neck*]. Come now, I'll have
a leg and you'll have a leg, and we'll draw lots for the wish-bone.
I'll be praising you, I'll be praising you while we're eating it, for
your good plans and for your good cooking. There's nobody in
the world like you, Blind Man. Come, come. Wait a minute. I
shouldn't have closed the door. There are some that look for me,
and I wouldn't like them not to find me. Don't tell it to anybody,
Blind Man. There are some that follow me. Boann herself out of
the river and Fand out of the deep sea. Witches they are, and
they come by in the wind, and they cry, 'Give a kiss, Fool, give a
kiss', that's what they cry. That's wide enough. All the witches
can come in now. I wouldn't have them beat at the door and say,
'Where is the Fool? Why has he put a lock on the door?' Maybe
they'll hear the bubbling of the pot and come in and sit on the
ground. But we won't give them any of the fowl. Let them go
back to the sea, let them go back to the sea.

Blind Man [*feeling legs of big chair with his hands*]. Ah! [*Then, in
a louder voice as he feels the back of it.*] Ah—ah—

Fool. Why do you say 'Ah-ah'?

Blind Man. I know the big chair. It is to-day the High King
Conchubar is coming. They have brought out his chair. He is
going to be Cuchulain's master in earnest from this day out. It
is that he's coming for.

Fool. He must be a great man to be Cuchulain's master.

Blind Man. So he is. He is a great man. He is over all the rest of
the kings of Ireland.

Fool. Cuchulain's master! I thought Cuchulain could do anything
he liked.

Blind Man. So he did, so he did. But he ran too wild, and
Conchubar is coming to-day to put an oath upon him that will
stop his rambling and make him as biddable as a house-dog

and keep him always at his hand. He will sit in this chair and put the oath upon him.

Fool. How will he do that?

Blind Man. You have no wits to understand such things. [*The Blind Man has got into the chair.*] He will sit up in this chair and he'll say: 'Take the oath, Cuchulain. I bid you take the oath. Do as I tell you. What are your wits compared with mine, and what are your riches compared with mine? And what sons have you to pay your debts and to put a stone over you when you die? Take the oath, I tell you. Take a strong oath.'

Fool [*crumpling himself up and whining*]. I will not. I'll take no oath. I want my dinner.

Blind Man. Hush, hush! It is not done yet.

Fool. You said it was done to a turn.

Blind Man. Did I, now? Well, it might be done, and not done. The wings might be white, but the legs might be red. The flesh might stick hard to the bones and not come away in the teeth. But, believe me, Fool, it will be well done before you put your teeth in it.

Fool. My teeth are growing long with the hunger.

Blind Man. I'll tell you a story—the kings have story-tellers while they are waiting for their dinner—I will tell you a story with a fight in it, a story with a champion in it, and a ship and a queen's son that has his mind set on killing somebody that you and I know.

Fool. Who is that? Who is he coming to kill?

Blind Man. Wait, now, till you hear. When you were stealing the fowl, I was lying in a hole in the sand, and I heard three men coming with a shuffling sort of noise. They were wounded and groaning.

Fool. Go on. Tell me about the fight.

Blind Man. There had been a fight, a great fight, a tremendous great fight. A young man had landed on the shore, the guardians of the shore had asked his name, and he had refused to tell it, and he had killed one, and others had run away.

Fool. That's enough. Come on now to the fowl. I wish it was bigger. I wish it was as big as a goose.

Blind Man. Hush! I haven't told you all. I know who that young man is. I heard the men who were running away say he had red hair, that he had come from Aoife's country, that he was coming to kill Cuchulain.

Fool. Nobody can do that.
[*To a tune*]
> Cuchulain has killed kings,
> Kings and sons of kings,
> Dragons out of the water,
> And witches out of the air,

Banachas and Bonachas and people of the woods.

Blind Man. Hush! hush!

Fool [*still singing*].
> Witches that steal the milk,
> Fomor that steal the children,
> Hags that have heads like hares,
> Hares that have claws like witches,
> All riding a-cock-horse
[*Spoken*]
Out of the very bottom of the bitter black North.

Blind Man. Hush, I say!

Fool. Does Cuchulain know that he is coming to kill him?

Blind Man. How would he know that with his head in the clouds? He doesn't care for common fighting. Why would he put himself out, and nobody in it but that young man? Now if it were a white fawn that might turn into a queen before morning—

Fool. Come to the fowl. I wish it was as big as a pig; a fowl with goose grease and pig's crackling.

Blind Man. No hurry, no hurry. I know whose son it is. I wouldn't tell anybody else, but I will tell you,—a secret is better to you than your dinner. You like being told secrets.

Fool. Tell me the secret.

Blind Man. That young man is Aoife's son. I am sure it is Aoife's son, it flows in upon me that it is Aoife's son. You have often heard me talking of Aoife, the great woman-fighter Cuchulain got the mastery over in the North?

Fool. I know, I know. She is one of those cross queens that live in hungry Scotland.

Blind Man. I am sure it is her son. I was in Aoife's country for a long time.

Fool. That was before you were blinded for putting a curse upon the wind.

Blind Man. There was a boy in her house that had her own red colour on him, and everybody said he was to be brought up to kill Cuchulain, that she hated Cuchulain. She used to put a helmet on a pillar-stone and call it Cuchulain and set him casting at it. There is a step outside—Cuchulain's step.
　　　　　[*Cuchulain passes by in the mist outside the big door.*

Fool. Where is Cuchulain going?

Blind Man. He is going to meet Conchubar that has bidden him to take the oath.

Fool. Ah, an oath, Blind Man. How can I remember so many things at once? Who is going to take an oath?

Blind Man. Cuchulain is going to take an oath to Conchubar who is High King.

Fool. What a mix-up you make of everything, Blind Man! You were telling me one story, and now you are telling me another story. . . . How can I get the hang of it at the end if you mix everything at the beginning? Wait till I settle it out. There now, there's Cuchulain [*he points to one foot*], and there is the young man [*he points to the other foot*] that is coming to kill him, and Cuchulain doesn't know. But where's Conchubar? [*Takes bag from side.*] That's Conchubar with all his riches—Cuchulain, young man, Conchubar.—And where's Aoife? [*Throws up cap.*] There is Aoife, high up on the mountains in high hungry

Scotland. Maybe it is not true after all. Maybe it was your own making up. It's many a time you cheated me before with your lies. Come to the cooking-pot, my stomach is pinched and rusty. Would you have it to be creaking like a gate?

Blind Man. I tell you it's true. And more than that is true. If you listen to what I say, you'll forget your stomach.

Fool. I won't.

Blind Man. Listen. I know who the young man's father is, but I won't say. I would be afraid to say. Ah, Fool, you would forget everything if you could know who the young man's father is.

Fool. Who is it? Tell me now quick, or I'll shake you. Come, out with it, or I'll shake you.

> [*A murmur of voices in the distance.*

Blind Man. Wait, wait. There's somebody coming. . . . It is Cuchulain is coming. He's coming back with the High King. Go and ask Cuchulain. He'll tell you. It's little you'll care about the cooking-pot when you have asked Cuchulain that . . .

> [*Blind Man goes out by side door.*

Fool. I'll ask him. Cuchulain will know. He was in Aoife's country. [*Goes up stage.*] I'll ask him. [*Turns and goes down stage.*] But, no, I won't ask him, I would be afraid. [*Going up again.*] Yes, I will ask him. What harm in asking? The Blind Man said I was to ask him. [*Going down.*] No, no. I'll not ask him. He might kill me. I have but killed hens and geese and pigs. He has killed kings. [*Goes up again almost to big door.*] Who says I'm afraid? I'm not afraid. I'm no coward. I'll ask him. No, no, Cuchulain, I'm not going to ask you.

> He has killed kings,
> Kings and the sons of kings,
> Dragons out of the water,
> And witches out of the air,

Banachas and Bonachas and people of the woods.

> [*Fool goes out by side door, the last words being heard outside. Cuchulain and Conchubar enter through the big door at the back. While they are still outside, Cuchulain's voice is heard raised in anger. He is a dark man, something over forty*

years of age. Conchubar is much older and carries a long staff,
elaborately carved or with an elaborate gold handle.

Cuchulain. Because I have killed men without your bidding
   And have rewarded others at my own pleasure,
   Because of half a score of trifling things,
   You'd lay this oath upon me, and now—and now
   You add another pebble to the heap,
   And I must be your man, well-nigh your bondsman,
   Because a youngster out of Aoife's country
   Has found the shore ill-guarded.

Conchubar.   He came to land
   While you were somewhere out of sight and hearing,
10   Hunting or dancing with your wild companions.

Cuchulain. He can be driven out. I'll not be bound.
   I'll dance or hunt, or quarrel or make love,
   Wherever and whenever I've a mind to.
   If time had not put water in your blood,
   You never would have thought it.

Conchubar.   I would leave
   A strong and settled country to my children.

Cuchulain. And I must be obedient in all things;
   Give up my will to yours; go where you please;
   Come when you call; sit at the council-board
20   Among the unshapely bodies of old men;
   I whose mere name has kept this country safe,
   I that in early days have driven out
   Maeve of Cruachan and the northern pirates,
   The hundred kings of Sorcha, and the kings
   Out of the Garden in the East of the World.
   Must I, that held you on the throne when all
   Had pulled you from it, swear obedience
   As if I were some cattle-raising king?
   Are my shins speckled with the heat of the fire,
30   Or have my hands no skill but to make figures
   Upon the ashes with a stick? Am I
   So slack and idle that I need a whip
   Before I serve you?

Conchubar.   No, no whip, Cuchulain,
  But every day my children come and say:
  'This man is growing harder to endure.
  How can we be at safety with this man
  That nobody can buy or bid or bind?
  We shall be at his mercy when you are gone;
  He burns the earth as if he were a fire,
  And time can never touch him.'

Cuchulain.   And so the tale   40
  Grows finer yet; and I am to obey
  Whatever child you set upon the throne,
  As if it were yourself!

Conchubar.   Most certainly.
  I am High King, my son shall be High King;
  And you for all the wildness of your blood,
  And though your father came out of the sun,
  Are but a little king and weigh but light
  In anything that touches government,
  If put into the balance with my children.

Cuchulain. It's well that we should speak our minds out plainly,   50
  For when we die we shall be spoken of
  In many countries. We in our young days
  Have seen the heavens like a burning cloud
  Brooding upon the world, and being more
  Than men can be now that cloud's lifted up,
  We should be the more truthful. Conchubar,
  I do not like your children—they have no pith,
  No marrow in their bones, and will lie soft
  Where you and I lie hard.

Conchubar.   You rail at them
  Because you have no children of your own.   60

Cuchulain. I think myself most lucky that I leave
  No pallid ghost or mockery of a man
  To drift and mutter in the corridors
  Where I have laughed and sung.

Conchubar.   That is not true.

For all your boasting of the truth between us;
For there is no man having house and lands,
That have been in the one family, called
By that one family's name for centuries,
But is made miserable if he know
70   They are to pass into a stranger's keeping,
As yours will pass.

Cuchulain.   The most of men feel that,
But you and I leave names upon the harp.

Conchubar. You play with arguments as lawyers do,
And put no heart in them. I know your thoughts,
For we have slept under the one cloak and drunk
From the one wine-cup. I know you to the bone,
I have heard you cry, aye, in your very sleep,
'I have no son', and with such bitterness
That I have gone upon my knees and prayed
That it might be amended.

80 *Cuchulain.*   For you thought
That I should be as biddable as others
Had I their reason for it; but that's not true;
For I would need a weightier argument
Than one that marred me in the copying,
As I have that clean hawk out of the air
That, as men say, begot this body of mine
Upon a mortal woman.

Conchubar.   Now as ever
You mock at every reasonable hope,
And would have nothing, or impossible things.
90   What eye has ever looked upon the child
Would satisfy a mind like that?

Cuchulain.   I would leave
My house and name to none that would not face
Even myself in battle.

Conchubar.   Being swift of foot,
And making light of every common chance,
You should have overtaken on the hills

Some daughter of the air, or on the shore
A daughter of the Country-under-Wave.

Cuchulain. I am not blasphemous.

Conchubar.   Yet you despise
Our queens, and would not call a child your own,
If one of them had borne him.

Cuchulain.   I have not said it.   100

Conchubar. Ah! I remember I have heard you boast,
When the ale was in your blood, that there was one
In Scotland, where you had learnt the trade of war,
That had a stone-pale cheek and red-brown hair;
And that although you had loved other women,
You'd sooner that fierce woman of the camp
Bore you a son than any queen among them.

Cuchulain. You call her a 'fierce woman of the camp',
For, having lived among the spinning-wheels,
You'd have no woman near that would not say,   110
'Ah! how wise!' 'What will you have for supper?'
'What shall I wear that I may please you, sir?'
And keep that humming through the day and night
For ever. A fierce woman of the camp!
But I am getting angry about nothing.
You have never seen her. Ah! Conchubar, had you seen her
With that high, laughing, turbulent head of hers
Thrown backward, and the bowstring at her ear,
Or sitting at the fire with those grave eyes
Full of good counsel as it were with wine,   120
Or when love ran through all the lineaments
Of her wild body—although she had no child,
None other had all beauty, queen or lover,
Or was so fitted to give birth to kings.

Conchubar. There's nothing I can say but drifts you farther
From the one weighty matter. That very woman—
For I know well that you are praising Aoife—
Now hates you and will leave no subtlety
Unknotted that might run into a noose

130   About your throat, no army in idleness
        That might bring ruin on this land you serve.

        Cuchulain. No wonder in that, no wonder at all in that.
        I never have known love but as a kiss
        In the mid-battle, and a difficult truce
        Of oil and water, candles and dark night,
        Hillside and hollow, the hot-footed sun
        And the cold, sliding, slippery-footed moon—
        A brief forgiveness between opposites
        That have been hatreds for three times the age
        Of this long-'stablished ground.

140   *Conchubar.*   Listen to me.
        Aoife makes war on us, and every day
        Our enemies grow greater and beat the walls
        More bitterly, and you within the walls
        Are every day more turbulent; and yet,
        When I would speak about these things, your fancy
        Runs as it were a swallow on the wind.
            [*Outside the door in the blue light of the sea-mist are many
            old and young Kings; amongst them are three Women, two of
            whom carry a bowl of fire. The third, in what follows, puts
            from time to time fragrant herbs into the fire so that it flickers
            up into brighter flame.*
        Look at the door and what men gather there—
        Old counsellors that steer the land with me,
        And younger kings, the dancers and harp-players
150   That follow in your tumults, and all these
        Are held there by the one anxiety.
        Will you be bound into obedience
        And so make this land safe for them and theirs?
        You are but half a king and I but half;
        I need your might of hand and burning heart,
        And you my wisdom.

        Cuchulain [*going near to door*]. Nestlings of a high nest,
        Hawks that have followed me into the air
        And looked upon the sun, we'll out of this
        And sail upon the wind once more. This king

Would have me take an oath to do his will,   160
And having listened to his tune from morning,
I will no more of it. Run to the stable
And set the horses to the chariot-pole,
And send a messenger to the harp-players.
We'll find a level place among the woods,
And dance awhile.

A Young King.   Cuchulain, take the oath.
There is none here that would not have you take it.

Cuchulain. You'd have me take it? Are you of one mind?

The Kings. All, all, all, all!

A Young King.   Do what the High King bids you.

Conchubar. There is not one but dreads this turbulence   170
Now that they're settled men.

Cuchulain.   Are you so changed,
Or have I grown more dangerous of late?
But that's not it. I understand it all.
It's you that have changed. You've wives and children now,
And for that reason cannot follow one
That lives like a bird's flight from tree to tree.—
It's time the years put water in my blood
And drowned the wildness of it, for all's changed,
But that unchanged.—I'll take what oath you will:
The moon, the sun, the water, light, or air,   180
I do not care how binding.

Conchubar.   On this fire
That has been lighted from your hearth and mine;
The older men shall be my witnesses,
The younger, yours. The holders of the fire
Shall purify the thresholds of the house
With waving fire, and shut the outer door,
According to the custom; and sing rhyme
That has come down from the old law-makers
To blow the witches out. Considering
That the wild will of man could be oath-bound,   190

But that a woman's could not, they bid us sing
Against the will of woman at its wildest
In the Shape-Changers that run upon the wind.
                    [*Conchubar has gone on to his throne.*

The Women. [*They sing in a very low voice after the first few*
    words so that the others all but drown their words.
                    May this fire have driven out
                    The Shape-Changers that can put
                    Ruin on a great king's house
                    Until all be ruinous.
                    Names whereby a man has known
                    The threshold and the hearthstone,
200   Gather on the wind and drive
                    The women none can kiss and thrive,
                    For they are but whirling wind,
                    Out of memory and mind.
                    They would make a prince decay
                    With light images of clay
                    Planted in the running wave;
                    Or, for many shapes they have,
                    They would change them into hounds
                    Until he had died of his wounds,
210   Though the change were but a whim;
                    Or they'd hurl a spell at him,
                    That he follow with desire
                    Bodies that can never tire
                    Or grow kind, for they anoint
                    All their bodies, joint by joint,
                    With a miracle-working juice
                    That is made out of the grease
                    Of the ungoverned unicorn.
                    But the man is thrice forlorn,
220   Emptied, ruined, wracked, and lost,
                    That they follow, for at most
                    They will give him kiss for kiss
                    While they murmur, 'After this
                    Hatred may be sweet to the taste'.
                    Those wild hands that have embraced
                    All his body can but shove

At the burning wheel of love
Till the side of hate comes up.
Therefore in this ancient cup
May the sword-blades drink their fill   230
Of the home-brew there, until
They will have for masters none
But the threshold and hearthstone.

Cuchulain [*speaking, while they are singing*]. I'll take and keep
    this oath, and from this day
  I shall be what you please, my chicks, my nestlings.
  Yet I had thought you were of those that praised
  Whatever life could make the pulse run quickly,
  Even though it were brief, and that you held
  That a free gift was better than a forced.—
  But that's all over.—I will keep it, too;   240
  I never gave a gift and took it again.
  If the wild horse should break the chariot-pole,
  It would be punished. Should that be in the oath?
    [*Two of the Women, still singing, crouch in front of him hold-
    ing the bowl over their heads. He spreads his hands over the
    flame.*
  I swear to be obedient in all things
  To Conchubar, and to uphold his children.

Conchubar. We are one being, as these flames are one:
  I give my wisdom, and I take your strength.
  Now thrust the swords into the flame, and pray
  That they may serve the threshold and the hearthstone
  With faithful service.
    [*The Kings kneel in a semicircle before the two Women and
    Cuchulain, who thrusts his sword into the flame. They all put
    the points of their swords into the flame. The third Woman is
    at the back near the big door.*

Cuchulain.   O pure, glittering ones   250
  That should be more than wife or friend or mistress,
  Give us the enduring will, the unquenchable hope,
  The friendliness of the sword!—
    [*The song grows louder, and the last words ring out clearly. There
    is a loud knocking at the door, and a cry of* 'Open! open!'

Conchubar. Some king that has been loitering on the way.
    Open the door, for I would have all know
    That the oath's finished and Cuchulain bound,
    And that the swords are drinking up the flame.
        [*The door is opened by the third Woman, and a Young Man
        with a drawn sword enters.*]

Young Man. I am of Aoife's country.
[*The Kings rush towards him. Cuchulain throws himself between.*]

Cuchulain.   Put up your swords.
    He is but one. Aoife is far away.

260 *Young Man.* I have come alone into the midst of you
    To weigh this sword against Cuchulain's sword.

Conchubar. And are you noble? for if of common seed,
    You cannot weigh your sword against his sword
    But in mixed battle.

Young Man.   I am under bonds
    To tell my name to no man; but it's noble.

Conchubar. But I would know your name and not your bonds.
    You cannot speak in the Assembly House,
    If you are not noble.

First Old King.   Answer the High King!

Young Man. I will give no other proof than the hawk gives
    That it's no sparrow!
                        [*He is silent for a moment, then speaks to all.*
270   Yet look upon me, kings.
    I, too, am of that ancient seed, and carry
    The signs about this body and in these bones.

Cuchulain. To have shown the hawk's grey feather is enough,
    And you speak highly, too. Give me that helmet.
    I'd thought they had grown weary sending champions.
    That sword and belt will do. This fighting's welcome.
    The High King there has promised me his wisdom;
    But the hawk's sleepy till its well-beloved
    Cries out amid the acorns, or it has seen

Its enemy like a speck upon the sun.   280
What's wisdom to the hawk, when that clear eye
Is burning nearer up in the high air?
    [*Looks hard at Young Man; then comes down steps and
    grasps Young Man by shoulder.*
Hither into the light.
[*To Conchubar.*]   The very tint
Of her that I was speaking of but now.
Not a pin's difference.
[*To Young Man.*]   You are from the North,
Where there are many that have that tint of hair—
Red-brown, the light red-brown. Come nearer, boy,
For I would have another look at you.
There's more likeness—a pale, a stone-pale cheek.
What brought you, boy? Have you no fear of death?   290

Young Man. Whether I live or die is in the gods' hands.

Cuchulain. That is all words, all words; a young man's talk.
    I am their plough, their harrow, their very strength;
    For he that's in the sun begot this body
    Upon a mortal woman, and I have heard tell
    It seemed as if he had outrun the moon
    That he must follow always through waste heaven,
    He loved so happily. He'll be but slow
    To break a tree that was so sweetly planted.
    Let's see that arm. I'll see it if I choose.   300
    That arm had a good father and a good mother,
    But it is not like this.

Young Man.   You are mocking me;
    You think I am not worthy to be fought.
    But I'll not wrangle but with this talkative knife.

Cuchulain. Put up your sword; I am not mocking you.
    I'd have you for my friend, but if it's not
    Because you have a hot heart and a cold eye,
    I cannot tell the reason.
    [*To Conchubar.*]   He has got her fierceness,
    And nobody is as fierce as those pale women.
    But I will keep him with me, Conchubar,   310

That he may set my memory upon her
When the day's fading.—You will stop with us,
And we will hunt the deer and the wild bulls;
And, when we have grown weary, light our fires
Between the wood and water, or on some mountain
Where the Shape-Changers of the morning come.
The High King there would make a mock of me
Because I did not take a wife among them.
Why do you hang your head? It's a good life:
320   The head grows prouder in the light of the dawn,
And friendship thickens in the murmuring dark
Where the spare hazels meet the wool-white foam.
But I can see there's no more need for words
And that you'll be my friend from this day out.

Conchubar. He has come hither not in his own name
     But in Queen Aoife's, and has challenged us
     In challenging the foremost man of us all.

Cuchulain. Well, well, what matter?

Conchubar.   You think it does not matter,
     And that a fancy lighter than the air,
330   A whim of the moment, has more matter in it.
     For, having none that shall reign after you,
     You cannot think as I do, who would leave
     A throne too high for insult.

Cuchulain.   Let your children
     Re-mortar their inheritance, as we have,
     And put more muscle on.—I'll give you gifts,
     But I'd have something too—that arm-ring, boy.
     We'll have this quarrel out when you are older.

Young Man. There is no man I'd sooner have my friend
     Than you, whose name has gone about the world
340   As if it had been the wind; but Aoife'd say
     I had turned coward.

Cuchulain.   I will give you gifts
     That Aoife'll know, and all her people know,
     To have come from me.   [Showing cloak.

My father gave me this.
He came to try me, rising up at dawn
Out of the cold dark of the rich sea.
He challenged me to battle, but before
My sword had touched his sword, told me his name,
Gave me this cloak, and vanished.
                              Say that I heard
A raven croak on the north side of the house
And was afraid.   350

Conchubar. Witchcraft has troubled his mind.

Cuchulain. No witchcraft. His head is like a woman's head
    I had a fancy for.

Conchubar.   A witch of the air
    Can make a leaf confound us with memories.
    They run upon the wind and hurl the spells
    That make us nothing, out of the invisible wind.
    They have gone to school to learn the trick of it.

Cuchulain. No, no—there's nothing out of common here;
    The winds are innocent.—That arm-ring, boy.

A King. If I've your leave I'll take this challenge up.   360

Another King. No, give it me, High King, for this wild Aoife
    Has carried off my slaves.

Another King.   No, give it me,
    For she has harried me in house and herd.

Another King. I claim this fight.

Other Kings [*together*].   And I! And I! And I!

Cuchulain. Back! back! Put up your swords! Put up your swords!
    There's none alive that shall accept a challenge
    I have refused. Laegaire, put up your sword!

Young Men. No, let them come. If they've a mind for it,
    I'll try it out with any two together.

Cuchulain. That's spoken as I'd have spoken it at your age.   370
    But you are in my house. Whatever man

Would fight with you shall fight it out with me.
They're dumb, they're dumb. How many of you would meet

[*Draws sword.*

This mutterer, this old whistler, this sand-piper,
This edge that's greyer than the tide, this mouse
That's gnawing at the timbers of the world,
This, this—Boy, I would meet them all in arms
If I'd a son like you. He would avenge me
When I have withstood for the last time the men
380   Whose fathers, brothers, sons, and friends I have killed
Upholding Conchubar, when the four provinces
Have gathered with the ravens over them.
But I'd need no avenger. You and I
Would scatter them like water from a dish.

Young Man. We'll stand by one another from this out.
Here is the ring.

Cuchulain.   No, turn and turn about.
But my turn's first because I am the older.

[*Spreading out cloak.*

Nine queens out of the Country-under-Wave
Have woven it with the fleeces of the sea
390   And they were long embroidering at it.—Boy,
If I had fought my father, he'd have killed me,
As certainly as if I had a son
And fought with him, I should be deadly to him;
For the old fiery fountains are far off
And every day there is less heat o' the blood.

Conchubar [*in a loud voice*]. No more of this. I will not have this
friendship.
Cuchulain is my man, and I forbid it.
He shall not go unfought, for I myself—

Cuchulain. I will not have it.

Conchubar.   You lay commands on me?

400   *Cuchulain* [*seizing Conchubar*]. You shall not stir, High King. I'll
hold you there.

Conchubar. Witchcraft has maddened you.

The Kings [*shouting*]. Yes, witchcraft! witchcraft!

First Old King. Some witch has worked upon your mind,
    Cuchulain.
  The head of that young man seemed like a woman's
  You'd had a fancy for. Then of a sudden
  You laid your hands on the High King himself!

Cuchulain. And laid my hands on the High King himself?

Conchubar. Some witch is floating in the air above us.

Cuchulain. Yes, witchcraft! witchcraft! Witches of the air!
  [*To Young Man.*] Why did you? Who was it set you to this
    work?
  Out, out! I say, for now it's sword on sword!   410

Young Man. But . . . but I did not.

Cuchulain. Out, I say, out, out!
  [*Young Man goes out followed by Cuchulain. The Kings follow
  them out with confused cries, and words one can hardly hear
  because of the noise. Some cry, 'Quicker, quicker!' 'Why are
  you so long at the door?' 'We'll be too late!' 'Have they begun
  to fight?' 'Can you see if they are fighting?' and so on. Their
  voices drown each other. The three Women are left alone.*

First Woman. I have seen, I have seen!

Second Woman. What do you cry aloud?

First Woman. The Ever-living have shown me what's to come.

Third Woman. How? Where?

First Woman. In the ashes of the bowl.

Second Woman. While you were holding it between your hands?

Third Woman. Speak quickly!

First Woman. I have seen Cuchulain's roof-tree
  Leap into fire, and the walls split and blacken.

Second Woman. Cuchulain has gone out to die.

Third Woman.   O! O!

Second Woman. Who could have thought that one so great as he
420   Should meet his end at this unnoted sword!

First Woman. Life drifts between a fool and a blind man
      To the end, and nobody can know his end.

Second Woman. Come, look upon the quenching of this greatness.
      [*The other two go to the door, but they stop for a moment
      upon the threshold and wail.*

First Woman. No crying out, for there'll be need of cries
      And rending of the hair when it's all finished.
      [*The Women go out. There is the sound of clashing swords
      from time to time during what follows.*

            Enter the Fool, dragging the Blind Man.

Fool. You have eaten it, you have eaten it! You have left me
      nothing but the bones.
                        [*He throws Blind Man down by big chair.*

Blind Man. O, that I should have to endure such a plague! O, I
      ache all over! O, I am pulled to pieces! This is the way you pay
      me all the good I have done you.

Fool. You have eaten it! You have told me lies. I might have
      known you had eaten it when I saw your slow, sleepy walk. Lie
      there till the kings come. O, I will tell Conchubar and
      Cuchulain and all the kings about you!

Blind Man. What would have happened to you but for me, and
      you without your wits? If I did not take care of you, what
      would you do for food and warmth?

Fool. You take care of me? You stay safe, and send me into every kind
      of danger. You sent me down the cliff for gulls' eggs while you
      warmed your blind eyes in the sun; and then you ate all that were
      good for food. You left me the eggs that were neither egg nor bird.
      [*Blind Man tries to rise; Fool makes him lie down again.*]
      Keep quiet now, till I shut the door. There is some noise
      outside—a high vexing noise, so that I can't be listening to
      myself. [*Shuts the big door.*] Why can't they be quiet? Why

can't they be quiet? [*Blind Man tries to get away.*] Ah! you
would get away, would you? [*Follows Blind Man and brings
him back.*] Lie there! lie there! No, you won't get away! Lie
there till the kings come. I'll tell them all about you. I will tell it
all. How you sit warming yourself, when you have made me
light a fire of sticks, while I sit blowing it with my mouth. Do
you not always make me take the windy side of the bush when
it blows, and the rainy side when it rains?

Blind Man. O, good Fool! listen to me. Think of the care I have
taken of you. I have brought you to many a warm hearth,
where there was a good welcome for you, but you would not
stay there; you were always wandering about.

Fool. The last time you brought me in, it was not I who wandered
away, but you that got put out because you took the crubeen
out of the pot when nobody was looking. Keep quiet, now!

Cuchulain [*rushing in*]. Witchcraft! There is no witchcraft on the
earth, or among the witches of the air, that these hands cannot
break.

Fool. Listen to me, Cuchulain. I left him turning the fowl at the
fire. He ate it all, though I had stolen it. He left me nothing but
the feathers.

Cuchulain. Fill me a horn of ale!

Blind Man. I gave him what he likes best. You do not know how
vain this Fool is. He likes nothing so well as a feather.

Fool. He left me nothing but the bones and feathers. Nothing but
the feathers, though I had stolen it.

Cuchulain. Give me that horn. Quarrels here, too! [*Drinks.*] What
is there between you two that is worth a quarrel? Out with it!

Blind Man. Where would he be but for me? I must be always
thinking—thinking to get food for the two of us, and when
we've got it, if the moon is at the full or the tide on the turn,
he'll leave the rabbit in the snare till it is full of maggots, or let
the trout slip back through his hands into the stream.
  [*The Fool has begun singing while the Blind Man is speaking.*

Fool [*singing*].

> When you were an acorn on the tree-top,
>> Then was I an eagle-cock;
> Now that you are a withered old block,
>> Still am I an eagle-cock.

Blind Man. Listen to him, now. That's the sort of talk I have to put up with day out, day in.

> [*The Fool is putting the feathers into his hair. Cuchulain takes a handful of feathers out of a heap the Fool has on the bench beside him, and out of the Fool's hair, and begins to wipe the blood from his sword with them.*]

Fool. He has taken my feathers to wipe his sword. It is blood that he is wiping from his sword.

Cuchulain [*goes up to door at back and throws away feathers*]. They are standing about his body. They will not awaken him, for all his witchcraft.

Blind Man. It is that young champion that he has killed. He that came out of Aoife's country.

Cuchulain. He thought to have saved himself with witchcraft.

Fool. That Blind Man there said he would kill you. He came from Aoife's country to kill you. That Blind Man said they had taught him every kind of weapon that he might do it. But I always knew that you would kill him.

Cuchulain [*to the Blind Man*]. You knew him, then?

Blind Man. I saw him, when I had my eyes, in Aoife's country.

Cuchulain. You were in Aoife's country?

Blind Man. I knew him and his mother there.

Cuchulain. He was about to speak of her when he died.

Blind Man. He was a queen's son.

Cuchulain. What queen? what queen? [*Seizes Blind Man, who is now sitting upon the bench.*] Was it Scathach? There were many queens. All the rulers there were queens.

Blind Man. No, not Scathach.

Cuchulain. It was Uathach, then? Speak! speak!

Blind Man. I cannot speak; you are clutching me too tightly. [*Cuchulain lets him go.*] I cannot remember who it was. I am not certain. It was some queen.

Fool. He said a while ago that the young man was Aoife's son.

Cuchulain. She? No, no! She had no son when I was there.

Fool. That Blind Man there said that she owned him for her son.

Cuchulain. I had rather he had been some other woman's son. What father had he? A soldier out of Alba? She was an amorous woman—a proud, pale, amorous woman.

Blind Man. None knew whose son he was.

Cuchulain. None knew! Did you know, old listener at doors?

Blind Man. No, no; I knew nothing.

Fool. He said a while ago that he heard Aoife boast that she'd never but the one lover, and he the only man that had overcome her in battle. [*Pause.*

Blind Man. Somebody is trembling, Fool! The bench is shaking. Why are you trembling? Is Cuchulain going to hurt us? It was not I who told you, Cuchulain.

Fool. It is Cuchulain who is trembling. It is Cuchulain who is shaking the bench.

Blind Man. It is his own son he has slain.

Cuchulain. 'Twas they that did it, the pale windy people.
Where? where? where? My sword against the thunder!
But no, for they have always been my friends;
And though they love to blow a smoking coal
Till it's all flame, the wars they blow aflame
Are full of glory, and heart-uplifting pride,
And not like this. The wars they love awaken
Old fingers and the sleepy strings of harps.
Who did it then? Are you afraid? Speak out!

10   For I have put you under my protection,
And will reward you well. Dubthach the Chafer?
He'd an old grudge. No, for he is with Maeve.
Laegaire did it! Why do you not speak?
What is this house? [*Pause.*] Now I remember all.
    [*Comes before Conchubar's chair, and strikes out with his
    sword, as if Conchubar was sitting upon it.*
'Twas you who did it—you who sat up there
With your old rod of kingship, like a magpie
Nursing a stolen spoon. No, not a magpie,
A maggot that is eating up the earth!
Yes, but a magpie, for he's flown away.
Where did he fly to?

20 *Blind Man.*   He is outside the door.

Cuchulain. Outside the door?

Blind Man.   Between the door and the sea.

Cuchulain. Conchubar, Conchubar! the sword into your heart!
    [*He rushes out. Pause. Fool creeps up to the big door and
    looks after him.*

Fool. He is going up to King Conchubar. They are all about the
young man. No, no, he is standing still. There is a great wave
going to break, and he is looking at it. Ah! now he is running
down to the sea, but he is holding up his sword as if he were
going into a fight. [*Pause.*] Well struck! well struck!

Blind Man. What is he doing now?

Fool. O! he is fighting the waves!

Blind Man. He sees King Conchubar's crown on every one of them.

Fool. There, he has struck at a big one! He has struck the crown
off it; he has made the foam fly. There again, another big one!

Blind Man. Where are the kings? What are the kings doing?

Fool. They are shouting and running down to the shore, and the
people are running out of the houses. They are all running.

Blind Man. You say they are running out of the houses? There will
be nobody left in the houses. Listen, Fool!

Fool. There, he is down! He is up again. He is going out in the deep water. There is a big wave. It has gone over him. I cannot see him now. He has killed kings and giants, but the waves have mastered him, the waves have mastered him!

Blind Man. Come here, Fool!

Fool. The waves have mastered him.

Blind Man. Come here!

Fool. The waves have mastered him.

Blind Man. Come here, I say.

Fool [*coming towards him, but looking backwards towards the door*]. What is it?

Blind Man. There will be nobody in the houses. Come this way; come quickly! The ovens will be full. We will put our hands into the ovens. [*They go out.*

Deirdre

(1907)

TO
MRS. PATRICK CAMPBELL
WHO IN THE GENEROSITY OF HER GENIUS HAS PLAYED MY
DEIRDRE IN DUBLIN AND LONDON WITH THE ABBEY COMPANY,
AS WELL AS WITH HER OWN PEOPLE,
AND
IN MEMORY OF
ROBERT GREGORY
WHO DESIGNED THE BEAUTIFUL SCENE SHE PLAYED IT IN.

Persons in the Play

Musicians

Fergus, *an old man*

Naoise (*pronounced* Neesh-e), *a young king*

Deirdre, *his queen*

A Dark-faced Messenger

Conchubar (*pronounced* Conochar),
the old King of Ulad, who is still strong and vigorous

A Dark-faced Executioner

A Guest-house in a wood. It is a rough house of timber; through the doors and some of the windows one can see the great spaces of the wood, the sky dimming, night closing in. But a window to the left shows the thick leaves of a coppice; the landscape suggests silence and loneliness. There is a door to right and left, and through the side windows one can see anybody who approaches either door, a moment before he enters. In the centre, a part of the house is curtained off; the curtains are drawn. There are unlighted torches in brackets on the walls. There is, at one side, a small table with a chess-

board and chessmen upon it. At the other side of the room there is a
brazier with a fire; two women, with musical instruments beside
them, crouch about the brazier: they are comely women of about
forty. Another woman, who carries a stringed instrument, enters hur-
riedly; she speaks, at first standing in the doorway.

First Musician. I have a story right, my wanderers,
    That has so mixed with fable in our songs
    That all seemed fabulous. We are come, by chance,
    Into King Conchubar's country, and this house
    Is an old guest-house built for travellers
    From the seashore to Conchubar's royal house,
    And there are certain hills among these woods
    And there Queen Deirdre grew.

Second Musician.   That famous queen
    Who has been wandering with her lover Naoise
    Somewhere beyond the edges of the world?   10

First Musician [*going nearer to the brazier*]. Some dozen years
      ago, King Conchubar found
    A house upon a hillside in this wood,
    And there a child with an old witch to nurse her,
    And nobody to say if she were human,
    Or of the gods, or anything at all
    Of who she was or why she was hidden there,
    But that she'd too much beauty for good luck.
    He went up thither daily, till at last
    She put on womanhood, and he lost peace,
    And Deirdre's tale began. The King was old.   20
    A month or so before the marriage-day,
    A young man, in the laughing scorn of his youth,
    Naoise, the son of Usna, climbed up there,
    And having wooed, or, as some say, been wooed,
    Carried her off.

Second Musician. The tale were well enough
    Had it a finish.

First Musician.   Hush! I have more to tell;
    But gather close about that I may whisper
    The secrets of a king.

Second Musician.   There's none to hear!

First Musician. I have been to Conchubar's house and followed up
30   A crowd of servants going out and in
    With loads upon their heads: embroideries
    To hang upon the walls, or new-mown rushes
    To strew upon the floors, and came at length
    To a great room.

Second Musician.   Be silent; there are steps!

    *Enter Fergus, an old man, who moves about from door to
       window excitedly through what follows.*

Fergus. I thought to find a message from the King.
    You are musicians by these instruments,
    And if as seems—for you are comely women—
    You can praise love, you'll have the best of luck,
    For there'll be two, before the night is in,
40   That bargained for their love, and paid for it
    All that men value. You have but the time
    To weigh a happy music with a sad,
    To find what is most pleasing to a lover,
    Before the son of Usna and his queen
    Have passed this threshold.

First Musician.   Deirdre and her man!

Fergus. I was to have found a message in this house,
    And ran to meet it. Is there no messenger
    From Conchubar to Fergus, son of Rogh?

First Musician. Are Deirdre and her lover tired of life?

50 *Fergus.* You are not of this country, or you'd know
    That they are in my charge and all forgiven.

First Musician. We have no country but the roads of the world.

Fergus. Then you should know that all things change in the world,
    And hatred turns to love and love to hate,
    And even kings forgive.

First Musician.   An old man's love
    Who casts no second line is hard to cure;
    His jealousy is like his love.

Fergus.   And that's but true.
  You have learned something in your wanderings.
  He was so hard to cure that the whole court,
  But I alone, thought it impossible;   60
  Yet after I had urged it at all seasons,
  I had my way, and all's forgiven now;
  And you shall speak the welcome and the joy
  That I lack tongue for.

First Musician.   Yet old men are jealous.

Fergus [*going to door*]. I am Conchubar's near friend, and that
      weighed somewhat,
  And it was policy to pardon them.
  The need of some young, famous, popular man
  To lead the troops, the murmur of the crowd,
  And his own natural impulse, urged him to it.
  They have been wandering half a dozen years.   70

First Musician. And yet old men are jealous.

Fergus [*coming from door*].   Sing the more sweetly
  Because, though age is arid as a bone,
  This man has flowered. I've need of music, too;
  If this grey head would suffer no reproach,
  I'd dance and sing—
      [*Dark-faced men with strange, barbaric dress and arms begin to
      pass by the doors and windows. They pass one by one and in silence.*
                  and dance till the hour ran out,
  Because I have accomplished this good deed.

First Musician. Look there—there at the window, those dark men,
  With murderous and outlandish-looking arms—
  They've been about the house all day.

Fergus [*looking after them*].   What are you?
  Where do you come from, who is it sent you here?   80

First Musician. They will not answer you.

Fergus.   They do not hear.

First Musician. Forgive my open speech, but to these eyes
  That have seen many lands they are such men

As kings will gather for a murderous task
That neither bribes, commands, nor promises
Can bring their people to.

Fergus.   And that is why
You harped upon an old man's jealousy.
A trifle sets you quaking. Conchubar's fame
Brings merchandise on every wind that blows.
90   They may have brought him Libyan dragon-skin,
Or the ivory of the fierce unicorn.

First Musician. If these be merchants, I have seen the goods
They have brought to Conchubar, and understood
His murderous purpose.

Fergus.   Murderous, you say?
Why, what new gossip of the roads is this?
But I'll not hear.

First Musician.   It may be life or death.
There is a room in Conchubar's house, and there——

Fergus. Be silent, or I'll drive you from the door.
There's many a one that would do more than that,
100   And make it prison, or death, or banishment
To slander the High King.
                    [*Suddenly restraining himself and speaking gently.*
                         He is my friend;
I have his oath, and I am well content.
I have known his mind as if it were my own
These many years, and there is none alive
Shall buzz against him, and I there to stop it.
I know myself, and him, and your wild thought
Fed on extravagant poetry, and lit
By such a dazzle of old fabulous tales
That common things are lost, and all that's strange
110   Is true because 'twere pity if it were not.
                                        [*Going to the door again.*
Quick! quick! your instruments! they are coming now.
I hear the hoofs a-clatter. Begin that song!
But what is it to be? I'd have them hear
A music foaming up out of the house

Like wine out of a cup. Come now, a verse
Of some old time not worth remembering,
And all the lovelier because a bubble.
Begin, begin, of some old king and queen,
Of Lugaid Redstripe or another; no, not him,
He and his lady perished wretchedly.   120

> *First Musician* [*singing*]
> 'Why is it', Queen Edain said,
>   'If I do but climb the stair . . .

Fergus. Ah! that is better. . . . They are alighted now.
Shake all your cockscombs, children; these are lovers.

> [*Fergus goes out.*

> *First Musician*
> 'Why is it', Queen Edain said,
>   'If I do but climb the stair
> To the tower overhead,
>   When the winds are calling there,
> Or the gannets calling out
>   In waste places of the sky,   130
> There's so much to think about
>   That I cry, that I cry?'

> *Second Musician*
> But her goodman answered her:
>   'Love would be a thing of naught
> Had not all his limbs a stir
>   Born out of immoderate thought;
> Were he anything by half,
>   Were his measure running dry.
> Lovers, if they may not laugh,
>   Have to cry, have to cry.'   140

[*Deirdre, Naoise, and Fergus have been seen for a moment
through the windows, but now they have entered.*

> *The Three Musicians* [*together*]
> But is Edain worth a song
>   Now the hunt begins anew?
> Praise the beautiful and strong;
>   Praise the redness of the yew;

>   Praise the blossoming apple-stem.
>   But our silence had been wise.
>   What is all our praise to them
>   That have one another's eyes?

Deirdre. Silence your music, though I thank you for it;
150   But the wind's blown upon my hair, and I
         Must set the jewels on my neck and head
         For one that's coming.

Naoise.   Your colour has all gone
         As 'twere with fear, and there's no cause for that.

Deirdre. These women have the raddle that they use
         To make them brave and confident, although
         Dread, toil, or cold may chill the blood o' their cheeks.
         You'll help me, women. It is my husband's will
         I show my trust in one that may be here
         Before the mind can call the colour up.
160   My husband took these rubies from a king
         Of Surracha that was so murderous
         He seemed all glittering dragon. Now wearing them
         Myself wars on myself, for I myself—
         That do my husband's will, yet fear to do it—
         Grow dragonish to myself.
             [*The women have gathered about her. Naoise has stood look-
             ing at her, but Fergus brings him to the chess table.*

Naoise.   No messenger!
         It's strange that there is none to welcome us.

Fergus. King Conchubar has sent no messenger
         That he may come himself.

Naoise.   And being himself,
         Being High King, he cannot break his faith.
170   I have his word and I must take that word,
         Or prove myself unworthy of my nurture
         Under a great man's roof.

Fergus.   We'll play at chess
         Till the King comes. It is but natural
         That she should doubt him, for her house has been
         The hole of the badger and the den of the fox.

Naoise. If I had not King Conchubar's word I'd think
    That chess-board ominous.

Fergus.   How can a board
    That has been lying there these many years
    Be lucky or unlucky?

Naoise.   It is the board
    Where Lugaid Redstripe and that wife of his,   180
    Who had a seamew's body half the year,
    Played at the chess upon the night they died.

Fergus. I can remember now, a tale of treachery,
    A broken promise and a journey's end—
    But it were best forgot.
        [*Deirdre has been standing with the women about her. They*
        have been helping her to put on her jewels and to put the pig-
        ment on her cheeks and arrange her hair. She has gradually
        grown attentive to what Fergus is saying.

Naoise.   If the tale's true,
    When it was plain that they had been betrayed,
    They moved the men and waited for the end
    As it were bedtime, and had so quiet minds
    They hardly winked their eyes when the sword flashed.

Fergus. She never could have played so, being a woman,   190
    If she had not the cold sea's blood in her.

Deirdre. The gods turn clouds and casual accidents
    Into omens.

Naoise.   It would but ill become us,
    Now that King Conchubar has pledged his word,
    Should we be startled by a cloud or a shadow.

Deirdre. There's none to welcome us.

Naoise.   Being his guest,
    Words that would wrong him can but wrong ourselves.

Deirdre. An empty house upon the journey's end!
    Is that the way a king that means no mischief
    Honours a guest?

200 *Fergus.*   He is but making ready
         A welcome in his house, arranging where
         The moorhen and the mallard go, and where
         The speckled heathcock on a golden dish.

Deirdre. Had he no messenger?

Naoise.   Such words and fears
         Wrong this old man who's pledged his word to us.
         We must not speak or think as women do,
         That when the house is all abed sit up
         Marking among the ashes with a stick
         Till they are terrified.—Being what we are
210   We must meet all things with an equal mind.
         [*To Fergus.*] Come, let us look if there's a messenger
         From Conchubar. We cannot see from this
         Because we are blinded by the leaves and twigs,
         But it may be the wood will thin again.
         It is but kind that when the lips we love
         Speak words that are unfitting for kings' ears
         Our ears be deaf.

Fergus.   But now I had to threaten
         These wanderers because they would have weighed
         Some crazy fantasy of their own brain
220   Or gossip of the road with Conchubar's word.
         If I had thought so little of mankind
         I never could have moved him to this pardon.
         I have believed the best of every man,
         And find that to believe it is enough
         To make a bad man show him at his best,
         Or even a good man swing his lantern higher.
             [*Naoise and Fergus go out. The last words are spoken as they
             go through the door. One can see them through part of what
             follows, either through door or window. They move about,
             talking or looking along the road towards Conchubar's house.*

First Musician. If anything lies heavy on your heart,
         Speak freely of it, knowing it is certain
         That you will never see my face again.

Deirdre. You've been in love?

First Musician. If you would speak of love   230
    Speak freely. There is nothing in the world
    That has been friendly to us but the kisses
    That were upon our lips, and when we are old
    Their memory will be all the life we have.

Deirdre. There was a man that loved me. He was old;
    I could not love him. Now I can but fear.
    He has made promises, and brought me home;
    But though I turn it over in my thoughts,
    I cannot tell if they are sound and wholesome,
    Or hackles on the hook.

First Musician. I have heard he loved you   240
    As some old miser loves the dragon-stone
    He hides among the cobwebs near the roof.

Deirdre. You mean that when a man who has loved like that
    Is after crossed, love drowns in its own flood,
    And that love drowned and floating is but hate;
    And that a king who hates sleeps ill at night
    Till he has killed; and that, though the day laughs,
    We shall be dead at cock-crow.

First Musician. You've not my thought.
    When I lost one I loved distractedly,
    I blamed my crafty rival and not him,
    And fancied, till my passion had run out,   250
    That could I carry him away with me,
    And tell him all my love, I'd keep him yet.

Deirdre. Ah! now I catch your meaning, that this king
    Will murder Naoise, and keep me alive.

First Musician. 'Tis you that put that meaning upon words
    Spoken at random.

Deirdre. Wanderers like you,
    Who have their wit alone to keep their lives,
    Speak nothing that is bitter to the ear
    At random; if they hint at it at all   260
    Their eyes and ears have gathered it so lately
    That it is crying out in them for speech.

First Musician. We have little that is certain.

Deirdre.   Certain or not,
    Speak it out quickly, I beseech you to it;
    I never have met any of your kind
    But that I gave them money, food, and fire.

First Musician. There are strange, miracle-working, wicked stones,
    Men tear out of the heart and the hot brain
    Of Libyan dragons.

Deirdre.   The hot Istian stone,
270   And the cold stone of Fanes, that have power
    To stir even those at enmity to love.

First Musician. They have so great an influence, if but sewn
    In the embroideries that curtain in
    The bridal bed.

Deirdre.   O Mover of the stars
    That made this delicate house of ivory,
    And made my soul its mistress, keep it safe!

First Musician. I have seen a bridal bed, so curtained in,
    So decked for miracle in Conchubar's house,
    And learned that a bride's coming.

Deirdre.   And I the bride?
280   Here is worse treachery than the seamew suffered,
    For she but died and mixed into the dust
    Of her dear comrade, but I am to live
    And lie in the one bed with him I hate.
    Where is Naoise? I was not alone like this
    When Conchubar first chose me for his wife;
    I cried in sleeping or waking and he came,
    But now there is worse need.

Naoise [*entering with Fergus*]. Why have you called?
    I was but standing there, without the door.

Deirdre. I have heard terrible mysterious things,
290   Magical horrors and the spells of wizards.

Fergus. Why, that's no wonder. You have been listening

To singers of the roads that gather up
The stories of the world.

Deirdre.   But I have one
To make the stories of the world but nothing.

Naoise. Be silent if it is against the King
Whose guest you are.

Fergus.   No, let her speak it out.
I know the High King's heart as it were my own,
And can refute a slander, but already
I have warned these women that it may be death.

Naoise. I will not weigh the gossip of the roads   300
With the King's word. I ask your pardon for her:
She has the heart of the wild birds that fear
The net of the fowler or the wicker cage.

Deirdre. Am I to see the fowler and the cage
And speak no word at all?

Naoise.   You would have known,
Had they not bred you in that mountainous place,
That when we give a word and take a word
Sorrow is put away, past wrong forgotten.

Deirdre. Though death may come of it?

Naoise.   Though death may come.

Deirdre. When first we came into this empty house   310
You had foreknowledge of our death, and even
When speaking of the paleness of my cheek
Your own cheek blanched.

Naoise.   Listen to this old man.
He can remember all the promises
We trusted to.

Deirdre.   You speak from the lips out,
And I am pleading for your life and mine.

Naoise. Listen to this old man, for many think
He has a golden tongue.

Deirdre.   Then I will say
　　What it were best to carry to the grave.
320　Look at my face where the leaf raddled it
　　And at these rubies on my hair and breast.
　　It was for him, to stir him to desire,
　　I put on beauty; yes, for Conchubar.

Naoise. What frenzy put these words into your mouth?

Deirdre. No frenzy, for what need is there for frenzy
　　To change what shifts with every change of the wind,
　　Or else there is no truth in men's old sayings?
　　Was I not born a woman?

Naoise.   You're mocking me.

Deirdre. And is there mockery in this face and eyes,
330　Or in this body, in these limbs that brought
　　So many mischiefs? Look at me and say
　　If that that shakes my limbs be mockery.

Naoise. What woman is there that a man can trust
　　But at the moment when he kisses her
　　At the first midnight?

Deirdre.   Were it not most strange
　　That woman should put evil in men's hearts
　　And lack it in themselves? And yet I think
　　That being half good I might change round again
　　Were we aboard our ship and on the sea.

340　*Naoise.* We'll to the horses and take ship again.

Fergus. Fool, she but seeks to rouse your jealousy
　　With crafty words.

Deirdre.   Were we not born to wander?
　　These jewels have been reaped by the innocent sword
　　Upon a mountain, and a mountain bred me;
　　But who can tell what change can come to love
　　Among the valleys? I speak no falsehood now.
　　Away to windy summits, and there mock
　　The night-jar and the valley-keeping bird!

Fergus. Men blamed you that you stirred a quarrel up
   That has brought death to many. I have made peace,   350
   Poured water on the fire, but if you fly
   King Conchubar may think that he is mocked
   And the house blaze again: and in what quarter,
   If Conchubar were the treacherous man you think,
   Would you find safety now that you have come
   Into the very middle of his power,
   Under his very eyes?

Deirdre.   Under his eyes
   And in the very middle of his power!
   Then there is but one way to make all safe:
   I'll spoil this beauty that brought misery   360
   And houseless wandering on the man I loved.
   These wanderers will show me how to do it;
   To clip this hair to baldness, blacken my skin
   With walnut juice, and tear my face with briars.
   O that the creatures of the woods had torn
   My body with their claws!

Fergus.   What, wilder yet!

Deirdre [*to Naoise*]. Whatever were to happen to my face
   I'd be myself, and there's not any way
   But this to bring all trouble to an end.

Naoise. Leave the gods' handiwork unblotched, and wait   370
   For their decision, our decision is past.
         [*A Dark-faced Messenger comes to the threshold.*

Fergus. Peace, peace; the messenger is at the door;
   He stands upon the threshold; he stands there;
   He stands, King Conchubar's purpose on his lips.

Messenger. Supper is on the table. Conchubar
   Is waiting for his guests.

Fergus.   All's well again!
   All's well! All's well! You cried your doubts so loud
   That I had almost doubted.

Naoise.   We doubted him,

And he the while but busy in his house
For the more welcome.

380 *Deirdre.*   The message is not finished.

Fergus. Come quickly, Conchubar will laugh, that I——
Although I held out boldly in my speech—
That I, even I——

Deirdre.   Wait, wait! He is not done.

Messenger. Deirdre and Fergus, son of Roigh, are summoned;
But not the traitor that bore off the Queen.
It is enough that the King pardon her,
And call her to his table and his bed.

Naoise. So, then, it's treachery.

Fergus.   I'll not believe it.

Naoise. Lead on and I will follow at your heels
390   That I may challenge him before his court
To match me there, or match me in some place
Where none can come between us but our swords,
For I have found no truth on any tongue
That's not of iron.

Messenger.   I am Conchubar's man,
I am content to serve an iron tongue:
That Tongue commands that Fergus, son of Roigh,
And Deirdre come this night into his house,
And none but they.   [*He goes, followed by Naoise.*

Fergus.   Some rogue, some enemy,
Has bribed him to embroil us with the King;
400   I know that he has lied because I know
King Conchubar's mind as if it were my own,
But I'll find out the truth.
          [*He is about to follow Naoise, but Deirdre stops him.*

Deirdre.   No, no, old man.
You thought the best, and the worst came of it;
We listened to the counsel of the wise,
And so turned fools. But ride and bring your friends.

Go, and go quickly. Conchubar has not seen me;
It may be that his passion is asleep,
And that we may escape.

Fergus.   But I'll go first,
And follow up that Libyan heel, and send
Such words to Conchubar that he may know   410
At how great peril he lays hands upon you.

                    Naoise enters

Naoise. The Libyan, knowing that a servant's life
Is safe from hands like mine, but turned and mocked.

Fergus. I'll call my friends, and call the reaping-hooks,
And carry you in safety to the ships.
My name has still some power. I will protect,
Or, if that is impossible, revenge.
                    [*Goes out by other door.*

Naoise [*who is calm, like a man who has passed beyond life*].
The crib has fallen and the birds are in it;
There is not one of the great oaks about us
But shades a hundred men.

Deirdre.   Let's out and die,   420
Or break away, if the chance favour us.

Naoise. They would but drag you from me, stained with blood.
Their barbarous weapons would but mar that beauty,
And I would have you die as a queen should—
In a death-chamber. You are in my charge.
We will wait here, and when they come upon us,
I'll hold them from the doors, and when that's over,
Give you a cleanly death with this grey edge.

Deirdre. I will stay here; but you go out and fight.
Our way of life has brought no friends to us,   430
And if we do not buy them leaving it,
We shall be ever friendless.

Naoise.   What do they say?
That Lugaid Redstripe and that wife of his
Sat at this chess-board, waiting for their end.

They knew that there was nothing that could save them,
And so played chess as they had any night
For years, and waited for the stroke of sword.
I never heard a death so out of reach
Of common hearts, a high and comely end.
440   What need have I, that gave up all for love,
To die like an old king out of a fable,
Fighting and passionate? What need is there
For all that ostentation at my setting?
I have loved truly and betrayed no man.
I need no lightning at the end, no beating
In a vain fury at the cage's door.
[*To Musicians.*] Had you been here when that man and his queen
Played at so high a game, could you have found
An ancient poem for the praise of it?
450   It should have set out plainly that those two,
Because no man and woman have loved better,
Might sit on there contentedly, and weigh
The joy comes after. I have heard the seamew
Sat there, with all the colour in her cheeks,
As though she'd say: 'There's nothing happening
But that a king and queen are playing chess.'

Deirdre. He's in the right, though I have not been born
Of the cold, haughty waves, my veins being hot,
And though I have loved better than that queen,
460   I'll have as quiet fingers on the board.
O, singing women, set it down in a book,
That love is all we need, even though it is
But the last drops we gather up like this;
And though the drops are all we have known of life,
For we have been most friendless—praise us for it,
And praise the double sunset, for naught's lacking
But a good end to the long, cloudy day.

Naoise. Light torches there and drive the shadows out,
For day's grey end comes up.
      [*A Musician lights a torch in the fire and then crosses before
      the chess-players, and slowly lights the torches in the sconces.
      The light is almost gone from the wood, but there is a clear*

*evening light in the sky, increasing the sense of solitude and
loneliness.*

Deirdre.   Make no sad music.
  What is it but a king and queen at chess?   470
  They need a music that can mix itself
  Into imagination, but not break
  The steady thinking that the hard game needs.
    [*During the chess, the Musicians sing this song*]
        Love is an immoderate thing
          And can never be content
        Till it dip an ageing wing
          Where some laughing element
        Leaps and Time's old lanthorn dims.
          What's the merit in love-play,
        In the tumult of the limbs   480
          That dies out before 'tis day,
        Heart on heart, or mouth on mouth,
          All that mingling of our breath,
        When love-longing is but drouth
          For the things come after death?
  [*During the last verses Deirdre rises from the board and
kneels at Naoise's feet.*

Deirdre. I cannot go on playing like that woman
  That had but the cold blood of the sea in her veins.

Naoise. It is your move. Take up your man again.

Deirdre. Do you remember that first night in the woods
  We lay all night on leaves, and looking up,   490
  When the first grey of the dawn awoke the birds,
  Saw leaves above us? You thought that I still slept,
  And bending down to kiss me on the eyes,
  Found they were open. Bend and kiss me now,
  For it may be the last before our death.
  And when that's over, we'll be different;
  Imperishable things, a cloud or a fire.
  And I know nothing but this body, nothing
  But that old vehement, bewildering kiss.
                [*Conchubar comes to the door.*

First Musician. Children, beware!

500   *Naoise* [*laughing*].   He has taken up my challenge;
          Whether I am a ghost or living man
          When day has broken, I'll forget the rest,
          And say that there is kingly stuff in him.
               [*Turns to fetch spear and shield, and then sees that Conchubar
               has gone.*

First Musician. He came to spy upon you, not to fight.

Naoise. A prudent hunter, therefore, but no king.
          He'd find if what has fallen in the pit
          Were worth the hunting, but has come too near,
          And I turn hunter. You're not man, but beast.
          Go scurry in the bushes, now, beast, beast,
510   For now it's topsy-turvy, I upon you.
                              [*He rushes out after Conchubar.*

Deirdre. You have a knife there, thrust into your girdle.
          I'd have you give it me.

First Musician.   No, but I dare not.

Deirdre. No, but you must.

First Musician.   If harm should come to you,
          They'd know I gave it.

Deirdre [*snatching knife*]. There is no mark on this
          To make it different from any other
          Out of a common forge.
                              [*Goes to the door and looks out.*

First Musician.   You have taken it,
          I did not give it you; but there are times
          When such a thing is all the friend one has.

Deirdre. The leaves hide all, and there's no way to find
520   What path to follow. Why is there no sound?
                              [*She goes from door to window.*

First Musician. Where would you go?

Deirdre.   To strike a blow for Naoise,

If Conchubar call the Libyans to his aid.
But why is there no clash? They have met by this!

First Musician. Listen. I am called wise. If Conchubar win,
You have a woman's wile that can do much,
Even with men in pride of victory.
He is in love and old. What were one knife
Among a hundred?

Deirdre [*going towards them*]. Women, if I die,
If Naoise die this night, how will you praise?
What words seek out? for that will stand to you; 530
For being but dead we shall have many friends.
All through your wanderings, the doors of kings
Shall be thrown wider open, the poor man's hearth
Heaped with new turf, because you are wearing this
                                  [*Gives Musician a bracelet.*
To show that you have Deirdre's story right.

First Musician. Have you not been paid servants in love's house
To sweep the ashes out and keep the doors?
And though you have suffered all for mere love's sake
You'd live your lives again.

Deirdre.   Even this last hour.

      Conchubar enters with dark-faced men

Conchubar. One woman and two men; that is the quarrel 540
That knows no mending. Bring in the man she chose
Because of his beauty and the strength of his youth.
         [*The dark-faced men drag in Naoise entangled in a net.*

Naoise. I have been taken like a bird or a fish.

Conchubar. He cried 'Beast, beast!' and in a blind-beast rage
He ran at me and fell into the nets,
But we were careful for your sake, and took him
With all the comeliness that woke desire
Unbroken in him. I being old and lenient,
I would not hurt a hair upon his head.

Deirdre. What do you say? Have you forgiven him? 550

Naoise. He is but mocking us. What's left to say
    Now that the seven years' hunt is at an end?

Deirdre. He never doubted you until I made him,
    And therefore all the blame for what he says
    Should fall on me.

Conchubar.   But his young blood is hot,
    And if we're of one mind, he shall go free,
    And I ask nothing for it, or, if something,
    Nothing I could not take. There is no king
    In the wide world that, being so greatly wronged,
560   Could copy me, and give all vengeance up.
    Although her marriage-day had all but come,
    You carried her away; but I'll show mercy.
    Because you had the insolent strength of youth
    You carried her away; but I've had time
    To think it out through all these seven years.
    I will show mercy.

Naoise.   You have many words.

Conchubar. I will not make a bargain; I but ask
    What is already mine.
        [Deirdre moves slowly towards Conchubar while he is speaking, her eyes fixed upon him.
               You may go free
    If Deirdre will but walk into my house
570   Before the people's eyes, that they may know,
    When I have put the crown upon her head,
    I have not taken her by force and guile.
    The doors are open, and the floors are strewed
    And in the bridal chamber curtains sewn
    With all enchantments that give happiness
    By races that are germane to the sun,
    And nearest him, and have no blood in their veins—
    For when they're wounded the wound drips with wine—
    Nor speech but singing. At the bridal door
580   Two fair king's daughters carry in their hands
    The crown and robe.

Deirdre.   O no! Not that, not that!
  Ask any other thing but that one thing.
  Leave me with Naoise. We will go away
  Into some country at the ends of the earth.
  We'll trouble you no more; and there is no one
  That will not praise you if you pardon us.
  'He is good, he is good', they'll say to one another;
  'There's nobody like him, for he forgave
  Deirdre and Naoise.'

Conchubar.   Do you think that I
  Shall let you go again, after seven years   590
  Of longing and of planning here and there,
  And trafficking with merchants for the stones
  That make all sure, and watching my own face
  That none might read it?

Deirdre [*to Naoise*].   It's better to go with him.
  Why should you die when one can bear it all?
  My life is over; it's better to obey.
  Why should you die? I will not live long, Naoise.
  I'd not have you believe I'd long stay living;
  O no, no, no! You will go far away.
  You will forget me. Speak, speak, Naoise, speak,   600
  And say that it is better that I go.
  I will not ask it. Do not speak a word,
  For I will take it all upon myself.
  Conchubar, I will go.

Naoise.   And do you think
  That, were I given life at such a price,
  I would not cast it from me? O my eagle!
  Why do you beat vain wings upon the rock
  When hollow night's above?

Deirdre.   It's better, Naoise.
  It may be hard for you, but you'll forget.
  For what am I, to be remembered always?   610
  And there are other women. There was one,
  The daughter of the King of Leodas;
  I could not sleep because of her. Speak to him;

Tell it out plain, and make him understand.
And if it be he thinks I shall stay living,
Say that I will not.

Naoise.   Would I had lost life
  Among those Scottish kings that sought it of me
  Because you were my wife, or that the worst
  Had taken you before this bargaining!
620 O eagle! If you were to do this thing,
  And buy my life of Conchubar with your body,
  Love's law being broken, I would stand alone
  Upon the eternal summits, and call out,
  And you could never come there, being banished.

Deirdre [kneeling to Conchubar]. I would obey, but cannot.
      Pardon us.
  I know that you are good. I have heard you praised
  For giving gifts; and you will pardon us,
  Although I cannot go into your house.
  It was my fault. I only should be punished.
                    [Unseen by Deirdre, Naoise is gagged.
630 The very moment these eyes fell on him,
  I told him; I held out my hands to him;
  How could he refuse? At first he would not—
  I am not lying—he remembered you.
  What do I say? My hands?—No, no, my lips—
  For I had pressed my lips upon his lips—
  I swear it is not false—my breast to his;
      [Conchubar motions; Naoise, unseen by Deirdre, is taken
      behind the curtain.
  Until I woke the passion that's in all,
  And how could he resist? I had my beauty.
  You may have need of him, a brave, strong man,
640 Who is not foolish at the council-board,
  Nor does he quarrel by the candle-light
  And give hard blows to dogs. A cup of wine
  Moves him to mirth, not madness.
                          [She stands up.
                    What am I saying?
  You may have need of him, for you have none

Who is so good a sword, or so well loved
Among the common people. You may need him,
And what king knows when the hour of need may come?
You dream that you have men enough. You laugh.
Yes; you are laughing to yourself. You say,
'I am Conchubar—I have no need of him.'   650
You will cry out for him some day and say,
'If Naoise were but living'—[*she misses Naoise*]. Where is he?
Where have you sent him? Where is the son of Usna?
Where is he, O, where is he?

> [*She staggers over to the Musicians. The Executioner has*
> *come out with a sword on which there is blood; Conchubar*
> *points to it. The Musicians give a wail.*

Conchubar. The traitor who has carried off my wife
   No longer lives. Come to my house now, Deirdre,
   For he that called himself your husband's dead.

Deirdre. O, do not touch me. Let me go to him.

> [*Pause.*

   King Conchubar is right. My husband's dead.
   A single woman is of no account,
   Lacking array of servants, linen cupboards,   660
   The bacon hanging—and King Conchubar's house
   All ready, too—I'll to King Conchubar's house.
   It is but wisdom to do willingly
   What has to be.

Conchubar.   But why are you so calm?
   I thought that you would curse me and cry out,
   And fall upon the ground and tear your hair.

Deirdre [*laughing*]. You know too much of women to think so;
   Though, if I were less worthy of desire,
   I would pretend as much; but, being myself,   670
   It is enough that you were master here.
   Although we are so delicately made,
   There's something brutal in us, and we are won
   By those who can shed blood. It was some woman
   That taught you how to woo: but do not touch me:
   I shall do all you bid me, but not yet,

Because I have to do what's customary.
We lay the dead out, folding up the hands,
Closing the eyes, and stretching out the feet,
680   And push a pillow underneath the head,
Till all's in order; and all this I'll do
For Naoise, son of Usna.

Conchubar.   It is not fitting.
You are not now a wanderer, but a queen,
And there are plenty that can do these things.

Deirdre [*motioning Conchubar away*]. No, no. Not yet. I cannot
        be your queen
Till the past's finished, and its debts are paid.
When a man dies, and there are debts unpaid,
He wanders by the debtor's bed and cries,
'There's so much owing.'

Conchubar.   You are deceiving me.
690   You long to look upon his face again.
Why should I give you now to a dead man
That took you from a living?

                                [*He makes a step towards her.*

Deirdre.   In good time.
You'll stir me to more passion than he could,
And yet, if you are wise, you'll grant me this:
That I go look upon him that was once
So strong and comely and held his head so high
That women envied me. For I will see him
All blood-bedabbled and his beauty gone.
It's better, when you're beside me in your strength,
700   That the mind's eye should call up the soiled body,
And not the shape I loved. Look at him, women.
He heard me pleading to be given up,
Although my lover was still living, and yet
He doubts my purpose. I will have you tell him
How changeable all women are; how soon
Even the best of lovers is forgot
When his day's finished.

Conchubar.   No; but I will trust
   The strength that you have praised, and not your purpose.

Deirdre [*almost with a caress*]. It is so small a gift and you will
     grant it
   Because it is the first that I have asked.   710
   He has refused. There is no sap in him;
   Nothing but empty veins. I thought as much.
   He has refused me the first thing I have asked—
   Me, me, his wife. I understand him now;
   I know the sort of life I'll have with him;
   But he must drag me to his house by force.
   If he refuses [*she laughs*], he shall be mocked of all.
   They'll say to one another, 'Look at him
   That is so jealous that he lured a man
   From over sea, and murdered him, and yet   720
   He trembled at the thought of a dead face!'
                [*She has her hand upon the curtain.*

Conchubar. How do I know that you have not some knife,
   And go to die upon his body?

Deirdre.   Have me searched,
   If you would make so little of your queen.
   It may be that I have a knife hid here
   Under my dress. Bid one of these dark slaves
   To search me for it.   [*Pause.*

Conchubar.   Go to your farewells, Queen.

Deirdre. Now strike the wire, and sing to it a while,
   Knowing that all is happy, and that you know
   Within what bride-bed I shall lie this night,   730
   And by what man, and lie close up to him,
   For the bed's narrow, and there outsleep the cock-crow.
                [*She goes behind the curtain.*

First Musician. They are gone, they are gone. The proud may lie
   by the proud.

Second Musician. Though we were bidden to sing, cry nothing
   loud.

First Musician. They are gone, they are gone.

Second Musician.   Whispering were enough.

First Musician. Into the secret wilderness of their love.

Second Musician. A high, grey cairn. What more is to be said?

First Musician. Eagles have gone into their cloudy bed.
    [*Shouting outside. Fergus enters. Many men with scythes and
    sickles and torches gather about the doors. The house is lit
    with the glare of their torches.*

Fergus. Where's Naoise, son of Usna, and his queen?
740   I and a thousand reaping-hooks and scythes
     Demand him of you.

Conchubar.   You have come too late.
    I have accomplished all. Deirdre is mine;
    She is my queen, and no man now can rob me.
    I had to climb the topmost bough, and pull
    This apple among the winds. Open the curtain
    That Fergus learn my triumph from her lips.
       [*The curtain is drawn back. The Musicians begin to keen with
       low voices.*
    No, no; I'll not believe it. She is not dead—
    She cannot have escaped a second time!

Fergus. King, she is dead; but lay no hand upon her.
750   What's this but empty cage and tangled wire,
     Now the bird's gone? But I'll not have you touch it.

Conchubar. You are all traitors, all against me—all.
    And she has deceived me for a second time;
    And every common man can keep his wife,
    But not the King.
       [*Loud shouting outside: 'Death to Conchubar!' 'Where is
       Naoise?' etc. The dark-faced men gather round Conchubar
       and draw their swords; but he motions them away.*
           I have no need of weapons,
    There's not a traitor that dare stop my way.
    Howl, if you will; but I, being King, did right
    In choosing her most fitting to be Queen,
    And letting no boy lover take the sway.

At the Hawk's Well

(1917)

Persons in the Play

Three Musicians *(their faces made up to resemble masks)*

The Guardian of the Well *(with face made up to resemble a mask)*

An Old Man *(wearing a mask)*

A Young Man *(wearing a mask)*

Time—*The Irish Heroic Age*

The stage is any bare space before a wall against which stands a patterned screen. A drum and a gong and a zither have been laid close to the screen before the play begins. If necessary, they can be carried in, after the audience is seated, by the First Musician, who also can attend to the lights if there is any special lighting. We had two lanterns upon posts—designed by Mr. Dulac—at the outer corners of the stage, but they did not give enough light, and we found it better to play by the light of a large chandelier. Indeed, I think, so far as my present experience goes, that the most effective lighting is the lighting we are most accustomed to in our rooms. These masked players seem stranger when there is no mechanical means of separating them from us. The First Musician carries with him a folded black cloth and goes to the centre of the stage towards the front and stands motionless, the folded cloth hanging from between his hands. The two other Musicians enter and, after standing a moment at either side of the stage, go towards him and slowly unfold the cloth, singing as they do so:

> I call to the eye of the mind
> A well long choked up and dry
> And boughs long stripped by the wind,
> And I call to the mind's eye
> Pallor of an ivory face,

Its lofty dissolute air,
A man climbing up to a place
The salt sea wind has swept bare.

*As they unfold the cloth, they go backward a little so that the
stretched cloth and the wall make a triangle with the First Musician
at the apex supporting the centre of the cloth. On the black cloth is a
gold pattern suggesting a hawk. The Second and Third Musicians
now slowly fold up the cloth again, pacing with a rhythmic move-
ment of the arms towards the First Musician and singing:*

What were his life soon done!
10   Would he lose by that or win?
A mother that saw her son
Doubled over a speckled shin,
Cross-grained with ninety years,
Would cry, 'How little worth
Were all my hopes and fears
And the hard pain of his birth!'

*The words 'a speckled shin' are familiar to readers of Irish leg-
endary stories in descriptions of old men bent double over the fire.
While the cloth has been spread out, the Guardian of the Well has
entered and is now crouching upon the ground. She is entirely cov-
ered by a black cloak; beside her lies a square blue cloth to represent
a well. The three Musicians have taken their places against the wall
beside their instruments of music; they will accompany the move-
ments of the players with gong or drum or zither.*

First Musician [*singing*].
The boughs of the hazel shake,
The sun goes down in the west.

Second Musician [*singing*].
The heart would be always awake,
20   The heart would turn to its rest.
[*They now go to one side of the stage rolling up the cloth.*

First Musician [*speaking*]. Night falls;
The mountain-side grows dark;
The withered leaves of the hazel
Half choke the dry bed of the well;

The guardian of the well is sitting
Upon the old grey stone at its side,
Worn out from raking its dry bed,
Worn out from gathering up the leaves.
Her heavy eyes
Know nothing, or but look upon stone. 30
The wind that blows out of the sea
Turns over the heaped-up leaves at her side;
They rustle and diminish.

Second Musician. I am afraid of this place.

Both Musicians [*singing*].
        'Why should I sleep?' the heart cries,
        'For the wind, the salt wind, the sea wind,
        Is beating a cloud through the skies;
        I would wander always like the wind.'

    An Old Man enters through the audience

First Musician [*speaking*]. That old man climbs up hither,
    Who has been watching by his well 40
    These fifty years.
    He is all doubled up with age;
    The old thorn-trees are doubled so
    Among the rocks where he is climbing.
    [*The Old Man stands for a moment motionless by the side of
    the stage with bowed head. He lifts his head at the sound of a
    drum-tap. He goes towards the front of the stage moving to
    the taps of the drum. He crouches and moves his hands as if
    making a fire. His movements, like those of the other persons
    in the play, suggest a marionette.*

First Musician [*speaking*]. He has made a little heap of leaves;
    He lays the dry sticks on the leaves
    And, shivering with cold, he has taken up
    The fire-stick and socket from its hole.
    He whirls it round to get a flame;
    And now the dry sticks take the fire, 50
    And now the fire leaps up and shines
    Upon the hazels and the empty well.

Musicians [*singing*].

> 'O wind, O salt wind, O sea wind!'
> Cries the heart, 'it is time to sleep;
> Why wander and nothing to find?
> Better grow old and sleep.'

Old Man [*speaking*]. Why don't you speak to me? Why don't you
    say:
'Are you not weary gathering those sticks?
Are not your fingers cold?' You have not one word,
60   While yesterday you spoke three times. You said:
'The well is full of hazel leaves.' You said:
'The wind is from the west.' And after that:
'If there is rain it's likely there'll be mud.'
To-day you are as stupid as a fish,
No, worse, worse, being less lively and as dumb.

                      [*He goes nearer.*

Your eyes are dazed and heavy. If the Sidhe
Must have a guardian to clean out the well
And drive the cattle off, they might choose somebody
That can be pleasant and companionable
70   Once in the day. Why do you stare like that?
You had that glassy look about the eyes
Last time it happened. Do you know anything?
It is enough to drive an old man crazy
To look all day upon these broken rocks,
And ragged thorns, and that one stupid face,
And speak and get no answer.

Young Man [*who has entered through the audience during the last
    speech*].   Then speak to me,
For youth is not more patient than old age;
And though I have trod the rocks for half a day
I cannot find what I am looking for.

Old Man.   Who speaks?
80   Who comes so suddenly into this place
Where nothing thrives? If I may judge by the gold
On head and feet and glittering in your coat,
You are not of those who hate the living world.

Young Man. I am named Cuchulain, I am Sualtim's son.

Old Man. I have never heard that name.

Young Man. It is not unknown.
    I have an ancient house beyond the sea.

Old Man. What mischief brings you hither?—you are like those
    Who are crazy for the shedding of men's blood,
    And for the love of women.

Young Man. A rumour has led me,
    A story told over the wine towards dawn. 90
    I rose from table, found a boat, spread sail,
    And with a lucky wind under the sail
    Crossed waves that have seemed charmed, and found this shore.

Old Man. There is no house to sack among these hills
    Nor beautiful woman to be carried off.

Young Man. You should be native here, for that rough tongue
    Matches the barbarous spot. You can, it may be,
    Lead me to what I seek, a well wherein
    Three hazels drop their nuts and withered leaves,
    And where a solitary girl keeps watch 100
    Among grey boulders. He who drinks, they say,
    Of that miraculous water lives for ever.

Old Man. And are there not before your eyes at the instant
    Grey boulders and a solitary girl
    And three stripped hazels?

Young Man. But there is no well.

Old Man. Can you see nothing yonder?

Young Man. I but see
    A hollow among stones half-full of leaves.

Old Man. And do you think so great a gift is found
    By no more toil than spreading out a sail,
    And climbing a steep hill? O, folly of youth, 110
    Why should that hollow place fill up for you,
    That will not fill for me? I have lain in wait
    For more than fifty years, to find it empty,

Or but to find the stupid wind of the sea
Drive round the perishable leaves.

Young Man.   So it seems
There is some moment when the water fills it.

Old Man. A secret moment that the holy shades
That dance upon the desolate mountain know,
And not a living man, and when it comes
120   The water has scarce plashed before it is gone.

Young Man. I will stand here and wait. Why should the luck
Of Sualtim's son desert him now? For never
Have I had long to wait for anything.

Old Man. No! Go from this accursed place! This place
Belongs to me, that girl there, and those others,
Deceivers of men.

Young Man.   And who are you who rail
Upon those dancers that all others bless?

Old Man. One whom the dancers cheat. I came like you
When young in body and in mind, and blown
130   By what had seemed to me a lucky sail.
The well was dry, I sat upon its edge,
I waited the miraculous flood, I waited
While the years passed and withered me away.
I have snared the birds for food and eaten grass
And drunk the rain, and neither in dark nor shine
Wandered too far away to have heard the plash,
And yet the dancers have deceived me. Thrice
I have awakened from a sudden sleep
To find the stones were wet.

Young Man.   My luck is strong,
140   It will not leave me waiting, nor will they
That dance among the stones put me asleep;
If I grow drowsy I can pierce my foot.

Old Man. No, do not pierce it, for the foot is tender,
It feels pain much. But find your sail again
And leave the well to me, for it belongs
To all that's old and withered.

Young Man.   No, I stay.
　　　[The Guardian of the Well gives the cry of the hawk.
　　There is that bird again.

Old Man.   There is no bird.

Young Man. It sounded like the sudden cry of a hawk,
　　But there's no wing in sight. As I came hither
　　A great grey hawk swept down out of the sky,   150
　　And though I have good hawks, the best in the world
　　I had fancied, I have not seen its like. It flew
　　As though it would have torn me with its beak,
　　Or blinded me, smiting with that great wing.
　　I had to draw my sword to drive it off,
　　And after that it flew from rock to rock.
　　I pelted it with stones, a good half-hour,
　　And just before I had turned the big rock there
　　And seen this place, it seemed to vanish away.
　　Could I but find a means to bring it down   160
　　I'd hood it.

Old Man.   The Woman of the Sidhe herself,
　　The mountain witch, the unappeasable shadow.
　　She is always flitting upon this mountain-side,
　　To allure or to destroy. When she has shown
　　Herself to the fierce women of the hills
　　Under that shape they offer sacrifice
　　And arm for battle. There falls a curse
　　On all who have gazed in her unmoistened eyes;
　　So get you gone while you have that proud step
　　And confident voice, for not a man alive   170
　　Has so much luck that he can play with it.
　　Those that have long to live should fear her most,
　　The old are cursed already. That curse may be
　　Never to win a woman's love and keep it;
　　Or always to mix hatred in the love;
　　Or it may be that she will kill your children,
　　That you will find them, their throats torn and bloody,
　　Or you will be so maddened that you kill them
　　With your own hand.

Young Man.   Have you been set down there

180   To threaten all who come, and scare them off?
    You seem as dried up as the leaves and sticks,
    As though you had no part in life.
                    [*The Guardian of the Well gives hawk cry again.*
                         That cry!
    There is that cry again. That woman made it,
    But why does she cry out as the hawk cries?

Old Man. It was her mouth, and yet not she, that cried.
    It was that shadow cried behind her mouth;
    And now I know why she has been so stupid
    All the day through, and had such heavy eyes.
    Look at her shivering now, the terrible life

190   Is slipping through her veins. She is possessed.
    Who knows whom she will murder or betray
    Before she awakes in ignorance of it all,
    And gathers up the leaves? But they'll be wet;
    The water will have come and gone again;
    That shivering is the sign. O, get you gone,
    At any moment now I shall hear it bubble.
    If you are good you will leave it. I am old,
    And if I do not drink it now, will never;
    I have been watching all my life and maybe

200   Only a little cupful will bubble up.

Young Man. I'll take it in my hands. We shall both drink,
    And even if there are but a few drops,
    Share them.

Old Man.   But swear that I may drink the first;
    The young are greedy, and if you drink the first
    You'll drink it all. Ah, you have looked at her;
    She has felt your gaze and turned her eyes on us;
    I cannot bear her eyes, they are not of this world,
    Nor moist, nor faltering; they are no girl's eyes.
        [*He covers his head. The Guardian of the Well throws off her*
        cloak and rises. Her dress under the cloak suggests a hawk.

Young Man. Why do you fix those eyes of a hawk upon me?

210   I am not afraid of you, bird, woman, or witch.

[*He goes to the side of the well, which the Guardian of the
Well has left.*

Do what you will, I shall not leave this place
Till I have grown immortal like yourself.
[*He has sat down; the Guardian of the Well has begun to
dance, moving like a hawk. The Old Man sleeps. The dance
goes on for some time.*

First Musician [*singing or half-singing*].
        O God, protect me
        From a horrible deathless body
        Sliding through the veins of a sudden.
[*The dance goes on for some time. The Young Man rises slowly.*

First Musician [*speaking*]. The madness has laid hold upon him
    now,
    For he grows pale and staggers to his feet.
                       [*The dance goes on.*

Young Man. Run where you will,
    Grey bird, you shall be perched upon my wrist.
    Some were called queens and yet have been perched there.   220
                       [*The dance goes on.*

First Musician [*speaking*]. I have heard water plash; it comes, it
    comes;
    Look where it glitters. He has heard the plash;
    Look, he has turned his head.
       [*The Guardian of the Well has gone out. The Young Man
       drops his spear as if in a dream and goes out.*

Musicians [*singing*].
        He has lost what may not be found
        Till men heap his burial-mound
        And all the history ends.
        He might have lived at his ease,
        An old dog's head on his knees,
        Among his children and friends.
           [*The Old Man creeps up to the well.*

Old Man. The accursed shadows have deluded me,   230
    The stones are dark and yet the well is empty;

The water flowed and emptied while I slept.
You have deluded me my whole life through,
Accursed dancers, you have stolen my life.
That there should be such evil in a shadow!

Young Man [*entering*]. She has fled from me and hidden in the rocks.

Old Man. She has but led you from the fountain. Look!
Though stones and leaves are dark where it has flowed,
There's not a drop to drink.
                    [*The Musicians cry* 'Aoife!' 'Aoife!' *and strike gong.*

Young Man.   What are those cries?
240   What is that sound that runs along the hill?
Who are they that beat a sword upon a shield?

Old Man. She has roused up the fierce women of the hills,
Aoife, and all her troop, to take your life,
And never till you are lying in the earth
Can you know rest.

Young Man.   The clash of arms again!

Old Man. O, do not go! The mountain is accursed;
Stay with me, I have nothing more to lose,
I do not now deceive you.

Young Man.   I will face them.
    [*He goes out, no longer as if in a dream, but shouldering his
    spear and calling:*

He comes! Cuchulain, son of Sualtim, comes!
    [*The Musicians stand up; one goes to centre with folded cloth.
    The others unfold it. While they do so they sing. During the
    singing, and while hidden by the cloth, the Old Man goes out.
    When the play is performed with Mr. Dulac's music, the Musi-
    cians do not rise or unfold the cloth till after they have sung
    the words* 'a bitter life'.

[*Songs for the unfolding and folding of the cloth*]

Come to me, human faces,   250
Familiar memories;
I have found hateful eyes
Among the desolate places,
Unfaltering, unmoistened eyes.

Folly alone I cherish,
I choose it for my share;
Being but a mouthful of air,
I am content to perish;
I am but a mouthful of sweet air.

O lamentable shadows,   260
Obscurity of strife!
I choose a pleasant life
Among indolent meadows,
Wisdom must live a bitter life.
                    [*They then fold up the cloth, singing.*
'The man that I praise',
Cries out the empty well,
'Lives all his days
Where a hand on the bell
Can call the milch cows
To the comfortable door of his house.   270
Who but an idiot would praise
Dry stones in a well?'

'The man that I praise',
Cries out the leafless tree,
'Has married and stays
By an old hearth, and he
On naught has set store
But children and dogs on the floor.
Who but an idiot would praise
A withered tree?'   [*They go out.*   280

The Words upon the Window-pane

(1930)

IN MEMORY OF
LADY GREGORY
IN WHOSE HOUSE IT WAS WRITTEN

Persons in the Play

Dr. Trench

Miss Mackenna

John Corbet

Cornelius Patterson

Abraham Johnson

Mrs. Mallet

Mrs. Henderson

A lodging-house room, an armchair, a little table in front of it, chairs on either side. A fireplace and window. A kettle on the hob and some tea-things on a dresser. A door to back and towards the right. Through the door one can see an entrance hall. The sound of a knocker. Miss Mackenna passes through and then she re-enters the hall together with John Corbet, a man of twenty-two or twenty-three, and Dr. Trench, a man of between sixty and seventy.

Dr. Trench [*in hall*]. May I introduce John Corbet, one of the Corbets of Ballymoney, but at present a Cambridge student? This is Miss Mackenna, our energetic secretary. [*They come into room, take off their coats.*]

Miss Mackenna. I thought it better to let you in myself. This country is still sufficiently medieval to make spiritualism an undesirable theme for gossip. Give me your coats and hats, I will put them in my own room. It is just across the hall. Better sit down; your watches must be fast. Mrs. Henderson is lying down, as she always does before a séance. We won't begin for ten minutes yet. [*She goes out with hats and coats.*]

Dr. Trench. Miss Mackenna does all the real work of the Dublin Spiritualists' Association. She did all the correspondence with Mrs. Henderson, and persuaded the landlady to let her this big room and a small room upstairs. We are a poor society and could not guarantee anything in advance. Mrs. Henderson has come from London at her own risk. She was born in Dublin and wants to spread the movement here. She lives very economically and does not expect a great deal. We all give what we can. A poor woman with the soul of an apostle.

John Corbet. Have there been many séances?

Dr. Trench. Only three so far.

John Corbet. I hope she will not mind my scepticism. I have looked into Myer's *Human Personality* and a wild book by Conan Doyle, but am unconvinced.

Dr. Trench. We all have to find the truth for ourselves. Lord Dunraven, then Lord Adare, introduced my father to the famous David Home. My father often told me that he saw David Home floating in the air in broad daylight, but I did not believe a word of it. I had to investigate for myself, and I was very hard to convince. Mrs. Piper, an American trance medium, not unlike Mrs. Henderson, convinced me.

John Corbet. A state of somnambulism and voices coming through her lips that purport to be those of dead persons?

Dr. Trench. Exactly: quite the best kind of mediumship if you want to establish the identity of a spirit. But do not expect too much. There has been a hostile influence.

John Corbet. You mean an evil spirit?

Dr. Trench. The poet Blake said that he never knew a bad man that had not something very good about him. I say a hostile influence, an influence that disturbed the last séance very seriously. I cannot tell you what happened, for I have not been at any of Mrs. Henderson's séances. Trance mediumship has nothing new to show me—I told the young people when they made me their President that I would probably stay at home, that I could get more out of Emanuel Swedenborg than out of any séance. [*A knock.*] That is probably old Cornelius Patterson; he thinks they race horses and whippets in the other world, and is, so they tell me, so anxious to find out if he is right that he is always punctual. Miss Mackenna will keep him to herself for some minutes. He gives her tips for Harold's Cross.

[*Miss Mackenna crosses to hall door and admits Cornelius Patterson. She brings him to her room across the hall.*

John Corbet [*who has been wandering about*]. This is a wonderful room for a lodging-house.

Dr. Trench. It was a private house until about fifty years ago. It was not so near the town in those days, and there are large stables at the back. Quite a number of notable people lived here. Grattan was born upstairs; no, not Grattan, Curran perhaps—I forget—but I do know that this house in the early part of the eighteenth century belonged to friends of Jonathan Swift, or rather of Stella. Swift chaffed her in the *Journal to Stella* because of certain small sums of money she lost at cards probably in this very room. That was before Vanessa appeared upon the scene. It was a country-house in those days, surrounded by trees and gardens. Somebody cut some lines from a poem of hers upon the window-pane—tradition says Stella herself. [*A knock.*] Here they are, but you will hardly make them out in this light. [*They stand in the window. Corbet stoops down to see better. Miss Mackenna and Abraham Johnson enter and stand near door.*]

Abraham Johnson. Where is Mrs. Henderson?

Miss Mackenna. She is upstairs; she always rests before a séance.

Abraham Johnson. I must see her before the séance. I know exactly what to do to get rid of this evil influence.

Miss Mackenna. If you go up to see her there will be no séance at all. She says it is dangerous even to think, much less to speak, of an evil influence.

Abraham Johnson. Then I shall speak to the President.

Miss Mackenna. Better talk the whole thing over first in my room. Mrs. Henderson says that there must be perfect harmony.

Abraham Johnson. Something must be done. The last séance was completely spoiled. [*A knock.*]

Miss Mackenna. That may be Mrs. Mallet; she is a very experienced spiritualist. Come to my room, old Patterson and some others are there already. [*She brings him to the other room and later crosses to hall door to admit Mrs. Mallet.*]

John Corbet. I know those lines well—they are part of a poem Stella wrote for Swift's fifty-fourth birthday. Only three poems of hers—and some lines she added to a poem of Swift's—have come down to us, but they are enough to prove her a better poet than Swift. Even those few words on the window make me think of a seventeenth-century poet, Donne or Crashaw. [*He quotes*]
> 'You taught how I might youth prolong
> By knowing what is right and wrong,
> How from my heart to bring supplies
> Of lustre to my fading eyes.'

How strange that a celibate scholar, well on in life, should keep the love of two such women! He met Vanessa in London at the height of his political power. She followed him to Dublin. She loved him for nine years, perhaps died of love, but Stella loved him all her life.

Dr. Trench. I have shown that writing to several persons, and you are the first who has recognised the lines.

John Corbet. I am writing an essay on Swift and Stella for my doctorate at Cambridge. I hope to prove that in Swift's day men of intellect reached the height of their power—the greatest position they ever attained in society and the State, that everything great in Ireland and in our character, in what remains of our architecture, comes from that day; that we have kept its seal longer than England.

Dr. Trench. A tragic life: Bolingbroke, Harley, Ormonde, all those great Ministers that were his friends, banished and broken.

John Corbet. I do not think you can explain him in that way—his tragedy had deeper foundations. His ideal order was the Roman Senate, his ideal men Brutus and Cato. Such an order and such men had seemed possible once more, but the moment passed and he foresaw the ruin to come, Democracy, Rousseau, the French Revolution; that is why he hated the common run of men,—'I hate lawyers, I hate doctors,' he said, 'though I love Dr. So-and-so and Judge So-and-so'—that is why he wrote *Gulliver,* that is why he wore out his brain, that is why he felt *saeva indignatio,* that is why he sleeps under the greatest epitaph in history. You remember how it goes? It is almost finer in English than in Latin: 'He has gone where fierce indignation can lacerate his heart no more.'
   [*Abraham Johnson comes in, followed by Mrs. Mallet and Cornelius Patterson.*

Abraham Johnson. Something must be done, Dr. Trench, to drive away the influence that has destroyed our séances. I have come here week after week at considerable expense. I am from Belfast. I am by profession a minister of the Gospel, I do a great deal of work among the poor and ignorant. I produce considerable effect by singing and preaching, but I know that my effect should be much greater than it is. My hope is that I shall be able to communicate with the great Evangelist Moody. I want to ask him to stand invisible beside me when I speak or sing, and lay his hands upon my head and give me such a portion of his power that my work may be blessed as the work of Moody and Sankey was blessed.

Mrs. Mallet. What Mr. Johnson says about the hostile influence is quite true. The last two séances were completely spoilt. I am thinking of starting a tea-shop in Folkestone. I followed Mrs. Henderson to Dublin to get my husband's advice, but two spirits kept talking and would not let any other spirit say a word.

Dr. Trench. Did the spirits say the same thing and go through the same drama at both séances?

Mrs. Mallet. Yes—just as if they were characters in some kind of horrible play.

Dr. Trench. That is what I was afraid of.

Mrs. Mallet. My husband was drowned at sea ten years ago, but constantly speaks to me through Mrs. Henderson as if he were still alive. He advises me about everything I do, and I am utterly lost if I cannot question him.

Cornelius Patterson. I never did like the Heaven they talk about in churches; but when somebody told me that Mrs. Mallet's husband ate and drank and went about with his favourite dog, I said to myself, 'That is the place for Corney Patterson'. I came here to find out if it was true, and I declare to God I have not heard one word about it.

Abraham Johnson. I ask you, Dr. Trench, as President of the Dublin Spiritualists' Association, to permit me to read the ritual of exorcism appointed for such occasions. After the last séance I copied it out of an old book in the library of Belfast University. I have it here.   [*He takes paper out of his pocket.*

Dr. Trench. The spirits are people like ourselves, we treat them as our guests and protect them from discourtesy and violence, and every exorcism is a curse or a threatened curse. We do not admit that there are evil spirits. Some spirits are earth-bound— they think they are still living and go over and over some action of their past lives, just as we go over and over some painful thought, except that where they are thought is reality. For instance, when a spirit which has died a violent death comes to a medium for the first time, it re-lives all the pains of death.

Mrs. Mallet. When my husband came for the first time the medium gasped and struggled as if she was drowning. It was terrible to watch.

Dr. Trench. Sometimes a spirit re-lives not the pain of death but some passionate or tragic moment of life. Swedenborg describes this and gives the reason for it. There is an incident of the kind in the *Odyssey,* and many in Eastern literature; the murderer repeats his murder, the robber his robbery, the lover his serenade, the soldier hears the trumpet once again. If I were a Catholic I would say that such spirits were in Purgatory. In vain do we write *requiescat in pace* upon the tomb, for they must suffer, and we in our turn must suffer until God gives peace. Such spirits do not often come to séances unless those séances are held in houses where those spirits lived, or where the event took places. This spirit which speaks those incomprehensible words and does not answer when spoken to is of such a nature. The more patient we are, the more quickly will it pass out of its passion and its remorse.

Abraham Johnson. I am still convinced that the spirit which disturbed the last séance is evil. If I may not exorcise it I will certainly pray for protection.

Dr. Trench. Mrs. Henderson's control, Lulu, is able and experienced and can protect both medium and sitters, but it may help Lulu if you pray that the spirit find rest.
    [*Abraham Johnson sits down and prays silently, moving his lips. Mrs. Henderson comes in with Miss Mackenna and others. Miss Mackenna shuts the door.*

Dr. Trench. Mrs. Henderson, may I introduce to you Mr. Corbet, a young man from Cambridge and a sceptic, who hopes that you will be able to convince him?

Mrs. Henderson. We were all sceptics once. He must not expect too much from a first séance. He must persevere. [*She sits in the armchair, and the others begin to seat themselves. Miss Mackenna goes to John Corbet and they remain standing.*]

Miss Mackenna. I am glad that you are a sceptic.

John Corbet. I thought you were a spiritualist.

Miss Mackenna. I have seen a good many séances, and sometimes think it is all coincidence and thought-transference. [*She says this in a low voice.*] Then at other times I think as Dr. Trench does, and then I feel like Job—you know the quotation—the hair of my head stands up. A spirit passes before my face.

Mrs. Mallet. Turn the key, Dr. Trench, we don't want anybody blundering in here. [*Dr. Trench locks door.*] Come and sit here, Miss Mackenna.

Miss Mackenna. No, I am going to sit beside Mr. Corbet.
                     [*Corbet and Miss Mackenna sit down.*

John Corbet. You feel like Job to-night?

Miss Mackenna. I feel that something is going to happen, that is why I am glad that you are a sceptic.

John Corbet. You feel safer?

Miss Mackenna. Yes, safer.

Mrs. Henderson. I am glad to meet all my dear friends again and to welcome Mr. Corbet amongst us. As he is a stranger I must explain that we do not call up spirits: we make the right conditions and they come. I do not know who is going to come; sometimes there are a great many and the guides choose between them. The guides try to send somebody for everybody but do not always succeed. If you want to speak to some dear friend who has passed over, do not be discouraged. If your friend cannot come this time, maybe he can next time. My control is a dear little girl called Lulu who died when she was five or six years old. She describes the spirits present and tells us what spirit wants to speak. Miss Mackenna, a verse of a hymn, please, the same we had last time, and will everyone join in the singing?
    [*They sing the following lines from Hymn 564, Irish Church Hymnal.*

                'Sun of my soul, Thou Saviour dear,
                  It is not night if Thou be near:
                  O may no earth-born cloud arise
                  To hide Thee from Thy servant's eyes.'
        [*Mrs. Henderson is leaning back in her chair asleep.*

Miss Mackenna [*to John Corbet*]. She always snores like that when she is going off.

Mrs. Henderson [*in a child's voice*]. Lulu so glad to see all her friends.

Mrs. Mallet. And we are glad you have come, Lulu.

Mrs. Henderson [*in a child's voice*]. Lulu glad to see new friend.

Miss Mackenna [*to John Corbet*]. She is speaking to you.

John Corbet. Thank you, Lulu.

Mrs. Henderson [*in a child's voice*]. You mustn't laugh at the way I talk.

John Corbet. I am not laughing, Lulu.

Mrs. Henderson [*in a child's voice*]. Nobody must laugh. Lulu does her best but can't say big long words. Lulu sees a tall man here, lots of hair on face [*Mrs. Henderson passes her hands over her cheeks and chin*], not much on the top of his head [*Mrs. Henderson passes her hand over the top of her head*], red necktie, and such a funny sort of pin.

Mrs. Mallet. Yes. . . . Yes. . . .

Mrs. Henderson [*in a child's voice*]. Pin like a horseshoe.

Mrs Mallet. It's my husband.

Mrs. Henderson [*in a child's voice*]. He has a message.

Mrs. Mallet. Yes.

Mrs. Henderson [*in a child's voice*]. Lulu cannot hear. He is too far off. He has come near. Lulu can hear now. He says . . . he says, 'Drive that man away!' He is pointing to somebody in the corner, that corner over there. He says it is the bad man who spoilt everything last time. If they won't drive him away, Lulu will scream.

Miss Mackenna. That horrible spirit again.

Abraham Johnson. Last time he monopolised the séance.

Mrs. Mallet. He would not let anybody speak but himself.

Mrs. Henderson [*in a child's voice*]. They have driven that bad man away. Lulu sees a young lady.

Mrs. Mallet. Is not my husband here?

Mrs. Henderson [*in a child's voice*]. Man with funny pin gone away. Young lady here—Lulu thinks she must be at a fancy dress party, such funny clothes, hair all in curls—all bent down on floor near that old man with glasses.

Dr. Trench. No, I do not recognize her.

Mrs. Henderson [*in a child's voice*]. That bad man, that bad old man in the corner, they have let him come back. Lulu is going to scream. O. . . . O. . . . [*In a man's voice*]. How dare you write to her? How dare you ask if we were married? How dare you question her?

Dr. Trench. A soul in its agony—it cannot see us or hear us.

Mrs. Henderson [*upright and rigid, only her lips moving, and still in a man's voice*]. You sit crouching there. Did you not hear what I said? How dared you question her? I found you an ignorant little girl without intellect, without moral ambition. How many times did I not stay away from great men's houses, how many times forsake the Lord Treasurer, how many times neglect the business of the State that we might read Plutarch together!

> [*Abraham Johnson half rises. Dr. Trench motions him to remain seated.*

Dr. Trench. Silence!

Abraham Johnson. But, Dr. Trench . . .

Dr. Trench. Hush—we can do nothing.

Mrs. Henderson [*speaking as before*]. I taught you to think in every situation of life not as Hester Vanhomrigh would think in that situation, but as Cato or Brutus would, and now you behave like some common slut with her ear against the keyhole.

John Corbet [*to Miss Mackenna*]. It is Swift, Jonathan Swift, talking to the woman he called Vanessa. She was christened Hester Vanhomrigh.

Mrs. Henderson [*in Vanessa's voice*]. I questioned her, Jonathan, because I love. Why have you let me spend hours in your company if you did not want me to love you? [*In Swift's voice.*] When I rebuilt Rome in your mind it was as though I walked its streets. [*In Vanessa's voice.*] Was that all, Jonathan? Was I nothing but a painter's canvas? [*In Swift's voice.*] My God, do you think it was easy? I was a man of strong passions and I had sworn never to marry. [*In Vanessa's voice.*] If you and she are not married, why should we not marry like other men and women? I loved you from the first moment when you came to my mother's house and began to teach me. I thought it would be enough to look at you, to speak to you, to hear you speak. I followed you to Ireland five years ago and I can bear it no longer. It is not enough to look, to speak, to hear. Jonathan, Jonathan, I am a woman, the women Brutus and Cato loved were not different. [*In Swift's voice.*] I have something in my blood that no child must inherit. I have constant attacks of dizziness; I pretend they come from a surfeit of fruit when I was a child. I had them in London. . . . There was a great doctor there, Dr. Arbuthnot; I told him of those attacks of dizziness, I told him of worse things. It was he who explained. There is a line of Dryden's. . . . [*In Vanessa's voice.*] O, I know—'Great wits are sure to madness near allied'. If you had children, Jonathan, my blood would make them healthy. I will take your hand, I will lay it upon my heart—upon the Vanhomrigh blood that has been healthy for generations. [*Mrs. Henderson slowly raises her left hand.*] That is the first time you have touched my body, Jonathan. [*Mrs. Henderson stands up and remains rigid. In Swift's voice.*] What do I care if it be healthy? What do I care if it could make mine healthy? Am I to add another to the healthy rascaldom and knavery of the world? [*In Vanessa's voice.*] Look at me, Jonathan. Your arrogant intellect separates us. Give me both your hands. I will put them upon my breast. [*Mrs. Henderson raises her right hand to the level of her left and then raises both to her breast.*] O, it is white—white as the gambler's dice—white ivory dice. Think of the uncertainty. Perhaps a mad child—perhaps a rascal—perhaps a knave— perhaps not, Jonathan. The dice of the intellect are loaded, but I am the common ivory dice. [*Her hands are stretched out as though drawing somebody towards her.*] It is not my hands that draw you back. My hands are weak, they could not draw you back if you did not love as I love. You said that you have strong passions; that is true, Jonathan—no man in Ireland is so passionate. That is why you need me, that is why you need children, nobody has greater need. You are growing old. An old man without children is very solitary. Even his friends, men as old as he, turn away, they turn towards the young, their children or their children's children. They cannot endure an old man like themselves. [*Mrs. Henderson moves away from the chair, her movements gradually growing convulsive.*] You are not too old for the dice, Jonathan, but a few years if you turn away will make you an old miserable childless man. [*In Swift's voice.*] O God, hear the prayer of Jonathan Swift, that afflicted man, and grant that he may leave to posterity nothing but his intellect that came to him from Heaven. [*In Vanessa's voice.*] Can you face solitude with that mind, Jonathan? [*Mrs. Henderson goes to the door, finds that it is closed.*] Dice, white ivory dice. [*In Swift's voice.*] My God, I am left alone with my enemy. Who locked the door, who locked me in with my enemy? [*Mrs. Henderson beats upon the door, sinks to the floor and then speaks as Lulu.*] Bad old man! Do not let him come back. Bad old man does not know he is dead. Lulu cannot find fathers, mothers, sons that have passed over. Power almost gone. [*Mrs. Mallet leads Mrs. Henderson, who seems very exhausted, back to her chair. She is still asleep. She speaks again as Lulu.*] Another verse of hymn. Everybody sing. Hymn will bring good influence.

[*They sing*]
'If some poor wandering child of Thine
Have spurned to-day the voice divine,
Now, Lord, the gracious work begin;
Let him no more lie down in sin.'

[*During the hymn Mrs. Henderson has been murmuring 'Stella', but the singing has almost drowned her voice. The singers draw one another's attention to the fact that she is speaking. The singing stops.*]

Dr. Trench. I thought she was speaking.

Mrs. Mallet. I saw her lips move.

Dr. Trench. She would be more comfortable with a cushion, but we might wake her.

Mrs. Mallet. Nothing can wake her out of a trance like that until she wakes up herself. [*She brings a cushion, and she and Dr. Trench put Mrs. Henderson into a more comfortable position.*]

Mrs. Henderson [*in Swift's voice*]. Stella.

Miss Mackenna [*to John Corbet*]. Did you hear that? She said 'Stella'.

John Corbet. Vanessa has gone, Stella has taken her place.

Miss Mackenna. Did you notice the change while we were singing? The new influence in the room?

John Corbet. I thought I did, but it must have been fancy.

Mrs. Mallet. Hush!

Mrs. Henderson [*in Swift's voice*]. Have I wronged you, beloved Stella? Are you unhappy? You have no children, you have no lover, you have no husband. A cross and ageing man for friend—nothing but that. But no, do not answer—you have answered already in that poem you wrote for my last birthday. With what scorn you speak of the common lot of women 'with no adornment but a face—'
> 'Before the thirtieth year of life
> A maid forlorn or hated wife.'
It is the thought of the great Chrysostom, who wrote in a famous passage that women loved according to the soul, loved as saints can love, keep their beauty longer, have greater happiness than women loved according to the flesh. That thought has comforted me, but it is a terrible thing to be responsible for another's happiness. There are moments when I doubt, when I think Chrysostom may have been wrong. But now I have your poem to drive doubt away. You have addressed me in these noble words:
> 'You taught how I might youth prolong
> By knowing what is right and wrong;
> How from my heart to bring supplies
> Of lustre to my fading eyes;
>
> How soon a beauteous mind repairs
> The loss of chang'd or falling hairs;

How wit and virtue from within
Can spread a smoothness o'er the skin.'

John Corbet. The words upon the window-pane!

Mrs. Henderson [*in Swift's voice*]. Then, because you understand
that I am afraid of solitude, afraid of outliving my friends—and
myself—you comfort me in that last verse—you overpraise my
moral nature when you attribute to it a rich mantle, but O how
touching those words which describe your love:

'Late dying may you cast a shred
Of that rich mantle o'er my head;
To bear with dignity my sorrow,
One day alone, then die to-morrow.'

Yes, you will close my eyes, Stella. O, you will live long after
me, dear Stella, for you are still a young woman, but you will
close my eyes. [*Mrs. Henderson sinks back in chair and speaks
as Lulu.*] Bad old man gone. Power all used up. Lulu can do no
more. Good-bye, friends. [*Mrs. Henderson, speaking in her
own voice.*] Go away, go away! [*She wakes.*] I saw him a
moment ago, has he spoilt the séance again?

Mrs. Mallet. Yes, Mrs. Henderson, my husband came, but he was
driven away.

Dr. Trench. Mrs. Henderson is very tired. We must leave her to
rest. [*To Mrs. Henderson.*] You did your best and nobody can
do more than that. [*He takes out money.*]

Mrs. Henderson. No. . . . No. . . . I cannot take any money, not
after a séance like that.

Dr. Trench. Of course you must take it, Mrs. Henderson. [*He puts
money on table, and Mrs. Henderson gives a furtive glance to
see how much it is. She does the same as each sitter lays down
his or her money.*]

Mrs. Mallet. A bad séance is just as exhausting as a good séance,
and you must be paid.

Mrs. Henderson. No. . . . No. . . . Please don't. It is very wrong to
take money for such a failure.

[*Mrs. Mallet lays down money.*

Cornelius Patterson. A jockey is paid whether he wins or not. [*He lays down money.*]

Miss Mackenna. That spirit rather thrilled me. [*She lays down money.*]

Mrs. Henderson. If you insist, I must take it.

Abraham Johnson. I shall pray for you to-night. I shall ask God to bless and protect your séances. [*He lays down money.*]
[*All go out except John Corbet and Mrs. Henderson.*

John Corbet. I know you are tired, Mrs. Henderson, but I must speak to you. I have been deeply moved by what I have heard. This is my contribution to prove that I am satisfied, completely satisfied. [*He puts a note on the table.*]

Mrs. Henderson. A pound note—nobody ever gives me more than ten shillings, and yet the séance was a failure.

John Corbet [*sitting down near Mrs. Henderson*]. When I say I am satisfied I do not mean that I am convinced it was the work of spirits. I prefer to think that you created it all, that you are an accomplished actress and scholar. In my essay for my Cambridge doctorate I examine all the explanations of Swift's celibacy offered by his biographers and prove that the explanation you selected was the only plausible one. But there is something I must ask you. Swift was the chief representative of the intellect of his epoch, that arrogant intellect free at last from superstition. He foresaw its collapse. He foresaw Democracy, he must have dreaded the future. Did he refuse to beget children because of that dread? Was Swift mad? Or was it the intellect itself that was mad?

Mrs. Henderson. Who are you talking of, sir?

John Corbet. Swift, of course.

Mrs. Henderson. Swift? I do not know anybody called Swift.

John Corbet. Jonathan Swift, whose spirit seemed to be present to-night.

Mrs. Henderson. What? That dirty old man?

John Corbet. He was neither old nor dirty when Stella and
Vanessa loved him.

Mrs. Henderson. I saw him very clearly just as I woke up. His
clothes were dirty, his face covered with boils. Some disease had
made one of his eyes swell up, it stood out from his face like a
hen's egg.

John Corbet. He looked like that in his old age. Stella had been
dead a long time. His brain had gone, his friends had deserted
him. The man appointed to take care of him beat him to keep
him quiet.

Mrs. Henderson. Now they are old, now they are young. They
change all in a moment as their thought changes. It is sometimes
a terrible thing to be out of the body, God help us all.

Dr. Trench [*at doorway*]. Come along, Corbet. Mrs. Henderson is
tired out.

John Corbet. Good-bye, Mrs. Henderson. [*He goes out with Dr.
Trench. All the sitters except Miss Mackenna, who has
returned to her room, pass along the passage on their way to
the front door. Mrs. Henderson counts the money, finds her
purse, which is in a vase on the mantelpiece, and puts the
money in it.*]

Mrs. Henderson. How tired I am! I'd be the better of a cup of tea.
[*She finds the teapot and puts kettle on fire, and then as she
crouches down by the hearth suddenly lifts up her hands and
counts her fingers, speaking in Swift's voice.*] Five great
Ministers that were my friends are gone, ten great Ministers that
were my friends are gone. I have not fingers enough to count the
great Ministers that were my friends and that are gone.
　　　　　[*She wakes with a start and speaks in her own voice.*]
Where did I put that tea-caddy? Ah! there it is. And there
should be a cup and saucer. [*She finds the saucer.*] But where's
the cup? [*She moves aimlessly about the stage and then, letting
the saucer fall and break, speaks in Swift's voice.*] Perish the day
on which I was born!

The Resurrection

(1931)

who gave me a sword

Persons in the Play
The Hebrew
The Greek
The Syrian
Christ
Three Musicians

Before I had finished this play I saw that its subject-matter might make it unsuited for the public stage in England or in Ireland. I had begun it with an ordinary stage scene in the mind's eye, curtained walls, a window and door at back, a curtained door at left. I now changed the stage directions and wrote songs for the unfolding and folding of the curtain that it might be played in a studio or a drawing-room like my dance plays, or at the Peacock Theatre before a specially chosen audience. If it is played at the Peacock Theatre the Musicians may sing the opening and closing songs, as they pull apart or pull together the proscenium curtain; the whole stage may be hung with curtains with an opening at the left. While the play is in progress the Musicians will sit towards the right of the audience; if at the Peacock, on the step which separates the stage from the audience, or one on either side of the proscenium.

[Song for the unfolding and folding of the curtain]

I

I saw a staring virgin stand
Where holy Dionysus died,
And tear the heart out of his side,
And lay the heart upon her hand
And bear that beating heart away;
And then did all the Muses sing
Of Magnus Annus at the spring,
As though God's death were but a play.

II

Another Troy must rise and set,
Another lineage feed the crow,
Another Argo's painted prow
Drive to a flashier bauble yet.
The Roman Empire stood appalled:
It dropped the reins of peace and war
When that fierce virgin and her Star
Out of the fabulous darkness called.

10

[*The Hebrew is discovered alone upon the stage; he has a sword or spear. The Musicians make faint drum-taps, or sound a rattle; the Greek enters through the audience from the left.*

The Hebrew. Did you find out what the noise was?

The Greek. Yes, I asked a Rabbi.

The Hebrew. Were you not afraid?

The Greek. How could he know that I am called a Christian? I wore the cap I brought from Alexandria. He said the followers of Dionysus were parading the streets with rattles and drums; that such a thing had never happened in this city before; that the Roman authorities were afraid to interfere. The followers of Dionysus have been out among the fields tearing a goat to pieces and drinking its blood, and are now wandering through the streets like a pack of wolves. The mob was so terrified of their frenzy that it left them alone, or, as seemed more likely, so busy hunting Christians it had time for nothing else. I turned to go, but he called me back and asked where I lived. When I said outside the gates, he asked if it was true that the dead had broken out of the cemeteries.

The Hebrew. We can keep the mob off for some minutes, long enough for the Eleven to escape over the roofs. I shall defend the narrow stair between this and the street until I am killed, then you will take my place. Why is not the Syrian here?

The Greek. I met him at the door and sent him on a message; he will be back before long.

The Hebrew. The three of us will be few enough for the work in hand.

The Greek [*glancing towards the opening at the left*]. What are they doing now?

The Hebrew. While you were down below, James brought a loaf out of a bag, and Nathanael found a skin of wine. They put them on the table. It was a long time since they had eaten anything. Then they began to speak in low voices, and John spoke of the last time they had eaten in that room.

The Greek. They were thirteen then.

The Hebrew. He said that Jesus divided bread and wine amongst them. When John had spoken they sat still, nobody eating or drinking. If you stand here you will see them. That is Peter close to the window. He has been quite motionless for a long time, his head upon his breast.

The Greek. Is it true that when the soldier asked him if he were a follower of Jesus he denied it?

The Hebrew. Yes, it is true. James told me. Peter told the others what he had done. But when the moment came they were all afraid. I must not blame. I might have been no braver. What are we all but dogs who have lost their master?

The Greek. Yet you and I if the mob come will die rather than let it up that stair.

The Hebrew. Ah! That is different. I am going to draw that curtain; they must not hear what I am going to say. [*He draws curtain.*]

The Greek. I know what is in your mind.

The Hebrew. They are afraid because they do not know what to think. When Jesus was taken they could no longer believe him the Messiah. We can find consolation, but for the Eleven it was always complete light or complete darkness.

The Greek. Because they are so much older.

The Hebrew. No, no. You have only to look into their faces to see they were intended to be saints. They are unfitted for anything else. What makes you laugh?

The Greek. Something I can see through the window. There, where I am pointing. There, at the end of the street. [*They stand together looking out over the heads of the audience.*]

The Hebrew. I cannot see anything.

The Greek. The hill.

The Hebrew. That is Calvary.

The Greek. And the three crosses on the top of it. [*He laughs again.*]

The Hebrew. Be quiet. You do not know what you are doing. You have gone out of your mind. You are laughing at Calvary.

The Greek. No, no. I am laughing because they thought they were nailing the hands of a living man upon the Cross, and all the time there was nothing there but a phantom.

The Hebrew. I saw him buried.

The Greek. We Greeks understand these things. No god has ever been buried; no god has ever suffered. Christ only seemed to be born, only seemed to eat, seemed to sleep, seemed to walk, seemed to die. I did not mean to tell you until I had proof.

The Hebrew. Proof?

The Greek. I shall have proof before nightfall.

The Hebrew. You talk wildly, but a masterless dog can bay the moon.

The Greek. No Jew can understand these things.

The Hebrew. It is you who do not understand. It is I and those men in there, perhaps, who begin to understand at last. He was nothing more than a man, the best man who ever lived. Nobody before him had so pitied human misery. He preached the coming of the Messiah because he thought the Messiah would take it all upon himself. Then some day when he was very tired, after a long journey perhaps, he thought that he himself was the Messiah. He thought it because of all destinies it seemed the most terrible.

The Greek. How could a man think himself the Messiah?

The Hebrew. It was always foretold that he would be born of a woman.

The Greek. To say that a god can be born of a woman, carried in her womb, fed upon her breast, washed as children are washed, is the most terrible blasphemy.

The Hebrew. If the Messiah were not born of a woman he could not take away the sins of man. Every sin starts a stream of suffering, but the Messiah takes it all away.

The Greek. Every man's sins are his property. Nobody else has a right to them.

The Hebrew. The Messiah is able to exhaust human suffering as though it were all gathered together in the spot of a burning-glass.

The Greek. That makes me shudder. The utmost possible suffering as an object of worship! You are morbid because your nation has no statues.

The Hebrew. What I have described is what I thought until three days ago.

The Greek. I say that there is nothing in the tomb.

The Hebrew. I saw him carried up the mountain and the tomb shut upon him.

The Greek. I have sent the Syrian to the tomb to prove that there is nothing there.

The Hebrew. You knew the danger we were all in and yet you weakened our guard?

The Greek. I have risked the apostles' lives and our own. What I have sent the Syrian to find out is more important.

The Hebrew. None of us are in our right mind to-day. I have got something in my own head that shocks me.

The Greek. Something you do not want to speak about?

The Hebrew. I am glad that he was not the Messiah; we might all have been deceived to our lives' end, or learnt the truth too late. One had to sacrifice everything that the divine suffering might, as it were, descend into one's mind and soul and make them pure. [*A sound of rattles and drums, at first in short bursts that come between sentences, but gradually growing continuous.*] One had to give up all worldly knowledge, all ambition, do nothing of one's own will. Only the divine could have any reality. God had to take complete possession. It must be a terrible thing when one is old, and the tomb round the corner, to think of all the ambitions one has put aside; to think, perhaps, a great deal about women. I want to marry and have children.

The Greek [*who is standing facing the audience, and looking out over their heads*]. It is the worshippers of Dionysus. They are under the window now. There is a group of women who carry upon their shoulders a bier with an image of the dead god upon it. No, they are not women. They are men dressed as women. I have seen something like it in Alexandria. They are all silent, as if something were going to happen. My God! What a spectacle! In Alexandria a few men paint their lips vermilion. They imitate women that they may attain in worship a woman's self-abandonment. No great harm comes of it—but here! Come and look for yourself.

The Hebrew. I will not look at such madmen.

The Greek. Though the music has stopped, some men are still
dancing, and some of the dancers have gashed themselves with
knives, imagining themselves, I suppose, at once the god and
the Titans that murdered him. A little further off a man and
woman are coupling in the middle of the street. She thinks the
surrender to some man the dance threw into her arms may
bring her god back to life. All are from the foreign quarter, to
judge by face and costume, and are the most ignorant and
excitable class of Asiatic Greeks, the dregs of the population.
Such people suffer terribly and seek forgetfulness in monstrous
ceremonies. Ah, that is what they were waiting for. The crowd
has parted to make way for a singer. It is a girl. No, not a girl; a
boy from the theatre. I know him. He acts girls' parts. He is
dressed as a girl, but his finger-nails are gilded and his wig is
made of gilded cords. He looks like a statue out of some
temple. I remember something of the kind in Alexandria. Three
days after the full moon, a full moon in March, they sing the
death of the god and pray for his resurrection.

> [*One of the Musicians sings the following song*]

> Astrea's holy child!
> A rattle in the wood
> Where a Titan strode!
> His rattle drew the child
> Into that solitude.
> Barrum, barrum, barrum.
>   [*Drum-taps accompany and follow the words.*]
> We wandering women,
> Wives for all that come,
> Tried to draw him home;
> And every wandering woman
> Beat upon a drum.
> Barrum, barrum, barrum.
>   [*Drum-taps as before.*]
> But the murderous Titans
> Where the woods grow dim
> Stood and waited him.
> The great hands of those Titans
> Tore limb from limb.
> Barrum, barrum, barrum.

10

[*Drum-taps as before.*]

On virgin Astrea
That can succour all
Wandering women call;
Call out to Astrea
That the moon stood at the full.   20
Barrum, barrum, barrum.

[*Drum-taps as before.*]

The Greek. I cannot think all that self-surrender and self-abasement is Greek, despite the Greek name of its god. When the goddess came to Achilles in the battle she did not interfere with his soul, she took him by his yellow hair. Lucretius thinks that the gods appear in the visions of the day and night but are indifferent to human fate; that, however, is the exaggeration of a Roman rhetorician. They can be discovered by contemplation, in their faces a high keen joy like the cry of a bat, and the man who lives heroically gives them the only earthly body that they covet. He, as it were, copies their gestures and their acts. What seems their indifference is but their eternal possession of themselves. Man, too, remains separate. He does not surrender his soul. He keeps his privacy.

[*Drum-taps to represent knocking at the door*]

The Hebrew. There is someone at the door, but I dare not open with that crowd in the street.

The Greek. You need not be afraid. The crowd has begun to move away. [*The Hebrew goes down into the audience towards the left.*] I deduce from our great philosophers that a god can overwhelm man with disaster, take health and wealth away, but man keeps his privacy. If that is the Syrian he may bring such confirmation that mankind will never forget his words.

The Hebrew [*from amongst the audience*]. It is the Syrian. There is something wrong. He is ill or drunk.

[*He helps the Syrian on to the stage.*]

The Syrian. I am like a drunken man. I can hardly stand upon my feet. Something incredible has happened. I have run all the way.

The Hebrew. Well?

The Syrian. I must tell the Eleven at once. Are they still in there? Everybody must be told.

The Hebrew. What is it? Get your breath and speak.

The Syrian. I was on my way to the tomb. I met the Galilean women, Mary the mother of Jesus, Mary the mother of James, and the other women. The younger women were pale with excitement and began to speak all together. I did not know what they were saying; but Mary the mother of James said that they had been to the tomb at daybreak and found that it was empty.

The Greek. Ah!

The Hebrew. The tomb cannot be empty. I will not believe it.

The Syrian. At the door stood a man all shining, and cried out that Christ had arisen. [*Faint drum-taps and the faint sound of a rattle.*] As they came down the mountain a man stood suddenly at their side; that man was Christ himself. They stooped down and kissed his feet. Now stand out of my way that I may tell Peter and James and John.

The Hebrew [*standing before the curtained entrance of the inner room*]. I will not stand out of the way.

The Syrian. Did you hear what I said? Our master has arisen.

The Hebrew. I will not have the Eleven disturbed for the dreams of women.

The Greek. The women were not dreaming. They told you the truth, and yet this man is in the right. He is in charge here. We must all be convinced before we speak to the Eleven.

The Syrian. The Eleven will be able to judge better than we.

The Greek. Though we are so much younger we know more of the world than they do.

The Hebrew. If you told your story they would no more believe it than I do, but Peter's misery would be increased. I have known him longer than you and I know what would happen. Peter would remember that the women did not flinch; that not one amongst them denied her master; that the dream proved their love and faith. Then he would remember that he had lacked both, and imagine that John was looking at him. He would turn away and bury his head in his hands.

The Greek. I said that we must all be convinced, but there is another reason why you must not tell them anything. Somebody else is coming. I am certain that Jesus never had a human body; that he is a phantom and can pass through that wall; that he will so pass; that he will pass through this room; that he himself will speak to the apostles.

The Syrian. He is no phantom. We put a great stone over the mouth of the tomb, and the women say that it has been rolled back.

The Hebrew. The Romans heard yesterday that some of our people planned to steal the body, and to put abroad a story that Christ had arisen; and so escape the shame of our defeat. They probably stole it in the night.

The Syrian. The Romans put sentries at the tomb. The women found the sentries asleep. Christ had put them asleep that they might not see him move the stone.

The Greek. A hand without bones, without sinews, cannot move a stone.

The Syrian. What matter if it contradicts all human knowledge?— another Argo seeks another fleece, another Troy is sacked.

The Greek. Why are you laughing?

The Syrian. What is human knowledge?

The Greek. The knowledge that keeps the road from here to Persia free from robbers, that has built the beautiful humane cities, that has made the modern world, that stands between us and the barbarian.

The Syrian. But what if there is something it cannot explain, something more important than anything else?

The Greek. You talk as if you wanted the barbarian back.

The Syrian. What if there is always something that lies outside knowledge, outside order? What if at the moment when knowledge and order seem complete that something appears?

[*He begins to laugh.*

The Hebrew. Stop laughing.

The Syrian. What if the irrational return? What if the circle begin again?

The Hebrew. Stop! He laughed when he saw Calvary through the window, and now you laugh.

The Greek. He too has lost control of himself.

The Hebrew. Stop, I tell you.   [*Drums and rattles.*]

The Syrian. But I am not laughing. It is the people out there who are laughing.

The Hebrew. No, they are shaking rattles and beating drums.

The Syrian. I thought they were laughing. How horrible!

The Greek [*looking out over heads of audience*]. The worshippers of Dionysus are coming this way again. They have hidden their image of the dead god, and have begun their lunatic cry, 'God has arisen! God has arisen!'
  [*The Musicians who have been saying* 'God has arisen!' *fall silent.*
They will cry 'God has arisen!' through all the streets of the city. They can make their god live and die at their pleasure; but why are they silent? They are dancing silently. They are coming nearer and nearer, dancing all the while, using some kind of ancient step unlike anything I have seen in Alexandria. They are almost under the window now.

The Hebrew. They have come back to mock us, because their god arises every year, whereas our god is dead for ever.

The Greek. How they roll their painted eyes as the dance grows quicker and quicker! They are under the window. Why are they all suddenly motionless? Why are all those unseeing eyes turned upon this house? Is there anything strange about this house?

The Hebrew. Somebody has come into the room.

The Greek. Where?

The Hebrew. I do not know; but I thought I heard a step.

The Greek. I knew that he would come.

The Hebrew. There is no one here. I shut the door at the foot of
the steps.

The Greek. The curtain over there is moving.

The Hebrew. No, it is quite still, and besides there is nothing
behind it but a blank wall.

The Greek. Look, look!

The Hebrew. Yes, it has begun to move. [*During what follows he
backs in terror towards the left-hand corner of the stage.*]

The Greek. There is someone coming through it.
[*The figure of Christ wearing a recognisable but stylistic mask
enters through the curtain. The Syrian slowly draws back the
curtain that shuts off the inner room where the apostles are.
The three young men are towards the left of the stage, the fig-
ure of Christ is at the back towards the right.*]

The Greek. It is the phantom of our master. Why are you afraid?
He has been crucified and buried, but only in semblance, and is
among us once more. [*The Hebrew kneels.*] There is nothing
here but a phantom, it has no flesh and blood. Because I know
the truth I am not afraid. Look, I will touch it. It may be hard
under my hand like a statue—I have heard of such things—or
my hand may pass through it—but there is no flesh and blood.
[*He goes slowly up to the figure and passes his hand over its
side.*] The heart of a phantom is beating! The heart of a
phantom is beating! [*He screams. The figure of Christ crosses
the stage and passes into the inner room.*]

The Syrian. He is standing in the midst of them. Some are afraid.
He looks at Peter and James and John. He smiles. He has
parted the clothes at his side. He shows them his side. There is
a great wound there. Thomas has put his hand into the wound.
He has put his hand where the heart is.

The Greek. O Athens, Alexandria, Rome, something has come to destroy you! The heart of a phantom is beating. Man has begun to die! Your words are clear at last, O Heraclitus. God and man die each other's life, live each other's death.

> [*The Musicians rise, one or more singing the following words. If the performance is in a private room or studio, they unfold and fold a curtain as in my dance plays; if at the Peacock Theatre, they draw the proscenium curtain across.*]

I

In pity for man's darkening thought
He walked that room and issued thence
In Galilean turbulence;
The Babylonian starlight brought
A fabulous, formless darkness in;
Odour of blood when Christ was slain
Made all Platonic tolerance vain
And vain all Doric discipline.

II

Everything that man esteems
Endures a moment or a day:
Love's pleasure drives his love away,
The painter's brush consumes his dreams;
The herald's cry, the soldier's tread
Exhaust his glory and his might:
Whatever flames upon the night
Man's own resinous heart has fed.

Purgatory

(1938)

Persons in the Play

A Boy

An Old Man

A ruined house and a bare tree in the background.

Boy. Half-door, hall door,
    Hither and thither day and night,
    Hill or hollow, shouldering this pack,
    Hearing you talk.

Old Man.   Study that house.
    I think about its jokes and stories;
    I try to remember what the butler
    Said to a drunken gamekeeper
    In mid-October, but I cannot.
    If I cannot, none living can.
    Where are the jokes and stories of a house,   10
    Its threshold gone to patch a pig-sty?

Boy. So you have come this path before?

Old Man. The moonlight falls upon the path,
    The shadow of a cloud upon the house,
    And that's symbolical; study that tree,
    What is it like?

Boy.   A silly old man.

Old Man. It's like—no matter what it's like.
    I saw it a year ago stripped bare as now,
    I saw it fifty years ago

20   Before the thunderbolt had riven it,
     Green leaves, ripe leaves, leaves thick as butter,
     Fat greasy life. Stand there and look,
     Because there is somebody in that house.
                    [*The Boy puts down pack and stands in the doorway.*

Boy. There's nobody here.

Old Man.   There's somebody there.

Boy. The floor is gone, the windows gone,
     And where there should be roof there's sky,
     And here's a bit of an egg-shell thrown
     Out of a jackdaw's nest.

Old Man.   But there are some
     That do not care what's gone, what's left:
30   The souls in Purgatory that come back
     To habitations and familiar spots.

Boy. Your wits are out again.

Old Man.   Re-live
     Their transgressions, and that not once
     But many times; they know at last
     The consequence of those transgressions
     Whether upon others, or upon themselves;
     Upon others, others may bring help
     For when the consequence is at an end
     The dream must end; upon themselves,
40   There is no help but in themselves
     And in the mercy of God.

Boy.   I have had enough!
     Talk to the jackdaws, if talk you must.

Old Man. Stop! Sit there upon that stone.
     That is the house where I was born.

Boy. The big old house that was burnt down?

Old Man. My mother that was your grand-dam owned it,
     This scenery and this countryside,
     Kennel and stable, horse and hound—

She had a horse at the Curragh, and there met
My father, a groom in a training stable;   50
Looked at him and married him.
Her mother never spoke to her again,
And she did right.

Boy.   What's right and wrong?
My grand-dad got the girl and the money.

Old Man. Looked at him and married him,
And he squandered everything she had.

She never knew the worst, because
She died in giving birth to me,
But now she knows it all, being dead.

Great people lived and died in this house;   60
Magistrates, colonels, members of Parliament,
Captains and Governors, and long ago
Men that had fought at Aughrim and the Boyne.
Some that had gone on government work
To London or to India came home to die,
Or came from London every spring
To look at the may-blossom in the park.
They had loved the trees that he cut down
To pay what he had lost at cards
Or spent on horses, drink and women;   70
Had loved the house, had loved all
The intricate passages of the house,
But he killed the house; to kill a house
Where great men grew up, married, died,
I here declare a capital offence.

Boy. My God, but you had luck! Grand clothes,
And maybe a grand horse to ride.

Old Man. That he might keep me upon his level
He never sent me to school, but some
Half-loved me for my half of her.   80
A gamekeeper's wife taught me to read,
A Catholic curate taught me Latin.

There were old books and books made fine
By eighteenth century French binding, books
Modern and ancient, books by the ton.

Boy. What education have you given me?

Old Man. I gave the education that befits
A bastard that a pedlar got
Upon a tinker's daughter in a ditch.

90 When I had come to sixteen years old
My father burned down the house when drunk.

Boy. But that is my age, sixteen years old
At the Puck Fair.

Old Man.   And everything was burnt;
Books, library, all were burnt.

Boy. Is what I have heard upon the road the truth,
That you killed him in the burning house?

Old Man. There's nobody here but our two selves?

Boy. Nobody, Father.

Old Man.   I stuck him with a knife,
That knife that cuts my dinner now,
100 And after that I left him in the fire;
They dragged him out, somebody saw
The knife-wound but could not be certain
Because the body was all black and charred.
Then some that were his drunken friends
Swore they would put me upon trial,
Spoke of quarrels, a threat I had made.
The gamekeeper gave me some old clothes,
I ran away, worked here and there
Till I became a pedlar on the roads,
110 No good trade, but good enough
Because I am my father's son,
Because of what I did or may do.

Listen to the hoof beats! Listen, listen!

Boy. I cannot hear a sound.

Old Man.   Beat! Beat!
This night is the anniversary
Of my mother's wedding night,
Or of the night wherein I was begotten.
My father is riding from the public house,
A whiskey bottle under his arm.
                    [*A window is lit showing a young girl.*
Look at the window; she stands there   120
Listening, the servants are all in bed,
She is alone, he has stayed late
Bragging and drinking in the public house.

Boy. There's nothing but an empty gap in the wall.
You have made it up. No, you are mad!
You are getting madder every day.

Old Man. It's louder now because he rides
Upon a gravelled avenue
All grass to-day. The hoof beat stops,
He has gone to the other side of the house,   130
Gone to the stable, put the horse up.
She has gone down to open the door.
This night she is no better than her man
And does not mind that he is half drunk,
She is mad about him. They mount the stairs;
She brings him into her own chamber.
And that is the marriage chamber. Now
The window is dimly lit again.

Do not let him touch you! It is not true
That drunken men cannot beget,   140
And if he touch he must beget
And you must bear his murderer.
Deaf! Both deaf! If I should throw
A stick or a stone they would not hear;
And that's a proof my wits are out.
But there's a problem: she must live
Through everything in exact detail,

Driven to it by remorse, and yet
Can she renew the sexual act
150 And find no pleasure in it, and if not,
If pleasure and remorse must both be there
Which is the greater?
                              I lack schooling.
Go fetch Tertullian; he and I
Will ravel all that problem out
Whilst those two lie upon the mattress
Begetting me.
                    Come back! Come back!
And so you thought to slip away,
My bag of money between your fingers,
And that I could not talk and see!
160 You have been rummaging in the pack.
                    [*The light in the window has faded out.*

Boy. You never gave me my right share.

Old Man. And had I given it, young as you are
    You would have spent it upon drink.

Boy. What if I did? I had a right
    To get it and spend it as I chose.

Old Man. Give me that bag and no more words.

Boy. I will not.

Old Man.   I will break your fingers.
    [*They struggle for the bag. In the struggle it drops, scattering
    the money. The old man staggers but does not fall. They stand
    looking at each other.*

Boy. What if I killed you? You killed my grand-dad,
    Because you were young and he was old.
170 Now I am young and you are old.
    [*A window is lit up. A man is seen pouring whiskey into a
    glass.*

Old Man [*staring at window*]. Better looking, those sixteen
    years—

Boy. What are you muttering?

Old Man.   Younger—and yet
  She should have known he was not her kind.

Boy. What are you saying? Out with it!
>   [*Old Man points to window.*

  My God! The window is lit up
  And somebody stands there, although
  The floorboards are all burnt away.

Old Man. The window is lit up because my father
  Has come to find a glass for his whiskey.
  He leans there like some tired beast.   180

Boy. A dead, living, murdered man.

Old Man. "Then the bride-sleep fell upon Adam:"
  Where did I read those words?
>   And yet
  There's nothing leaning in the window
  But the impression upon my mother's mind;
  Being dead she is alone in her remorse.

Boy. A body that was a bundle of old bones
  Before I was born. Horrible! Horrible!
>   [*He covers his eyes.*

Old Man. That beast there would know nothing, being nothing,
  If I should kill a man under the window;   190
  He would not even turn his head.
>   [*He stabs the Boy.*

  My father and my son on the same jack-knife!
  That finishes—there—there—there—
>   [*He stabs again and again. The window grows dark.*

Old Man. "Hush-a-bye baby, thy father's a knight,
  Thy mother a lady, lovely and bright."

  No, that is something that I read in a book,
  And if I sing it must be to my mother,
  And I lack rhyme.
>   [*The stage has grown dark except where the tree stands in*
>   *white light.*
>   Study that tree.

It stands there like a purified soul,
200 All cold, sweet, glistening light.
Dear mother, the window is dark again
But you are in the light because
I finished all that consequence.
I killed that lad because he had grown up.
He would have struck a woman's fancy,
Begot, and passed pollution on.
I am a wretched foul old man
And therefore harmless. When I have stuck
This old jack-knife into a sod
210 And pulled it out all bright again,
And picked up all the money that he dropped,
I'll to a distant place, and there
Tell my old jokes among new men.
              [*He cleans the knife and begins to pick up money.*
Hoof beats! Dear God,
How quickly it returns—beat—beat—

Her mind cannot hold up that dream.
Twice a murderer and all for nothing,
And she must animate that dead night
Not once but many times!
                    O God!
220 Release my mother's soul from its dream!
Mankind can do no more. Appease
The misery of the living and the remorse of the dead.

The Death
of Cuchulain

(1939)

Persons in the Play

Cuchulain

Eithne Inguba

Aoife

Emer

The Morrigu, *Goddess of War*

An Old Man

A Blind Man

A Servant

A Singer, a Piper, and

a Drummer

A bare stage of any period. A very old man looking like something out of mythology.

Old Man. I have been asked to produce a play called *The Death of Cuchulain.* It is the last of a series of plays which has for theme his life and death. I have been selected because I am out of fashion and out of date like the antiquated romantic stuff the thing is made of. I am so old that I have forgotten the name of my father and mother, unless indeed I am, as I affirm, the son of Talma, and he was so old that his friends and acquaintances still read Virgil and Homer. When they told me that I could have my own way I wrote certain guiding principles on a bit of newspaper. I wanted an audience of fifty or a hundred, and if there are more I beg them not to shuffle their feet or talk when the actors are speaking. I am sure that as I am producing a play for people I like it is not probable in this vile age that they will be more in number than those who listened to the first performance of Milton's *Comus*. On the present occasion they must know the old epics and Mr. Yeats' plays about them. Such people, however poor, have libraries of their own. If there are more than a hundred I won't be able to escape people who are educating themselves out of the book societies and the like, sciolists all, pickpockets and opinionated bitches. Why pickpockets? I will explain that, I will make it all quite clear.

> [*Drum and pipe behind the scene, then silence.*

That's from the musicians; I asked them to do that if I was getting excited. If you were as old you would find it easy to get excited. Before the night ends you will meet the music. There is a singer, a piper and a drummer. I have picked them up here and there about the streets, and I will teach them, if I live, the music of the beggar-man, Homer's music. I promise a dance. I wanted a dance because where there are no words there is less to spoil. Emer must dance, there must be severed heads—I am old, I belong to mythology—severed heads for her to dance before. I had thought to have had those heads carved, but no, if the dancer can dance properly no wood-carving can look as well as a parallelogram of painted wood. But I was at my wit's end to find a good dancer; I could have got such a dancer once, but she has gone; the tragi-comedian dancer, the tragic dancer, upon the same neck love and loathing, life and death. I spit three times. I spit upon the dancers painted by Degas. I spit upon their short bodices, their stiff stays, their toes whereon they spin like peg-tops, above all upon that chambermaid face. They might have looked timeless, Rameses the Great, but not the chambermaid, that old maid history. I spit! I spit! I spit!

> [*The stage is darkened, the curtain falls. Pipe and drum begin and continue until the curtain rises on a bare stage. Half a minute later Eithne Inguba enters.*

Eithne. Cuchulain! Cuchulain!

Cuchulain enters from back

       I am Emer's messenger,
I am your wife's messenger, she has bid me say
You must not linger here in sloth for Maeve
With all those Connacht ruffians at her back
Burns barns and houses up at Emain Macha:
Your house at Muirthemne already burns.
No matter what's the odds, no matter though
Your death may come of it, ride out and fight.
The scene is set and you must out and fight.

Cuchulain. You have told me nothing. I am already armed.   10
 I have sent a messenger to gather men,
 And wait for his return. What have you there?

Eithne. I have nothing.

Cuchulain.   There is something in your hand.

Eithne. No.

Cuchulain. Have you a letter in your hand?

Eithne. I do not know how it got into my hand.
 I am straight from Emer. We were in some place.
 She spoke. She saw.

Cuchulain.   This letter is from Emer,
 It tells a different story. I am not to move
 Until to-morrow morning, for, if now,
 I must face odds no man can face and live.   20
 To-morrow morning Conall Caernach comes
 With a great host.

Eithne.   I do not understand.
 Who can have put that letter in my hand?

Cuchulain. And there is something more to make it certain
 I shall not stir till morning; you are sent
 To be my bedfellow, but have no fear;
 All that is written, but I much prefer
 Your own unwritten words. I am for the fight,

I and my handful are set upon the fight;
30   We have faced great odds before, a straw decided.

The Morrigu enters and stands between them

Eithne. I know that somebody or something is there,
   Yet nobody that I can see.

Cuchulain.   There is nobody.

Eithne. Who among the gods of the air and upper air
   Has a bird's head?

Cuchulain.   Morrigu is headed like a crow.

Eithne [*dazed*]. Morrigu, war goddess, stands between.
   Her black wing touched me upon the shoulder, and now
   All is intelligible.   [*The Morrigu goes out.*
          Maeve put me in a trance.
   Though when Cuchulain slept with her as a boy
   She seemed as pretty as a bird, she has changed.
40   She has an eye in the middle of her forehead.

Cuchulain. A woman that has an eye in the middle of her forehead,
   A woman that is headed like a crow,
   But she that put those words into your mouth
   Had nothing monstrous; you put them there yourself.
   You need a younger man, a friendlier man,
   But fearing what my violence might do
   Thought out those words to send me to my death,
   And were in such excitement you forgot
   The letter in your hand.

Eithne.   Now that I wake
50   I say that Maeve did nothing out of error;
   What mouth could you believe if not my mouth?

Cuchulain. When I went mad at my son's death and drew
   My sword against the sea, it was my wife
   That brought me back.

Eithne.   Better women than I
   Have served you well, but 'twas to me you turned.

Cuchulain. You thought that if you changed I'd kill you for it,
    When everything sublunary must change,
    And if I have not changed that goes to prove
    That I am monstrous.

Eithne.   You're not the man I loved,
    That violent man forgave no treachery.   60
    If thinking what you think you can forgive
    It is because you are about to die.

Cuchulain. Spoken too loudly and too near the door;
    Speak low if you would speak about my death,
    Or not in that strange voice exulting in it.
    Who knows what ears listen behind the door?

Eithne. Some that would not forgive a traitor, some
    That have the passion necessary to life,
    Some not about to die. When you are gone
    I shall denounce myself to all your cooks,   70
    Scullions, armourers, bed-makers and messengers,
    Until they hammer me with a ladle, cut me with a knife,
    Impale me upon a spit, put me to death
    By what foul way best please their fancy,
    So that my shade can stand among the shades
    And greet your shade and prove it is no traitor.

Cuchulain. Women have spoken so plotting a man's death.

Enter a Servant

Servant. Your great horse is bitted. All wait the word.

Cuchulain. I come to give it, but must ask a question.
    This woman, wild with grief, declares that she   80
    Out of pure treachery has told me lies
    That should have brought my death. What can I do?
    How can I save her from her own wild words?

Servant. Is her confession true?

Cuchulain.   I make the truth.
    I say she brings a message from my wife.

Servant. What if I make her swallow poppy juice?

Cuchulain. What herbs seem suitable, but protect her life
    As it were your own and should I not return
    Give her to Conall Caernach because the women
    Have called him a good lover.

90   *Eithne.*   I might have peace that know
    The Morrigu, the woman like a crow,
    Stands to my defence and cannot lie,
    But that Cuchulain is about to die.
      [*Pipe and drum. The stage grows dark for a moment. When it
      lights up again, it is empty. Cuchulain enters wounded. He
      tries to fasten himself to a pillar-stone with his belt. Aoife, an
      erect white-haired woman, enters.*

Aoife. Am I recognised, Cuchulain?

Cuchulain.   You fought with a sword,
    It seemed that we should kill each other; then
    Your body wearied and I took your sword.

Aoife. But look again, Cuchulain! Look again!

Cuchulain. Your hair is white.

Aoife.   That time was long ago,
    And now it is my time. I have come to kill you.

Cuchulain. Where am I? Why am I here?

100 *Aoife.*   You asked their leave,
    When certain that you had six mortal wounds,
    To drink out of the pool.

Cuchulain.   I have put my belt
    About this stone and want to fasten it
    And die upon my feet, but am too weak.
    Fasten this belt.   [*She helps him to do so.*
          And now I know your name,
    Aoife, the mother of my son. We met
    At the Hawk's Well under the withered trees.
    I killed him upon Baile's Strand, that is why
    Maeve parted ranks that she might let you through.
    You have a right to kill me.

Aoife.   Though I have   110
   Her army did not part to let me through.
   The grey of Macha, that great horse of yours
   Killed in the battle, came out of the pool
   As though it were alive, and went three times
   In a great circle round you and that stone,
   Then leaped into the pool and not a man
   Of all that terrified army dare approach,
   But I approach.

Cuchulain.   Because you have the right.

Aoife. But I am an old woman now and that
   Your strength may not start up when the time comes   120
   I wind my veil about this ancient stone
   And fasten down your hands.

Cuchulain.   But do not spoil your veil:
   Your veils are beautiful, some with threads of gold.

Aoife. I am too old to care for such things now.
               [She has wound the veil about him.

Cuchulain. There was no reason so to spoil your veil:
   I am weak from loss of blood.

Aoife.   I was afraid,
   But now that I have wound you in the veil
   I am not afraid. Our son—How did he fight?

Cuchulain. Age makes more skilful but not better men.

Aoife. I have been told you did not know his name,   130
   And wanted, because he had a look of me,
   To be his friend, but Conchubar forbade it.

Cuchulain. Forbade it and commanded me to fight;
   That very day I had sworn to do his will,
   Yet I refused him and spoke about a look;
   But somebody spoke of witchcraft and I said
   Witchcraft had made the look, and fought and killed him.
   Then I went mad, I fought against the sea.

Aoife. I seemed invulnerable; you took my sword;
140   You threw me on the ground and left me there.
I searched the mountain for your sleeping-place
And laid my virgin body at your side,
And yet, because you had left me, hated you
And thought that I would kill you in your sleep
And yet begot a son that night between
Two black thorn trees.

Cuchulain.   I cannot understand.

Aoife. Because about to die.
                  Somebody comes,
Some countryman, and when he finds you there,
And none to protect him, will be terrified.
150   I will keep out of his sight for I have things
That I must ask questions on before I kill you.
     [*She goes. The Blind Man of "On Baile's Strand" comes in. He
     moves his stick about until he finds the standing stone; he lays
     his stick down, stoops and touches Cuchulain's feet. He feels the
     legs.*

Blind Man. Ah! Ah!

Cuchulain.   I think you are a blind old man.

Blind Man. A blind old beggar-man. What is your name?

Cuchulain. Cuchulain.

Blind Man.   They say that you are weak with wounds.
I stood between a fool and the sea at Baile's Strand
When you went mad. What's bound about your hands
So that they cannot move? Some womanish stuff.
I have been fumbling with my stick since the dawn
And then heard many voices. I began to beg.
160   Somebody said that I was in Maeve's tent,
And somebody else, a big man by his voice,
That if I brought Cuchulain's head in a bag
I would be given twelve pennies; I had the bag
To carry what I get at kitchen doors,
Somebody told me how to find the place;

I thought it would have taken till the night
But this has been my lucky day.

Cuchulain.   Twelve pennies!

Blind Man. I would not promise anything until the woman,
The great Queen Maeve herself, repeated the words.

Cuchulain. Twelve pennies. What better reason for killing a man?   170
You have a knife, but have you sharpened it?

Blind Man. I keep it sharp because it cuts my food.
    [*He lays bag on ground and begins feeling Cuchulain's body,
    his hands mounting upward.*

Cuchulain. I think that you know everything, Blind Man.
My mother or my nurse said that the blind
Know everything.

Blind Man.   No, but they have good sense.
How could I have got twelve pennies for your head
If I had not good sense?

Cuchulain.   There floats out there
The shape that I shall take when I am dead,
My soul's first shape, a soft feathery shape,
And is not that a strange shape for the soul   180
Of a great fighting-man?

Blind Man.   Your shoulder is there,
This is your neck. Ah! Ah! Are you ready, Cuchulain!

Cuchulain. I say it is about to sing.

                              [*The stage darkens.*

Blind Man.   Ah! Ah!
    [*Music of pipe and drum, the curtain falls, the music ceases as
    the curtain rises upon a bare stage. There is nobody upon the
    stage except a woman with a crow's head. She is the Morrigu.
    She stands towards the back. She holds a black parallelogram
    the size of a man's head. There are six other parallelograms
    near the backcloth.*

The Morrigu. The dead can hear me, and to the dead I speak.
This head is great Cuchulain's, those other six

Gave him six mortal wounds. This man came first,
Youth lingered though the years ran on, that season
A woman loves the best, Maeve's latest lover;
This man had given him the second wound,
190   He had possessed her once; these were her sons,
Two valiant men that gave the third and fourth;
These other men were men of no account,
They saw that he was weakening and crept in,
One gave him the sixth wound and one the fifth.
Conall avenged him. I arranged the dance.

[*Emer enters. The Morrigu places the head of Cuchulain upon
the ground and goes out. Emer runs in and begins to dance.
She so moves that she seems to rage against the heads of those
that had wounded Cuchulain, perhaps makes movements as
though to strike them, going three times round the circle of
the heads. She then moves towards the head of Cuchulain,—
It may, if need be, be raised above the others on a pedestal—
she moves as if in adoration or in triumph. She is about to
prostrate herself before it, perhaps does so, then rises, looking
up as though listening. She seems to hesitate between the head
and what she hears. Then she stands motionless. There is
silence and in the silence a few faint bird notes. The stage
darkens slowly. Then comes loud music, but now it is quite
different. It is the music of some Irish fair of our day. The
stage brightens. Emer and the head are gone. There is none
there but the three Musicians. They are in ragged street-
singers' clothes; two of them play pipe and drum. They cease.
The Street-Singer begins to sing.*

Singer.   The harlot sang to the beggar-man.
             I meet them face to face,
             Conall, Cuchulain, Usna's boys,
             All that most ancient race;
200   Maeve had three in an hour they say;
             I adore those clever eyes,
             Those muscular bodies, but can get
             No grip upon their thighs.
             I meet those long pale faces,
             Hear their great horses, then

Recall what centuries have passed
Since they were living men,
That there are still some living
That do my limbs unclothe,
But that the flesh my flesh has gripped   210
I both adore and loathe.

                        [Pipe and drum music.

Singer.   Are those things that men adore and loathe
Their sole reality?
What stood in the Post Office
With Pearse and Connolly?
What comes out of the mountain
Where men first shed their blood?
Who thought Cuchulain till it seemed
He stood where they had stood?

No body like his body   220
Has modern woman borne,
But an old man looking back on life
Imagines it in scorn.
A statue's there to mark the place
By Oliver Sheppard done.
So ends the tale that the harlot
Sang to the beggar-man.

                        [Music from pipe and drum.

Autobiographical Writings

FROM Reveries Over Childhood and Youth

(1916)

[I]

MY FIRST memories are fragmentary and isolated and contemporaneous, as though one remembered some first moments of the Seven Days. It seems as if time had not yet been created, for all thoughts are connected with emotion and place without sequence.

I remember sitting upon somebody's knee, looking out of an Irish window at a wall covered with cracked and falling plaster, but what wall I do not remember, and being told that some relation once lived there. I am looking out of a window in London. It is in Fitzroy Road. Some boys are playing in the road and among them a boy in uniform, a telegraph-boy perhaps. When I ask who the boy is, a servant tells me that he is going to blow the town up, and I go to sleep in terror.

After that come memories of Sligo, where I live with my grandparents. I am sitting on the ground looking at a mastless toy boat with the paint rubbed and scratched, and I say to myself in great melancholy, 'It is further away than it used to be', and while I am saying it I am looking at a long scratch in the stern, for it is especially the scratch which is further away. Then one day at dinner my great-uncle, William Middleton, says, 'We should not make light of the troubles of children. They are worse than ours, because we can see the end of our trouble and they can never see any end', and I feel grateful, for I know that I am very unhappy and have often said to myself, 'When you grow up, never talk as grown-up people do of the happiness of childhood'. I may have already had the night of misery when, having prayed for several days that I might die, I began to be afraid that I was dying and prayed that I might live.

There was no reason for my unhappiness. Nobody was unkind, and my grandmother has still after so many years my gratitude and my reverence. The house was so big that there was always a room to hide in, and I had a red pony and a garden where I could wander, and there were two dogs to follow at my heels, one white with some black spots on his head and the other with long black hair all over him. I used to think about God and fancy that I was very wicked, and one day when I threw a stone and hit a duck in the yard by mischance and broke its wing, I was full of wonder when I was told that the duck would be cooked for dinner and that I should not be punished.

Some of my misery was loneliness and some of it fear of old William Pollexfen, my grandfather. He was never unkind, and I cannot remember that he ever spoke harshly to me, but it was the custom to fear and admire him. He had won the freedom of some Spanish city, for saving life perhaps, but was so silent that his wife never knew it till he was near eighty, and then from the chance visit of an old sailor. She asked him if it was true and he said it was true, but she knew him too well to question and his old shipmate had left the town. She too had the habit of fear. We knew that he had been in many parts of the world, for there was a great scar on his hand made by a whaling-hook, and in the dining-room was a cabinet with bits of coral in it and a jar of water from the Jordan for the baptizing of his children and Chinese pictures upon rice-paper and an ivory walking-stick from India that came to me after his death. He had great physical strength and had the reputation of never ordering a man to do anything he would not do himself. He owned many sailing-ships and once, when a captain just come to anchor at Rosses Point reported something wrong with the rudder, had sent a messenger to say, 'Send a man down to find out what's wrong'. 'The crew all refuse' was the answer, and to that my grandfather answered, 'Go down yourself', and not being obeyed, he dived from the main deck, all the neighbourhood lined along the pebbles of the shore. He came up with his skin torn but well informed about the rudder. He had a violent temper and kept a hatchet at his bedside for burglars and would knock a man down instead of going to law, and I once saw him hunt a party of men with a horsewhip. He had no relation, for he was an only child, and, being solitary and silent, he had few friends. He corresponded with Campbell of Islay who had befriended him and his crew after a shipwreck, and Captain Webb, the first man who had swum the Channel and who was drowned swimming the Niagara Rapids, had been a mate in his employ and a close friend. That is all the friends I can remember, and yet he was so looked up to and admired that when he returned from taking the waters of Bath his men would light bonfires along the railway line for miles; while his partner, William Middleton, whose father after the great famine had attended the sick for weeks, and taken cholera from a man he carried in his arms into his own house and died of it, and was himself civil to everybody and a cleverer man than my grandfather, came and went without notice. I think I confused my grandfather with God, for I remember in one of my attacks of melancholy praying that he might punish me for my sins, and I was shocked and astonished when a daring little girl—a cousin, I think—having waited under a group of trees in the avenue, where she knew he would pass near four o'clock on the way to his dinner, said to him, 'If I were you and you were a little girl, I would give you a doll'.

Yet for all my admiration and alarm, neither I nor any one else thought it wrong to outwit his violence or his rigour; and his lack of suspicion and something helpless about him made that easy while it stirred our affection. When I must have been still a very little boy, seven or eight years old perhaps, an uncle called me out of bed one night, to ride the five or six miles to Rosses Point to borrow a railway-pass from a cousin. My grandfather had one, but thought it dishonest to let another use it, but the cousin was not so particular. I was let out through a gate that opened upon a little lane beside the garden away from earshot of the house, and rode delighted through the moonlight, and awoke my cousin in the small hours by tapping on his window with a whip. I was home again by two or three in the morning and found the coachman waiting in the little lane. My grandfather would not have thought such an adventure possible, for every night at eight he believed that the stable-yard was locked, and he knew that he was brought the key. Some servant had once got into trouble at night and so he had arranged that they should all be locked in. He never knew, what everybody else in the house knew, that for all the ceremonious bringing of the key the gate was never locked.

Even to-day when I read *King Lear* his image is always before me, and I often wonder if the delight in passionate men in my plays and in my poetry is more than his memory. He must have been ignorant, though I could not judge him in my childhood, for he had run away to sea when a boy, 'gone to sea through the hawse-hole' as he phrased it, and I can but remember him with two books—his Bible and Falconer's *Shipwreck,* a little green-covered book that lay always upon his table; he belonged to some younger branch of an old Cornish family. His father had been in the Army, had retired to become an owner of sailing-ships, and an engraving of some old family place my grandfather thought should have been his hung next a painted coat of arms in the little back parlour. His mother had been a Wexford woman, and there was a tradition that his family had been linked with Ireland for generations and once had their share in the old Spanish trade with Galway. He had a good deal of pride and disliked his neighbours, whereas his wife, a Middleton, was gentle and patient and did many charities in the little back parlour among frieze coats and shawled heads, and every night when she saw him asleep went the round of the house alone with a candle to make certain there was no burglar in danger of the hatchet. She was a true lover of her garden, and before the care of her house had grown upon her, would choose some favourite among her flowers and copy it upon rice-paper. I saw some of her handiwork the other day and I wondered at the delicacy of form and colour and at a handling that may have needed a magnifying-glass it was so minute. I can remember no other pictures but the Chinese paintings, and some coloured prints of battles in the Crimea upon the wall of a passage, and the painting of a ship at the passage end darkened by time.

My grown-up uncles and aunts, my grandfather's many sons and daughters, came and went, and almost all they said or did has faded from my memory, except a few harsh words that convince me by a vividness out of proportion to their harshness that all were habitually kind and considerate. The youngest of my uncles was stout and humorous and had a tongue of leather over the keyhole of his door to keep the draught out, and another whose bedroom was at the end of a long stone passage had a model turret-ship in a glass case. He was a clever man and had designed the Sligo quays, but was now going mad and inventing a vessel of war that could not be sunk, his pamphlet explained, because of a hull of solid wood. Only six months ago my sister awoke dreaming that she held a wingless sea-bird in her arms and presently she heard that he had died in his mad-house, for a sea-bird is the omen that announces the death or danger of a Pollexfen. An uncle, George Pollexfen, afterwards astrologer and mystic, and my dear friend, came but seldom from Ballina, once to a race-meeting with two postilions dressed in green; and there was that younger uncle who had sent me for the railway-pass. He was my grandmother's favourite, and had, the servants told me, been sent away from school for taking a crowbar to a bully.

I can only remember my grandmother punishing me once. I was playing in the kitchen and a servant in horseplay pulled my shirt out of my trousers in front just as my grandmother came in, and I, accused of I knew not what childish indecency, was given my dinner in a room by myself. But I was always afraid of my uncles and aunts, and once the uncle who had taken the crowbar to the bully found me eating lunch which my grandmother had given me and reproved me for it and made me ashamed. We breakfasted at nine and dined at four and it was considered self-indulgent to eat anything between meals; and once an aunt told me that I had reined in my pony and struck it at the same moment that I might show it off as I rode through the town, and I, because I had been accused of what I thought a very dark crime, had a night of misery. Indeed I remember little of childhood but its pain. I have grown happier with every year of life as though gradually conquering something in myself, for certainly my miseries were not made by others but were a part of my own mind.

VII

Two pictures come into my memory. I have climbed to the top of a tree by the edge of the playing-field, and am looking at my schoolfellows and am as proud of myself as a March cock when it crows to its first sunrise. I am saying to myself, 'If when I grow up I am as clever among grown-up men as I am among these boys, I shall be a famous man'. I remind myself how they think all the same things and cover the school walls at election times with the opinions their fathers find in the newspapers. I remind myself that I am an artist's son and must take some work as the whole end of life and not think as the others do of becoming well off and living pleasantly. The other picture is of a hotel sitting-room in the Strand, where a man is hunched up over the fire. He is a cousin who has speculated with another cousin's money and has fled from Ireland in danger of arrest. My father has brought us to spend the evening with him, to distract him from the remorse that he must be suffering.

IX

My father read out poetry, for the first time, when I was eight or nine years old. Between Sligo and Rosses Point, there is a tongue of land covered with coarse grass that runs out into the sea or the mud according to the state of the tide. It is the place where dead horses are buried. Sitting there, my father read me the *Lays of Ancient Rome.* It was the first poetry that had moved me after the stable-boy's Orange rhymes. Later on he read me *Ivanhoe* and *The Lay of the Last Minstrel,* and they are still vivid in the memory. I re-read *Ivanhoe* the other day, but it has all vanished except Gurth, the swineherd, at the outset and Friar Tuck and his venison pasty, the two scenes that laid hold of me in childhood. *The Lay of the Last Minstrel* gave me a wish to turn magician that competed for years with the dream of being killed upon the sea-shore. When I first went to school, he tried to keep me from reading boys' papers, because a paper, by its very nature, as he explained to me, had to be made for the average boy or man and so could not but thwart one's growth. He took away my paper and I had not courage to say that I was but reading and delighting in a prose retelling of the *Iliad.* But after a few months, my father said he had been too anxious and became less urgent about my lessons and less violent if I had learnt them badly, and he ceased to notice what I read. From that on I shared the excitement which ran through all my fellows on Wednesday afternoons when the boys' papers were published, and I read endless stories I have forgotten as I have forgotten *Grimm's Fairy-Tales* that I read at Sligo, and all of Hans Andersen except *The Ugly Duckling* which my mother had read to me and to my sisters. I remember vaguely that I liked Hans Andersen better than Grimm because he was less homely, but even he never gave me the knights and dragons and beautiful ladies that I longed for. I have remembered nothing that I read, but only those things that I heard or saw. When I was ten or twelve my father took me to see Irving play Hamlet, and did not understand why I preferred Irving to Ellen

Terry, who was, I can now see, the idol of himself and his friends. I could not think of her, as I could of Irving's Hamlet, as but myself, and I was not old enough to care for feminine charm and beauty. For many years Hamlet was an image of heroic self-possession for the poses of youth and childhood to copy, a combatant of the battle within myself. My father had read me the story of the little boy murdered by the Jews in Chaucer and the tale of Sir Thopas, explaining the hard words, and though both excited me, I had liked Sir Thopas best and been disappointed that it left off in the middle. As I grew older, he would tell me plots of Balzac's novels, using incident or character as an illustration for some profound criticism of life. Now that I have read all the *Comédie Humaine,* certain pages have an unnatural emphasis, straining and overbalancing the outline, and I remember how, in some suburban street, he told me of Lucien de Rubempré's duel after the betrayal of his master, and how the wounded Lucien hearing some one say that he was not dead had muttered, 'So much the worse'.

I now can but share with a friend my thoughts and my emotions, and there is a continual discovery of difference, but in those days, before I had found myself, we could share adventures. When friends plan and do together, their minds become one mind and the last secret disappears. I was useless at games. I cannot remember that I ever kicked a goal or made a run, but I was a mine of knowledge when I and the athlete and those two notoriously gentlemanly boys—theirs was the name that I remember without a face—set out for Richmond Park, or Coombe Wood or Twyford Abbey to look for butterflies and moths and beetles. Sometimes to-day I meet people at lunch or dinner whose address sounds familiar and I remember of a sudden that a gamekeeper chased me from the plantation behind their house, or that I turned over the cow-dung in their paddock in the search for some rare beetle believed to haunt the spot. The athlete was our watchman and our safety. He would suggest, should we meet a carriage on the drive, that we take off our hats and walk on as though about to pay a call. And once when we were sighted by a gamekeeper at Coombe Wood, he persuaded the elder of the brothers to pretend to be a schoolmaster taking his boys for a walk, and the keeper, instead of swearing and threatening the law, was sad and argumentative. No matter how charming the place (and there is a little stream in a hollow where Wimbledon Common flows into Coombe Wood that is pleasant in the memory), I knew that those other boys saw something I did not see. I was a stranger there. There was something in their way of saying the names of places that made me feel this.

XIV

The great event of a boy's life is the awakening of sex. He will bathe many times a day, or get up at dawn and having stripped leap to and fro over a stick laid upon two chairs, and hardly know, and never admit, that he had begun to take pleasure in his own naked-ness, nor will he understand the change until some dream discovers it. He may never understand at all the greater change in his mind.

It all came upon me when I was close upon seventeen like the bursting of a shell. Somnambulistic country girls, when it is upon them, throw plates about or pull them with long hairs in simulation of the poltergeist, or become mediums for some genuine spirit-mischief, sur-rendering to their desire of the marvellous. As I look backward, I seem to discover that my passions, my loves and my despairs, instead of being my enemies, a disturbance and an attack, became so beautiful that I had to be constantly alone to give them my whole attention. I notice that now, for the first time, what I saw when alone is more vivid in my memory than what I did or saw in company.

A herd had shown me a cave some hundred and fifty feet below the cliff path and a couple of hundred above the sea, and told me that an evicted tenant called Macrom, dead some fifteen years, had lived there many years, and shown me a rusty nail in the rock which had served perhaps to hold up some wooden protection from wind and weather. Here I stored a tin of cocoa and some biscuits, and instead of going to my bed, would slip out on warm nights and sleep in the cave on the excuse of catching moths. One had to pass over a rocky ledge, safe enough for any one with a fair head, yet seeming, if looked at from above, narrow and sloping; and a remonstrance from a stranger who had seen me climbing along it doubled my delight in the adventure. When, however, upon a bank holiday, I found lovers in my cave, I was not content with it again till I heard that the ghost of Macrom had been seen a little before the dawn, stooping over his fire in the cave-mouth. I had been trying to cook eggs, as I had read in some book, by burying them in the earth under a fire of sticks.

At other times, I would sleep among the rhododendrons and rocks in the wilder part of the grounds of Howth Castle. After a while my father said I must stay indoors half the night, meaning that I should get some sleep in my bed; but I, knowing that I would be too sleepy and comfortable to get up again, used to sit over the kitchen fire till half the night was gone. Exaggerated accounts spread through the school, and sometimes when I did not know a lesson some master would banter me about the way my nights were spent. My interest in science began to fade, and presently I said to myself, 'It has all been a misunderstanding'. I remembered how soon I tired of my specimens, and how little I knew after all my years of collecting, and I came to believe that I had gone through so much labour because of a text, heard for the first time in Saint John's Church in Sligo, and copied Solomon, who had knowledge of hyssop and of tree, that I might be certain of my own wisdom. I still carried my green net, but I began to play at being a sage, a magician or a poet. I had many idols, and as I climbed along the narrow ledge I was now Manfred on his glacier, and now Prince Athanase with his solitary lamp, but I soon chose Alastor for my chief of men and longed to share his melancholy, and maybe at last to disappear from everybody's sight as he disappeared drifting in a boat along some slow-moving river between great trees. When I thought of women they were modelled on those in my favourite poets and loved in brief tragedy, or like the girl in *The Revolt of Islam,* accompanied their lovers through all manner of wild places, lawless women without homes and without children.

XV

My father's influence upon my thoughts was at its height. We went to Dublin by train every morning, breakfasting in his studio. He had taken a large room with a beautiful eighteenth-century mantelpiece in a York Street tenement-house, and at breakfast he read passages from the poets, and always from the play or poem at its most passionate moment. He never read me a passage because of its speculative interest, and indeed did not care at all for poetry where there was generalization or abstraction however impassioned. He would read out the first speeches of the *Prometheus Unbound,* but never the ecstatic lyricism of that famous fourth act;

and another day the scene where Coriolanus comes to the house of Aufidius and tells the impudent servants that his home is under the canopy. I have seen *Coriolanus* played a number of times since then, and read it more than once, but that scene is more vivid than the rest, and it is my father's voice that I hear and not Irving's or Benson's. He did not care even for a fine lyric passage unless he felt some actual man behind its elaboration of beauty, and he was always looking for the lineaments of some desirable, familiar life. When the spirits sang their scorn of Manfred, and Manfred answered, 'O sweet and melancholy voices', I was told that they could not, even in anger, put off their spiritual sweetness. He thought Keats a greater poet than Shelley, because less abstract, but did not read him, caring little, I think, for any of that most beautiful poetry which has come in modern times from the influence of painting. All must be an idealization of speech, and at some moment of passionate action or somnambulistic reverie. I remember his saying that all contemplative men were in a conspiracy to overrate their state of life, and that all writers were of them, excepting the great poets. Looking backwards, it seems to me that I saw his mind in fragments, which had always hidden connections I only now begin to discover. He disliked the Victorian poetry of ideas, and Wordsworth but for certain passages or whole poems. He said one morning over his breakfast that he had discovered in the shape of the head of a Wordsworthian scholar, an old and greatly respected clergyman whose portrait he was painting, all the animal instincts of a prize-fighter. He despised the formal beauty of Raphael, that calm which is not an ordered passion but an hypocrisy, and attacked Raphael's life for its love of pleasure and its self-indulgence. In literature he was always Pre-Raphaelite, and carried into literature principles that, while the Academy was still unbroken, had made the first attack upon academic form.

He no longer read me anything for its story, and all our discussion was of style.

XVI

I began to make blunders when I paid calls or visits, and a woman I had known and liked as a child told me I had changed for the worse. I wanted to be wise and eloquent, an essay on the younger Ampère had helped me to this ambition, and when I was alone I exaggerated my blunders and was miserable. I had begun to write poetry in imitation of Shelley and of Edmund Spenser, play after play—for my father exalted dramatic poetry above all other kinds—and I invented fantastic and incoherent plots. My lines but seldom scanned, for I could not understand the prosody in the books, although there were many lines that taken by themselves had music. I spoke them slowly as I wrote and only discovered when I read them to somebody else that there was no common music, no prosody. There were, however, moments of observation; for, even when I caught moths no longer, I still noticed all that passed; how the little moths came out at sunset, and how after that there were only a few big moths till dawn brought little moths again; and what birds cried out at night as if in their sleep.

XXX

Some one at the Young Ireland Society gave me a newspaper that I might read some article or letter. I began idly reading verses describing the shore of Ireland as seen by a returning, dying emigrant. My eyes filled with tears and yet I knew the verses were badly written—vague, abstract words such as one finds in a newspaper. I looked at the end and saw the name of some political exile who had died but a few days after his return to Ireland. They had moved me because they contained the actual thoughts of a man at a passionate moment of life, and when I met my father I was full of the discovery. We should write out our own thoughts in as nearly as possible the language we thought them in, as though in a letter to an intimate friend. We should not disguise them in any way; for our lives give them force as the lives of people in plays give force to their words. Personal utterance, which had almost ceased in English literature, could be as fine an escape from rhetoric and abstraction as drama itself. But my father would hear of nothing but drama; personal utterance was only egotism. I knew it was not, but as yet did not know how to explain the difference. I tried from that on to write out of my emotions exactly as they came to me in life, not changing them to make them more beautiful. 'If I can be sincere and make my language natural, and without becoming discursive, like a novelist, and so indiscreet and prosaic,' I said to myself, 'I shall, if good luck or bad luck make my life interesting, be a great poet; for it will be no longer a matter of literature at all.' Yet when I re-read those early poems which gave me so much trouble, I find little but romantic convention, unconscious drama. It is so many years before one can believe enough in what one feels even to know what the feeling is.

XXXIII

For some months now I have lived with my own youth and childhood, not always writing indeed but thinking of it almost every day, and I am sorrowful and disturbed. It is not that I have accomplished too few of my plans, for I am not ambitious; but when I think of all the books I have read, and of the wise words I have heard spoken, and of the anxiety I have given to parents and grandparents, and of the hopes that I have had, all life weighed in the scales of my own life seems to me a preparation for something that never happens.

FROM The Trembling of the Veil

(1922)

FROM Book I: Four Years, 1887–1891

II

I could not understand where the charm had gone that I had felt, when as a schoolboy of twelve or thirteen I had played among the unfinished houses, once leaving the marks of my two hands, blacked by a fall among some paint, upon a white balustrade.

Yet I was in all things Pre-Raphaelite. When I was fifteen or sixteen my father had told me about Rossetti and Blake and given me their poetry to read; and once at Liverpool on my way to Sligo I had seen *Dante's Dream* in the gallery there, a picture painted when Rossetti had lost his dramatic power and to-day not very pleasing to me, and its colour, its people, its romantic architecture had blotted all other pictures away. It was a perpetual bewilderment that when my father, moved perhaps by some memory of his youth, chose some theme from poetic tradition, he would soon weary and leave it unfinished. I had seen the change coming bit by bit and its defence elaborated by young men fresh from the Paris art schools. 'We must paint what is in front of us', or 'A man must be of his own time', they would say, and if I spoke of Blake or Rossetti they would point out his bad drawing and tell me to admire Carolus Duran and Bastien-Lepage. Then, too, they were very ignorant men; they read nothing, for nothing mattered but 'knowing how to paint', being in reaction against a generation that seemed to have wasted its time upon so many things. I thought myself alone in hating these young men, their contempt for the past, their monopoly of the future, but in a few months I was to discover others of my own age who thought as I did, for it is not true that youth looks before it with the mechanical gaze of a well-drilled soldier. Its quarrel is not with the past, but with the present, where its elders are so obviously powerful and no cause seems lost if it seem to threaten that power. Does cultivated youth ever really love the future, where the eye can discover no persecuted Royalty hidden among oak leaves, though from it certainly does come so much proletarian rhetoric?

I was unlike others of my generation in one thing only. I am very religious, and deprived by Huxley and Tyndall, whom I detested, of the simple-minded religion of my childhood, I had made a new religion, almost an infallible Church of poetic tradition, of a fardel of stories, and of personages, and of emotions, inseparable from their first expression, passed on from generation to generation by poets and painters with some help from philosophers and theologians. I wished for a world where I could discover this tradition perpetually, and not in pictures and in poems only, but in tiles round the chimney-piece and in the hangings that kept out the draught. I had even created a dogma: 'Because those imaginary people are created out of the deepest instinct of man, to be his measure and his norm, whatever I can imagine those mouths speaking may be the nearest I can go to truth'. When I listened they seemed always to speak of one thing only: they, their loves, every incident of their lives, were steeped in the supernatural. Could even Titian's *Ariosto* that I loved beyond other portraits have its grave look, as if waiting for some perfect final event, if the painters before Titian had not learned portraiture while painting into the corner of compositions full of saints and Madonnas their kneeling patrons? At seventeen years old I was already an old-fashioned brass cannon full of shot, and nothing had kept me from going off but a doubt as to my capacity to shoot straight.

V

Presently a hansom drove up to our door at Bedford Park with Miss Maud Gonne, who brought an introduction to my father from old John O'Leary, the Fenian leader. She vexed my father by praise of war, war for its own sake, not as the creator of certain virtues but as if there were some virtue in excitement itself. I supported her against my father, which vexed him the more, though he might have understood that, apart from the fact that Carolus Duran and Bastien-Lepage were somehow involved, a man young as I could not have differed from a woman so beautiful and so young. To-day, with her great height and the unchangeable lineaments of her form, she looks the Sibyl I would have had played by Florence Farr, but in that day she seemed a classical impersonation of the Spring, the Virgilian commendation 'She walks like a goddess' made for her alone. Her complexion was luminous, like that of apple-blossom through which the light falls, and I remember her standing that first day by a great heap of such blossoms in the window. In the next few years I saw her always when she passed to and fro between Dublin and Paris, surrounded, no matter how rapid her journey and how brief her stay at either end of it, by cages full of birds, canaries, finches of all kinds, dogs, a parrot, and once a full-grown hawk from Donegal. Once when I saw her to her railway carriage I noticed how the cages obstructed racks and cushions and wondered what her fellow-travellers would say, but the carriage remained empty. It was years before I could see into the mind that lay hidden under so much beauty and so much energy.

VIII

My first meeting with Oscar Wilde was an astonishment. I never before heard a man talking with perfect sentences, as if he had written them all overnight with labour and yet all spontaneous. There was present that night at Henley's, by right of propinquity or of accident, a man full of the secret spite of dullness, who interrupted from time to time, and always to check or disorder thought; and I noticed with what mastery he was foiled and thrown. I noticed, too, that the impression of artificiality that I think all Wilde's listeners have recorded came from the perfect rounding of the sentences and from the deliberation that made it possible. That very impression helped him, as the effect of metre, or of the antithetical prose of the seventeenth century, which is itself a true metre, helped its writers, for he could pass without incongruity from some unforeseen, swift stroke of wit to elaborate reverie. I heard him say a few nights later: 'Give me *The Winter's Tale*, "Daffodils that come before the swallow dares", but not *King Lear*. What is *King Lear* but poor life staggering in the fog?'

and the slow, carefully modulated cadence sounded natural to my ears. That first night he praised Walter Pater's *Studies in the History of the Renaissance*: 'It is my golden book; I never travel anywhere without it; but it is the very flower of decadence: the last trumpet should have sounded the moment it was written.' 'But', said the dull man, 'would you not have given us time to read it?' 'O no,' was the retort, 'there would have been plenty of time afterwards—in either world.' I think he seemed to us, baffled as we were by youth, or by infirmity, a triumphant figure, and to some of us a figure from another age, an audacious Italian fifteenth-century figure. A few weeks before I had heard one of my father's friends, an official in a publishing firm that had employed both Wilde and Henley as editors, blaming Henley, who was 'no use except under control', and praising Wilde, 'so indolent but such a genius'; and now the firm became the topic of our talk. 'How often do you go to the office?' said Henley. 'I used to go three times a week', said Wilde, 'for an hour a day, but I have since struck off one of the days.' 'My God,' said Henley, 'I went five times a week for five hours a day and when I wanted to strike off a day they had a special committee meeting.' 'Furthermore,' was Wilde's answer, 'I never answered their letters. I have known men come to London full of bright prospects and seen them complete wrecks in a few months through a habit of answering letters.' He too knew how to keep our elders in their place, and his method was plainly the more successful, for Henley had been dismissed. 'No, he is not an aesthete', Henley commented later, being somewhat embarrassed by Wilde's Pre-Raphaelite entanglement; 'one soon finds that he is a scholar and a gentleman.' And when I dined with Wilde a few days afterwards he began at once, 'I had to strain every nerve to equal that man at all'; and I was too loyal to speak my thought: 'You and not he said all the brilliant things'. He, like the rest of us, had felt the strain of an intensity that seemed to hold life at the point of drama. He had said on that first meeting, 'The basis of literary friendship is mixing the poisoned bowl'; and for a few weeks Henley and he became close friends till, the astonishment of their meeting over, diversity of character and ambition pushed them apart, and, with half the cavern helping, Henley began mixing the poisoned bowl for Wilde. Yet Henley never wholly lost that first admiration, for after Wilde's downfall he said to me: 'Why did he do it? I told my lads to attack him and yet we might have fought under his banner.'

XXI

I generalized a great deal and was ashamed of it. I thought it was my business in life to be an artist and a poet, and that there could be no business comparable to that. I refused to read books and even to meet people who excited me to generalization, all to no purpose. I said my prayers much as in childhood, though without the old regularity of hour and place, and I began to pray that my imagination might somehow be rescued from abstraction and become as preoccupied with life as had been the imagination of Chaucer. For ten or twelve years more I suffered continual remorse, and only became content when my abstractions had composed themselves into picture and dramatization. My very remorse helped to spoil my early poetry, giving it an element of sentimentality through my refusal to permit it any share of an intellect which I considered impure. Even in practical life I only very gradually began to use generalizations, that have since become the foundation of all I have done, or shall do, in Ireland. For all I know all men may have been so timid, for I am persuaded that our intellects at twenty contain all the truths we shall ever find, but as yet we do not know truths that belong to us from opinions caught up in casual irritation or momentary fantasy. As life goes on we discover that certain thoughts sustain us in defeat, or give us victory, whether over ourselves or others, and it is these thoughts, tested by passion, that we call convictions. Among subjective men (in all those, that is, who must spin a web out of their own bowels) the victory is an intellectual daily re-creation of all that exterior fate snatches away, and so that fate's antithesis; while what I have called 'the Mask' is an emotional antithesis to all that comes out of their internal nature. We begin to live when we have conceived life as tragedy.

XXII

A conviction that the world was now but a bundle of fragments possessed me without ceasing. I had tried this conviction on the Rhymers, thereby plunging into greater silence an already too-silent evening. 'Johnson,' I was accustomed to say, 'you are the only man I know whose silence has beak and claw.' I had lectured on it to some London Irish society, and I was to lecture upon it later on in Dublin, but I never found but one interested man, an official of the Primrose League, who was also an active member of the Fenian Brotherhood. 'I am an extreme conservative apart from Ireland', I have heard him explain; and I have no doubt that personal experience made him share the sight of any eye that saw the world in fragments. I had been put into a rage by the followers of Huxley, Tyndall, Carolus Duran, and Bastien-Lepage, who not only asserted the unimportance of subject whether in art or literature, but the independence of the arts from one another. Upon the other hand, I delighted in every age where poet and artist confined themselves gladly to some inherited subject-matter known to the whole people, for I thought that in man and race alike there is something called 'Unity of Being', using that term as Dante used it when he compared beauty in the *Convito* to a perfectly proportioned human body. My father, from whom I had learned the term, preferred a comparison to a musical instrument so strung that if we touch a string all the strings murmur faintly. There is not more desire, he had said, in lust than in true love, but in true love desire awakens pity, hope, affection, admiration, and, given appropriate circumstance, every emotion possible to men. When I began, however, to apply this thought to the State and to argue for a law-made balance among trades and occupations my father displayed at once the violent Free Trader and propagandist of liberty. I thought that the enemy of this unity was abstraction, meaning by abstraction not the distinction but the isolation of occupation, or class or faculty:—

> Call down the hawk from the air,
> Let him be hooded or caged
> Till the yellow eye has grown mild,
> For larder and spit are bare,
> The old cook enraged,
> The scullion gone wild.

I knew no mediaeval cathedral, and Westminster, being a part of abhorred London, did not interest me, but I thought constantly of Homer and Dante, and the tombs of Mausolus and Artemisia, the great figures of King and Queen and the lesser figures of Greek and Amazon, Centaur and Greek. I thought that all art should be a Centaur finding in the popular lore its back and its strong legs. I got great pleasure, too, from remembering that Homer was sung, and from that tale of Dante hearing a common man sing some stanza from the *Divine Comedy,* and from Don Quixote's meeting with some common man that sang Ariosto. Morris had never seemed to care greatly for any poet later than Chaucer and though I preferred Shakespeare to Chaucer I begrudged my own preference. Had not Europe shared one mind and heart, until both mind and heart began to break into fragments a little before Shakespeare's birth? Music and verse began to fall apart when Chaucer robbed verse of its speed that he might give it greater meditation, though for another generation or so minstrels were to sing his lengthy elaborated *Troilus and Criseyde;* painting parted from religion in the later Renaissance that it might study effects of tangibility undisturbed; while, that it might characterize, where it had once personified, it renounced, in our own age, all that inherited subject-matter which we have named poetry. Presently I was indeed to number character itself among the abstractions, encouraged by Congreve's saying that 'passions are too powerful in the fair sex to let humour', or, as we say, character, 'have its course'. Nor have we fared better under the common daylight, for pure reason has notoriously made but light of practical reason, and has been made light of in its turn from that morning when Descartes discovered that he could think better in his bed than out of it; nor needed I original thought to discover, being so late of the school of Morris, that machinery had not separated from handicraft wholly for the world's good, nor to notice that the distinction of classes had become their isolation. If the London merchants of our day competed together in writing lyrics they would not, like the Tudor merchants, dance in the open street before the house of the victor; nor do the great ladies of London finish their balls on the pavement before their doors as did the great Venetian ladies, even in the eighteenth century, conscious of an all-enfolding sympathy. Doubtless because fragments broke into ever smaller fragments we saw one another in a light of bitter comedy, and in the arts, where now one technical element reigned and now another, generation hated generation, and accomplished beauty was snatched away when it had most engaged our affections. One thing I did not foresee, not having the courage of my own thought: the growing murderousness of the world.

> Turning and turning in the widening gyre
> The falcon cannot hear the falconer;

Things fall apart; the centre cannot hold;
Mere anarchy is loosed upon the world,
The blood-dimmed tide is loosed, and everywhere
The ceremony of innocence is drowned;
The best lack all conviction, while the worst
Are full of passionate intensity.

XXIII

If abstraction had reached, or all but reached its climax, escape might be possible for many, and if it had not, individual men might still escape. If Chaucer's personages had disengaged themselves from Chaucer's crowd, forgot their common goal and shrine, and after sundry magnifications became each in turn the centre of some Elizabethan play, and had after split into their elements and so given birth to romantic poetry, must I reverse the cinematograph? I thought that the general movement of literature must be such a reversal, men being there displayed in casual, temporary, contact as at the Tabard door. I had lately read Tolstoy's *Anna Karenina* and thought that where his theoretical capacity had not awakened there was such a turning back: but a nation or an individual with great emotional intensity might follow the pilgrims, as it were, to some unknown shrine, and give to all those separated elements, and to all that abstract love and melancholy, a symbolical, a mythological coherence. Not Chaucer's rough-tongued riders, but rather an ended pilgrimage, a procession of the Gods! Arthur Symons brought back from Paris stories of Verhaeren and Maeterlinck, and so brought me confirmation, as I thought, and I began to announce a poetry like that of the Sufis. I could not endure, however, an international art, picking stories and symbols where it pleased. Might I not, with health and good luck to aid me, create some new *Prometheus Unbound*; Patrick or Columcille, Oisin or Finn, in Prometheus' stead; and, instead of Caucasus, Cro-Patrick or Ben Bulben? Have not all races had their first unity from a mythology that marries them to rock and hill? We had in Ireland imaginative stories, which the uneducated classes knew and even sang, and might we not make those stories current among the educated classes, rediscovering for the work's sake what I have called 'the applied arts of literature', the association of literature, that is, with music, speech, and dance; and at last, it might be, so deepen the political passion of the nation that all, artist and poet, craftsman and day-labourer would accept a common design? Perhaps even these images, once created and associated with river and mountain, might move of themselves and with some powerful, even turbulent life, like those painted horses that trampled the rice-fields of Japan.

XXIV

I used to tell the few friends to whom I could speak these secret thoughts that I would make the attempt in Ireland but fail, for our civilization, its elements multiplying by division like certain low forms of life, was all-powerful; but in reality I had the wildest hopes. To-day I add to that first conviction, to that first desire for unity, this other conviction, long a mere opinion vaguely or inter-mittently apprehended: Nations, races, and individual men are uni-fied by an image, or bundle of related images, symbolical or evocative of the state of mind which is, of all states of mind not impossible, the most difficult to that man, race, or nation; because only the greatest obstacle that can be contemplated without despair rouses the will to full intensity.

A powerful class by terror, rhetoric, and organized sentimental-ity may drive their people to war, but the day draws near when they cannot keep them there; and how shall they face the pure nations of the East when the day comes to do it with but equal arms? I had seen Ireland in my own time turn from the bragging rhetoric and gregarious humour of O'Connell's generation and school, and offer herself to the solitary and proud Parnell as to her anti-self, buskin followed hard on sock, and I had begun to hope, or to half hope, that we might be the first in Europe to seek unity as deliberately as it had been sought by theologian, poet, sculptor, architect, from the eleventh to the thirteenth century. Doubtless we must seek it differ-ently, no longer considering it convenient to epitomize all human knowledge, but find it we well might could we first find philosophy and a little passion.

FROM Book II: Ireland After Parnell

X

I was at Sligo when I received a letter from John O'Leary, saying that I could do no more in Dublin, for even the younger men had turned against me, were 'jealous', his letter said, though what they had to be jealous of God knows. He said further that it was all my own fault, that he had warned me what would happen if I lived on terms of intimacy with those I tried to influence. I should have kept myself apart and alone. It was all true; through some influence from an earlier generation, from Walt Whitman, perhaps, I had sat talking in public bars, had talked late into the night at many men's houses, showing all my convictions to men that were but ready for one, and used conversation to explore and discover among men who looked for authority. I did not yet know that intellectual freedom and social equality are incompatible; and yet, if I had, could hardly have lived otherwise, being too young for silence. The trouble came from half a dozen obscure young men, who having nothing to do attended every meeting and were able to overturn a project that seemed my only bridge to other projects, including a travelling theatre. We had planned small libraries of Irish literature in connection with our country branches; we collected books and money, sending a lecturer to every branch and taking half the proceeds of that lecture to buy books. Maud Gonne, whose beauty could draw a great audience in any country town, had been the lecturer. The scheme was very nearly self-supporting, and six or seven bundles of books, chosen after much disputation by John O'Leary, J. F. Taylor, and myself, had been despatched to some six or seven branches. 'The country will support this work', Taylor had said somewhere on some public platform, 'because we are the most inflammable people on God's earth', his harsh voice giving almost a quality of style to Carlylean commonplace; but we are also a very jealous people. The half a dozen young men, if a little jealous of me, were still more jealous of those country branches which were getting so much notice, and where there was so much of that peasant mind their schoolmasters had taught them to despise. One must be

English or Irish, they would have said. I returned to find a great box of books appropriated for some Dublin purpose and the whole scheme abandoned. I knew that it was a bitter moment because I remember with gratitude words spoken not to my ear, but for my ear, by a young man who had lately joined our Society, Mr. Stephen MacKenna, now well known amongst scholars for his distinguished translations of Plotinus, and I seem to remember that I lost through anger what gift of persuasion I may possess, and that I was all the more helpless because I felt that even the best of us disagreed about everything at heart. I began to feel that I needed a hostess more than a society, but that I was not to find for years to come. I tried to persuade Maud Gonne to be that hostess, but her social life was in Paris, and she had already formed a new ambition, the turning of French public opinion against England. Without intellectual freedom there can be no agreement, and in Nationalist Dublin there was not—indeed there still is not—any society where a man is heard by the right ears, but never overheard by the wrong, and where he speaks his whole mind gaily, and is not the cautious husband of a part; where fantasy can play before matured into conviction; where life can shine and ring, and lack utility. Mere life lacking the protection of wealth or rank, or some beauty's privilege of caprice, cannot choose its company, taking up and dropping men merely because it likes or dislikes their manners and their looks, and in its stead opinion crushes and rends, and all is hatred and bitterness: wheel biting upon wheel, a roar of steel or iron tackle, a mill of argument grinding all things down to mediocrity.

If, as I think, minds and metals correspond, the goldsmiths of Paris foretold the French Revolution when they substituted steel for that unserviceable gold in the manufacture of the more expensive jewel work, and made those large, flat steel buttons for men of fashion wherein the card-sharpers were able to study the reflections of the cards.

FROM Book III: Hodos Chameliontos

IX

I know now that revelation is from the self, but from that age-long memoried self, that shapes the elaborate shell of the mollusc and the child in the womb, that teaches the birds to make their nest; and that genius is a crisis that joins that buried self for certain moments to our trivial daily mind. There are, indeed, personifying spirits that we had best call but Gates and Gate-keepers, because through their dramatic power they bring our souls to crisis, to Mask and Image, caring not a straw whether we be Juliet going to her wedding, or Cleopatra to her death; for in their eyes nothing has weight but passion. We have dreamed a foolish dream these many centuries in thinking that they value a life of contemplation, for they scorn that more than any possible life, unless it be but a name for the worst crisis of all. They have but one purpose, to bring their chosen man to the greatest obstacle he may confront without despair. They contrived Dante's banishment, and snatched away his Beatrice, and thrust Villon into the arms of harlots, and sent him to gather cronies at the foot of the gallows, that Dante and Villon might through passion become conjoint to their buried selves, turn all to Mask and Image, and so be phantoms in their own eyes. In great lesser writers like Landor and like Keats we are shown that Image and that Mask as something set apart; Andromeda and her Perseus—though not the sea-dragon—but in a few in whom we recognize supreme masters of tragedy, the whole contest is brought into the circle of their beauty. Such masters—Villon and Dante, let us say— would not, when they speak through their art, change their luck; yet they are mirrored in all the suffering of desire. The two halves of their nature are so completely joined that they seem to labour for their objects, and yet to desire whatever happens, being at the same instant predestinate and free, creation's very self. We gaze at such men in awe, because we gaze not at a work of art, but at the re-creation of the man through that art, the birth of a new species of man, and it may even seem that the hairs of our heads stand up, because that birth, that re-creation, is from terror. Had not Dante and Villon understood that their fate wrecked what life could not rebuild, had they lacked their Vision of Evil, had they cherished any species of optimism, they could but have found a false beauty, or some momentary instinctive beauty, and suffered no change at all, or but changed as do the wild creatures, or from Devil well to Devil sick, and so round the clock.

They and their sort alone earn contemplation, for it is only when the intellect has wrought the whole of life to drama, to crisis, that we may live for contemplation, and yet keep our intensity.

And these things are true also of nations, but the Gatekeepers who drive the nation to war or anarchy that it may find its Image are different from those who drive individual men, though I think at times they work together. And as I look backward upon my own writing, I take pleasure alone in those verses where it seems to me I have found something hard and cold, some articulation of the Image which is the opposite of all that I am in my daily life, and all that my country is; yet man or nation can no more make this Mask or Image[1] than the seed can be made by the soil into which it is cast.

ILLE

What portion in the world can the artist have
Who has awakened from the common dream
But dissipation and despair?

HIC

And yet
No one denies to Keats love of the world;
Remember his deliberate happiness.

ILLE

His art is happy, but who knows his mind?
I see a schoolboy when I think of him
With face and nose pressed to a sweet-shop window,
For certainly he sank into his grave
His senses and his heart unsatisfied,
And made—being poor, ailing and ignorant,
Shut out from all the luxury of the world,
The coarse-bred son of a livery-stable keeper—
Luxuriant song.

[1] There is a form of Mask or Image that comes from life and is fated, but there is a form that is chosen.

FROM Book IV: The Tragic Generation

III

Somewhere about 1450, though later in some parts of Europe by a hundred years or so, and in some earlier, men attained to personality in great numbers, 'Unity of Being', and became like 'a perfectly proportioned human body', and as men so fashioned held places of power, their nations had it too, prince and ploughman sharing that thought and feeling. What afterwards showed for rifts and cracks were there already, but imperious impulse held all together. Then the scattering came, the seeding of the poppy, bursting of pea-pod, and for a time personality seemed but the stronger for it. Shakespeare's people make all things serve their passion, and that passion is for the moment the whole energy of their being—birds, beasts, men, women, landscape, society, are but symbols and metaphors, nothing is studied in itself, the mind is a dark well, no surface, depth only. The men that Titian painted, the men that Jongsen painted, even the men of Van Dyck seemed at moments like great hawks at rest. In the Dublin National Gallery there hung, perhaps there still hang, upon the same wall, a portrait of some Venetian gentleman by Strozzi, and Mr. Sargent's painting of President Wilson. Whatever thought broods in the dark eyes of that Venetian gentleman has drawn its life from his whole body; it feeds upon it as the flame feeds upon the candle—and should that thought be changed, his pose would change, his very cloak would rustle, for his whole body thinks. President Wilson lives only in the eyes, which are steady and intent; the flesh about the mouth is dead, and the hands are dead, and the clothes suggest no movement of his body, nor any movement but that of the valet, who has brushed and folded in mechanical routine. There all was an energy flowing outward from the nature itself; here all is the anxious study and slight deflection of external force; there man's mind and body were predominantly subjective; here all is objective, using those words not as philosophy uses them, but as we use them in conversation.

The bright part of the moon's disk, to adopt the symbolism of a certain poem, is subjective mind, and the dark, objective mind, and we have eight-and-twenty Phases for our classification of mankind, and of the movement of its thought. At the first Phase—the night where there is no moonlight—all is objective, while when, upon the fifteenth night, the moon comes to the full, there is only subjective mind. The mid-Renaissance could but approximate to the full moon, 'For there's no human life at the full or the dark', but we may attribute to the next three nights of the moon the men of Shakespeare, of Titian, of Strozzi, and of Van Dyck, and watch them grow more reasonable, more orderly, less turbulent, as the nights pass; and it is well to find before the fourth—the nineteenth night counting from the start—a sudden change, as when a cloud becomes rain, or water freezes, for the great transitions are sudden; popular, typical men have grown more ugly and more argumentative; the face that Van Dyck called a fatal face has faded before Cromwell's warty opinionated head. Henceforth no mind made like 'a perfectly proportioned human body' shall sway the public, for great men must live in a portion of themselves, become professional and abstract; but seeing that the moon's third quarter is scarce passed; that abstraction has attained but not passed its climax; that a half, as I affirm it, of the twenty-second night still lingers, they may subdue and conquer, cherish even some Utopian dream, spread abstraction ever further till thought is but a film, and there is no dark depth any more, surface only. But men who belong by nature to the nights near to the full are still born, a tragic minority, and how shall they do their work when too ambitious for a private station, except as Wilde of the nineteenth Phase, as my symbolism has it, did his work? He understood his weakness, true personality was impossible, for that is born in solitude, and at his moon one is not solitary; he must project himself before the eyes of others, and, having great ambition, before some great crowd of eyes; but there is no longer any great crowd that cares for his true thought. He must humour and cajole and pose, take worn-out stage situations, for he knows that he may be as romantic as he please, so long as he does not believe in his romance, and all that he may get their ears for a few strokes of contemptuous wit in which he does believe.

We Rhymers did not humour and cajole; but it was not wholly from demerit, it was in part because of different merit, that he refused our exile. Shaw, as I understand him, has no true quarrel with his time, its moon and his almost exactly coincide. He is quite content to exchange Narcissus and his Pool for the signal-box at a railway junction, where goods and travellers pass perpetually upon their logical glittering road. Wilde was a monarchist, though content that monarchy should turn demagogue for its own safety, and he held a theatre by the means whereby he held a London dinner-table. 'He who can dominate a London dinner-table', he had boasted, 'can dominate the world.' While Shaw has but carried his street-corner Socialist eloquence on to the stage, and in him one discovers, in his writing and his public speech, as once—before their outline had been softened by prosperity or the passage of the years—in his clothes and in his stiff joints, the civilization that Sargent's picture has explored. Neither his crowd nor he have yet made a discovery that brought President Wilson so near his death, that the moon draws to its fourth quarter. But what happens to the individual man whose moon has come to that fourth quarter, and what to the civilization . . . ?

I can but remember pipe music to-night, though I can half-hear beyond it in the memory a weightier music, but this much at any rate is certain—the dream of my early manhood, that a modern nation can return to Unity of Culture, is false; though it may be we can achieve it for some small circle of men and women, and there leave it till the moon bring round its century.

> The cat went here and there
> And the moon spun round like a top,
> And the nearest kin of the moon,
> The creeping cat, looked up.
>
> ·   ·   ·   ·   ·
>
> Minnaloushe creeps through the grass
> From moonlit place to place,
> The sacred moon overhead
> Has taken a new phase.
> Does Minnaloushe know that his pupils
> Will pass from change to change,
> And that from round to crescent,
> From crescent to round they range?
> Minnaloushe creeps through the grass
> Alone, important and wise,
> And lifts to the changing moon
> His changing eyes.

IX

Two men are always at my side, Lionel Johnson and John Synge whom I was to meet a little later; but Johnson is to me the more vivid in memory, possibly because of the external finish, the clearly-marked lineaments of his body, which seemed but to express the clarity of his mind. I think Dowson's best verse immortal, bound, that is, to outlive famous novels and plays and learned histories and other discursive things, but he was too vague and gentle for my affections. I understood him too well, for I had been like him but for the appetite that made me search out strong condiments. Though I cannot explain what brought others of my generation to such misfortune, I think that (falling backward upon my parable of the moon) I can explain some part of Dowson's and Johnson's dissipation:—

> What portion in the world can the artist have
> Who has awakened from the common dream
> But dissipation and despair?

When Edmund Spenser described the islands of Phaedria and of Acrasia he aroused the indignation of Lord Burleigh, that 'rugged forehead', and Lord Burleigh was in the right if morality were our only object.

In those islands certain qualities of beauty, certain forms of sensuous loveliness were separated from all the general purposes of life, as they had not been hitherto in European literature—and would not be again, for even the historical process has its ebb and flow, till Keats wrote his *Endymion*. I think that the movement of our thought has more and more so separated certain images and regions of the mind, and that these images grow in beauty as they grow in sterility. Shakespeare leaned, as it were, even as craftsman, upon the general fate of men and nations, had about him the excitement of the playhouse; and all poets, including Spenser in all but a few pages, until our age came, and when it came almost all, have had some propaganda or traditional doctrine to give companionship with their fellows. Had not Matthew Arnold his faith in what he described as the best thought of his generation, Browning his psychological curiosity, Tennyson, as before him Shelley and Wordsworth, moral values that were not aesthetic values? But Coleridge of the *Ancient Mariner*, and *Kubla Khan*, and Rossetti in all his writings, made what

Arnold has called that 'morbid effort', that search for 'perfection of thought and feeling, and to unite this to perfection of form', sought this new, pure beauty, and suffered in their lives because of it. The typical men of the classical age (I think of Commodus, with his half-animal beauty, his cruelty, and his caprice) lived public lives, pursuing curiosities of appetite, and so found in Christianity, with its Thebaid and its Mareotic Sea, the needed curb. But what can the Christian confessor say to those who more and more must make all out of the privacy of their thought, calling up perpetual images of desire, for he cannot say, 'Cease to be artist, cease to be poet', where the whole life is art and poetry, nor can he bid men leave the world, who suffer from the terrors that pass before shut eyes. Coleridge, and Rossetti, though his dull brother did once persuade him that he was an agnostic, were devout Christians, and Stenbock and Beardsley were so towards their lives' end, and Dowson and Johnson always, and yet I think it but deepened despair and multiplied temptation.

> Dark Angel, with thine aching lust
> To rid the world of penitence:
> Malicious angel, who still dost
> My soul such subtil violence!
>
> When music sounds, then changest thou
> A silvery to a sultry fire:
> Nor will thine envious heart allow
> Delight untortured by desire.
>
> Through thee, the gracious Muses turn
> To Furies, O mine Enemy!
> And all the things of beauty burn
> With flames of evil ecstasy.
>
> Because of thee, the land of dreams
> Becomes a gathering-place of fears:
> Until tormented slumber seems
> One vehemence of useless tears.

Why are these strange souls born everywhere to-day, with hearts that Christianity, as shaped by history, cannot satisfy? Our love-letters wear out our love; no school of painting outlasts its founders, every stroke of the brush exhausts the impulse, Pre-Raphaelitism had some twenty years; Impressionism thirty perhaps. Why should we believe that religion can never bring round its antithesis? Is it true that our air is disturbed, as Mallarmé said, by 'the trembling of the veil of the Temple', or that 'our whole age is seeking to bring forth a sacred book'? Some of us thought that book near towards the end of last century, but the tide sank again.

XIX

I am certain of one date, for I have gone to much trouble to get it right. I met John Synge for the first time in the autumn of 1896, when I was one-and-thirty, and he four-and-twenty. I was at the Hôtel Corneille instead of my usual lodging, and why I cannot remember, for I thought it expensive. Synge's biographer says that you boarded there for a pound a week, but I was accustomed to cook my own breakfast, and dine at an Anarchist restaurant in the Boulevard St. Jacques for little over a shilling. Some one, whose name I forget, told me there was a poor Irishman at the top of the house, and presently introduced us. Synge had come lately from Italy, and had played his fiddle to peasants in the Black Forest—six months of travel upon fifty pounds—and was now reading French literature and writing morbid and melancholy verse. He told me that he had learned Irish at Trinity College, so I urged him to go to the Aran Islands and find a life that had never been expressed in literature, instead of a life where all had been expressed. I did not divine his genius, but I felt he needed something to take him out of his morbidity and melancholy. Perhaps I would have given the same advice to any young Irish writer who knew Irish, for I had been that summer upon Inishmaan and Inishmore, and was full of the subject. My friends and I had landed from a fishing-boat to find ourselves among a group of islanders, one of whom said he would bring us to the oldest man upon Inishmaan. This old man, speaking very slowly, but with laughing eyes, had said, 'If any gentleman has done a crime, we'll hide him. There was a gentleman that killed his father, and I had him in my own house six months till he got away to America.'

From that on I saw much of Synge, and brought him to Maud Gonne's, under whose persuasion, perhaps, he joined the 'Young Ireland Society of Paris', the name we gave to half a dozen Parisian

Irish, but resigned after a few months because 'it wanted to stir up Continental nations against England, and England will never give us freedom until she feels she is safe', the one political sentence I ever heard him speak. Over a year was to pass before he took my advice and settled for a while in an Aran cottage, and became happy, having escaped at last, as he wrote, 'from the squalor of the poor and the nullity of the rich'. I almost forget the prose and verse he showed me in Paris, though I read it all through again when after his death I decided, at his written request, what was to be published and what not. Indeed, I have but a vague impression, as of a man trying to look out of a window and blurring all that he sees by breathing upon the window. According to my Lunar parable, he was a man of the twenty-third Phase; a man whose subjective lives—for a constant return to our life is a part of my dream—were over; who must not pursue an image, but fly from it, all that subjective dreaming, that had once been power and joy, now corrupting within him. He had to take the first plunge into the world beyond himself, the first plunge away from himself that is always pure technique, the delight in doing, not because one would or should, but merely because one can do.

He once said to me, 'A man has to bring up his family and be as virtuous as is compatible with so doing, and if he does more than that he is a puritan; a dramatist has to express his subject and to find as much beauty as is compatible with that, and if he does more he is an aesthete', that is to say, he was consciously objective. Whenever he tried to write drama without dialect he wrote badly, and he made several attempts, because only through dialect could he escape self-expression, see all that he did from without, allow his intellect to judge the images of his mind as if they had been created by some other mind. His objectivity was, however, technical only, for in those images paraded all the desires of his heart. He was timid, too shy for general conversation, an invalid and full of moral scruple, and he was to create now some ranting braggadocio, now some tipsy hag full of poetical speech, and now some young man or girl full of the most abounding health. He never spoke an unkind word, had admirable manners, and yet his art was to fill the streets with rioters, and to bring upon his dearest friends enemies that may last their lifetime.

No mind can engender till divided into two, but that of a Keats or a Shelley falls into an intellectual part that follows, and a hidden emotional flying image, whereas in a mind like that of Synge the emotional part is deadened and stagnant, while the intellectual part is a clear mirror-like technical achievement.

But in writing of Synge I have run far ahead, for in 1896 he was but one picture among many. I am often astonished when I think that we can meet unmoved some person, or pass some house, that in later years is to bear a chief part in our life. Should there not be some flutter of the nerve or stopping of the heart like that MacGregor Mathers experienced at the first meeting with a phantom?

FROM Book V: The Stirring of the Bones

VI

When in my twenty-second year I had finished *The Wanderings of Oisin*, my style seemed too elaborate, too ornamental, and I thought for some weeks of sleeping upon a board. Had I been anywhere but at Sligo, where I was afraid of my grandfather and grandmother, I would have made the attempt. When I had finished *Rosa Alchemica* for the *Savoy*, I had a return of the old trouble and went to consult a friend who, under the influence of my cabbalistic symbols, could pass into a condition between meditation and trance. A certain symbolic personality who called herself, if I remember rightly, Megarithma, said that I must 'live near water and avoid woods because they concentrate the solar ray'. I believed that this enigmatic sentence came from my own Daimon, my own buried self speaking through my friend's mind. 'Solar', according to all that I learnt from Mathers, meant elaborate, full of artifice, rich, all that resembles the work of a goldsmith, whereas 'water' meant 'lunar', and 'lunar' all that is simple, popular, traditional, emotional. But why should woods concentrate the solar ray? I did not understand why, nor do I now, and I decided to reject that part of the message as an error. I accepted the rest without difficulty, for after *The Wanderings of Oisin*, I had simplified my style by filling my imagination with country stories. My friends believed that the dark portion of the mind—the subconscious—had an incalculable power, and even over events. To influence events or one's own mind, one had to draw the attention of that dark portion, to turn it, as it were, into a new direction. Mathers described how as a boy he had drawn over and over again some event that he longed for; and called those drawings an instinctive magic. But for the most part one repeated certain names and drew or imagined certain symbolic forms which had acquired a precise meaning, and not only to the dark portion of one's own mind, but to the mind of the race. I decided to repeat the names associated with the moon in the cabbalistic tree of life, the divine name, the name of the angelic order, the name of the planetary sphere, and so on, and probably, though my memory is not clear upon the point, to draw certain geometrical forms. As Arthur Symons and I were about to stay with Mr. Edward Martyn at Tulira Castle, in Galway, I decided that it was there I must make my invocation of the moon. I made it night after night just before I went to bed, and after many nights—eight or nine perhaps—I saw between sleeping and waking, as in a kinematograph, a galloping centaur, and a moment later a naked woman of incredible beauty, standing upon a pedestal and shooting an arrow at a star. I still remember the tint of that marvellous flesh which makes all human flesh seem unhealthy, and remember that others who have seen such forms have remembered the same characteristic. Next morning before breakfast Arthur Symons took me out on to the lawn to recite a scrap of verse, the only verse he had ever written to a dream. He had dreamt the night before of a woman of great beauty, but she was clothed and had not a bow and arrow. When he got back to London, he found awaiting him a story sent to the *Savoy* by Fiona Macleod and called, I think, *The Archer.* Some one in the story had a vision of a woman shooting an arrow into the sky and later of an arrow shot at a faun that pierced the faun's body and remained, the faun's heart torn out and clinging to it, embedded in a tree. Some weeks later I, too, was in London, and found among Mathers' pupils a woman whose little child—perhaps at the time of my vision, perhaps a little later—had come running in from the garden calling out, 'O, mother, I have seen a woman shooting an arrow into the sky and I am afraid that she has killed God'. I have somewhere among my papers a letter from a very old friend describing how her little cousin—perhaps a few months later—dreamed of a man who shot at a star with a gun and that the star fell down, but, 'I do not think', the child said, 'it minded dying because it was so very old', and how presently the child saw the star lying in a cradle. Had some great event taken place in some world where myth is reality and had we seen some portion of it? One of my fellow-students quoted a Greek saying, 'Myths are the activities of the Daimons', or had we but seen in the memory of the race something believed thousands of years ago, or had somebody—I myself perhaps—but dreamed a fantastic dream which had come to those others by transference of thought? I came to no conclusion, but I was sure there was some symbolic meaning could I but find it. I went to my friend who had spoken to Megarithma, and she went once more into her trance-like meditation and heard but a single unexplained sentence: 'There were three that saw; three will attain a wisdom older than the serpent, but the child will die.' Did this refer to myself, to Arthur Symons, to Fiona Macleod, to the child who feared that the archer had killed God? I thought not, for Symons had no deep interest in the subject, and there was the second child to account for. It was probably some new detail of the myth or an interpretation of its meaning. There was a London coroner in those days, learned in the Cabbala, whom I had once known though we had not met for some years. I called upon him and told all that I have set down here. He opened a drawer and took out of it two water-colour paintings, made by a clumsy painter who had no object but a symbolical record: one was of a centaur, the other of a woman standing upon a stone pedestal and shooting her arrow at what seemed a star. He asked me to look carefully at the star, and I saw that it was a little golden heart. He said: 'You have hit upon things that you can never have read of in any book; these symbols belong to a part of the Christian Cabbala'—perhaps this was not his exact term—'that you know nothing of. The centaur is the elemental spirit and the woman the divine spirit of the path Samekh, and the golden heart is the central point upon the cabbalistic Tree of Life and corresponds to the Sephiroth Tiphareth.' I was full of excitement, for now at last I began to understand. The Tree of Life is a geometrical figure made up of ten circles or spheres called Sephiroth joined by straight lines. Once men must have thought of it as like some great tree covered with its fruit and its foliage, but at some period, in the thirteenth century perhaps, touched by the mathematical genius of Arabia in all likelihood, it had lost its natural form. The Sephiroth Tiphareth, attributed to the sun, is joined to the Sephiroth Yesod, attributed to the moon, by a straight line called the path Samekh, and this line is attributed to the constellation Sagittarius. He would not or could not tell me more, but when I repeated what I had heard to one of my fellow-students, a yachtsman and yacht-designer and cabbalist, he said, 'Now you know what was meant by a wisdom older than the serpent'. He reminded me that the cabbalistic tree has a green serpent winding through it which represents the winding path of nature or of instinct, and that the path Samekh is part of the long straight line that goes up through the centre of the tree, and that it was interpreted as the path of 'deliberate effort'. The three who saw must, he said, be those who could attain to wisdom by the study of magic, for that was 'deliberate effort'. I remember that I quoted Balzac's description of the straight line as the line of man, but he could not throw light on the other symbols except that the shot arrow must symbolise effort, nor did I get any further light.

A couple of weeks after my vision, Lady Gregory, whom I had met once in London for a few minutes, drove over to Tulira, and after Symons's return to London I stayed at her house. When I saw her great woods on the edge of a lake, I remembered the saying about avoiding woods and living near the water. Had this new friend come because of my invocation, or had the saying been but prevision and my invocation no act of will, but prevision also? Were those unintelligible words—'avoid woods because they concentrate the solar ray'—but a dream-confusion, an attempt to explain symbolically an actual juxtaposition of wood and water? I could not say nor can I now. I was in poor health, the strain of youth had been greater than it commonly is, even with imaginative men, who must always, I think, find youth bitter, and I had lost myself besides, as I had done periodically for years, upon Hodos Chameliontos. The first time was in my eighteenth or nineteenth year, when I tried to create a more multitudinous dramatic form, and now I had got there through a novel that I could neither write nor cease to write which had Hodos Chameliontos for its theme. My chief person was to see all the modern visionary sects pass before his bewildered eyes, as Flaubert's Saint Anthony saw the Christian sects, and I was as helpless to create artistic, as my chief person to create philosophic, order. It was not that I do not love order, or that I lack capacity for it, but that—and not in the arts and in thought only—I outrun my strength. It is not so much that I choose too many elements, as that the possible unities themselves seem without number, like those angels that, in Henry More's paraphrase of the schoolman's problem, dance spurred and booted upon the point of a needle. Perhaps fifty years ago I had been in less trouble, but what can one do when the age itself has come to Hodos Chameliontos?

Lady Gregory, seeing that I was ill, brought me from cottage to cottage to gather folk-belief, tales of the faeries, and the like, and wrote down herself what we had gathered, considering that this work, in which one let others talk, and walked about the fields so much, would lie, to use a country phrase, 'very light upon the mind'. She asked me to return there the next year, and for years to come I was to spend my summers at her house. When I was in good health again, I found myself indolent, partly perhaps because I was affrighted by that impossible novel, and asked her to send me to my work every day at eleven, and at some other hour to my letters, rating me with idleness if need be, and I doubt if I should have done much with my life but for her firmness and her care. After a time, though not very quickly, I recovered tolerable industry, though it has only been of late years that I have found it possible to face an hour's verse without a preliminary struggle and much putting off.

Certain woods at Sligo, the woods above Dooney Rock and those above the waterfall at Ben Bulben, though I shall never perhaps walk there again, are so deep in my affections that I dream about them at night; and yet the woods at Coole, though they do not come into my dream, are so much more knitted to my thought that when I am dead they will have, I am persuaded, my longest visit. When we are dead, according to my belief, we live our lives backward for a certain number of years, treading the paths that we have trodden, growing young again, even childish again, till some attain an innocence that is no longer a mere accident of nature, but the human intellect's crowning achievement. It was at Coole that the first few simple thoughts that now, grown complex through their contact with other thoughts, explain the world, came to me from beyond my own mind. I practised meditations, and these, as I think, so affected my sleep that I began to have dreams that differed from ordinary dreams in seeming to take place amid brilliant light, and by their invariable coherence, and certain half-dreams, if I can call them so, between sleep and waking. I have noticed that such experiences come to me most often amid distraction, at some time that seems of all times the least fitting, as though it were necessary for the exterior mind to be engaged elsewhere, and it was during 1897 and 1898, when I was always just arriving from or just setting out to some political meeting, that the first dreams came. I was crossing a little stream near Inchy Wood and actually in the middle of a stride from bank to bank, when an emotion never experienced before swept down upon me. I said, 'That is what the devout Christian feels, that is how he surrenders his will to the will of God'. I felt an extreme surprise, for my whole imagination was preoccupied with the pagan mythology of ancient

Ireland, I was marking in red ink, upon a large map, every sacred mountain. The next morning I awoke near dawn, to hear a voice saying, 'The love of God is infinite for every human soul because every human soul is unique; no other can satisfy the same need in God'.

Lady Gregory and I had heard many tales of changelings, grown men and women as well as children, who, as the people believe, are taken by the faeries, some spirit or inanimate object bewitched into their likeness remaining in their stead, and I constantly asked myself what reality there could be in these tales, often supported by so much testimony. I woke one night to find myself lying upon my back with all my limbs rigid, and to hear a ceremonial measured voice, which did not seem to be mine, speaking through my lips. 'We make an image of him who sleeps', it said, 'and it is not he who sleeps, and we call it Emmanuel.' After many years that thought, others often found as strangely being added to it, became the thought of the Mask, which I have used in these memoirs to explain men's characters. A few months ago at Oxford I was asking myself why it should be 'an image of him who sleeps', and took down from the shelf, not knowing what I did, Burkitt's *Early Eastern Christianity,* and opened it at random. I had opened it at a Gnostic Hymn that told of a certain King's son who, being exiled, slept in Egypt—a symbol of the natural state—and how an Angel while he slept brought him a royal mantle; and at the bottom of the page I found a footnote saying that the word mantle did not represent the meaning properly, for that which the Angel gave had the exile's own form and likeness. I did not, however, find in the Gnostic Hymn my other conviction that Egypt and that which the Mask represents are antithetical. That, I think, became clear when a countryman told Lady Gregory and myself that he had heard the crying of new-dropped lambs in November— spring in the world of Faery being November with us.

•   •   •   •   •   •   •

On the sea-coast at Duras, a few miles from Coole, an old French Count, Florimond de Basterot, lived for certain months in every year. Lady Gregory and I talked over my project of an Irish Theatre, looking out upon the lawn of his house, watching a large flock of ducks that was always gathered for his arrival from Paris, and that would be a very small flock, if indeed it were a flock at all, when he set out for Rome in the autumn. I told her that I had given up my project because it was impossible to get the few pounds necessary for a start in little halls, and she promised to collect or give the money necessary. That was her first great service to the Irish intellectual movement. She reminded me the other day that when she first asked me what she could do to help our movement I suggested nothing; and, certainly, I no more foresaw her genius than I foresaw that of John Synge, nor had she herself foreseen it. Our theatre had been established before she wrote or had any ambition to write, and yet her little comedies have merriment and beauty, an unusual combination, and those two volumes where the Irish heroic tales are arranged and translated in an English so simple and so noble may do more than other books to deepen Irish imagination. They contain our ancient literature, are something better than our *Mabinogion,* are almost our *Morte d'Arthur.* It is more fitting, however, that in a book of memoirs I should speak of her personal influence, and especially as no witness is likely to arise better qualified to speak. If that influence were lacking, Ireland would be greatly impoverished, so much has been planned out in the library or among the woods at Coole; for it was there that John Shawe-Taylor found the independence from class and family that made him summon the conference between landlord and tenant that brought Land Purchase, and it was there that Hugh Lane formed those Irish ambitions that led to his scattering many thousands, and gathering much ingratitude; and where, but for that conversation at Florimond de Basterot's, had been the genius of Synge?

I have written these words instead of leaving all to posterity, and though my friend's ear seems indifferent to praise or blame, that young men, to whom recent events are often more obscure than those long past, may learn what debts they owe and to what creditor.

FROM *Dramatis Personae*

(1935)

VI

I must have spent the summer of 1897 at Coole. I was involved in a miserable love affair, that had but for one brief interruption absorbed my thoughts for years past, and would for some years yet. My devotion might as well have been offered to an image in a milliner's window, or to a statue in a museum, but romantic doctrine had reached its extreme development. Dowson was in love with a girl in an Italian restaurant, courted her for two years; at first she was too young, then he too disreputable; she married the waiter and Dowson's life went to wreck. Sober, he looked on no woman; drunk, he picked the cheapest whore. 'He did not even want them clean', said a friend. 'I have been faithful to thee, Cynara, in my fashion.' My health was giving way, my nerves had been wrecked. Finding that I could not work, and thinking the open air salutary, Lady Gregory brought me from cottage to cottage collecting folk-lore. Every night she wrote out what we had heard in the dialect of the cottages. She wrote, if my memory does not deceive me, two hundred thousand words, discovering that vivid English she was the first to use upon the stage. My object was to find actual experience of the supernatural, for I did not believe, nor do I now, that it is possible to discover in the text-books of the schools, in the manuals sold by religious booksellers, even in the subtle reverie of saints, the most violent force in history. I have described elsewhere our discovery that when we passed the door of some peasant's cottage, we passed out of Europe as that word is understood. 'I have longed', she said once, 'to turn Catholic, that I might be nearer to the people, but you have taught me that paganism brings me nearer still.' Yet neither she nor those peasants were pagans. Christianity begins to recognize the validity of experiences that preceded its birth and were, in some sense, shared by its founders. When later she asked me to annotate and introduce her book,

Visions and Beliefs, I began a study of 'Spiritualism' not only in its scientific form but as it is found among the London poor, and discovered that there was little difference except that the experience of the cottagers was the richer. Requiring no proof that we survive the grave, they could turn to what was dramatic or exciting and, though more ignorant than the townsmen, lacked vulgarity. Do the cottagers still live that mysterious life? Has it been driven away by exciting tales of ambush and assassination or has it become more inaccessible? When I was yet a very young man Sligo people told me whatever I asked, because all knew my mother's father, and some still remembered my father's grandfather. The people of South Galway did the same because Lady Gregory was my friend; an old witch-doctor in Clare said to us both: 'I have told you now what I have not told my own wife'; but if a stranger, or a neighbour that might mock, questioned them, they would say that all such things had long disappeared through the influence of the school. Once when I heard an old shepherd at Doneraile, where I spent a few days, give Lord Castletown such an answer, I said: 'Has anybody ever gone from here to consult Biddy Early?'—a famous Clare witch—and in a moment the man's face became excited; he himself had stood at the roadside, watching spirits playing hurley in a field, until one came and pulled the cap over his eyes. What he saw, what he did not see but thought he saw, does not concern me here, being but a part of that traditional experience which I have discussed only too much elsewhere. That experience is my obsession, as Coole and its history, her hope that her son or her grandson might live there, were Lady Gregory's.

XV

I saw Moore daily, we were at work on *Diarmuid and Grania.* Lady Gregory thought such collaboration would injure my own art, and was perhaps right. Because his mind was argumentative, abstract, diagrammatic, mine sensuous, concrete, rhythmical, we argued about words. In later years, through much knowledge of the stage, through the exfoliation of my own style, I learnt that occasional prosaic words gave the impression of an active man speaking. In dream poetry, in *Kubla Khan,* in *The Stream's Secret,* every line, every word, can carry its unanalysable, rich associations; but if we dramatize some possible singer or speaker we remember that he is moved by one thing at a time, certain words must be dull and numb. Here and there in correcting my early poems I have introduced such numbness and dullness, turned, for instance, 'the curd-pale moon' into the 'brilliant moon', that all might seem, as it were, remembered with indifference, except some one vivid image. When I began to rehearse a play I had the defects of my early poetry; I insisted upon obvious all-pervading rhythm. Later on I found myself saying that only in those lines or words where the beauty of the passage came to its climax, must rhythm be obvious. Because Moore thought all drama should be about possible people set in their appropriate surroundings, because he was fundamentally a realist ('Who are his people?' he said after a performance of George Russell's *Deirdre*. 'Ours were cattle merchants') he required many dull, numb words. But he put them in more often than not because he had no feeling for words in themselves, none for their historical associations. He insisted for days upon calling the Fianna 'soldiers'. In *A Story-teller's Holiday* he makes a young man in the thirteenth century go to the 'salons' of 'the fashionable ladies' in Paris, in his last story men and women of the Homeric age read books. Our worst quarrels, however, were when he tried to be poetical, to write in what he considered my style. He made the dying Diarmuid say to Finn: 'I will kick you down the stairway of the stars'. My letters to Lady Gregory show that we made peace at last, Moore accepting my judgment upon words, I his upon construction. To that he would sacrifice what he had thought the day before not only his best scene but 'the best scene in any modern play', and without regret: all must receive its being from the central idea; nothing be in itself anything. He would have been a master of construction, but that his practice as a novelist made him long for descriptions and reminiscences. If *Diarmuid and Grania* failed in performance, and I am not sure that it did, it failed because the second act, instead of moving swiftly from incident to incident, was reminiscent and descriptive; almost a new first act. I had written enough poetical drama to know this and to point it out to Moore. After the performance and just before our final quarrel the letters speak of an agreement to rewrite this act. I had sent Moore a scenario.

XXIII

During these first years Lady Gregory was friend and hostess, a centre of peace, an adviser who never overestimated or underestimated trouble, but neither she nor we thought her a possible creator. And now all in a moment, as it seemed, she became the founder of modern Irish dialect literature. When her husband died she had sold her London house, hiring instead a small flat in Queen Anne's Mansions, lived most of the year at Coole, cutting down expenses that her son might inherit an unencumbered estate. In early life she had written two or three articles, such as many clever fashionable women write, more recently had edited her husband, Sir William Gregory's, *Autobiography* and *Mr. Gregory's Letter-Box,* a volume of letters to William Gregory, Irish Under-Secretary at the beginning of the nineteenth century, from Palmerston, Wellesley, many famous men, drawn from the Coole archives. Some slight desire to create had been put aside until her son reached manhood; but now he had left the university and she was fifty. I told her that Alfred Nutt had offered to supply me with translations of the Irish heroic cycles if I would pick the best versions and put my English upon them, attempting what Malory had done for the old French narratives. I told her that I was too busy with my own work. Some days later she asked if I would object to her attempting it, making or finding the translations herself. An eminent Trinity College professor had described ancient Irish literature as 'silly, religious, or indecent', and she thought such work necessary for the dignity of Ireland. 'We work to add dignity to Ireland' was a favourite phrase of hers. I hesitated, I saw nothing in her past to fit her for that work; but in a week or two she brought a translation of some heroic tale, what tale I cannot now remember, in the dialect of the neighbourhood, where one discovers the unemphatic cadence, the occasional poignancy of Tudor English. Looking back, *Cuchulain of Muirthemne* and *Gods and Fighting Men* at my side, I can see that they were made possible by her past; semi-feudal Roxborough, her inherited sense of caste, her knowledge of that top of the world where men and women are valued for their manhood and their charm, not for their opinions, her long study of Scottish Ballads, of Percy's *Reliques,* of the *Morte d'Arthur.* If she had not found those tales, or finding them had not found the dialect of Kiltartan, that past could not, as it were, have drawn itself together, come to birth as present personality. Sometimes in her letters, in her books when she wrote ordinary English, she was the late-Victorian woman turning aside from reality to what seems pleasing, or to a slightly sentimental persiflage as a form of politeness—in society, to discover 'eternity glaring', as Carlyle did when he met Charles Lamb for the first time, is scarcely in good taste—but in her last years, when speaking in her own character, she seemed always her greater self. A writer must die every day he lives, be reborn, as it is said in the Burial Service, an incorruptible self, that self opposite of all that he has named 'himself'. George Moore, dreading the annihilation of an impersonal bleak realism, used life like a mediaeval ghost making a body for itself out of drifting dust and vapour; and have I not sung in describing guests at Coole—'There one that ruffled in a manly pose, For all his timid heart'—that one myself? Synge was a sick man picturing energy, a doomed man picturing gaiety; Lady Gregory, in her life much artifice, in her nature much pride, was born to see the glory of the world in a peasant mirror. 'I saw the household of Finn; it was not the household of a soft race; I had a vision of that man yesterday. . . . A King of heavy blows; my law; my adviser, my sense and my wisdom, prince and poet, braver than kings, King of the Fianna, brave in all countries; golden salmon of the sea, clean hawk of the air . . . a high messenger in bravery and in music. His skin lime-white, his hair golden; ready to work, gentle to women. His great green vessels full of rough sharp wine, it is rich the king was, the head of his people.' And then Grania's song over the sleeping Diarmuid:—

' "Sleep a little, sleep a little, for there is nothing at all to fear, Diarmuid, grandson of Duibhne; sleep here soundly, soundly, Diarmuid, to whom I have given my love. It is I will keep watch for you, grandchild of shapely Duibhne; sleep a little, a blessing on you, beside the well of the strong field; my lamb from above the lake, from the banks of the strong streams. Let your sleep be like the sleep in the North of fair comely Fionnchadh of Ess Ruadh, the time he took Slaine with bravery as we think, in spite of Failbhe of the Hard Head.

"Let your sleep be like the sleep in the West of Aine, daughter of Gailian, the time she went on a journey in the night with Dubhthach from Dorinis, by the light of torches.

"Let your sleep be like the sleep in the East of Deaghadh the proud, the brave fighter, the time he took Coincheann, daughter of Binn, in spite of fierce Decheall of Duibhreann.

"O heart of the valour of the world to the west of Greece, my heart will go near to breaking if I do not see you every day. The parting of us two will be the parting of two children of the one house; it will be the parting of life from the body."

'And then to rouse him she would make another song, and it is what she would say: "Caoinche will be loosed on your track; it is not slow the running of Caoilte will be; do not let death reach to you, do not give yourself to sleep forever.

"The stag to the East is not asleep, he does not cease from bellowing; the bog lark is not asleep to-night on the high stormy bogs; the sound of her clear voice is sweet; she is not sleeping between the streams." '

FROM The Bounty of Sweden

(1925)

Early in November [1923] a journalist called to show me a
printed paragraph saying that the Nobel Prize would probably be
conferred upon Herr Mann, the distinguished novelist, or upon
myself. I did not know that the Swedish Academy had ever heard my
name; tried to escape an interview by talking of Rabindranath
Tagore, of his gift to his School of the seven thousand pounds
awarded him; almost succeeded in dismissing the whole Reuter
paragraph from my memory. Herr Mann has many readers, is a
famous novelist with his fixed place in the world, and, said I to myself,
well fitted for such an honour; whereas I am but a writer of plays
which are acted by players with a literary mind for a few evenings,
and I have altered them so many times that I doubt the value of every
passage. I am more confident of my lyrics, or of some few amongst
them, but then I have got into the habit of recommending or com-
mending myself to general company for anything rather than my gift
of lyric writing, which concerns such a meagre troop.

Every now and then, when something has stirred my imagination,
I begin talking to myself. I speak in my own person and dramatize
myself, very much as I have seen a mad old woman do upon the Dublin
quays, and sometimes detect myself speaking and moving as if I were
still young, or walking perhaps like an old man with fumbling steps.
Occasionally, I write out what I have said in verse, and generally for
no better reason than because I remember that I have written no verse
for a long time. I do not think of my soliloquies as having different
literary qualities. They stir my interest, by their appropriateness to

the men I imagine myself to be, or by their accurate description of some emotional circumstance, more than by any aesthetic value. When I begin to write I have no object but to find for them some natural speech, rhythm and syntax, and to set it out in some pattern, so seeming old that it may seem all men's speech, and though the labour is very great, I seem to have used no faculty peculiar to myself, certainly no special gift. I print the poem and never hear about it again, until I find the book years after with a page dog-eared by some young man, or marked by some young girl with a violet, and when I have seen that, I am a little ashamed, as though somebody were to attribute to me a delicacy of feeling I should but do not possess. What came so easily at first, and amidst so much drama, and was written so laboriously at the last, cannot be counted among my possessions.

On the other hand, if I give a successful lecture, or write a vigorous, critical essay, there is immediate effect; I am confident that on some one point, which seems to me of great importance, I know more than other men, and I covet honour.

III

Then some eight days later, between ten and eleven at night, comes a telephone message from the *Irish Times* saying that the prize has indeed been conferred upon me; and some ten minutes after that comes a telegram from the Swedish Ambassador; then journalists come for interviews. At half past twelve my wife and I are alone, and search the cellar for a bottle of wine, but it is empty, and as a celebration is necessary we cook sausages. A couple of days pass and a letter from the Ambassador invites me to receive the prize at Stockholm, but a letter from the Swedish Academy offers to send medal, money, and diploma to Dublin.

I question booksellers in vain for some history of Sweden, or of Swedish literature. Even Gosse's *Studies in the Literature of Northern Europe,* which I read twenty years ago, is out of print, and among my own books there is nothing but the Life of Swedenborg, which contains photographs of Swedenborg's garden and garden-house, and of the Stockholm House of Nobles, built in Dutch style, and beautiful, with an ornament that never insists upon itself, and a dignity that has no pomp. It had housed in Swedenborg's day that

Upper Chamber of the Swedish Parliament where he had voted and spoken upon finance, after the ennoblement of his family.

XII

On Thursday I give my official lecture to the Swedish Royal Academy. I have chosen 'The Irish Theatre' for my subject, that I may commend all those workers, obscure or well-known, to whom I owe much of whatever fame in the world I may possess. If I had been a lyric poet only, if I had not become through this Theatre the representative of a public movement, I doubt if the English committees would have placed my name upon that list from which the Swedish Academy selects its prize-winner. They would not have acknowledged a thought so irrelevant, but those dog-eared pages, those pressed violets, upon which the fame of a lyric poet depends at the last, might without it have found no strong voice. I have seen so much beautiful lyric poetry pass unnoticed for years, and indeed at this very moment a little book of exquisite verse lies upon my table, by an author who died a few years ago, whom I knew slightly, and whose work I ignored, for chance had shown me only that part of it for which I could not care.

On my way to the lecture hall I ask an Academician what kind of audience I will have, and he replies, 'An audience of women, a fit audience for a poet'; but there are men as well as women. I had thought it would be difficult to speak to an audience in a language they had learnt at school, but it is exceedingly easy. All I say seems to be understood, and I am conscious of that sympathy which makes a speaker forget all but his own thoughts, and soliloquize aloud. I am speaking without notes and the image of old fellow-workers comes upon me as if they were present, above all of the embittered life and death of one, and of another's laborious, solitary age, and I say, 'When your King gave me medal and diploma, two forms should have stood, one at either side of me, an old woman sinking into the infirmity of age and a young man's ghost. I think when Lady Gregory's name and John Synge's name are spoken by future generations, my name, if remembered, will come up in the talk, and that if my name is spoken first their names will come in their turn because of the years we worked together. I think that both had been well pleased to have stood beside me at the great reception at your Palace, for their work and mine has delighted in history and tradition.' I think as I speak these words of how deep down we have gone, below all that is individual, modern and restless, seeking foundations for an Ireland that can only come into existence in a Europe that is still but a dream.

X

I was twenty-three years old when the troubling of my life began. I had heard from time to time in letters from Miss O'Leary, John O'Leary's old sister, of a beautiful girl who had left the society of the Viceregal Court for Dublin nationalism. In after years I persuaded myself that I felt premonitory excitement at the first reading of her name. Presently she drove up to our house in Bedford Park with an introduction from John O'Leary to my father. I had never thought to see in a living woman so great beauty. It belonged to famous pictures, to poetry, to some legendary past. A complexion like the blossom of apples, and yet face and body had the beauty of lineaments which Blake calls the highest beauty because it changes least from youth to age, and a stature so great that she seemed of a divine race. Her movements were worthy of her form, and I understood at last why the poet of antiquity, where we would but speak of face and form, sings, loving some lady, that she paces like a goddess. I remember nothing of her speech that day except that she vexed my father by praise of war, for she too was of the Romantic movement and found those uncontrovertible Victorian reasons, that seemed to announce so prosperous a future, a little grey. As I look backward, it seems to me that she brought into my life in those days—for as yet I saw only what lay upon the surface—the middle of the tint, a sound as of a Burmese gong, an overpowering tumult that had yet many pleasant secondary notes.

She asked [me] to dine with her that evening in her rooms in Ebury Street, and I think that I dined with her all but every day during her stay in London of perhaps nine days, and there was something so exuberant in her ways that it seemed natural she should give her hours in overflowing abundance. She had heard of me from O'Leary; he had praised me, and it was natural that she should give and take without stint. She lived surrounded by cages of innumerable singing birds and with these she always travelled, it seemed, taking them even upon short journeys, and they and she were now returning to Paris where their home was.

She spoke to me of her wish for a play that she could act in Dublin. Somebody had suggested Todhunter's *Helena in Troas,* but he had refused. I told her of a story I had found when compiling my *Fairy and Folk Tales of the Irish Peasantry,* and offered to write for her the play I have called *The Countess Cathleen.* When I told her I wished to become an Irish Victor Hugo, was I wholly sincere?—for though a volume of bad verse translations from Hugo had been my companion at school, I had begun to simplify myself with great toil. I had seen upon her table *Tristram of Lyonesse* and *Les Contemplations,* and besides it was natural to commend myself by claiming a very public talent, for her beauty as I saw it in those days seemed incompatible with private, intimate life.

She, like myself, had received the political tradition of Davis with an added touch of hardness and heroism from the hand of O'Leary, and when she spoke of William O'Brien, [who] was in jail making a prolonged struggle against putting on the prison clothes, she said, 'There was a time when men sacrificed their lives for their country, but now they sacrifice their dignity.' But mixed with this feeling for what is permanent in human life there was something declamatory, Latin in a bad sense, and perhaps even unscrupulous. She spoke of her desire for power, apparently for its own sake, and when we talked of politics spoke much of mere effectiveness, or the mere winning of this or that election. Her two and twenty years had taken some colour, I thought, from French Boulangist adventurers and journalist *arrivistes* of whom she had seen too much, and [she] already had made some political journey into Russia in their interest. I was full of that thought of the 'Animula Vagula' chapter, I had heard it at the feet of a young Brahmin in Dublin, 'Only the means can justify the end.' She meant her ends to be unselfish, but she thought almost any means justified in their success. We were seeking different things: she, some memorable action for final consecration of her youth, and I, after all, but to discover and communicate a state of being. Perhaps even in politics it would in the end be enough to have lived and thought passionately and have, like O'Leary, a head worthy of a Roman coin.

I spoke much of my spiritual philosophy. How important it all seemed to me; what would I not have given that she might think exactly right on all those great questions of the day? All is but faint to me beside a moment when she passed before a window, dressed in white, and rearranged a spray of flowers in a vase. Twelve years afterwards I put that impression into verse: ('she pulled down the pale blossom'. Quote):

> [Blossom pale, she pulled down the pale blossom
> At the moth hour and hid it in her bosom.]

I felt in the presence of a great generosity and courage, and of a mind without peace, and when she and all her singing birds had gone my melancholy was not the mere melancholy of love. I had what I thought was a 'clairvoyant' perception but was, I can see now, but an obvious deduction of an awaiting immediate disaster. I was compiling for an American publisher a selection from the Irish novelists, and I can remember that all the tribulations of their heroes but reminded me of that dread. They too, according to a fashion of the writers of early Victoria, had been so often thrown without father or mother or guardian amid a world of deception, and they too, in their different way, were incurably romantic. I was in love but had not spoken of love and never meant to speak, and as the months passed I grew master of myself again. 'What wife could she make,' I thought, 'what share could she have in the life of a student?'

<h2 style="text-align:center">XII</h2>

A few months later I was again in Ireland and I heard that she was in Dublin. I called and waited for her at a little hotel in Nassau Street, which no longer exists, in a room overlooking the College Park. At the first sight of her as she came through the door, her great height seeming to fill it, I was overwhelmed with emotion, an intoxication of pity. She did not seem to have any beauty, her face was wasted, the form of the bones showing, and there was no life in her manner. As our talk became intimate, she hinted at some unhappiness, some disillusionment. The old hard resonance had gone and she had become gentle and indolent. I was in love once more and no longer wished to fight against it. I no longer thought what kind of wife would this woman make, but of her need for protection and for peace.

Yet I left Dublin next day to stay somewhere in Orange Ulster with the brilliant student of my old Dublin school, Charles Johnston, and spent a week or ten days with him and his elder brother, making fire balloons. We made the fire balloons of tissue paper and then chased them over the countryside, our chase becoming longer and longer as our skill in manufacture improved. I was not, it seems—not altogether—captive; but presently came from her a letter touching a little upon her sadness, and telling of a dream of some past life. She and I had been brother and sister somewhere on the edge of the Arabian desert, and sold together into slavery. She had an impression of some long journey and of miles upon miles of the desert sand. I returned to Dublin at once, and that evening, but a few minutes after we had met, asked her to marry me. I remember a curious thing. I had come into the room with that purpose in my mind, and hardly looked at her or thought of her beauty. I sat there holding her hand and speaking vehemently. She did not take away her hand for a while. I ceased to speak, and presently as I sat in silence I felt her nearness to me and her beauty. At once I knew that my confidence had gone, and an instant later she drew her hand away. No, she could not marry—there were reasons—she would never marry; but in words that had no conventional ring she asked for my friendship. We spent the next day upon the cliff paths at Howth and dined at a little cottage near the Baily Lighthouse, where her old nurse lived, and I overheard the old nurse asking if we were engaged to be married. At the day's end I found I had spent ten shillings, which seemed to me a very great sum.

I saw her day after day. I read her my unfinished *The Countess Cathleen*, and I noticed that she became moved at the passage, 'the joy of losing joy, of ceasing all resistance'—and thought, she is burdened by a sense of responsibility for herself. I told her after meeting her in London I had come to understand the tale of a woman selling her soul to buy food for a starving people as a symbol of all souls who lose their peace, or their fineness, or any beauty of the spirit in political service, but chiefly of her soul that had seemed so incapable of rest. For the moment she had no political work nor plan of any, and we saw each other continually. Suddenly she was called back to France, and she told me in confidence that she had joined a secret political society and though she had come to look upon its members as self-seekers and adventurers she could not disobey this, the first definite summons it had sent to her. I stayed on in Ireland, probably at Sligo with my uncle, George Pollexfen, finishing *The Countess Cathleen* that had become but the symbolical song of my pity. Then came a letter of wild sorrow. She had adopted a little child, she told me, some three years ago, and now this child had died. Mixed into her incoherent grief were accounts of the death bird that had pecked at the nursery window the day when it was taken ill, and how at sight of the bird she had brought doctor after doctor.

XIII

She returned to Ireland in the same ship with Parnell's body, arriving at Kingstown a little after six in the morning. I met her on the pier and went with her to her hotel, where we breakfasted. She was dressed in extravagantly deep mourning, for Parnell, people thought, thinking her very theatrical. We spoke of the child's death. She had built a memorial chapel, using some of her capital. 'What did money matter to her now?' From another I learned later on that she had the body embalmed. That day and on later days she went over again the details of the death—speech was a relief to her. She was plainly very ill. She had for the first days of her grief lost the power of speaking French, which she knew almost as well as English, and she had acquired the habit, unlearned afterwards with great difficulty, of taking chloroform in order to sleep. We were continually together; my spiritual philosophy was evidently a great comfort to her. We spoke often of the state of death, and it was plain that she was thinking of the soul of her 'Georgette'.

One evening we were joined by a friend I had made at the art school in Kildare Street. This was George Russell. He had given up art and was now an accountant in a draper's shop, for his will was weak and an emotional occupation would have weakened it still further. He had seen many visions, and some of them had contained information about matters of fact that were afterwards verified; but, though his own personal revelation was often original and very remarkable, he accepted in the main the conclusions of Theosophy. He spoke of reincarnation, and Maud Gonne asked him, 'How soon a child was reborn, and if [reborn], where?' He said, 'It may be reborn in the same family.' I could see that Maud Gonne was deeply impressed, and I quieted my more sceptical intelligence, as I have so often done in her presence. I remember a pang of conscience. Ought I not to say, 'The whole doctrine of the reincarnation of the soul is hypothetical. It is the most plausible of the explanations of the world, but can we say more than that?' or some like sentence?

I had already taken a decision that will not suggest scepticism. She now told me of an apparition of a woman dressed in grey and with a grey veil covering the lower part of her face, which had appeared to her [in] childhood. Perhaps when one loves one is not quite sane, or perhaps one can pierce—in sudden intuition—behind the veil. I decided to make this woman visible at will. I had come to believe that she was an evil spirit troubling Maud Gonne's life unseen, weakening affections and above all creating a desire for power and excitement. But, if it were visible, it would speak, it would put its temptation into words and she would face it with her intellect, and at last banish it. I made a symbol according to the rules of my Order, considering it as an inhabitant of the fifth element with another element subordinate, and almost at once it became visible. I of course saw nothing beyond an uncertain impression on the mind, but Maud Gonne saw it almost as if palpably present. It told its story, taking up what was perhaps a later event of her dream of the desert. It was a past personality of hers, now seeking to be reunited with her. She had been priestess in a temple somewhere in Egypt and under the influence of a certain priest who was her lover gave false oracles for money, and because of this the personality of that life had split off from the soul and remained a half-living shadow. I would have taken all this for but a symbolic event, expressing a psychological state or spirit (is not Rahab 'an Eternal State' in William Blake?), but for a coincidence. When I had been in the Esoteric Section of the Theosophical Society, I had been taught as one of the secrets of that initiation that a just such separated, half-living personality might haunt the soul in its new life and seek a reunion that must be always refused. I had not then the evidence that I have now of the most profound knowledge of all that passes in our minds and in the minds of those with whom we are even in remote contact, upon the part of beings of whom I know nothing except that they are invisible, subtle, and perhaps full of a secret laughter.

She had come [to] have need of me, as it seemed, and I had no doubt that need would become love, that it was already coming so. I had even as I watched her a sense of cruelty, as though I were a hunter taking captive some beautiful wild creature. We went to London and were initiated in the Hermetic Students, and I began to form plans of our lives devoted to mystic truth, and spoke to her of Nicholas Flamel and his wife, Pernella. In a propaganda, secret and seeking out only the most profound and subtle minds, that great beauty would be to others, as it was always to me, symbolic and mysterious. She stayed with her sister in London. I noticed that one evening when I paid her some compliment her face was deeply tinted. She returned to Paris, and her cousin, a young girl of like age, meeting me in the street, asked me 'why I was not in Paris'. I had no money. I had spent in Ireland all my earnings, and now instead of earning more as quickly as possible I spent more than half my time writing to her. Surely if I told her all my thoughts, all my hopes and my ambitions, she would never leave me.

I knew indeed that energies would return and that I must set her to some work—a secret, mystic propaganda might be insufficient. And now the death of Parnell had shown me, as I thought, what that work would be. When I had gone to London with my father and mother, it had been with the thought of returning some day to begin some movement like that of Young Ireland, though less immediately political. I had not thought out the details and during my years in London I had come to think of societies and movements to encourage literature, or create it where it was not, as absurd—is not the artist always solitary?—and yet now I wished to found societies and to influence newspapers. I began to justify this plan to that newer, mocking self by saying that Ireland, which could not support a critical press, must find a substitute. A moment later that newer self would convict me of insincerity and show me that I was seeking to find a work that would not be demoralizing, as I thought that even the most necessary politics were, not for all, but mostly for her whose soul I partly judged from her physical beauty and partly knew to be distinguished and subtle. I knew by a perception that seemed to come into my mind from without, so sudden it was, that the romance of Irish public life had gone and that the young, perhaps for many years to come, would seek some unpolitical form for national feeling.

I had occasionally lectured to a little patriotic society of young

Irish men and women at Southwark, clerks for the most part, and
their sisters and sweethearts. I made an appointment with the most
energetic of them to explain my new plan. He was very ready for it,
for his society had ceased to meet. The women had taken to laugh-
ing at the lectures—they were always the same and they had heard
them so often—and nobody would give another lecture. I invited
these men to meet in my study in Bedford Park to plan a new pro-
paganda, and invited to meet them a man I had met in Dublin when
he edited the *Dublin University Review*. He had indeed been
appointed at my suggestion, and I had seen his admirable transla-
tions from the German. I had been impressed also by his physical
beauty, as of a Greek statue. This man, T. W. Rolleston, came to be
what Russell calls 'an intimate enemy'; without passion, though in
mind and in body he seemed a vessel shaped for fiery use, I came to
think him, in Ben Jonson's phrase, 'a hollow image'. And yet after
five and twenty years I continually murmur to myself his lyric, 'In a
quiet watered land, a land of roses'. He was the true founder of the
Irish Literary Society, though the first general idea was mine, under-
standing all about resolutions and amendments and the like.

I had a plan for a series of books like the old National Library of
Davis, and found that Sir Charles Gavan Duffy had suggested a
similar scheme to one or two of the young Southwark Irishmen. We
decided to amalgamate the schemes and to organize the sales
through the Irish Literary Society in London and a similar society to
be founded in Dublin. I sent Rolleston there and he got together a
group of learned [men], many our political opponents, who decided
that one really necessary thing was to raise more money for a cer-
tain learned society they all belonged to. I had not set my thoughts
on learned men and went to Dublin in a passion. The first man I
sought out was a butter merchant, whose name I had been given in
Southwark, and a society, the National Literary Society, which
afflicts me now by its permanence and by its dullness, so changed it
is from its fiery youth, was planned out over a butter tub.

XVI

While I was working out these plans, in which there was much
patriotism and more desire for a fair woman, and watching them
prosper beyond my hopes, Maud Gonne had found more exciting

work. After the fall of Parnell, tenants evicted during the Land War were abandoned, or so it seemed, by their leaders. There was no longer any money from America and the energies of political Ireland were absorbed in the dispute between Parnellite and anti-Parnellite. She felt responsible for certain of these tenants as she had been among those who advised them to join the Plan of Campaign, and she began lecturing in France for their benefit. She spoke of the wrongs of Ireland and much of certain Irishmen who were in jail for attempting to blow up public buildings. Some of these men, who had already served many years, were in bad health, and seven or seventeen had, it was said, lost their reason. Neither of the Irish parties would take up their cause for fear of compromising the Home Rule movement with the English electorate. Perhaps her lectures, besides bringing in a little money for the evicted tenants, might make England anxious enough for her good name in France to release some of these men.

She lectured first in Paris and then in the French provinces, and her success was exceedingly great. Michael Davitt had come to her help with certain letters: M. Magnard had placed the *Figaro* at her disposal. Everywhere old journalists and young students spoke of the cruelty of England, and the English Embassy had begun to show signs of uneasiness. I was touched at her success and read with pleasure of her 'mysterious eye' that drew some journalist to say it contained the shadow of battles yet to come. I also knew that vague look in the eyes and had often wondered at its meaning—the wisdom that must surely accompany its symbol, her beauty, or lack of any thought? Looking backward now I see that a mastery over popular feeling, abandoned by the members of Parliament through a quarrel that was to last for nine years, was about to pass into her hands. At the moment I was jealous of all those unknown helpers who arranged her lectures—had she not told me too a French friend, seeing her unhappy, had suggested her first lecture? And then too I saw no sufficient gain for so much toil—a few more tenants restored, perhaps a few dynamite prisoners released—and I had begun to dream of a co-ordination of intellectual and political forces. Her oratory, by its emotional temper, was an appeal to herself and also to something uncontrollable, something that could never be co-ordinated. I also, as Hyde later on with more success, had begun to bid for that forsaken leadership.

My Dublin world was even blinder. O'Leary saw but a beautiful woman seeking excitement, and Miss Sarah Purser said, continuing her pictorial interpretation, 'Maud Gonne talks politics in Paris, and literature to you, and at the Horse Show she would talk of a clinking brood mare.' I always defended her, though I was full of disquiet, and said often, 'None of you understands her force of character.' She came to Ireland again and again and often to the West where, through her efforts, all the tenants who had joined some combination through her influence were restored to their houses and farms. When in Dublin, we were always together and she collected books for our country branches and founded, I think, three of the seven branches, which were all we ever attained to. But it was no longer possible for her to become that 'fiery hand'. Till some political project came into her head she was the woman I had come to love. She lived as ever, surrounded by dogs and birds, and I became gradually aware of many charities—old women or old men past work were always seeking her out; and I began to notice a patience beyond my reach in handling birds or beasts. I could play with bird or beast half the day, but I was not patient with its obstinacy.

XXIII

I was tortured by sexual desire and had been for many years. I have often said to myself that some day I would put it all down in a book that some young man of talent might not think as I did that my shame was mine alone. It began when I was fifteen years old. I had been bathing, and lay down in the sun on the sand on the Third Rosses and covered my body with sand. Presently the weight of the sand began to affect the organ of sex, though at first I did not know what the strange, growing sensation was. It was only at the orgasm that I knew, remembering some boy's description or the description in my grandfather's encyclopedia. It was many days before I discovered how to renew that wonderful sensation. From that on it was a continual struggle against an experience that almost invariably left me with exhausted nerves. Normal sexual intercourse does not affect me more than other men, but that, though never frequent, was plain ruin. It filled me with loathing of myself; and yet at first pride and perhaps, a little, lack of obvious opportunity, and now love kept me in unctuous celibacy. When I returned to London in my twenty-seventh year I think my love seemed almost hopeless, and I knew that my friends had all mistresses of one kind or another and that most, at need, went home with harlots. Henley, indeed, mocked at any other life. I had never since childhood kissed a woman's lips. At Hammersmith I saw a woman of the town walking up and down in the empty railway station. I thought of offering myself to her, but the old thought came back, 'No, I love the most beautiful woman in the world.'

XXIV

At a literary dinner where there were some fifty or sixty guests I noticed opposite me, between celebrated novelists, a woman of great beauty. Her face had a perfectly Greek regularity, though her skin was a little darker than a Greek's would have been and her hair was very dark. She was exquisitely dressed with what seemed to me very old lace over her breast, and had the same sensitive look of distinction I had admired in Eva Gore-Booth. She was, it seemed, about my own age, but suggested to me an incomparable distinction. I was not introduced to her, but found that she was related to a member of the Rhymers' Club and had asked my name.

I began to write *The Land of Heart's Desire* to supply the niece of a new friend, Miss Florence Farr, with a part, and put into it my own despair. I could not tell why Maud Gonne had turned from me unless she had done so from some vague desire for some impossible life, for some unvarying excitement like that of the heroine of my play. Before it was finished I went to Paris to stay with MacGregor Mathers, now married to Bergson's sister. The decay of his character that came later had not set in, though I noticed that his evocations were a dangerous strain. One day a week he and his wife were shut up together evoking, trying to influence the politics of the world, I believe now, rearranging nations according to his own grandiose phantasy, and on this day I noticed that he would spit blood. He had a small income, three or four hundred a year, allowed him by a member of the Order, and there was some provision for some frater or soror, as we are called, staying with him.

Maud Gonne was of course my chief interest; she had not left France for a long time now and was, I was told, ill again. I saw her, and our relations, which were friendly enough, had not our old intimacy.

I remember going with her to call upon some friend and noting that she mounted the stairs slowly and with difficulty. She had not gone on with her work in the Order, and was soon to withdraw altogether, disliking, she said, our absorption in biblical symbolism, but MacGregor Mathers was her firm admirer. I remember little of the time but that I went here and there murmuring the lines of my play, and Bergson came to call, very well dressed and very courteous. He was but an obscure professor and MacGregor Mathers was impatient. 'I have shown him all that my magic can do and I have no effect upon him.' Sometimes in the evening we would play a curious form of chess at which there should be four players. My partner would be Mrs Mathers, and Mathers would declare that he had a spirit for his. He would cover his eyes with his hands or gaze at the empty chair at the opposite corner of the board before moving his partner's piece. I found him a gay, companionable man, very learned in his own subject, but [without] the standards of a scholar. He would sometimes come down to breakfast with a Horace in his hands and sometimes with Macpherson's *Ossian*, and it made him angry to doubt the perfect authenticity of *Ossian*.

XXV

On my return from France came a performance of my play and it had a measure of success, keeping the stage in part perhaps from the kindness of the management, my friend Florence Farr, for nearly seven weeks. Presently the member of the Rhymers' Club introduced me to the lady I had seen between the two famous novelists, and a friendship I hope to keep till death began. In this book I cannot give her her real name—Diana Vernon sounds pleasantly in my ears and will suit her as well as any other. When I went to see her she said, 'So-and-so seemed disinclined to introduce us; after I saw your play I made up my mind to write to you if [I] could not meet you otherwise.' She had profound culture, a knowledge of French, English, and Italian literature, and seemed always at leisure. Her nature was gentle and contemplative, and she was content, it seems, to have no more of life than leisure and the talk of her friends. Her husband, whom I saw but once, was much older and seemed a little heavy, a little without life. As yet I did not know how utterly estranged they were. I told her of my love sorrow, indeed it was my obsession, never leaving by day or night.

XXX

I had received while at Sligo many letters from Diana Vernon, kind letters that gave me a sense of half-conscious excitement. I remember after one such letter asking some country woman to throw the tea leaves for me and my disappointment at the vagueness of the oracle. (I think Mary Battle, my uncle's second-sighted servant, was again ill and away.) She was to tell me later on that my letters were unconscious love-letters, and I was taken by surprise at the description. I do not know how long after my return the conversation that was to decide so much in my life took place. I had found the Rhymer who had introduced me under the influence of drink, speaking vaguely and with vague movements, and while we were speaking this recent memory came back. She spoke of her pagan life in a way that made me believe that she had had many lovers and loathed her life. I thought of that young man so nearly related. Here is the same weakness, I thought; two souls so distinguished and contemplative that the common world seems empty. What is there left but sanctity, or some satisfying affection, or mere dissipation?—'Folly the comforter,' some Elizabethan had called it. Her beauty, dark and still, had the nobility of defeated things, and how could it help but wring my heart? I took a fortnight to decide what I should do.

I was poor and it would be a hard struggle if I asked her [to] come away, and perhaps after all I would but add my tragedy to hers, for she might return to that evil life. But, after all, if I could not get the woman I loved, it would be a comfort even but for a little while to devote myself to another. No doubt my excited senses had their share in the argument, but it was an unconscious one. At the end of the fortnight I asked her to leave home with me. She became very gay and joyous and a few days later praised me [for] what she thought my beautiful tact in giving at the moment but a brother's kiss. Doubtless at the moment I was exalted above the senses, and yet I do not [think] I knew any better way of kissing, for when on our first railway journey together—we were to spend the day at Kew—she gave me the long passionate kiss of love I was startled and a little shocked.

Presently I told something of my thoughts during that fortnight, and she [was] perplexed and ashamed that I should have had such imagination of her. Her wickedness had never gone further than her own mind; I would be her first lover. We decided that we should be but friends till she could leave her home for mine, but agreed to wait until her mother, a very old woman, had died. We decided to consult each a woman friend that we might be kept to these resolutions, as sponsors of our adventure, and for nearly a year met in railway carriages and at picture galleries and occasionally at her house. At Dulwich Gallery she taught me to care for Watteau—she too was of Pater's school—and at the National Gallery for the painter who pleased her best of all, Mantegna. I wrote her several poems, all curiously elaborate in style, 'The Shadowy Horses', and—— and——, and thought I was once more in love. I noticed that she was like the mild heroines of my plays. She seemed a part of myself.

I noticed that she did not talk so well as when I had at first known her, her mind seemed more burdened, but she would show in her movements an unforeseen youth; she seemed to have gone back to her twentieth year. For a short time, a few months I think, I shared a flat with Arthur Symons in the Temple. Symons knew I had such a friend and plan, but did [not] know her name. He indeed met my friend somewhere in society and asked if he might call, and came back with her praises. At last she and her sponsor were to come to tea. I do not think I had asked Symons, for I went myself to buy the cake. As I came home with the parcel I began to think of Maud Gonne till my thought was interrupted by my finding the door locked. I had forgotten the key and I went off in a great fuss to find a locksmith and found instead a man who climbed along the roof and in at an attic window.

That night at twelve o'clock I said to Symons, who had just come in, 'Did I ever tell you about Maud Gonne?' and till two or three in the morning I spoke of my love for her. Of all the men I have known he was the best listener; he could listen as a woman listens, never meeting one's thought as a man does with a rival thought, but taking up what one said and changing [it], giving it as it were flesh and bone. A couple of days later I got a wild letter from Maud Gonne, who was in Dublin. 'Was I ill? Had some accident happened?' On a day that was, I found, the day I had had those guests and lost the key, I had walked into the room in her hotel where she was sitting with friends. At first she thought I was really there, but presently on finding that no one else saw me knew that it was my ghost. She told me to return at twelve that night and I vanished. At twelve I had stood, dressed in some strange, priest-like costume, at her bedside and brought her soul away, and we had wandered round the cliffs [of] Howth where we had been together years before. I remember one phrase very clearly, 'It was very sad, and all the seagulls were asleep.' All my old love had returned and began to struggle with the new.

Presently I was asked to call and see my friend's sponsor. She condemned our idea of going away from home. There were various arguments that I cannot recall without perhaps, against my will, revealing Diana Vernon's true name. My sponsor came to see me and used the same arguments, and both, people of the world, advised us to live together without more ado. Then Diana Vernon tried to get a separation from the husband who had for her, she believed, aversion or indifference. 'He ceased to pay court to me from the day of our marriage,' she had said. He was deeply distressed and became ill, and she gave up the project and said to me, 'It will be kinder to deceive him.' Our senses were engaged now, and though we spoke of parting it was but to declare it impossible. I took my present rooms at Woburn Buildings and furnished them very meagrely with such cheap furniture as I could throw away without regret as I grew more prosperous. She came with me to make every purchase, and I remember an embarrassed conversation in the presence of some Tottenham Court [Road] shop man upon the width of the bed—every inch increased the expense.

At last she came to me in I think January of my thirtieth year, and I was impotent from nervous excitement. The next day we met at the British Museum—we were studying together—and I wondered that there seemed no change in me or in her. A week later she came to me again, and my nervous excitement was so painful that it seemed best but to sit over our tea and talk. I do not think we kissed each other except at the moment of her leaving. She understood instead of, as another would, changing liking for dislike—was only troubled by my trouble. My nervousness did not return again and we had many days of happiness. It will always be a grief to me that I could not give the love that was her beauty's right, but she was too near my soul, too salutary and wholesome to my inmost being. All our lives long, as da Vinci says, we long, thinking it is but the moon that we long [for], for our destruction, and how, when we meet [it] in the shape of a most fair woman, can we do less than leave all others for her? Do we not seek our dissolution upon her lips?

My liaison lasted but a year, interrupted by one journey to Italy upon her part and by one of mine also to Paris. I had a struggle to earn my living, and that made it harder for me, I was so often preoccupied when she came. Then Maud Gonne wrote to me; she was in London and would I come to dine? I dined with her and my trouble increased—she certainly had no thought of the mischief she was doing. And at last one morning instead of reading much love poetry, as my way was to bring the right mood round, I wrote letters. My friend found my mood did not answer hers and burst into tears. 'There is someone else in your heart,' she said. It was the breaking between us for many years.

XL

On a visit to Dr Hyde I had seen the Castle Rock, as it was called, in Lough Key. There is this small island entirely covered by what was a still habitable but empty castle. The last man who had lived there had been Dr Hyde's father who, when a young man, lived there for a few weeks. All round were the wooded and hilly shores, a place of great beauty. I believed that the castle could be hired for little money, and had long been dreaming of making it an Irish Eleusis or Samothrace. An obsession more constant than anything but my love itself was the need of mystical rites—a ritual system of evocation and meditation—to reunite the perception of the spirit, of the divine, with natural beauty. I believed that instead of thinking of Judea as holy we should [think] our own land holy, and most holy where most beautiful. Commerce and manufacture had made the world ugly; the death of pagan nature-worship had robbed visible beauty of its inviolable sanctity. I was convinced that all lonely and lovely places were crowded with invisible beings and that it would be possible to communicate with them. I meant to initiate young men and women in this worship, which would unite the radical truths of Christianity to those of a more ancient world, and to use the Castle Rock for their occasional retirement from the world.

For years to come it was in my thought, as in much of my writing, to seek also to bring again in[to] imaginative life the old sacred places—Slievenamon, Knocknarea—all that old reverence that hung—above all—about conspicuous hills. But I wished by my writings and those of the school I hoped to found to have a secret symbolical relation to these mysteries, for in that way, I thought, there will be a greater richness, a greater claim upon the love of the soul, doctrine without exhortation and rhetoric. Should not religion hide within the work of art as God is within His world, and how can the interpreter do more than whisper? I did not wish to compose rites as if for the theatre. They must in their main outline be the work of invisible hands.

My own seership was, I thought, inadequate; it was to be Maud Gonne's work and mine. Perhaps that was why we had been thrown together. Were there not strange harmonies amid discord? My outer nature was passive—but for her I should never perhaps have left my desk—but I knew my spiritual nature was passionate, even violent. In her all this was reversed, for it was her spirit only that was gentle and passive and full of charming fantasy, as though it touched the world only with the point of its finger. When I had first met her I had used as a test the death symbol, imagining it in my own mind, but not wishing to alarm her had asked that it should take the form not of a human but of a dog's skull. She said, 'I see a figure holding out its hand with a skull on it. No, there is a bruise on the hand, but I was compelled to say it was a skull.' I, who could not influence her actions, could dominate her inner being. I could therefore use her clairvoyance to produce forms that would arise from both minds, though mainly seen by one, and escape therefore from what is mere[ly] personal. There would be, as it were, a spiritual birth from the soul of a man and a woman. I knew that the incomprehensible life could select from our memories and, I believed, from the memory of the race itself; could realize of ourselves, beyond personal predilection, all it required, of symbol and of myth. I believed we were about to attain a revelation.

Maud Gonne entirely shared these ideas, and I did not doubt that in carrying them out I should win her for myself. Politics were merely a means of meeting, but this was a link so perfect that [it] would restore at once, even [after] a quarrel, the sense of intimacy. At every moment of leisure we obtained in vision long lists of symbols. Various trees corresponded to cardinal points, and the old gods and heroes took their places gradually in a symbolic fabric that had for its centre the four talismans of the Tuatha de Danaan, the sword, the stone, the spear and the cauldron, which related themselves in my mind with the suits of the Tarot. George Pollexfen, though already an old man, shared my plans, and his slow and difficult clairvoyance added certain symbols. He and Maud Gonne only met once—in politics he was an extreme Unionist—but he and she worked with each other's symbols and I did much of the work in his house. The forms became very continuous in my thoughts, and when AE came to stay at Coole he asked who was the white jester he had seen about the corridors. It was a form I associated with the god Aengus.

It was a time of great personal strain and sorrow. Since my mistress had left me, no other woman had come into my life, and for nearly seven years none did. I was tortured by sexual desire and disappointed love. Often as I walked in the woods at Coole it would have been a relief to have screamed aloud. When desire became an unendurable torture, I would masturbate, and that, no matter how moderate I was, would make me ill. It never occurred to me to seek another love. I would repeat to myself again and again the last confession of Lancelot, and indeed it was my greatest pride, 'I have loved a queen beyond measure and exceeding long.' I was never before or since so miserable as in those years that followed my first visit to Coole. In the second as during the first visit my nervous system was worn out. The toil of dressing in the morning exhausted me, and Lady Gregory began to send me cups of soup when I was called.

Instead of the work which I could not make myself do, I began with her that great collection of faery belief which is now passing through the press. I lived amid mystery. It seemed as if these people possessed an ancient knowledge. Ah, if we could but speak face to face with those they spoke to. 'That old man,' Lady Gregory said to me of an old man who passed us in the wood, 'may have the mystery of the ages.' I began to have visions and dreams full of wisdom or beauty. Much of my thought since is founded upon certain sentences that came in this way. Once I asked when going to sleep what was the explanation of those curious tales of people 'away', of which Lady Gregory [and] I had so many. In all these tales some man, woman, or child was believed to be carried off bodily by the faery world, a changeling, some old man or woman perhaps, or perhaps [a] mere heap of shavings bewitched into their likeness, being left instead. I awoke enough to know that I lay in bed and had the familiar objects round, but to hear a strange voice speaking through my lips: 'We make an image of him who sleeps, and it is not him who sleeps but it is like him who sleeps, and we call it Emmanuel.'

I was crossing one afternoon a little stream, and as I leaped I felt an emotion very strange to me—for all my thoughts were pagan—a sense of utter dependence on the divine will. It was over in an instant, and I said to myself, 'That is the way Christians feel.' That night I seemed to wake in my bed to hear a voice saying, 'The love of God for every soul is infinite, for every soul is unique; no other soul can satisfy the same need in God.' At other times I received fragments of poems, partly hearing and partly seeing. I saw in a dream a young shepherdess among many goats and sheep.

Somebody passed and spoke the name of some young man whom she had never seen. In my dream she stood up and said good-bye to each goat and sheep by name, and set out upon a journey. While I saw I seemed to hear also at moments the words [of] the poem, but only one sentence remained with me: 'She had but just heard his name, and yet it seemed as if he had long lain between her arms.'

Sometimes as I awoke marvellous illuminated pages seemed to be held before [me], with symbolic pictures that seemed profound, but when I tried to read the text all would vanish or but a sentence remain. I remember, 'The secret of the world is so simple that it could be written on a blade of grass with the juice of a berry'; and 'The rivers of Eden are in the midst of our rivers.' Sometimes when I lay in bed seeming awake, but always on my back as one lies when in nightmare, but with a feeling of wonder and delight, I would see forms at my bedside: once a fair woman who said she was Aedain, and both man and woman; and once a young boy and a young girl dressed in olive green, with sad, gentle faces; once my mother holding a cup in her hand; once a woman with an Elizabethan ruff.

A sexual dream was very rare, I neither then nor at any other time told the woman I loved to come to me [in] such a dream; I think I surrounded her with too great reverence and fear. One night I heard a voice, while I lay on my back, say I would be shown a secret, the secret of life and of death, but I must not speak of it. The room seemed to brighten and as I looked towards the foot of the bed I saw that it was changed into precious stones and yet these stones had a familiar look—they reminded me of the raised glass fruit on the bottles of lime-juice in my childhood. I never associated this growing brightness with sex, until all became suddenly dark and I found I had emitted seed.

I dreamed that I was lying on my back in a great stone trough in a great round house. I knew it was an initiation, and a wind was blowing over [me], I think from the feet up. Round me stood forms I could not see, and certain currents of influence were being directed through my eyes and various points of my body. These influences were painful. I heard a voice say, 'We are doing this to find out if it is worth going on doing this.' I knew my fitness for initiation was being questioned. Another night I thought I was taken out of my body and into a world of light, and while in this light, which was also complete happiness, I was told I would now be shown the passage of the soul at its incarnation. I saw the mystic elements gather about my soul in a certain order, a whole elaborate process, but the details vanished as I awoke. Little remained but a sentence I seemed to have spoken to myself: 'Beauty is becoming beautiful objects, and truth is becoming truths.'

I found I could call dreams by my symbols, though I think the most profound came unsought, and I would go to sleep, say with a spray of apple blossoms on my pillow. Sometimes, when I had gone to sleep with the endeavour to send my soul to that of Maud Gonne, using some symbol, which I forget, I would wake dreaming of a shower of precious stones. Sometimes she would have some corresponding experience in Paris and upon the same night, but always with more detail. I thought we became one in a world of emotion eternalized by its own intensity and purity, and that this world had for its symbol precious stones. No physical, sexual sensation ever accompanied these dreams and I noticed that once the excitement of the genital ceased, a visionary form, that of Aedain, approached.

I tried to describe some vision to Lady Gregory, and to my great surprise could not. I felt a difficulty in articulation and became confused. I had wanted to tell her of some beautiful sight, and could see no reason for this. I remembered then what I had read of mystics not being always [able] to speak, and remembered some tale of a lecturer on mysticism having to stop in the middle of a sentence. Even to this moment, though I can sometimes speak without difficulty, I am more often unable to. I am a little surprised that I can write what I please.

XLIII

I joined Maud Gonne from time to time, once at Belfast, where she [had] gone on some political mission, sometimes at Paris, often in Dublin. In Dublin I never went to the same hotel, fearing to compromise her, though she often laughed at my scruple. Once she complained that she saw too much of me. 'I do not say', she said, 'that the crowds are in love with me, but they would hate anybody who was.' But I never failed to get my letter saying when we could meet. One morning I woke in my hotel somewhere near Rutland Square with the fading vision of her face bending over mine and the knowledge that she had just kissed me. I joined her after breakfast in the Nassau Hotel. We were to spend the day together and visit in the afternoon the old Fenian leader, James Stephens. She said, 'Had you a strange dream last night?' I said, 'I dreamed this morning for the first time in my life that you kissed me.' She made no answer, but late that night when dinner was over and I was about to return home she said, 'I will tell you now what happened. When I fell asleep last night I saw standing at my bedside a great spirit. He took me to a great throng of spirits, and you were among them. My hand was put into yours and I was told that we were married. After that I remember nothing.' Then and there for the first time with the bodily mouth, she kissed me.

The next day I found her sitting very gloomily over the fire. 'I should not have spoken to you in that way,' she said, 'for I can never be your wife in reality.' I said, 'Do you love anyone else?' and she said 'No' but added that there was somebody else, and that she had to be a moral nature for two. Then bit by bit came out the story of her life, things I had heard all twisted awry by scandal, and disbelieved.

She had met in the South of France the French Boulangist deputy, Millevoye, while staying with a relative in her nineteenth year, and had at once and without any urging on his part fallen in love with him. She then returned to Dublin where her father had a military command. She had sat one night over the fire thinking over her future life. She longed to have control over her own life, and chance discovery of some book on magic among her father's books had made her believe that the Devil, if she prayed to him, might help her. He was rather a real personage to her, for in her earlier girlhood she had wanted to join a convent. She asked the Devil to give her control of her own life and offered in return her soul. At that moment the clock struck twelve, and she felt of a sudden that the prayer had been heard and answered. Within a fortnight her father died suddenly, and she was stricken with remorse.

She had control of her life now, and when she was of age settled in Paris, and after some months became Millevoye's mistress. She was often away from him, for sexual love soon began to repel her, but was for all that very much in love. Then he failed her in various ways. But [she] gave me no coherent account and when I asked some questions clenched her hands together and said it was not well to speak of such things. He had, I discovered, at one time urged her to become the mistress of one man to help his political projects, and that she had refused. Then a little boy was born, the adopted child I had been told of—she thought that sexual love was only justified by children. If the boy had not died, she would have broken with Millevoye altogether and lived in Ireland. As it was, after its death she had thought of breaking with him, and had engaged herself for a week to someone else—I thought, I may have had that poor betrothal for my reward—but had broken it off. The idea came to her that the lost child might be reborn, and she had gone back to Millevoye, in the vault under the memorial chapel. A girl child was born, now two years old. Since the child's birth, I understood her to say amid so much broken speech, she and Millevoye had lived apart.

But she was necessary to him, 'She did not know what would happen to him if her influence was not there.' I wonder as I write these words if I rightly understood, if she had not [in] mind some service he might fall from, to a political ideal. I thought at the time that [she] was appeasing a troubled conscience by performing to the last tittle every duty, and Lady Gregory confirmed me later in this thought. And in all that followed I was careful to touch [her] as one might a sister. If she was to come to me, it must be from no temporary passionate impulse, but with the approval of her conscience. Many a time since then, as I lay awake at night, have I accused myself of acting, not as I thought from a high scruple, but from a dread of moral responsibility, and my thoughts have gone round and round, as do miserable thoughts, coming to no solution.

A little later, how many days I do not remember, we were sitting together when she said, 'I hear a voice saying, "You are about to receive the initiation of the spear." ' We became silent; a double vision unfolded itself, neither speaking till all was finished. She thought herself a great stone statue through which passed flame, and I felt myself becoming flame and mounting up through and looking out of the eyes of a great stone Minerva. Were the beings which stand behind human life trying to unite us, or had we brought it by our own dreams? She was now always very emotional, and would kiss me very tenderly, but when I spoke of marriage on the eve of her leaving said, 'No, it seems to me impossible.' And then, with clenched hands, 'I have a horror and terror of physical love.' Lady Gregory was in Venice, but had come home at once on receiving from me an incoherent letter. She offered me money to travel, and told me not to leave Maud Gonne till I had her promise of marriage, but I said, 'No, I am too exhausted; I can do no more.'

FROM Journal

(WRITTEN 1909–30, PUBLISHED 1972)

10

Today the thought came to me that PIAL never really understands my plans, or nature, or ideas. Then came the thought, what matter? How much of the best I have done and still do is but the attempt to explain myself to her? If she understood, I should lack a reason for writing, and one never can have too many reasons for doing what is so laborious.

34

There is a relation between discipline and the theatrical sense. If we cannot imagine ourselves as different from what we are and try to assume that second self, we cannot impose a discipline upon ourselves, though we may accept one from others. Active virtue as distinguished from the passive acceptance of a current code is therefore theatrical, consciously dramatic, the wearing of a mask. It is the condition of arduous full life. One constantly notices in very active natures a tendency to pose, or a preoccupation with the effect they are producing if the pose has become a second self. One notices this in Plutarch's heroes, and every now and then in some modern who has tried to live by classical ideas, in Oscar Wilde, for instance, and less obviously in men like Walt Whitman. Wordsworth is so often flat and heavy partly because his moral sense has no theatrical element, it is an obedience, a discipline which he has not created. This increases his popularity with the better sort of journalists, the *Spectator* writers, for instance, with all who are part of the machine and yet care for poetry.

35

All my life I have been haunted with the idea that the poet should know all classes of men as one of themselves, that he should combine the greatest possible personal realization with the greatest possible knowledge of the speech and circumstance of the world. Fifteen or twenty years ago I remember longing, with this purpose, to disguise myself as a peasant and wander through the West, and then shipping as a sailor. But when one shrinks from even talking business with a stranger, and is unnatural till one knows a man for months, because one underrates or overrates all unknown people, one cannot adventure far. The artist grows more and more distinct, more and more a being in his own right as it were, but more and more loses grasp of the always more complex world. Some day setting out to find knowledge, like some pilgrim to the Holy Land, he will become the most romantic of all characters. He will play with all masks.

36

Tragedy is passion alone and, instead of character, it gets form from motives, the wandering of passion; while comedy is the clash of character. Eliminate character from comedy and you get farce. Farce is bound together by incident alone. (Eliminate passion from tragedy and you get melodrama.) In practice most works are mixed: Shakespeare being tragicomedy. Comedy is joyous because all assumption of a part, of a personal mask, whether the individualized face of comedy or the grotesque face of farce, is a display of energy, and all energy is joyous. A poet creates tragedy from his own soul, that soul which is alike in all men, and at moments it has no joy, as we understand that word, for the soul is an exile and without will. It attains to ecstasy, which is from the contemplation of things which are vaster than the individual and imperfectly seen, perhaps, by all those that still live. The masks of tragedy contain neither character nor personal energy. They are allied to decoration and to the abstract figures of Egyptian temples. Before the mind can look out of their eyes the active will perishes, hence their sorrowful calm. Joy is of the will which does things, which overcomes obstacles, which is victorious. The soul only knows changes of state. These changes of state, or this gradually enlarging consciousness, is the self-realization of modern culture. I think the motives of tragedy are connected more with these changes of state than with action. I feel this but cannot see my way clearly. But I am hunting truth too far into its thicket. It is my business to keep close to the impression of the senses, and to daily thought. Yet is not always the tragic ecstasy some realization or fulfilment of the soul in itself, some slow or sudden expansion of it like an overflowing well? Is not that what we mean by beauty?

50 (On 6 and 7 of month ♂♂♃ ♃p)

Feb. 4 [1909]. This morning I got a letter telling me of Lady Gregory's illness. I did not recognize her son's writing at first, and my mind wandered, I suppose because I am not well. I thought my mother was ill and that my sister was asking me to come at once: then I remembered that my mother died years ago and that more than kin was at stake. She has been to me mother, friend, sister and brother. I cannot realize the world without her—she brought to my wavering thoughts steadfast nobility. All day the thought of losing her is like a conflagration in the rafters. Friendship is all the house I have.

61

Feb. 12 [1909]. By implication the philosophy of Irish faery lore declares that all power is from the body, all intelligence from the spirit. Western civilization, religion and magic alike insist on power and therefore body and these three doctrines—efficient rule, the Incarnation, and thaumaturgy. Eastern asceticism answers to these with indifference to rule, scorn of the flesh, contemplation of the formless. Western minds who follow the Eastern way become weak and vapoury because they become unfit for the work forced upon them by Western life. Every symbol is an invocation which produces its equivalent expression in all worlds. The Incarnation involved modern science and modern efficiency and also modern lyric feeling which gives body to the most spiritual emotions. It produced a solidification of all things that grew from the individual will. It did not, however, produce the idea of the State; that comes from another evocation, polytheistic Greece and Rome. The historical truth of the Incarnation is indifferent, though the belief in that truth was essential to the power of the evocation. All civilization is held together by a series of suggestions made by an invisible hypnotist, artificially created illusions. The knowledge of reality is always by some means or other a secret knowledge. It is a kind of death.

78

Tonight Henderson said to me that he has always thought the bad luck of Ireland comes from hatred being the foundation of our politics. It is possible that emotion is an evocation and in ways beyond the senses alters events—creating good or evil luck. Certain individuals who hate much seem to be followed by violent events outside their control. Maud Gonne has been so followed always. It is possible to explain it by saying that hatred brings certain associates and causes a tendency to violent action. But there are times when there seems to be more than this—an actual stream of ill-luck. Certainly evocation with symbol has taught me that much that we think of as limited to certain obvious effects influences the whole being. A meditation on sunlight, for instance, affects the nature throughout, producing all that follows from the symbolical nature of the sun. Hate must, in the same way, make sterile, producing many effects which would follow from the meditation on a symbol capable of giving hate. Such symbol would produce not merely hate but associated effects. At least so I think. An emotion produces a symbol—sensual emotion dreams of water, for instance—just as a symbol produces emotion. The symbol is, however, perhaps more powerful than an emotion without symbol. Hatred as a basis of imagination, in ways which one could explain even without magic, helps to dry up the nature and makes the sexual abstinence, so common among young men and women in Ireland, possible. This abstinence reacts in its turn on the imagination, so that we get at last that strange eunuch-like tone and temper. For the last ten or twenty years there has been a perpetual drying of the Irish mind, with the resultant dust-cloud.

87

I cry out continually against my life. I have sleepless nights, thinking of the time that I must take from my poetry, from the harvest of the Lord—last night I could not sleep—and yet perhaps I must do all these things that I may set myself into a life of action, so as to express not the traditional poet but that forgotten thing, the normal active man.

107

I think all happiness depends on having the energy to assume the mask of some other self, that all joyous or creative life is a rebirth as something not oneself, something created in a moment and perpetually renewed in playing a game like that of a child where one loses the infinite pain of self-realization, a grotesque or solemn painted face put on that one may hide from the terrors of judgment, an imaginative Saturnalia that makes one forget reality. Perhaps all the sins and energies of the world are but the world's flight from an infinite blinding beam.

246

A good writer should be so simple that he has no faults, only sins.

October 1914

FROM *Pages from a Diary Written in Nineteen Hundred and Thirty*

(1944)

XXI

I think that two conceptions, that of reality as a congeries of beings, that of reality as a single being, alternate in our emotion and in history, and must always remain something that human reason, because subject always to one or the other, cannot reconcile. I am always, in all I do, driven to a moment which is the realisation of myself as unique and free, or to a moment which is the surrender to God of all that I am. I think that there are historical cycles wherein one or the other predominates, and that a cycle approaches where all shall [be] as particular and concrete as human intensity permits. Again and again I have tried to sing that approach—*The Hosting of the Sidhe,* 'O sweet everlasting voices', and those lines about 'The lonely, majestical multitude'—and have almost understood my intention. Again and again with remorse, a sense of defeat, I have failed when I would write of God, written coldly and conventionally. Could those two impulses, one as much a part of truth as the other, be reconciled, or if one or the other could prevail, all life would cease.

XL
THREE ESSENTIALS

I would found literature on the three things which Kant thought we must postulate to make life livable—Freedom, God, Immortality. The fading of these three before 'Bacon, Newton, Locke' has made literature decadent. Because Freedom is gone we have Stendhal's 'mirror dawdling down a lane'; because God has gone we have realism, the accidental, because Immortality is gone we can no longer write those tragedies which have always seemed to me alone legitimate—those that are a joy to the man who dies. Recent Irish literature has only delighted me in so far as it implies one or the other, in so far as it has been a defiance of all else, in so far as it has created those extravagant characters and emotions which have always arisen spontaneously from the human mind when it sees itself exempt from death and decay, responsible to its source alone.

James Joyce differs from Arnold Bennett and Galsworthy, let us say, because he can isolate the human mind and its vices as if in eternity. So could Synge, so could O'Casey till he caught the London contagion in *The Silver Tassie* and changed his mountain into a mouse. The movement began with A. E.'s first little verses made out of the Upanishads, and my *Celtic Twilight,* a bit of ornamental trivial needlework sewn on a prophetic fury got by Blake and Boehme. James Stephens has read the *Tain* in the light of the *Veda* but the time is against him and he is silent.

Between Berkeley's account of his exploration of certain Kilkenny laws which speak of the 'natives' came that intellectual crisis which led up to the sentence in the *Commonplace Book:* 'We Irish do not hold with this'. That was the birth of the national intellect and it caused the defeat in Berkeley's philosophical secret society of English materialism, the Irish Salamis.

The capture of a Spanish treasure ship in the time of Elizabeth made England a capitalist nation. A nation of country gentlemen, who were paid more in kind than in money and had traditional uses for their money, were to find themselves in control of free power over labour, a power that could be used anywhere and for anything.

*   *   *

The first nation that can affirm the three convictions affirmed by Kant as free powers—*i.e.* without associations of language, dogma, and ritual—will be able to control the moral energies of the soul.

Critical Writings

FROM Ideas of Good and Evil

(1903)

What is 'Popular Poetry'?
(1902)

I THINK IT was a Young Ireland Society that set my mind running on 'popular poetry.' We used to discuss everything that was known to us about Ireland, and especially Irish literature and Irish history. We had no Gaelic, but paid great honour to the Irish poets who wrote in English, and quoted them in our speeches. I could have told you at that time the dates of the birth and death, and quoted the chief poems, of men whose names you have not heard, and perhaps of some whose names I have forgotten. I knew in my heart that the most of them wrote badly, and yet such romance clung about them, such a desire for Irish poetry was in all our minds, that I kept on saying, not only to others but to myself, that most of them wrote well, or all but well. I had read Shelley and Spenser and had tried to mix their styles together in a pastoral play which I have now come to dislike much, and yet I do not think Shelley or Spenser ever moved me as did these poets. I thought one day—I can remember the very day when I thought it—'If somebody could make a style which would not be an English style and yet would be musical and full of colour, many others would catch fire from him, and we would have a really great school of ballad poetry in Ireland. If these poets, who have never ceased to fill the newspapers and the ballad-books with their verses, had a good tradition they would write beautifully and move everybody as they move me.' Then a little later on I thought, 'If they had

363

something else to write about besides political opinions, if more of them would write about the beliefs of the people like Allingham, or about old legends like Ferguson, they would find it easier to get a style.' Then with a deliberateness that still surprises me, for in my heart of hearts I have never been quite certain that one should be more than an artist, that even patriotism is more than an impure desire in an artist, I set to work to find a style and things to write about that the ballad-writers might be the better.

They are no better, I think, and my desire to make them so was, it may be, one of the illusions Nature holds before one, because she knows that the gifts she has to give are not worth troubling about. It is for her sake that we must stir ourselves, but we would not trouble to get out of bed in the morning, or to leave our chairs once we are in them, if she had not her conjuring bag. She wanted a few verses from me, and because it would not have seemed worth while taking so much trouble to see my books lie on a few drawing-room tables, she filled my head with thoughts of making a whole literature, and plucked me out of the Dublin art schools where I should have stayed drawing from the round, and sent me into a library to read bad translations from the Irish, and at last down into Connacht to sit by turf fires. I wanted to write 'popular poetry' like those Irish poets, for I believed that all good literatures were popular, and even cherished the fancy that the Adelphi melodrama, which I had never seen, might be good literature, and I hated what I called the coteries. I thought that one must write without care, for that was of the coteries, but with a gusty energy that would put all straight if it came out of the right heart. I had a conviction, which indeed I have still, that one's verses should hold, as in a mirror, the colours of one's own climate and scenery in their right proportion; and, when I found my verses too full of the reds and yellows Shelley gathered in Italy, I thought for two days of setting things right, not as I should now by making my rhythms faint and nervous and filling my images with a certain coldness, a certain wintry wildness, but by eating little and sleeping upon a board. I felt indignant with Matthew Arnold because he complained that somebody, who had translated Homer into a ballad measure, had tried to write epic to the tune of 'Yankee Doodle.' It seemed to me that it did not matter what tune one wrote to, so long as that gusty energy came often enough and strongly enough. And I delighted in Victor Hugo's book upon Shakespeare, because he abused critics and coteries and thought that Shakespeare wrote without care or premeditation and to please everybody. I would indeed have had every illusion had I believed in that straightforward logic, as of newspaper articles, which so tickles an ignorant ear; but I always knew that the line of Nature is crooked, that, though we dig the canal-beds as straight as we can, the rivers run hither and thither in their wildness.

From that day to this I have been busy among the verses and stories that the people make for themselves, but I had been busy a very little while before I knew that what we call 'popular poetry' never came from the people at all. Longfellow, and Campbell, and Mrs. Hemans, and Macaulay in his *Lays,* and Scott in his longer poems are the poets of a predominant portion of the middle class, of people who have unlearned the unwritten tradition which binds the unlettered, so long as they are masters of themselves, to the beginning of time and to the foundation of the world, and who have not learned the written tradition which has been established upon the unwritten. I became certain that Burns, whose greatness has been used to justify the littleness of others, was in part a poet of this portion of the middle class, because though the farmers he sprang from and lived among had been able to create a little tradition of their own, less a tradition of ideas than of speech, they had been divided by religious and political changes from the images and emotions which had once carried their memories backward thousands of years. Despite his expressive speech which sets him above all other popular poets, he has the triviality of emotion, the poverty of ideas, the imperfect sense of beauty of a poetry whose most typical expression is in Longfellow. Longfellow has his popularity, in the main, because he tells his story or his idea so that one needs nothing but his verses to understand it. No words of his borrow their beauty from those that used them before, and one can get all that there is in story and idea without seeing them as if moving before a half-faded curtain embroidered with kings and queens, their loves and battles and their days out hunting, or else with holy letters and images of so great antiquity that nobody can tell the god or goddess they would commend to an unfading memory. Poetry that is not 'popular poetry' presupposes, indeed, more than it says, though we, who cannot know what it is to be disinherited, only understand how much more, when we read it in its most typical expressions, in the *Epipsychidion* of Shelley, or in Spenser's description of the gardens of Adonis, or when we meet the misunderstandings of others. Go down into the street and read to your baker or your candlestick-maker any poem which is not 'popular poetry.' I have heard a baker, who was clever enough with his oven, deny that Tennyson could have known what he was writing when he wrote, 'Warming his five wits, the white owl in the belfry sits,' and once when I read out Omar Khayyám to one of the best of candlestick-makers, he said, 'What is the meaning of "I came like water and like wind I go"?' Or go down into the street with some thought whose bare meaning must be plain to everybody; take with you Ben Jonson's 'Beauty like sorrow dwelleth everywhere,' and find out how utterly its enchantment depends on an association of beauty with sorrow which written tradition has from the unwritten, which had it in its turn from ancient religion; or take with you these lines in whose bare meaning also there is nothing to stumble over, and find out what men lose who are not in love with Helen—

> Brightness falls from the air,
> Queens have died young and fair,
> Dust hath closed Helen's eye.

I pick my examples at random, for I am writing where I have no books to turn the pages of, but one need not go east of the sun or west of the moon in so simple a matter.

On the other hand, when Walt Whitman writes in seeming defiance of tradition, he needs tradition for protection, for the butcher and the baker and the candlestick-maker grow merry over him when they meet his work by chance. Nature, being unable to endure emptiness, has made them gather conventions which cannot hide that they are low-born things though copies, as from far off, of the dress and manners of the well-bred and the well-born. The gatherers mock all expression that is wholly unlike their own, just as little boys in the street mock at strangely dressed people and at old men who talk to themselves.

There is only one kind of good poetry, for the poetry of the coteries, which presupposes the written tradition, does not differ in kind from the true poetry of the people, which presupposes the unwritten tradition. Both are alike strange and obscure, and unreal to all who have not understanding, and both, instead of that manifest logic, that clear rhetoric of the 'popular poetry,' glimmer with thoughts and images whose 'ancestors were stout and wise,' 'anigh to Paradise' 'ere yet men knew the gift of corn.' It may be that we know as little of their descent as men knew of 'the man born to be a king' when they found him in that cradle marked with the red lion crest, and yet we know somewhere in the heart that they have been sung in temples, in ladies' chambers, and quiver with a recognition our nerves have been shaped to by a thousand emotions. If men did not remember or half remember impossible things, and, it may be, if the worship of sun and moon had not left a faint reverence behind it, what Aran fisher-girl would sing:—

'It is late last night the dog was speaking of you; the snipe was speaking of you in her deep marsh. It is you are the lonely bird throughout the woods; and that you may be without a mate until you find me.

'You promised me and you said a lie to me, that you would be before me where the sheep are flocked. I gave a whistle and three hundred cries to you; and I found nothing there but a bleating lamb.

'You promised me a thing that was hard for you, a ship of gold under a silver mast; twelve towns and a market in all of them, and a fine white court by the side of the sea.

'You promised me a thing that is not possible; that you would give me gloves of the skin of a fish; that you would give me shoes of the skin of a bird, and a suit of the dearest silk in Ireland.

'My mother said to me not to be talking with you, to-day or to-morrow or on Sunday. It was a bad time she took for telling me that, it was shutting the door after the house was robbed. . . .

'You have taken the east from me, you have taken the west from me, you have taken what is before me and what is behind me; you have taken the moon, you have taken the sun from me, and my fear is great you have taken God from me.'

The Gael of the Scottish islands could not sing his beautiful song over a bride, had he not a memory of the belief that Christ was the only man who measured six feet and not a little more or less, and was perfectly shaped in all other ways, and if he did not remember old symbolical observances:—

> I bathe thy palms
> In showers of wine,
> In the cleansing fire,

In the juice of raspberries,
In the milk of honey.

  •   •   •   •   •

Thou art the joy of all joyous things,
Thou art the light of the beam of the sun,
Thou art the door of the chief of hospitality,
Thou art the surpassing pilot star,
Thou art the step of the deer of the hill,
Thou art the step of the horse of the plain,
Thou art the grace of the sun rising,
Thou art the loveliness of all lovely desires.

The lovely likeness of the Lord
Is in thy pure face,
The loveliest likeness that was upon earth.

I soon learned to cast away one other illusion of 'popular poetry.' I learned from the people themselves, before I learned it from any book, that they cannot separate the idea of an art or a craft from the idea of a cult with ancient technicalities and mysteries. They can hardly separate mere learning from witchcraft, and are fond of words and verses that keep half their secret to themselves. Indeed, it is certain that before the counting-house had created a new class and a new art without breeding and without ancestry, and set this art and this class between the hut and the castle, and between the hut and the cloister, the art of the people was as closely mingled with the art of the coteries as was the speech of the people that delighted in rhythmical animation, in idiom, in images, in words full of far-off suggestion, with the unchanging speech of the poets.

Now I see a new generation in Ireland which discusses Irish literature and history in Young Ireland Societies, and societies with newer names, and there are far more than when I was a boy who would make verses for the people. They have the help, too, of a vigorous journalism, and this journalism sometimes urges them to desire the direct logic, the clear rhetoric of 'popular poetry.' It sees that Ireland has no cultivated minority, and it does not see, though it would cast out all English things, that its literary ideal belongs more to England than to other countries. I have hope that the new writers will not fall into its illusion, for they write in Irish, and for a people the counting-house has not made forgetful. Among the seven or eight hundred thousand who have had Irish from the cradle, there is, perhaps, nobody who has not enough of the unwritten tradition to know good verses from bad ones, if he have enough mother-wit. Among all that speak English in Australia, in America, in Great Britain, are there many more than the ten thousand the prophet saw who have enough of the written tradition education has set in room of the unwritten to know good verses from bad ones, even though their mother-wit has made them Ministers of the Crown or what you will? Nor can things be better till that ten thousand have gone hither and thither to preach their faith that 'the imagination is the man himself,' and that the world as imagination sees it is the durable world, and have won men as did the disciples of Him who—

> His seventy disciples sent
> Against religion and government.

FROM Magic
(1901)

I

I believe in the practice and philosophy of what we have agreed to call magic, in what I must call the evocation of spirits, though I do not know what they are, in the power of creating magical illusions, in the visions of truth in the depths of the mind when the eyes are closed; and I believe in three doctrines, which have, as I think, been handed down from early times, and been the foundations of nearly all magical practices. These doctrines are:—

(1) That the borders of our mind are ever shifting, and that many minds can flow into one another, as it were, and create or reveal a single mind, a single energy.

(2) That the borders of our memories are as shifting, and that our memories are a part of one great memory, the memory of Nature herself.

(3) That this great mind and great memory can be evoked by symbols.

I often think I would put this belief in magic from me if I could, for I have come to see or to imagine, in men and women, in houses, in handicrafts, in nearly all sights and sounds, a certain evil, a certain ugliness, that comes from the slow perishing through the centuries of a quality of mind that made this belief and its evidences common over the world.

VIII

I have now described that belief in magic which has set me all but unwilling among those lean and fierce minds who are at war with their time, who cannot accept the days as they pass, simply and gladly; and I look at what I have written with some alarm, for I have told more of the ancient secret than many among my fellow-students think it right to tell. I have come to believe so many strange things because of experience, that I see little reason to doubt the truth of many things that are beyond my experience; and it may be that there are beings who watch over that ancient secret, as all tradition affirms, and resent, and perhaps avenge, too fluent speech. They say in the Aran Islands that if you speak over-much of the things of Faery your tongue becomes like a stone, and it seems to me, though doubtless naturalistic reason would call it auto-suggestion or the like, that I have often felt my tongue become just so heavy and clumsy. More than once, too, as I wrote this very essay I have become uneasy, and have torn up some paragraph, not for any literary reason, but because some incident or some symbol that would perhaps have meant nothing to the reader, seemed, I know not why, to belong to hidden things. Yet I must write or be of no account to any cause, good or evil; I must commit what merchandise of wisdom I have to this ship of written speech, and after all, I have many a time watched it put out to sea with not less alarm when all the speech was rhyme. We who write, we who bear witness, must often hear our hearts cry out against us, complaining because of their hidden things, and I know not but he who speaks of wisdom may sometimes, in the change that is coming upon the world, have to fear the anger of the people of Faery, whose country is the heart of the world—'The Land of the Living Heart.' Who can keep always to the little pathway between speech and silence, where one meets none but discreet revelations? And surely, at whatever risk, we must cry out that imagination is always seeking to remake the world according to the impulses and the patterns in that Great Mind, and that Great Memory? Can there be anything so important as to cry out that what we call romance, poetry, intellectual beauty, is the only signal that the supreme Enchanter, or some one in His councils, is speaking of what has been, and shall be again, in the consummation of time?

William Blake and the Imagination
(1897)

THERE HAVE been men who loved the future like a mistress, and the future mixed her breath into their breath and shook her hair about them, and hid them from the understanding of their times. William Blake was one of these men, and if he spoke confusedly and obscurely it was because he spoke of things for whose speaking he could find no models in the world he knew. He announced the religion of art, of which no man dreamed in the world he knew; and he understood it more perfectly than the thousands of subtle spirits who have received its baptism in the world we know, because in the beginning of important things—in the beginning of love, in the beginning of the day, in the beginning of any work—there is a moment when we understand more perfectly than we understand again until all is finished. In his time educated people believed that they amused themselves with books of imagination, but that they 'made their souls' by listening to sermons and by doing or by not doing certain things. When they had to explain why serious people like themselves honoured the great poets greatly they were hard put to it for lack of good reasons. In our time we are agreed that we 'make our souls' out of some one of the great poets of ancient times, or out of Shelley or Wordsworth, or Goethe or Balzac, or Flaubert, or Count Tolstoy, in the books he wrote before he became a prophet and fell into a lesser order, or out of Mr. Whistler's pictures, while we amuse ourselves, or, at best, make a poorer sort of soul, by listening to sermons or by doing or by not doing certain things. We write of great writers, even of writers whose beauty would once have seemed an unholy beauty, with rapt sentences like those our fathers kept for the beatitudes and mysteries of the Church; and no matter what we believe with our lips, we believe with our hearts that beautiful things, as Browning said in his one prose essay that was not in verse, have 'lain burningly on the Divine hand,' and that when time has begun to wither, the Divine hand will fall heavily on bad taste and vulgarity. When no man believed these things William Blake believed them, and began that preaching against the Philistines which is as the preaching of the Middle Ages against the Saracen.

He had learned from Jacob Boehme and from old alchemist writers that imagination was the first emanation of divinity, 'the body of God,' 'the Divine members,' and he drew the deduction, which they did not draw, that the imaginative arts were therefore the greatest of Divine revelations, and that the sympathy with all living things, sinful and righteous alike, which the imaginative arts awaken, is that forgiveness of sins commanded by Christ. The reason, and by the reason he meant deductions from the observations of the senses, binds us to mortality because it binds us to the senses, and divides us from each other by showing us our clashing interests; but imagination divides us from mortality by the immortality of beauty, and binds us to each other by opening the secret doors of all hearts. He cried again and again that everything that lives is holy, and that nothing is unholy except things that do not live—lethargies, and cruelties, and timidities, and that denial of imagination which is the root they grew from in old times. Passions, because most living, are most holy—and this was a scandalous paradox in his time—and man shall enter eternity borne upon their wings.

And he understood this so literally that certain drawings to *Vala*, had he carried them beyond the first faint pencillings, the first faint washes of colour, would have been a pretty scandal to his time and to our time. The sensations of this 'foolish body,' this 'phantom of the earth and water,' were in themselves but half-living things, 'vegetative' things, but passion, that 'eternal glory,' made them a part of the body of God.

This philosophy kept him more simply a poet than any poet of his time, for it made him content to express every beautiful feeling that came into his head without troubling about its utility or chaining it to any utility. Sometimes one feels, even when one is reading poets of a better time—Tennyson or Wordsworth, let us say—that they have troubled the energy and simplicity of their imaginative passions by asking whether they were for the helping or for the hindrance of the world, instead of believing that all beautiful things have 'lain burningly on the Divine hand.' But when one reads Blake, it is as though the spray of an inexhaustible fountain of beauty was blown into our faces, and not merely when one reads the *Songs of Innocence,* or the lyrics he wished to call 'Ideas of Good and Evil,' but when one reads those 'Prophetic Books' in which he spoke confusedly and obscurely because he spoke of things for whose speaking he could find no models in the world about him. He was a symbolist who had to invent his symbols; and his counties of England, with their correspondence to tribes of Israel, and his mountains and rivers, with their correspondence to parts of a man's body, are arbitrary as some of the symbolism in the *Axël* of the symbolist Villiers de l'Isle-Adam is arbitrary, while they mix incongruous things as *Axël* does not. He was a man crying out for a mythology, and trying to make one because he could not find one to his hand. Had he been a Catholic of Dante's time he would have been well content with Mary and the angels; or had he been a scholar of our time he would have taken his symbols where Wagner took his, from Norse mythology; or have followed, with the help of Professor Rhys, that pathway into Welsh mythology which he found in *Jerusalem;* or have gone to Ireland and chosen for his symbols the sacred mountains, along whose sides the peasant still sees enchanted fires, and the divinities which have not faded from the belief, if they have faded from the prayers, of simple hearts; and have spoken without mixing incongruous things because he spoke of things that had been long steeped in emotion; and have been less obscure because a traditional mythology stood on the threshold of his meaning and on the margin of his sacred darkness. If Enitharmon had been named Freia, or Gwydeon, or Dana, and made live in Ancient Norway, or Ancient Wales, or Ancient Ireland, we would have forgotten that her maker was a mystic; and the hymn of her harping, that is in *Vala,* would but have reminded us of many ancient hymns.

> The joy of woman is the death of her most best beloved,
> Who dies for love of her,
> In torments of fierce jealousy and pangs of adoration.
> The lovers' night bears on my song,
> And the nine spheres rejoice beneath my powerful control.

They sing unceasing to the notes of my immortal hand.
The solemn, silent moon
Reverberates the living harmony upon my limbs.
The birds and beasts rejoice and play,
And every one seeks for his mate to prove his inmost joy.

Furious and terrible they sport and red the nether deep.
The deep lifts up his rugged head,
And lost in infinite humming wings vanishes with a cry.
The fading cry is ever dying,
The living voice is ever living in its inmost joy.

The Symbolism of Poetry
(1900)

I

Symbolism, as seen in the writers of our day, would have no value
if it were not seen also, under one 'disguise or another, in every great
imaginative writer,' writes Mr. Arthur Symons in *The Symbolist
Movement in Literature,* a subtle book which I cannot praise as I
would, because it has been dedicated to me; and he goes on to show
how many profound writers have in the last few years sought for a
philosophy of poetry in the doctrine of symbolism, and how even in
countries where it is almost scandalous to seek for any philosophy
of poetry, new writers are following them in their search. We do not
know what the writers of ancient times talked of among themselves,
and one bull is all that remains of Shakespeare's talk, who was on the
edge of modern times; and the journalist is convinced, it seems, that
they talked of wine and women and politics, but never about their
art, or never quite seriously about their art. He is certain that no one
who had a philosophy of his art, or a theory of how he should write,
has ever made a work of art, that people have no imagination who
do not write without forethought and afterthought as he writes his
own articles. He says this with enthusiasm, because he has heard it
at so many comfortable dinner-tables, where some one had mentioned
through carelessness, or foolish zeal, a book whose difficulty had
offended indolence, or a man who had not forgotten that beauty is

an accusation. Those formulas and generalisations, in which a hidden sergeant has drilled the ideas of journalists and through them the ideas of all but all the modern world, have created in their turn a forgetfulness like that of soldiers in battle, so that journalists and their readers have forgotten, among many like events, that Wagner spent seven years arranging and explaining his ideas before he began his most characteristic music; that opera, and with it modern music, arose from certain talks at the house of one Giovanni Bardi of Florence; and that the Pléiade laid the foundations of modern French literature with a pamphlet. Goethe has said, 'a poet needs all philosophy, but he must keep it out of his work,' though that is not always necessary; and almost certainly no great art, outside England, where journalists are more powerful and ideas less plentiful than elsewhere, has arisen without a great criticism, for its herald or its interpreter and protector, and it may be for this reason that great art, now that vulgarity has armed itself and multiplied itself, is perhaps dead in England.

All writers, all artists of any kind, in so far as they have had any philosophical or critical power, perhaps just in so far as they have been deliberate artists at all, have had some philosophy, some criticism of their art; and it has often been this philosophy, or this criticism, that has evoked their most startling inspiration, calling into outer life some portion of the divine life, or of the buried reality, which could alone extinguish in the emotions what their philosophy or their criticism would extinguish in the intellect. They have sought for no new thing, it may be, but only to understand and to copy the pure inspiration of early times, but because the divine life wars upon our outer life, and must needs change its weapons and its movements as we change ours, inspiration has come to them in beautiful startling shapes. The scientific movement brought with it a literature which was always tending to lose itself in externalities of all kinds, in opinion, in declamation, in picturesque writing, in word-painting, or in what Mr. Symons has called an attempt 'to build in brick and mortar inside the covers of a book'; and now writers have begun to dwell upon the element of evocation, of suggestion, upon what we call the symbolism in great writers.

II

In 'Symbolism in Painting,' I tried to describe the element of symbolism that is in pictures and sculpture, and described a little the symbolism in poetry, but did not describe at all the continuous indefinable symbolism which is the substance of all style.

There are no lines with more melancholy beauty than these by Burns:—

> The white moon is setting behind the white wave,
> And Time is setting with me, O!

and these lines are perfectly symbolical. Take from them the whiteness of the moon and of the wave, whose relation to the setting of Time is too subtle for the intellect, and you take from them their beauty. But, when all are together, moon and wave and whiteness and setting Time and the last melancholy cry, they evoke an emotion which cannot be evoked by any other arrangement of colours and sounds and forms. We may call this metaphorical writing, but it is better to call it symbolical writing, because metaphors are not profound enough to be moving, when they are not symbols, and when they are symbols they are the most perfect of all, because the most subtle, outside of pure sound, and through them one can best find out what symbols are. If one begins the reverie with any beautiful lines that one can remember, one finds they are like those by Burns. Begin with this line by Blake:—

> The gay fishes on the wave when the moon sucks up the dew;

or these lines by Nash:—

> Brightness falls from the air,
> Queens have died young and fair,
> Dust hath closed Helen's eye;

or these lines by Shakespeare:—

> Timon hath made his everlasting mansion
> Upon the beached verge of the salt flood;
> Who once a day with his embossed froth
> The turbulent surge shall cover;

or take some line that is quite simple, that gets its beauty from its place in a story, and see how it flickers with the light of the many symbols that have given the story its beauty, as a sword-blade may flicker with the light of burning towers.

All sounds, all colours, all forms, either because of their preordained energies or because of long association, evoke indefinable and yet precise emotions, or, as I prefer to think, call down among us certain disembodied powers, whose footsteps over our hearts we call emotions; and when sound, and colour, and form are in a musical relation, a beautiful relation to one another, they become, as it were, one sound, one colour, one form, and evoke an emotion that is made out of their distinct evocations and yet is one emotion. The same relation exists between all portions of every work of art, whether it be an epic or a song, and the more perfect it is, and the more various and numerous the elements that have flowed into its perfection, the more powerful will be the emotion, the power, the god it calls among us. Because an emotion does not exist, or does not become perceptible and active among us, till it has found its expression, in colour or in sound or in form, or in all of these, and because no two modulations or arrangements of these evoke the same emotion, poets and painters and musicians, and in a less degree because their effects are momentary, day and night and cloud and shadow, are continually making and unmaking mankind. It is indeed only those things which seem useless or very feeble that have any power, and all those things that seem useful or strong, armies, moving wheels, modes of architecture, modes of government, speculations of the reason, would have been a little different if some mind long ago had not given itself to some emotion, as a woman gives herself to her lover, and shaped sounds or colours or forms, or all of these, into a musical relation, that their emotion might live in other minds. A little lyric evokes an emotion, and this emotion gathers others about it and melts into their being in the making of some great epic; and at last, needing an always less delicate body, or symbol, as it grows more powerful, it flows out, with all it has gathered, among the blind instincts of daily life, where it moves a power within powers, as one sees ring within ring in the stem of an old tree. This is maybe what Arthur O'Shaughnessy meant when he made his poets say they had built Nineveh with their sighing; and I am certainly never sure, when I hear of some war, or of some religious excitement, or of some new manufacture, or of anything else that fills the ear of the world, that it has not all happened because of something that a boy piped in Thessaly. I remember once telling a seeress to ask one among the gods who, as she believed, were standing about her in their symbolic bodies, what would come of a charming but seeming trivial labour of a friend, and the form answering, 'the devastation of peoples and the overwhelming of cities.' I doubt indeed if the crude circumstance of the world, which seems to create all our emotions, does more than reflect, as in multiplying mirrors, the emotions that have come to solitary men in moments of poetical contemplation; or that love itself would be more than an animal hunger but for the poet and his shadow the priest, for unless we believe that outer things are the reality, we must believe that the gross is the shadow of the subtle, that things are wise before they become foolish, and secret before they cry out in the market-place. Solitary men in moments of contemplation receive, as I think, the creative impulse from the lowest of the Nine Hierarchies, and so make and unmake mankind, and even the world itself, for does not 'the eye altering alter all'?

> Our towns are copied fragments from our breast;
> And all man's Babylons strive but to impart
> The grandeurs of his Babylonian heart.

III

The purpose of rhythm, it has always seemed to me, is to prolong the moment of contemplation, the moment when we are both asleep and awake, which is the one moment of creation, by hushing us with an alluring monotony, while it holds us waking by variety, to keep us in that state of perhaps real trance, in which the mind liberated from the pressure of the will is unfolded in symbols. If certain sensitive persons listen persistently to the ticking of a watch, or gaze persistently on the monotonous flashing of a light, they fall into the hypnotic trance; and rhythm is but the ticking of a watch made softer, that one must needs listen, and various, that one may not be swept beyond memory or grow weary of listening; while the patterns of the artist are but the monotonous flash woven to take the eyes in a subtler enchantment. I have heard in meditation voices that were forgotten the moment they had spoken; and I have been swept, when in more profound meditation, beyond all memory but of those things that came from beyond the threshold of waking life. I was writing once at a very symbolical and abstract poem, when my pen fell on the ground; and as I stooped to pick it up, I remembered some fantastic adventure that yet did not seem fantastic, and then another like adventure, and when I asked myself when these things had happened, I found that I was remembering my dreams for many nights. I tried to remember what I had done the day before, and then what I had done that morning; but all my waking life had perished from me, and it was only after a struggle that I came to remember it again, and as I did so that more powerful and startling life perished in its turn. Had my pen not fallen on the ground and so made me turn from the images that I was weaving into verse, I would never have known that meditation had become trance, for I would have been like one who does not know that he is passing through a wood because his eyes are on the pathway. So I think that in the making and in the understanding of a work of art, and the more easily if it is full of patterns and symbols and music, we are lured to the threshold of sleep, and it may be far beyond it, without knowing that we have ever set our feet upon the steps of horn or of ivory.

IV

Besides emotional symbols, symbols that evoke emotions alone,—and in this sense all alluring or hateful things are symbols, although their relations with one another are too subtle to delight us fully, away from rhythm and pattern,—there are intellectual symbols, symbols that evoke ideas alone, or ideas mingled with emotions; and outside the very definite traditions of mysticism and the less definite criticism of certain modern poets, these alone are called symbols. Most things belong to one or another kind, according to the way we speak of them and the companions we give them, for symbols, associated with ideas that are more than fragments of the shadows thrown upon the intellect by the emotions they evoke, are the playthings of the allegorist or the pedant, and soon pass away. If I say 'white' or 'purple' in an ordinary line of poetry, they evoke emotions so exclusively that I cannot say why they move me; but if I bring them into the same sentence with such obvious intellectual symbols as a cross or a crown of thorns, I think of purity and sovereignty. Furthermore, innumerable meanings, which are held to 'white' or to 'purple' by bonds of subtle suggestion, and alike in the emotions and in the intellect, move visibly through my mind, and move invisibly beyond the threshold of sleep, casting lights and shadows of an indefinable wisdom on what had seemed before, it may be, but sterility and noisy violence. It is the intellect that decides where the reader shall ponder over the procession of the symbols, and if the symbols are merely emotional, he gazes from amid the accidents and destinies of the world; but if the symbols are intellectual too, he becomes himself a part of pure intellect, and he is himself mingled with the procession. If I watch a rushy pool in the moonlight, my emotion at its beauty is mixed with memories of the man that I have seen ploughing by its margin, or of the lovers I saw there a night ago; but if I look at the moon herself and remember any of her ancient names and meanings, I move among divine people, and things that have shaken off our mortality, the tower of ivory, the queen of waters, the shining stag among enchanted woods, the white hare sitting upon the hilltop, the fool of Faery with his shining cup full of dreams, and it may be 'make a friend of one of these images of wonder,' and 'meet the Lord in the air.' So, too, if one is moved by Shakespeare, who is content with emotional symbols that he may come the nearer to our sympathy, one is mixed with the whole spectacle of the world; while if one is moved by Dante, or by the myth of Demeter, one is mixed into the shadow of God or of a goddess. So, too, one is furthest from symbols when one is busy doing this or that, but the soul moves among symbols and unfolds in symbols when trance, or madness, or deep meditation has withdrawn it from every impulse but its own. 'I then saw,' wrote Gérard de Nerval of his madness, 'vaguely drifting into form, plastic images of antiquity, which outlined themselves, became definite, and seemed to represent symbols of which I only seized the idea with difficulty.' In an earlier time he would have been of that multitude whose souls austerity withdrew, even more perfectly than madness could withdraw his soul, from hope and memory, from desire and regret, that they might reveal those processions of symbols that men bow to before altars, and woo with incense and offerings. But being of our time, he has been like Maeterlinck, like Villiers de l'Isle-Adam in *Axël*, like all who are preoccupied with intellectual symbols in our time, a foreshadower of the new sacred book, of which all the arts, as somebody has said, are beginning to dream. How can the arts overcome the slow dying of men's hearts that we call the progress of the world, and lay their hands upon men's heartstrings again, without becoming the garment of religion as in old times?

V

If people were to accept the theory that poetry moves us because of its symbolism, what change should one look for in the manner of our poetry? A return to the way of our fathers, a casting out of descriptions of nature for the sake of nature, of the moral law for the sake of the moral law, a casting out of all anecdotes and of that brooding over scientific opinion that so often extinguished the central flame in Tennyson, and of that vehemence that would make us do or not do certain things; or, in other words, we should come to understand that the beryl stone was enchanted by our fathers that it might unfold the pictures in its heart, and not to mirror our own excited faces, or the boughs waving outside the window. With this change of substance, this return to imagination, this understanding that the laws of art, which are the hidden laws of the world, can alone bind the imagination, would come a change of style, and we would cast out of serious poetry those energetic rhythms, as of a man running, which are the invention of the will with its eyes always on something to be done or undone; and we would seek out those wavering, meditative, organic rhythms, which are the embodiment of the imagination, that neither desires nor hates, because it has done with time, and only wishes to gaze upon some reality, some beauty; nor would it be any longer possible for anybody to deny the importance of form, in all its kinds, for although you can expound an opinion, or describe a thing, when your words are not quite well chosen, you cannot give a body to something that moves beyond the senses, unless your words are as subtle, as complex, as full of mysterious life, as the body of a flower or of a woman. The form of sincere poetry, unlike the form of the 'popular poetry,' may indeed be sometimes obscure, or ungrammatical as in some of the best of the *Songs of Innocence and Experience,* but it must have the perfections that escape analysis, the subtleties that have a new meaning every day, and it must have all this whether it be but a little song made out of a moment of dreamy indolence, or some great epic made out of the dreams of one poet and of a hundred generations whose hands were never weary of the sword.

Ireland and the Arts
(1901)

THE ARTS HAVE FAILED; fewer people are interested in them every generation. The mere business of living, of making money, of amusing oneself, occupies people more and more, and makes them less and less capable of the difficult art of appreciation. When they buy a picture it generally shows a long-current idea, or some conventional form that can be admired in that lax mood one admires a fine carriage in or fine horses in; and when they buy a book it is so much in the manner of the picture that it is forgotten, when its moment is over, as a glass of wine is forgotten. We who care deeply about the arts find ourselves the priesthood of an almost forgotten faith, and we must, I think, if we would win the people again, take upon ourselves the method and the fervour of a priesthood. We must be half humble and half proud. We see the perfect more than others, it may be, but we must find the passions among the people. We must baptize as well as preach.

The makers of religions have established their ceremonies, their form of art, upon fear of death, upon the hope of the father in his child, upon the love of man and woman. They have even gathered into their ceremonies the ceremonies of more ancient faiths, for fear a grain of the dust turned into crystal in some past fire, a passion that had mingled with the religious idea, might perish if the ancient ceremony perished. They have re-named wells and images and given new meanings to ceremonies of spring and midsummer and harvest. In very early days the arts were so possessed by this method that they were almost inseparable from religion, going side by side with it into all life. But, to-day, they have grown, as I think, too proud, too anxious to live alone with the perfect, and so one sees them, as I think, like charioteers standing by deserted chariots and holding broken reins in their hands, or seeking to go upon their way drawn by that sexual passion which alone remains to them out of the passions of the world. We should not blame them, but rather a mysterious tendency in things which will have its end some day. In England, men like William Morris, seeing about them passions so long separated from the perfect that it seemed as if they could not be changed until society had been changed, tried to unite the arts once more to life by uniting them to use. They advised painters to paint fewer pictures upon canvas, and to burn more of them on plates; and they tried to persuade sculptors that a candlestick might be as beautiful as a statue. But here in Ireland, when the arts have grown humble, they will find two passions ready to their hands, love of the Unseen Life and love of country. I would have a devout writer or painter often content himself with subjects taken from his religious beliefs; and if his religious beliefs are those of the majority, he may at last move hearts in every cottage; while even if his religious beliefs are those of some minority, he will have a better welcome than if he wrote of the rape of Persephone, or painted the burning of Shelley's body. He will have founded his work on a passion which will bring him to many besides those who have been trained to care for beautiful things by a special education. If he is a painter or a sculptor he will find churches awaiting his hand everywhere, and if he follows the masters of his craft our other passion will come into his work also, for he will show his Holy Family winding among hills like those of Ireland, and his Bearer of the Cross among faces copied from the faces of his own town. Our art teachers should urge their pupils into this work, for I can remember, when I was myself a Dublin art student, how I used to despond, when youthful ardour burned low, at the general indifference of the town.

But I would rather speak to those who, while moved in other things than the arts by love of country, are beginning to write, as I was some sixteen years ago, without any decided impulse to one thing more than another, and especially to those who are convinced, as I was convinced, that art is tribeless, nationless, a blossom gathered in No Man's Land. The Greeks looked within their borders, and we, like them, have a history fuller than any modern history of imaginative events; and legends which surpass, as I think, all legends but theirs in wild beauty, and in our land, as in theirs, there is no river or mountain that is not associated in the memory with some event or legend; while political reasons have made love of country, as I think, even greater among us than among them. I would have our writers and craftsmen of many kinds master this history and these legends, and fix upon their memory the appearance of mountains and rivers and make it all visible again in their arts, so that Irishmen, even though they had gone thousands of miles away, would still be in their own country. Whether they chose for the subject the carrying off of the Brown Bull or the coming of Patrick, or the political struggle of later times, the other world comes so much into it all that their love of it would move in their hands also, and as much, it may be, as in the hands of the Greek craftsmen. In other words, I would have Ireland re-create the ancient arts, the arts as they were understood in Judaea, in India, in Scandinavia, in Greece and Rome, in every ancient land; as they were understood when they moved a whole people and not a few people who have grown up in a leisured class and made this understanding their business.

I think that my reader will have agreed with most that I have said up till now, for we all hope for arts like these. I think indeed I first learned to hope for them myself in Young Ireland Societies, or in reading the essays of Davis. An Englishman, with his belief in progress, with his instinctive preference for the cosmopolitan literature of the last century, may think arts like these parochial, but they are the arts we have begun the making of.

I will not, however, have all my readers with me when I say that no writer, no artist, even though he choose Brian Borúmha or Saint Patrick for his subject, should try to make his work popular. Once he has chosen a subject he must think of nothing but giving it such an expression as will please himself. As Walt Whitman has written:—

> The oration is to the orator, the acting is to the actor and actress, not to the audience:
> And no man understands any greatness or goodness, but his own or the indication of his own.

He must make his work a part of his own journey towards beauty and truth. He must picture saint or hero, or hillside, as he sees them, not as he is expected to see them, and he must comfort himself, when others cry out against what he has seen, by remembering that no two men are alike, and that there is no 'excellent beauty without strangeness.' In this matter he must be without humility. He may, indeed, doubt the reality of his vision if men do not quarrel with him as they did with the Apostles, for there is only one perfection and only one search for perfection, and it sometimes has the form of the religious life and sometimes of the artistic life; and I do not think these lives differ in their wages, for 'The end of art is peace,' and out of the one as out of the other comes the cry: *Sero te amavi, Pulchritudo tam antiqua et tam nova! Sero te amavi!*

The Catholic Church is not the less the Church of the people because the Mass is spoken in Latin, and art is not less the art of the people because it does not always speak in the language they are used to. I once heard my friend Mr. Ellis say, speaking at a celebration in honour of a writer whose fame had not come till long after his death, 'It is not the business of a poet to make himself understood, but it is the business of the people to understand him. That they are at last compelled to do so is the proof of his authority.' And certainly if you take from art its martyrdom, you will take from it its glory. It might still reflect the passing modes of mankind, but it would cease to reflect the face of God.

If our craftsmen were to choose their subjects under what we may call, if we understand faith to mean that belief in a spiritual life which is not confined to one Church, the persuasion of their faith and their country, they would soon discover that although their choice seemed arbitrary at first, it had obeyed what was deepest in them. I could not now write of any other country but Ireland, for my style has been shaped by the subjects I have worked on, but there was a time when my imagination seemed unwilling, when I found myself writing of some Irish event in words that would have better fitted some Italian or Eastern event, for my style had been shaped in that general stream of European literature which has come from so many watersheds, and it was slowly, very slowly, that I made a new style. It was years before I could rid myself of Shelley's Italian light, but now I think my style is myself. I might have found more of Ireland if I had written in Irish, but I have found a little, and I have found all myself. I am persuaded that if the Irishmen who are painting conventional pictures or writing conventional books on alien subjects, which have been worn away like pebbles on the shore, would do the same, they, too, might find themselves. Even the landscape-painter, who paints a place that he loves, and that no other man has painted, soon discovers that no style learned in the studios is wholly fitted to his purpose.

And I cannot but believe that if our painters of Highland cattle and moss-covered barns were to care enough for their country to care for what makes it different from other countries, they would discover, when struggling, it may be, to paint the exact grey of the bare Burren Hills,[1] and of a sudden, it may be, a new style, their very selves. And I admit, though in this I am moved by some touch of fanaticism, that even when I see an old subject written of or painted in a new way, I am yet jealous for Cuchulain, and for Baile and Aillinn, and for those grey mountains that still are lacking their celebration. I sometimes reproach myself because I cannot admire Mr. Hughes' beautiful, piteous *Orpheus and Eurydice* with an unquestioning mind. I say with my lips, 'The Spirit made it, for it is beautiful, and the Spirit bloweth where it listeth,' but I say in my heart, 'Aengus and Edain would have served his turn'; but one cannot, perhaps, love or believe at all if one does not love or believe a little too much.

And I do not think with unbroken pleasure of our scholars who write about German writers or about periods of Greek history. I always remember that they could give us a number of little books which would tell, each book for some one county, or some one parish, the verses, or the stories, or the events that would make every lake or mountain a man can see from his own door an excitement in his imagination. I would have some of them leave that work of theirs which will never lack hands, and begin to dig in Ireland the garden of the future, understanding that here in Ireland the spirit of man may be about to wed the soil of the world.

Art and scholarship like these I have described would give Ireland more than they received from her, for they would make love of the unseen more unshakable, more ready to plunge deep into the abyss, and they would make love of country more fruitful in the mind, more a part of daily life. One would know an Irishman into whose life they had come—and in a few generations they would come into the life of all, rich and poor—by something that set him apart among men. He himself would understand that more was expected of him than of others because he had greater possessions. The Irish race would have become a chosen race, one of the pillars that uphold the world.

---

[1]Robert Gregory painted the Burren Hills and thereby found what promised to grow into a great style, but he had hardly found it before he was killed. His few finished pictures, so full of austerity and sweetness, should find their way into Irish public galleries. 1924.

FROM Samhain

(1903)

The Reform of the Theatre

I THINK THE theatre must be reformed in its plays, its speaking, its acting, and its scenery. That is to say, I think there is nothing good about it at present.

First. We have to write or find plays that will make the theatre a place of intellectual excitement—a place where the mind goes to be liberated as it was liberated by the theatres of Greece and England and France at certain great moments of their history, and as it is liberated in Scandinavia to-day. If we are to do this we must learn that beauty and truth are always justified of themselves, and that their creation is a greater service to our country than writing that compromises either in the seeming service of a cause. We will, doubtless, come more easily to truth and beauty because we love some cause with all but all our heart; but we must remember when truth and beauty open their mouths to speak, that all other mouths should be as silent as Finn bade the son of Lugaidh be in the houses of the great. Truth and beauty judge and are above judgment. They justify and have no need of justification.

Such plays will require, both in writers and audiences, a stronger feeling for beautiful and appropriate language than one finds in the ordinary theatre. Sainte-Beuve has said that there is nothing immortal in literature except style, and it is precisely this sense of style, once common among us, that is hardest for us to recover. I do not mean by style words with an air of literature about them, what is ordinarily called eloquent writing. The speeches of Falstaff are as perfect in their style as the soliloquies of Hamlet. One must be able to make a king of Faery or an old countryman or a modern lover speak that language which is his and nobody else's, and speak it with so much of emotional subtlety that the hearer may find it hard to know whether it is the thought or the word that has moved him, or whether these could be separated at all.

If we do not know how to construct, if we cannot arrange much complicated life into a single action, our work will not hold the attention or linger in the memory, but if we are not in love with words it will lack the delicate movement of living speech that is the chief garment of life; and because of this lack the great realists seem to the lovers of beautiful art to be wise in this generation, and for the next generation, perhaps, but not for all generations that are to come.

Second. But if we are to restore words to their sovereignty we must make speech even more important than gesture upon the stage.

I have been told that I desire a monotonous chant, but that is not true, for though a monotonous chant may be a safer beginning for an actor than the broken and prosaic speech of ordinary recitation, it puts me to sleep none the less. The sing-song in which a child says a verse is a right beginning, though the child grows out of it. An actor should understand how so to discriminate cadence from cadence, and so to cherish the musical lineaments of verse or prose that he delights the ear with a continually varied music. Certain passages of lyrical feeling, or where one wishes, as in the Angel's part in *The Hour-Glass,* to make a voice sound like the voice of an Immortal, may be spoken upon pure notes which are carefully recorded and learned as if they were the notes of a song. Whatever method one adopts, one must always be certain that the work of art, as a whole, is masculine and intellectual, in its sound as in its form.

Third. We must simplify acting, especially in poetical drama, and in prose drama that is remote from real life like my *Hour-Glass.* We must get rid of everything that is restless, everything that draws the attention away from the sound of the voice, or from the few moments of intense expression, whether that expression is through the voice or through the hands; we must from time to time substitute for the movements that the eye sees the nobler movements that the heart sees, the rhythmical movements that seem to flow up into the imagination from some deeper life than that of the individual soul.

Fourth. Just as it is necessary to simplify gesture that it may accompany speech without being its rival, it is necessary to simplify both the form and colour of scenery and costume. As a rule the background should be but a single colour, so that the persons in the play, wherever they stand, may harmonise with it and preoccupy our attention. In other words, it should be thought out not as one thinks out a landscape, but as if it were the background of a portrait, and this is especially necessary on a small stage where the moment the stage is filled, the painted forms of the background are broken up and lost. Even when one has to represent trees or hills they should be treated in most cases decoratively, they should be little more than an unobtrusive pattern. There must be nothing unnecessary, nothing that will distract the attention from speech and movement. An art is always at its greatest when it is most human. Greek acting was great because it did all but everything with the voice, and modern acting may be great when it does everything with voice and movement. But an art which smothers these things with bad painting, with innumerable garish colours, with continual restless mimicries of the surface of life, is an art of fading humanity, a decaying art.

FROM Samhain

(1908)

First Principles

[I]

Some countrymen in Galway, whither we carried our plays in dialect a few weeks ago, said that it was no use going in to see them because they showed people that could be seen on the road every day; but these were but a few, and we had a great popular success, crowds being turned away every evening from the doors. Ireland is always Connacht to my imagination, for there more than elsewhere is the folk tradition that is the loftiest thing that has come down to us within the ring of Ireland. I knew an observant and cultivated French count, descendant of *émigrés,* who came for a few months in every summer to a property they had left him upon the Galway shore. He came from Paris or from Rome, but would not stay, if he could help it, even a few hours in Dublin, because Dublin was 'shabby England'. We find our most highly trained audiences of late in Dublin, but the majority of theatre-goers drift between what is Irish and what is English in confused uncertainty, and have not even begun the search for what is their own.

Somebody in *Un Grand Homme de province à Paris* says, with I know not what truth, that French actresses pay more for attacks than admiring criticism, for 'controversy is fame'. In Ireland this would be an unnecessary expense, and many of the attacks which have followed us from the beginning in such plenty have arisen out of conceptions of life which, unknown to the journalists who have made them, are essentially English, though of an England that has begun to change its clothes since Matthew Arnold and his contemporaries began a truer popular culture. Even at this moment the early Victorian thought is not so out of fashion that English newspapers would not revive it and talk of the duties of writers to preach and the like, all that old Utilitarianism, if the drama, let us say, were taken seriously enough for leading articles instead of being left to the criticism of a few writers who really know something of their business. Some fifteen years ago English critics themselves wrote of Ibsen very much as our more hysterical patriots write of us. These patriots, with an heretical preference for faith over works—for have not opinions and second- and third-hand conceptions of life, images of what we wish to be, a substance of things hoped for, come from the pawnshop of schismatical faith?—continually attack in the interest of some point of view popularised by Macaulay and his contemporaries, or of some reflection from English novelists and the like, Irish emotion and temperament discovered by some writer in himself after years of labour, for all reality comes to us as the reward of labour. Forms of emotion and thought which the future will recognise as peculiarly Irish, for no other country has had the like, are looked upon as un-Irish because of their novelty in a land that is so nearly conquered that it has all but nothing of its own. English provincialism shouts through the lips of Irish patriots who have no knowledge of other countries to give them a standard of comparison, and they, with the confidence of all who speak the opinions of others, labour to thwart everybody who would dig a well for Irish water to bubble in.

II

In 1892, when I started the National Literary Society, and began a movement that was intended to lead up to the establishment of an Irish Dramatic School, the songs and ballads of Young Ireland were used as examples to prove the personal, and therefore Irish, art of A. E., Lionel Johnson, Katharine Tynan, and myself (see Lionel Johnson's essay, *Poetry and Politics*), an un-Irish thing. And yet those songs and ballads, with the exception of a small number which are partly copied from Gaelic models, and a few, almost all by Mangan, that have a personal style, are imitations of the poetry of Burns and Macaulay and Scott. All literature in every country is derived from models, and as often as not these are foreign models, and it is the presence of a personal element alone that can give it nationality in a fine sense, the nationality of its maker. It is only before

personality has been attained that a race struggling towards self-con-
sciousness is the better for having, as in primitive times, nothing but
native models, for before this has been attained it can neither assim-
ilate nor reject. It was precisely at this passive moment, attainment
approaching but not yet come, that the Irish heart and mind surren-
dered to England, or rather to what is most temporary in England;
and Irish patriotism, content that the names and opinions should be
Irish, was deceived and satisfied. It is always necessary to affirm and
to reaffirm that nationality is in the things that escape analysis. We
discover it, as we do the quality of saltness or sweetness, by the taste,
and literature is a cultivation of taste.

III

The Irish novelists of the nineteenth century, who established
themselves, like the Young Ireland poets, upon various English
writers, without, except at rare moments—*Castle Rackrent* was, it
may be, the most inspired of those moments—attaining to person-
ality, have filled the popular mind with images of character, with
forms of construction, with a criticism of life, which are all so many
arguments to prove that some play that has arisen out of a fresh
vision is unlike every Irish thing. A real or fancied French influence
is pointed out at once and objected to, but the English influence
which runs through the patriotic reading of the people is not
noticed because it is everywhere. I say, with certainty, that *The Play-
boy of the Western World,* so rich in observation, so full of the tem-
perament of a unique man, has more of Ireland in its characters, in
its method of art, in its conception of morals, than all the novels of
Kickham, Michael Banim (I have much respect for his brother John,
perhaps because French influence in part annulled the influence of
Mrs. Radcliffe, and so helped him to personality); Gerald Griffin,
so full of amiable English sentiment; Carleton, in his longer tales,
powerful spirit though he was; and, of course, much more in any
page of it than in all those romances founded upon Walter Scott
which are, or used to be, published in Irish newspapers to make
boys and girls into patriots. Here and there, of course, one finds
Irish elements. In Lever, for instance, even after one has put aside all
that is second-hand, there is a rightful Irish gaiety, but one finds
these elements only just in so far as the writers had come to know

themselves in the Socratic sense. Of course, too, the tradition itself was not all English, but it is impossible to divide what is new, and therefore Irish, what is very old, and therefore Irish, from all that is foreign, from all that is an accident of imperfect culture, before we have had some revelation of Irish character, pure enough and varied enough to create a standard of comparison. I do not speak carelessly of the Irish novelists, for when I was in London during the first years of my literary life, I read them continually, seeking in them an image of Ireland that I might not forget what I meant to be the foundations of my art, trying always to winnow as I read. I only escaped from many misconceptions when, in 1897, I began an active Irish life, comparing what I saw about me with what I heard of in Galway cottages. Yet for all that, it was from the novelists and poets that I learned in part my symbols of expression. Somebody has said that all sound philosophy is but biography, and what I myself did, getting into an original relation to Irish life, creating in myself a new character, a new pose—in the French sense of the word—the literary mind of Ireland must do as a whole, always understanding that the result must be no bundle of formulas, not faggots but a fire. We never learn to know ourselves by thought, said Goethe, but by action only; and to a writer creation is action.

IV

A moment comes in every country when its character expresses itself through some group of writers, painters, or musicians, and it is this moment, the moment of Goethe in Germany, of the Elizabethan poets in England, of the Van Eycks in the Low Countries, of Corneille and Racine in France, of Ibsen and Björnson in Scandinavia, which fixes the finer elements of national character for generations. This moment is impossible until public opinion is ready to welcome in the mind of the artist a power, little affected by external things, being self-contained, self-created, self-sufficing, the seed of character. Generally up to that moment literature has tried to express everybody's thought, history being considered merely as a chronicle of facts, but now, at the instant of revelation, writers think the world is but their palette, and if history amuses them, it is but, as Goethe says, because they would do its personages the honour of naming after them their own thoughts.

In the same spirit they approach their contemporaries when they borrow for their own passions the images of living men, and, at times, external facts will be no more to them than the pewter pot gleaming in the sunlight that started Jacob Boehme into his seven days' trance.

There are moments, indeed, when they will give you more powerful and exact impressions of the outer world than any other can, but these impressions are always those which they have been the first to receive, and more often than not, to make them the more vivid, they will leave out everything that everybody can see every day. The man of genius may be Signor Mancini if he please, but never Mr. Lafayette.

Just as they use the life of their own times, they use past literature—their own and that of other countries—selecting here and there under what must always seem, until their revelation is understood, an impulse of mere caprice, and the more original, that is to say the more pure, the revelation, the greater the caprice. It was a moment of importance in Scandinavia when a certain pamphlet announced that an historical play could not find its justification in history alone, for it must contain an idea, meaning by an idea thought flowing out of character, as opinions are thought arising out of the necessities of organisation. We grow like others through opinions, but through ideas discover ourselves, for these are only true when images of our own power.

V

In no country has this independence of mind, this audacity I had almost said, been attained without controversy, for the men who affirm it seem the enemies of all other interests. In Ireland, in addition to the external art of our predecessors, full of the misunderstandings created by English influence, there is a preoccupation of a great part of the population with opinions and a habit of deciding that a man is useful to his country, or otherwise, not by what he is in himself or by what he does in his whole life, but by the opinions he holds on one or two subjects. Balzac, in *Les Comédiens sans le Savoir,* describes a sculptor, a follower of the Socialist Fourier, who has made an allegorical figure of Harmony, and got into his statue the doctrine of his master by giving it six breasts and by putting under its feet an enormous Savoy cabbage. One of his friends promises that when everybody is converted to their doctrine he will be the foremost man of his craft, but another and a wiser says of him that 'while opinions cannot give talent they inevitably spoil it', and adds that an artist's opinion ought to be a faith in works, and that there is no way for him to succeed but by work, 'while nature gives the sacred fire.' In Paris, according to Balzac, it is ambition that makes artists and writers identify themselves with a cause that gives them the help of politicians, of journalists, or of society, as the case may be, but in Ireland, so far as I am able to see, they do it for sociability's sake, to have a crowd to shout with, and therefore by half-deliberate sophistry they persuade themselves that the old tale is not true, and that art is not ruined so. I do not mean that the artist should not as a man be a good citizen and hold opinions like another; Balzac was a Catholic and a Monarchist. We, too, in following his great example, have not put away in anything the strong opinions that we set out with, but in our art they have no place. Every trouble of our Theatre in its earlier years, every attack on us in any year, has come directly or indirectly either from those who prefer Mr. Lafayette to Signor Mancini, or from those who believe, from a defective education, that the writer who does not help some cause, who does not support some opinion, is but an idler, or if his air be too serious for that, the supporter of some hidden wickedness. A principal actor left us in our first year because he believed *The Hour-Glass* to be a problem play. This is all natural enough in a country where the majority have been denied University teaching. I found precisely the same prejudices among the self-educated working-men about William Morris, and among some few educated persons, generally women, who took their tune from the working-men. One woman used to repeat as often as possible that to paint pictures or to write poetry in this age was to fiddle while Rome was burning. The artist who permits opinion to master his work is always insincere, always what Balzac calls an unconscious comedian, a man playing to a public for an end, or a philanthropist who has made the most tragic and the most useless of sacrifices.

VI

Certain among the Nationalist attacks have been the work of ignorant men, untruthful, imputing unworthy motives, the kind of thing one cannot answer. But the Unionist hostility, though better-mannered, has been more injurious. Our Nationalist pit has grown to understand us, and night after night we have not been able to find room for all who came, but except at rare moments and under exceptional circumstances our stalls have been almost empty, though the people who keep away from us in Ireland flock to us in London, where there is culture enough to make us a fashion. I think that tide is turning, however, for we played before many Unionists at Galway matinées, *Cathleen ni Houlihan*, *The Gaol Gate*, and *The Rising of the Moon*, all plays that have been objected to at some time or other by some section or other of official Dublin, or that we have been warned against in friendlier moods. When *Cathleen ni Houlihan* was first played in the Abbey I was hissed by a group of young men at the door; and we were offered a good deal of support once towards the filling of our empty stalls if we would drop it from our list. I heard a while ago we had lost financial support through *The Rising of the Moon*, but returned to tranquillity when I found that it would have been a donation to the National Literary Society—God save the mark!—given under the belief that we and it were the same body.

VII

In most modern countries when the moment has arrived for a personal impulse, either for the first time or in some art hitherto external and conventional, the cry has been raised against the writer that he is preaching sexual immorality, for that is the subject upon which the newspapers, at any rate, most desire to see certain opinions always in force, and a view of the world as sexually unex-citing as possible always displayed as if it were reality. Balzac in his preface to the *Comédie humaine* had to defend himself from this charge, but it is not the burning question with us at present, for politics are our national passion. We have to free our vision of reality from political prepossession, for entangled, as it were, with all that is exaggerated, lifeless, frozen, in the attitudes of party, there are true thoughts about all those things that Ireland is most interested in, a reverie over the emptiness and the fullness of Irish character which is not less a part of wisdom because politics, like art, have their exaggerations. We cannot renounce political subjects in renouncing mere opinions, for that pleasure in the finer culture of

England, that displeasure in Irish disunions and disorders, which are the root of reasoned Unionism, are as certainly high and natural thoughts as the self-denying enthusiasm that leads Michael Gillane to probable death or exile, and Dervorgilla to her remorse, and Patrick Sarsfield of *The White Cockade* to his sense of what a king should be; and we cannot renounce them because politicians believe that one thought or another may help their opponents, any more than Balzac could have refused to write the *Comédie humaine* because somebody was afraid Madame l'Épicière might run away from her husband.

VIII

At the close of my speech at one of the performances we were asked to give to the British Association, I used these words: 'When I was coming up in the train the other day from Galway, I began thinking how unlike your work was to my work, and then suddenly it struck me that it was all the same. A picture arose before my mind's eye: I saw Adam numbering the creatures of Eden; soft and terrible, foul and fair, they all went before him. That, I thought, is the man of science, naming and numbering, for our understanding, everything in the world. But then, I thought, we writers, do we not also number and describe, though with a difference? You are busy with the exterior world, and we with the interior. Science understands that everything must be known in the world our eyes look at; there is nothing too obscure, too common, too vile, to be the subject of knowledge. When a man of science discovers a new species, or a new law, you do not ask the value of the law, or the value of the species, before you do him honour; you leave all that to the judgment of the generations. It is your pride that in you the human race contemplates all things with so pure, so disinterested, an eyesight that it forgets its own necessities and infirmities, all its hopes and fears, in the contemplation of truth for the sake of truth, reality for the sake of reality.

'We, on the other hand, are Adams of a different Eden, a more terrible Eden, perhaps, for we must name and number the passions and motives of men. There, too, everything must be known, everything understood, everything expressed; there, also, there is nothing common, nothing unclean; every motive must be followed through all the obscure mystery of its logic. Mankind must be seen and understood in every possible circumstance, in every conceivable situation. There is no laughter too bitter, no irony too harsh for utterance, no passion too terrible to be set before the minds of men. The Greeks knew that. Only in this way can mankind be understood, only when we have put ourselves in all the possible positions of life, from the most miserable to those that are so lofty that we can only speak of them in symbols and in mysteries, will entire wisdom be possible. All wise government depends upon this knowledge not less than upon that other knowledge which is your business rather than ours; and we and you alike rejoice in battle, finding the sweetest of all music to be the stroke of the sword.'

The Cutting of an Agate

(1912)

The Tragic Theatre

I DID NOT FIND a word in the printed criticism of Synge's *Deirdre of the Sorrows* about the qualities that made certain moments seem to me the noblest tragedy, and the play was judged by what seemed to me but wheels and pulleys necessary to the effect, but in themselves nothing.

Upon the other hand, those who spoke to me of the play never spoke of these wheels and pulleys, but if they cared at all for the play, cared for the things I cared for. One's own world of painters, of poets, of good talkers, of ladies who delight in Ricard's portraits or Debussy's music, all those whose senses feel instantly every change in our mother the moon, saw the stage in one way; and those others who look at plays every night, who tell the general playgoer whether this play or that play is to his taste, saw it in a way so different that there is certainly some body of dogma—whether in the instincts or in the memory—pushing the ways apart. A printed criticism, for instance, found but one dramatic moment, that when Deirdre in the second act overhears her lover say that he may grow weary of her; and not one—if I remember rightly—chose for praise or explanation the third act which alone had satisfied the author, or contained in any abundance those sentences that were quoted at the fall of the curtain and for days after.

Deirdre and her lover, as Synge tells the tale, returned to Ireland, though it was nearly certain they would die there, because death was better than broken love, and at the side of the open grave that had been dug for one and would serve for both, quarrelled, losing all they had given their life to keep. 'Is it not a hard thing that we should miss the safety of the grave and we trampling its edge?' That is Deirdre's cry at the outset of a reverie of passion that mounts and mounts till grief itself has carried her beyond grief into pure contemplation. Up to this the play had been a Master's unfinished work, monotonous and melancholy, ill-arranged, little more than a sketch of what it would have grown to, but now I listened breathless to sentences that may never pass away, and as they filled or dwindled in their civility of sorrow, the player, whose art had seemed clumsy and incomplete, like the writing itself, ascended into that tragic ecstasy which is the best that art—perhaps that life—can give. And at last when Deirdre, in the paroxysm before she took her life, touched with compassionate fingers him that had killed her lover, we knew that the player had become, if but for a moment, the creature of that noble mind which had gathered its art in waste islands, and we too were carried beyond time and persons to where passion, living through its thousand purgatorial years, as in the wink of an eye, becomes wisdom; and it was as though we too had touched and felt and seen a disembodied thing.

One dogma of the printed criticism is that if a play does not contain definite character, its constitution is not strong enough for the stage, and that the dramatic moment is always the contest of character with character.

In poetical drama there is, it is held, an antithesis between character and lyric poetry, for lyric poetry—however much it move you when read out of a book—can, as these critics think, but encumber the action. Yet when we go back a few centuries and enter the great periods of drama, character grows less and sometimes disappears, and there is much lyric feeling, and at times a lyric measure will be wrought into the dialogue, a flowing measure that had well befitted music, or that more lumbering one of the sonnet. Suddenly it strikes us that character is continuously present in comedy alone, and that there is much tragedy, that of Corneille, that of Racine, that of Greece and Rome, where its place is taken by passions and motives, one person being jealous, another full of love or remorse or pride or anger. In writers of tragi-comedy (and Shakespeare is always a writer of tragi-comedy) there is indeed character, but we notice that it is in the moments of comedy that character is defined, in Hamlet's gaiety, let us say; while amid the great moments, when Timon orders his tomb, when Hamlet cries to Horatio 'Absent thee from felicity awhile,' when

Antony names 'Of many thousand kisses the poor last,' all is lyricism, unmixed passion, 'the integrity of fire.' Nor does character ever attain to complete definition in these lamps ready for the taper, no matter how circumstantial and gradual the opening of events, as it does in Falstaff, who has no passionate purpose to fulfil, or as it does in Henry V, whose poetry, never touched by lyric heat, is oratorical; nor when the tragic reverie is at its height do we say, 'How well that man is realised! I should know him were I to meet him in the street,' for it is always ourselves that we see upon the stage, and should it be a tragedy of love, we renew, it may be, some loyalty of our youth, and go from the theatre with our eyes dim for an old love's sake.

I think it was while rehearsing a translation of *Les Fourberies de Scapin* in Dublin, and noticing how passionless it all was, that I saw what should have been plain from the first line I had written, that tragedy must always be a drowning and breaking of the dykes that separate man from man, and that it is upon these dykes comedy keeps house. But I was not certain of the site of that house (one always hesitates when there is no testimony but one's own) till somebody told me of a certain letter of Congreve's. He describes the external and superficial expressions of 'humour' on which farce is founded and then defines 'humour' itself—the foundation of comedy—as a 'singular and unavoidable way of doing anything peculiar to one man only, by which his speech and actions are distinguished from all other men,' and adds to it that 'passions are too powerful in the sex to let humour have its course,' or, as I would rather put it, that you can find but little of what we call character in unspoiled youth, whatever be the sex, for, as he indeed shows in another sentence, it grows with time like the ash of a burning stick, and strengthens towards middle life till there is little else at seventy years.

Since then I have discovered an antagonism between all the old art and our new art of comedy and understand why I hated at nineteen years Thackeray's novels and the new French painting. A big picture of *cocottes* sitting at little tables outside a café, by some follower of Manet, was exhibited at the Royal Hibernian Academy while I was a student at a life class there, and I was miserable for days. I found no desirable place, no man I could have wished to be, no woman I could have loved, no Golden Age, no lure for secret hope, no adventure with myself for theme out of that endless tale I told myself all day long. Years after, I saw the *Olympia* of Manet at the Luxembourg and watched it without hostility indeed, but as I might some incomparable talker whose precision of gesture gave me pleasure, though I did not understand his language. I returned to it again and again at intervals of years, saying to myself, 'Some day I will understand'; and yet it was not until Sir Hugh Lane brought the *Eva Gonzales* to Dublin, and I had said to myself, 'How perfectly that woman is realised as distinct from all other women that have lived or shall live,' that I understood I was carrying on in my own mind that quarrel between a tragedian and a comedian which the Devil on Two Sticks in Le Sage showed to the young man who had climbed through the window.

There is an art of the flood, the art of Titian when his *Ariosto,* and his *Bacchus and Ariadne,* give new images to the dreams of youth, and of Shakespeare when he shows us Hamlet broken away from life by the passionate hesitations of his reverie. And we call this art poetical, because we must bring more to it than our daily mood if we would take our pleasure; and because it takes delight in the moment of exaltation, of excitement, of dreaming (or in the capacity for it, as in that still face of Ariosto's that is like some vessel soon to be full of wine). And there is an art that we call real, because character can only express itself perfectly in a real world, being that world's creature, and because we understand it best through a delicate discrimination of the senses which is but entire wakefulness, the daily mood grown cold and crystalline.

We may not find either mood in its purity, but in mainly tragic art one distinguishes devices to exclude or lessen character, to diminish the power of that daily mood, to cheat or blind its too clear perception. If the real world is not altogether rejected, it is but touched here and there, and into the places we have left empty we summon rhythm, balance, pattern, images that remind us of vast passions, the vagueness of past times, all the chimeras that haunt the edge of trance; and if we are painters, we shall express personal emotion through ideal form, a symbolism handled by the generations, a mask from whose eyes the disembodied looks, a style that remembers many masters that it may escape contemporary suggestion; or we shall leave out some element of reality as in Byzantine painting, where there is no mass, nothing in relief; and so it is that in the supreme moment of tragic art there comes upon one that strange sensation as though the hair of one's head stood up. And when we love, if it be in the excitement of youth, do we not also, that the flood may find no stone to convulse, no wall to narrow it, exclude character or the signs of it by choosing that beauty which seems unearthly because the individual woman is lost amid the labyrinth of its lines as though life were trembling into stillness and silence, or at last folding itself away? Some little irrelevance of line, some promise of character to come, may indeed put us at our ease, 'give more interest' as the humour of the old man with the basket does to Cleopatra's dying; but should it come, as we had dreamed in love's frenzy, to our dying for that woman's sake, we would find that the discord had its value from the tune. Nor have we chosen illusion in choosing the outward sign of that moral genius that lives among the subtlety of the passions, and can for her moment make her of the one mind with great artists and poets. In the studio we may indeed say to one another, 'Character is the only beauty,' but when we choose a wife, as when we go to the gymnasium to be shaped for woman's eyes, we remember academic form, even though we enlarge a little the point of interest and choose 'a painter's beauty,' finding it the more easy to believe in the fire because it has made ashes.

When we look at the faces of the old tragic paintings, whether it is in Titian or in some painter of mediaeval China, we find there sadness and gravity, a certain emptiness even, as of a mind that waited the supreme crisis (and indeed it seems at times as if the graphic art, unlike poetry which sings the crisis itself, were the celebration of waiting). Whereas in modern art, whether in Japan or Europe, 'vitality' (is not that the great word of the studios?), the energy, that is to say, which is under the command of our common moments, sings, laughs, chatters or looks its busy thoughts.

Certainly we have here the Tree of Life and that of the Knowledge of Good and Evil which is rooted in our interests, and if we have forgotten their differing virtues it is surely because we have taken delight in a confusion of crossing branches. Tragic art, passionate art, the drowner of dykes, the confounder of understanding, moves us by setting us to reverie, by alluring us almost to the intensity of trance. The persons upon the stage, let us say, greaten till they are humanity itself. We feel our minds expand convulsively or spread out slowly like some moon-brightened image-crowded sea. That which is before our eyes perpetually vanishes and returns again in the midst of the excitement it creates, and the more enthralling it is, the more do we forget it.

FROM Per Amica Silentia Lunae

(1918)

FROM *Anima Hominis*

I

When I come home after meeting men who are strange to me, and sometimes even after talking to women, I go over all I have said in gloom and disappointment. Perhaps I have overstated everything from a desire to vex or startle, from hostility that is but fear; or all my natural thoughts have been drowned by an undisciplined sympathy. My fellow-diners have hardly seemed of mixed humanity, and how should I keep my head among images of good and evil, crude allegories?

But when I shut my door and light the candle, I invite a Marmorean Muse, an art, where no thought or emotion has come to mind because another man has thought or felt something different, for now there must be no reaction, action only, and the world must move my heart but to the heart's discovery of itself, and I begin to dream of eyelids that do not quiver before the bayonet: all my thoughts have ease and joy, I am all virtue and confidence. When I come to put in rhyme what I have found it will be a hard toil, but for a moment I believe I have found myself and not my anti-self. It is only the shrinking from toil perhaps that convinces me that I have been no more myself than is the cat the medicinal grass it is eating in the garden.

How could I have mistaken for myself an heroic condition that from early boyhood has made me superstitious? That which comes as complete, as minutely organised, as are those elaborate, brightly lighted buildings and sceneries appearing in a moment, as I lie between sleeping and waking, must come from above me and beyond me. At times I remember that place in Dante where he sees in his chamber the 'Lord of Terrible Aspect', and how, seeming 'to rejoice inwardly that it was a marvel to see, speaking, he said, many things among the which I could understand but few, and of these this: ego dominus tuus'; or should the conditions come, not as it were in a gesture—as the image of a man—but in some fine land-scape, it is of Boehme, maybe, that I think, and of that country where we 'eternally solace ourselves in the excellent beautiful flour-ishing of all manner of flowers and forms, both trees and plants, and all kinds of fruit'.

V

We make out of the quarrel with others, rhetoric, but of the quarrel with ourselves, poetry. Unlike the rhetoricians, who get a confident voice from remembering the crowd they have won or may win, we sing amid our uncertainty; and, smitten even in the pres-ence of the most high beauty by the knowledge of our solitude, our rhythm shudders. I think, too, that no fine poet, no matter how dis-ordered his life, has ever, even in his mere life, had pleasure for his end. Johnson and Dowson, friends of my youth, were dissipated men, the one a drunkard, the other a drunkard and mad about women, and yet they had the gravity of men who had found life out and were awakening from the dream; and both, one in life and art and one in art and less in life, had a continual preoccupation with religion. Nor has any poet I have read of or heard of or met with been a sentimentalist. The other self, the anti-self or the antithetical self, as one may choose to name it, comes but to those who are no longer deceived, whose passion is reality. The sentimentalists are practical men who believe in money, in position, in a marriage bell, and whose understanding of happiness is to be so busy whether at work or at play, that all is forgotten but the momentary aim. They find their pleasure in a cup that is filled from Lethe's wharf, and for the awakening, for the vision, for the revelation of reality, tradition offers us a different word—ecstasy.' An old artist wrote to me of his wanderings by the quays of New York, and how he found there a woman nursing a sick child, and drew her story from her. She spoke, too, of other children who had died: a long tragic story. 'I wanted to paint her,' he wrote; 'if I denied myself any of the pain I could not believe in my own ecstasy'. We must not make a false faith by hiding from our thoughts the causes of doubt, for faith is the highest achievement of the human intellect, the only gift man can make to God, and therefore it must be offered in sincerity. Neither must we create, by hiding ugliness, a false beauty as our offering to the world. He only can create the greatest imaginable beauty who has endured all imaginable pangs, for only when we have seen and foreseen what we dread shall we be rewarded by that dazzling unforeseen wing-footed wanderer. We could not find him if he were not in some sense of our being and yet of our being but as water with fire, a noise with silence. He is of all things not impossible the most difficult, for that only which comes easily can never be a portion of our being, 'Soon got, soon gone', as the proverb says. I shall find the dark grow luminous, the void fruitful when I understand I have nothing, that the ringers in the tower have appointed for the hymen of the soul a passing bell.

The last knowledge has often come most quickly to turbulent men, and for a season brought new turbulence. When life puts away her conjuring tricks one by one, those that deceive us longest may well be the wine-cup and the sensual kiss, for our Chambers of Commerce and of Commons have not the divine architecture of the body, nor has their frenzy been ripened by the sun. The poet, because he may not stand within the sacred house but lives amid the whirlwinds that beset its threshold, may find his pardon.

VIII

I think that all religious men have believed that there is a hand not ours in the events of life, and that, as somebody says in *Wilhelm Meister*, accident is destiny; and I think it was Heraclitus who said: the Daemon is our destiny. When I think of life as a struggle with the Daemon who would ever set us to the hardest work among those not impossible, I understand why there is a deep enmity between a man and his destiny, and why a man loves nothing but his destiny. In an Anglo-Saxon poem a certain man is called, as though to call him something that summed up all heroism, 'Doom eager'. I am persuaded that the Daemon delivers and deceives us, and that he wove that netting from the stars and threw the net from his shoulder. Then my imagination runs from Daemon to sweetheart, and I divine an analogy that evades the intellect. I remember that Greek antiquity has bid us look for the principal stars, that govern enemy and sweetheart alike, among those that are about to set, in the Seventh House as the astrologers say; and that it may be 'sexual love', which is 'founded upon spiritual hate', is an image of the warfare of man and Daemon; and I even wonder if there may not be some secret communion, some whispering in the dark between Daemon and sweetheart. I remember how often women when in love, grow superstitious, and believe that they can bring their lovers good luck; and I remember an old Irish story of three young men who went seeking for help in battle into the house of the gods at Slieve-na-mon. 'You must first be married', some god told them, 'because a man's good or evil luck comes to him through a woman'.

I sometimes fence for half an hour at the day's end, and when I close my eyes upon the pillow I see a foil playing before me, the button to my face. We meet always in the deep of the mind, whatever our work, wherever our reverie carries us, that other Will.

XI

Many years ago I saw, between sleeping and waking, a woman of incredible beauty shooting an arrow into the sky, and from the moment when I made my first guess at her meaning I have thought much of the difference between the winding movement of nature and the straight line, which is called in Balzac's *Séraphita* the 'Mark of Man', but is better described as the mark of saint or sage. I think that we who are poets and artists, not being permitted to shoot beyond the tangible, must go from desire to weariness and so to desire again, and live but for the moment when vision comes to our weariness like terrible lightning, in the humility of the brutes. I do not doubt those heaving circles, those winding arcs, whether in one man's life or in that of an age, are mathematical, and that some in the world, or beyond the world, have foreknown the event and pricked upon the calendar the life-span of a Christ, a Buddha, a Napoleon: that every movement, in feeling or in thought, prepares in the dark by its own increasing clarity and confidence its own executioner. We seek reality with the slow toil of our weakness and are smitten from the boundless and the unforeseen. Only when we are saint or sage, and renounce Experience itself, can we, in imagery of the Christian Cabbala, leave the sudden lightning and the path of the serpent and become the bowman who aims his arrow at the centre of the sun.

XIII

A poet, when he is growing old, will ask himself if he cannot keep his mask and his vision without new bitterness, new disappointment. Could he if he would, knowing how frail his vigour from youth up, copy Landor who lived loving and hating, ridiculous and unconquered, into extreme old age, all lost but the favour of his muses?

> The mother of the muses we are taught
> Is memory; she has left me; they remain
> And shake my shoulder urging me to sing.

Surely, he may think, now that I have found vision and mask I need not suffer any longer. He will buy perhaps some small old house where like Ariosto he can dig his garden, and think that in the return of birds and leaves, or moon and sun, and in the evening flight of the rooks he may discover rhythm and pattern like those in sleep and so never awake out of vision. Then he will remember Wordsworth withering into eighty years, honoured and empty-witted, and climb to some waste room and find, forgotten there by youth, some bitter crust.

FROM *Anima Mundi*

I

I have always sought to bring my mind close to the mind of Indian and Japanese poets, old women in Connaught, mediums in Soho, lay brothers whom I imagine dreaming in some mediaeval monastery the dreams of their village, learned authors who refer all to antiquity; to immerse it in the general mind where that mind is scarce separable from what we have begun to call 'the subconscious'; to liberate it from all that comes of councils and committees, from the world as it is seen from universities or from populous towns; and that I might so believe I have murmured evocations and frequented mediums, delighted in all that displayed great problems through sensuous images, or exciting phrases, accepting from abstract schools but a few technical words that are so old they seem but broken architraves fallen amid bramble and grass, and have put myself to school where all things are seen: *A Tenedo Tacitae per Amica Silentia Lunae*. At one time I thought to prove my conclusions by quoting from diaries where I have recorded certain strange events the moment they happened, but now I have changed my mind—I will but say like the Arab boy that became Vizier: 'O brother, I have taken stock in the desert sand and of the sayings of antiquity.'

X

There are two realities, the terrestrial and the condition of fire.[1] All power is from the terrestrial condition, for there all opposites meet and there only is the extreme of choice possible, full freedom. And there the heterogeneous is, and evil, for evil is the strain one upon another of opposites; but in the condition of fire is all music and all rest. Between is the condition of air where images have but a borrowed life, that of memory or that reflected upon them when they symbolise colours and intensities of fire: the place of shades who are 'in the whirl of those who are fading', and who cry like those amorous shades in the Japanese play:

> That we may acquire power
> Even in our faint substance,
> We will show forth even now,
> And though it be but in a dream,
> Our form of repentance.

After so many rhythmic beats the soul must cease to desire its images, and can, as it were, close its eyes.

When all sequence comes to an end, time comes to an end, and

[1]When writing this essay I did not see how complete must be the antithesis between man and Daimon. The repose of man is the choice of the Daimon, and the repose of the Daimon the choice of man; and what I have called man's terrestrial state the Daimon's condition of fire. I might have seen this, as it all follows from the words written by the beggar in *The Hour-Glass* upon the walls of Babylon. 1924.

the soul puts on the rhythmic or spiritual body or luminous body and contemplates all the events of its memory and every possible impulse in an eternal possession of itself in one single moment. That condition is alone animate, all the rest is phantasy, and from thence come all the passions, and some have held, the very heat of the body.

> Time drops in decay,
> Like a candle burnt out,
> And the mountains and woods
> Have their day, have their day;
> What one in the rout
> Of the fire-born moods
> Has fallen away?

XVI

The Daemon, by using his mediatorial shades, brings man again and again to the place of choice, heightening temptation that the choice may be as final as possible, imposing his own lucidity upon events, leading his victim to whatever among works not impossible is the most difficult. He suffers with man as some firm-souled man suffers with the woman he but loves the better because she is extravagant and fickle. His descending power is neither the winding nor the straight line but zigzag, illuminating the passive and active properties, the tree's two sorts of fruit: it is the sudden lightning, for all his acts of power are instantaneous. We perceive in a pulsation of the artery, and after slowly decline.

XXI

When I remember that Shelley calls our minds 'mirrors of the fire for which all thirst', I cannot but ask the question all have asked, 'What or who has cracked the mirror?' I begin to study the only self that I can know, myself, and to wind the thread upon the perne again.

At certain moments, always unforeseen, I become happy, most commonly when at hazard I have opened some book of verse. Sometimes it is my own verse when, instead of discovering new technical flaws, I read with all the excitement of the first writing. Perhaps I am sitting in some crowded restaurant, the open book beside me, or closed, my excitement having over-brimmed the page. I look at the strangers near as if I had known them all my life, and it seems strange that I cannot speak to them: everything fills me with affection, I have no longer any fears or any needs; I do not even remember that this happy mood must come to an end. It seems as if the vehicle had suddenly grown pure and far extended and so luminous that the images from *Anima Mundi,* embodied there and drunk with that sweetness, would, like a country drunkard who has thrown a wisp into his own thatch, burn up time.

It may be an hour before the mood passes, but latterly I seem to understand that I enter upon it the moment I cease to hate. I think the common condition of our life is hatred—I know that this is so with me—irritation with public or private events or persons. There is no great matter in forgetfulness of servants, or the delays of tradesmen, but how forgive the ill-breeding of Carlyle, or the rhetoric of Swinburne, or that woman who murmurs over the din-ner-table the opinion of her daily paper? And only a week ago last Sunday, I hated the spaniel who disturbed a partridge on her nest, a trout who took my bait and yet broke away unhooked. The books say that our happiness comes from the opposite of hate, but I am not certain, for we may love unhappily. And plainly, when I have closed a book too stirred to go on reading, and in those brief intense visions of sleep, I have something about me that, though it makes me love, is more like innocence. I am in the place where the Dae-mon is, but I do not think he is with me until I begin to make a new personality, selecting among those images, seeking always to satisfy a hunger grown out of conceit with daily diet; and yet as I write the words 'I select', I am full of uncertainty not knowing when I am the finger, when the clay. Once, twenty years ago, I seemed to awake from sleep to find my body rigid, and to hear a strange voice speak-ing these words through my lips as through lips of stone: 'We make an image of him who sleeps, and it is not him who sleeps, and we call it Emmanuel.'

FROM *A Vision*

(1925, 1937)

FROM Introduction

XV

Some will ask whether I believe in the actual existence of my circuits of sun and moon. Those that include, now all recorded time in one circuit, now what Blake called "the pulsation of an artery", are plainly symbolical, but what of those that fixed, like a butterfly upon a pin, to our central date, the first day of our Era, divide actual history into periods of equal length? To such a question I can but answer that if sometimes, overwhelmed by miracle as all men must be when in the midst of it, I have taken such periods literally, my reason has soon recovered; and now that the system stands out clearly in my imagination I regard them as stylistic arrangements of experience comparable to the cubes in the drawing of Wyndham Lewis and to the ovoids in the sculpture of Brancusi. They have helped me to hold in a single thought reality and justice.

November 23rd 1928, and later

FROM BOOK I: THE GREAT WHEEL
FROM Part I: The Principal Symbol

II

According to Simplicius,[1] a late commentator upon Aristotle, the Concord of Empedocles fabricates all things into "an homogeneous sphere", and then Discord separates the elements and so makes the world we inhabit, but even the sphere formed by Concord is not the changeless eternity, for Concord or Love but offers us the image of that which is changeless.

If we think of the vortex attributed to Discord as formed by circles diminishing until they are nothing, and of the opposing sphere attributed to Concord as forming from itself an opposing vortex, the apex of each vortex in the middle of the other's base, we have the fundamental symbol of my instructors.

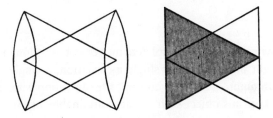

If I call the unshaded cone "Discord" and the other "Concord" and think of each as the bound of a gyre, I see that the gyre of "Concord" diminishes as that of "Discord" increases, and can imagine after that the gyre of "Concord" increasing while that of "Discord" diminishes, and so on, one gyre within the other always. Here the thought of Heraclitus dominates all: "Dying each other's life, living each other's death".

---

[1] Quoted by Pierre Duhem in *Le Système du monde*, vol. i, page 75.

FROM Part II: Examination of the Wheel

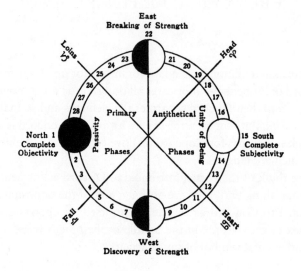

II

This wheel is every completed movement of thought or life, twenty-eight incarnations, a single incarnation, a single judgment or act of thought. Man seeks his opposite or the opposite of his condition, attains his object so far as it is attainable, at Phase 15 and returns[1] to Phase 1 again.

Phase 15 is called Sun in Moon because the solar or *primary tincture* is consumed by the lunar, but from another point of view it is *Mask* consumed in *Will*; all is beauty. The *Mask* as it were wills itself as beauty, but because, as Plotinus says, things that are of one kind are unconscious, it is an ideal or supernatural incarnation. Phase 1 is called Moon in Sun because the lunar or *antithetical tincture* is consumed in the *primary* or solar, but from another point of view it is the *Body of Fate*

---

[1] A similar circular movement fundamental in the works of Giovanni Gentile is, I read somewhere, the half-conscious foundation of the political thought of modern Italy. Individuals and classes complete their personality and then sink back to enrich the mass. Government must, it is held, because all good things have been created by class war, recognise that class war though it may be regulated must never end. It is the old saying of Heraclitus, "War is God of all, and Father of all, some it has made Gods and some men, some bond and some free," and the converse of Marxian Socialism.

414

consumed in *Creative Mind;* man is submissive and plastic: unless where supersensual power intervenes, the steel-like plasticity of water where the last ripple has been smoothed away. We shall presently have to consider the *Principles* where pure thought is possible, but in the *Faculties* the sole activity and the sole unity is natural or lunar, and in the *primary* phases that unity is moral. At Phase 1 morality is complete submission. All unity is from the *Mask,* and the *antithetical Mask* is described in the automatic script as a "form created by passion to unite us to ourselves", the self so sought is that Unity of Being compared by Dante in the *Convito* to that of "a perfectly proportioned human body". The *Body of Fate* is the sum, not the unity, of fact, fact as it affects a particular man. Only in the Four *Principles* shall we discover the concord of Empedocles. The *Will* is very much the Will described by Croce.[1] When not affected by the other *Faculties* it has neither emotion, morality nor intellectual interest, but knows how things are done, how windows open and shut, how roads are crossed, everything that we call utility. It seeks its own continuance. Only by the pursuit or acceptance of its direct opposite, that object of desire or moral ideal which is of all possible things the most difficult, and by forcing that form upon the *Body of Fate,* can it attain self-knowledge and expression. Phase 8 and Phase 22 are phases of struggle and tragedy, the first a struggle to find personality, the second to lose it. After Phase 22 and before Phase 1 there is a struggle to accept the fate-imposed unity, from Phase 1 to Phase 8 to escape it.

All such abstract statements are, however, misleading, for we are dealing always with a particular man, the man of Phase 13 or Phase 17 let us say. The *Four Faculties* are not the abstract categories of philosophy, being the result of the four memories of the *Daimon* or ultimate self of that man. His *Body of Fate,* the series of events forced upon him from without, is shaped out of the *Daimon's* memory of the events of his past incarnations; his *Mask* or object of desire or idea of the good, out of its memory of the moments of exaltation in his past lives; his *Will* or normal ego out of its memory of all the events of his present life, whether consciously remembered or not; his *Creative Mind* from its memory of ideas—or universals—displayed by actual men in past lives, or their spirits between lives.

---

[1] The *Four Faculties* somewhat resemble the four moments to which Croce has dedicated four books; that the resemblance is not closer is because Croce makes little use of antithesis and antinomy.

FROM Part III: The Twenty-eight Incarnations

PHASE FIFTEEN

Will.
Mask (from Phase 1).
Creative Mind (from Phase 15).
Body of Fate (from Phase 1).

No description except that this is a phase of complete beauty.

Body of Fate and *Mask* are now identical; and *Will* and *Creative Mind* identical; or rather the *Creative Mind* is dissolved in the *Will* and the *Body of Fate* in the *Mask*. Thought and will are indistinguishable, effort and attainment are indistinguishable; and this is the consummation of a slow process; nothing is apparent but dreaming *Will* and the Image that it dreams. Since Phase 12 all images, and cadences of the mind, have been satisfying to that mind just in so far as they have expressed this converging of will and thought, effort and attainment. The words "musical", "sensuous", are but descriptions of that converging process. Thought has been pursued, not as a means but as an end—the poem, the painting, the reverie has been sufficient of itself. It is not possible, however, to separate in the understanding this running into one of *Will* and *Creative Mind* from the running into one of *Mask* and *Body of Fate*. Without *Mask* and *Body of Fate* the *Will* would have nothing to desire, the *Creative Mind* nothing to apprehend. Since Phase 12 the *Creative Mind* has been so interfused by the *antithetical tincture* that it has more and more confined its contemplation of actual things to those that resemble images of the mind desired by the *Will*. The being has selected, moulded and remoulded, narrowed its circle of living, been more and more the artist, grown more and more "distinguished" in all preference. Now contemplation and desire, united into one, inhabit a world where every beloved image has bodily form, and every bodily form is loved. This love knows nothing of desire, for desire implies effort, and though there is still separation from the loved object, love accepts the separation as necessary to its own existence. *Fate* is known for the boundary that gives our *Destiny* its form, and—as we can desire nothing outside that form—as an expression of our freedom. Chance and Choice have become interchangeable without losing their identity. As all effort has ceased, all thought has become image, because no thought could exist if it were not carried towards its own extinction, amid fear or in contemplation; and every image is separate from every other, for if image were linked to image, the soul would awake from its immovable trance. All that the being has experienced as thought is visible to its eyes as a whole, and in this way it perceives, not as they are to others, but according to its own perception, all orders of existence. Its own body possesses the greatest possible beauty, being indeed that body which the soul will permanently inhabit, when all its phases have been repeated according to the number allotted: that which we call the clarified or Celestial Body. Where the being has lived out of phase, seeking to live through *antithetical* phases as though they had been *primary,* there is now terror of solitude, its forced, painful and slow acceptance, and a life haunted by terrible dreams. Even for the most perfect, there is a time of pain, a passage through a vision, where evil reveals itself in its final meaning. In this passage Christ, it is said, mourned over the length of time and the unworthiness of man's lot to man, whereas his forerunner mourned and his successor will mourn over the shortness of time and the unworthiness of man to his lot; but this cannot yet be understood.

PHASE SEVENTEEN

Will—The *Daimonic* Man.

Mask (from Phase 3). *True*—Simplification through intensity. *False*—Dispersal.

Creative Mind (from Phase 13). *True*—Creative imagination through *antithetical* emotion. *False*—Enforced self-realization.

Body of Fate (from Phase 27)—Enforced Loss.
Examples: Dante, Shelley, Landor.

He is called the *Daimonic* man because Unity of Being, and consequent expression of *Daimonic* thought, is now more easy than at any other phase. As contrasted with Phase 13 and Phase 14, where mental images were separated from one another that they might be subject to knowledge, all now flow, change, flutter, cry out, or mix into something else; but without, as at Phase 16, breaking and bruising one another, for Phase 17, the central phase of its triad, is without frenzy.

The *Will* is falling asunder, but without explosion and noise. The separated fragments seek images rather than ideas, and these the intellect, seated in Phase 13, must synthesise in vain, drawing with its compass-point a line that shall but represent the outline of a bursting pod. The being has for its supreme aim, as it had at Phase 16 (and as all subsequent *antithetical* phases shall have), to hide from itself and others this separation and disorder, and it conceals them under the emotional Image of Phase 3; as Phase 16 concealed its greater violence under that of Phase 2. When true to phase the intellect must turn all its synthetic power to this task. It finds, not the impassioned myth that Phase 16 found, but a *Mask* of simplicity that is also intensity. This *Mask* may represent intellectual or sexual passion; seem some Ahasuerus or Athanase; be the gaunt Dante of the *Divine Comedy;* its corresponding Image may be Shelley's Venus Urania, Dante's Beatrice, or even the Great Yellow Rose of the *Paradiso.* The *Will,* when true to phase, assumes, in assuming the *Mask,* an intensity which is never dramatic but always lyrical and personal, and this intensity, though always a deliberate assumption, is to others but the charm of the being; and yet the *Will* is always aware of the *Body of Fate,* which perpetually destroys this intensity, thereby leaving the *Will* to its own "dispersal".

At Phase 3, not as *Mask* but as phase, there should be perfect physical well-being or balance, though not beauty or emotional intensity, but at Phase 27 are those who turn away from all that Phase 3 represents and seek all those things it is blind to. The *Body of Fate,* therefore, derived from a phase of renunciation, is "loss", and works to make impossible "simplification through intensity". The being, through the intellect, selects some object of desire for a representation of the *Mask* as Image, some woman perhaps, and the *Body of Fate* snatches away the object. Then the intellect *(Creative Mind),* which in the most *antithetical* phases were better described as imagination, must substitute some new image of desire; and in the degree of its power and of its attainment of unity, relate that which is lost, that which has snatched it away, to the new image of desire, that which threatens the new image to the being's unity. If its unity be already past, or if unity be still to come, it may for all that be true to phase. It will then use its intellect merely to isolate *Mask* and Image, as chosen forms or as conceptions of the mind.

If it be out of phase it will avoid the subjective conflict, acquiesce, hope that the *Body of Fate* may die away; and then the *Mask* will cling to it and the Image lure it. It will feel itself betrayed, and persecuted till, entangled in *primary* conflict, it rages against all that destroys *Mask* and Image. It will be subject to nightmare, for its *Creative Mind* (deflected from the Image and *Mask* to the *Body of Fate*) gives an isolated mythological or abstract form to all that excites its hatred. It may even dream of escaping from ill-luck by possessing the impersonal *Body of Fate* of its opposite phase and of exchanging passion for desk and ledger. Because of the habit of synthesis, and of the growing complexity of the energy, which gives many interests, and the still faint perceptions of things in their weight and mass, men of this phase are almost always partisans, propagandists and gregarious; yet because of the *Mask* of simplification, which holds up before them the solitary life of hunters and of fishers and "the groves pale passion loves", they hate parties, crowds, propaganda. Shelley out of phase writes pamphlets, and dreams of converting the world, or of turning man of affairs and upsetting governments, and yet returns again and again to these two images of solitude, a young man whose hair has grown white from the burden of his thoughts, an old man in some shell-strewn cave whom it is possible to call, when speaking to the Sultan, "as inaccessible as God or thou". On the other hand, how subject he is to nightmare! He sees the devil leaning against a tree, is attacked by imaginary assassins, and, in obedience to what he considers a supernatural voice, creates *The Cenci* that he may give to Beatrice Cenci her incredible father. His political enemies are monstrous, meaningless images. And unlike Byron, who is two phases later, he can never see anything that opposes him as it really is. Dante, who lamented his exile as of all possible things the worst for such as he, and sighed for his lost solitude, and yet could never keep from politics, was, according to a contemporary, such a partisan that if a child, or a woman, spoke against his party he would pelt this child or woman with stones. Yet Dante, having attained, as poet, to Unity of Being, as poet saw all things set in order, had an intellect that served the *Mask* alone, that compelled even those things that opposed it to serve, and was content to see both good and evil. Shelley, upon the other hand, in whom even as poet unity was but in part attained, found compensation for his "loss", for the taking away of his children, for his quarrel with his first wife, for later sexual disappointment, for his exile, for his obloquy—there were but some three or four persons, he said, who did not consider him a monster of iniquity—in his hopes for the future of mankind. He lacked the Vision of Evil, could not conceive of the world as a continual conflict, so, though great poet he certainly was, he was not of the greatest kind. Dante suffering injustice and the loss of Beatrice, found divine justice and the heavenly Beatrice, but the justice of *Prometheus Unbound* is a vague propagandist emotion and the women that await its coming are but clouds. This is in part because the age in which Shelley lived was in itself so broken that true Unity of Being was almost impossible, but partly because, being out of phase so far as his practical reason was concerned, he was subject to an *automatonism* which he mistook for poetical invention, especially in his longer poems. *Antithetical* men (Phase 15 once passed) use this *automatonism* to evade hatred, or rather to hide it from their own eyes; perhaps all at some time or other, in moments of fatigue, give themselves up to fantastic, constructed images, or to an almost mechanical laughter.

Landor has been examined in *Per Amica Silentia Lunae.* The most violent of men, he uses his intellect to disengage a visionary image of perfect sanity (*Mask* at Phase 3) seen always in the most serene and classic art imaginable. He had perhaps as much Unity of Being as his age permitted, and possessed, though not in any full measure, the Vision of Evil.

FROM BOOK V: DOVE OR SWAN

IV
A.D. 1 TO A.D. 1050

I think if I could be given a month of Antiquity and leave to spend it where I chose, I would spend it in Byzantium a little before Justinian opened St. Sophia and closed the Academy of Plato. I think I could find in some little wine shop some philosophical worker in mosaic who could answer all my questions, the supernatural descending nearer to him than to Plotinus even, for the pride of his delicate skill would make what was an instrument of power to Princes and Clerics and a murderous madness in the mob, show as a lovely flexible presence like that of a perfect human body.

I think that in early Byzantium, maybe never before or since in recorded history, religious, aesthetic and practical life were one, that architect and artificers—though not, it may be, poets, for language had been the instrument of controversy and must have grown abstract—spoke to the multitude and the few alike. The painter, the mosaic worker, the worker in gold and silver, the illuminator of sacred books, were almost impersonal, almost perhaps without the consciousness of individual design, absorbed in their subject-matter and that the vision of a whole people. They could copy out of old Gospel books those pictures that seemed as sacred as the text, and yet weave all into a vast design, the work of many that seemed the work of one, that made building, picture, pattern, metal-work of rail and lamp, seem but a single image; and this vision, this proclamation of their invisible master, had the Greek nobility, Satan always the still half-divine Serpent, never the horned scarecrow of the didactic Middle Ages.

Essays for the Scribner Edition

(1937)

Introduction

I

THE FIRST PRINCIPLE

A poet writes always of his personal life, in his finest work out of its tragedies, whatever it be, remorse, lost love or mere loneliness; he never speaks directly as to someone at the breakfast table, there is always a phantasmagoria. Dante and Milton had mythologies, Shakespeare the characters of English history, of traditional romance; even when the poet seems most himself, when he is Raleigh and gives potentates the lie, or Shelley 'a nerve o'er which do creep the else unfelt oppressions of mankind', or Byron when 'the heart wears out the breast as the sword wears out the sheath', he is never the bundle of accident and incoherence that sits down to breakfast; he has been re-born as an idea, something intended, complete. A novelist might describe his accidence, his incoherence, he must not, he is more type than man, more passion than type. He is Lear, Romeo, Oedipus, Tiresias; he has stepped out of a play and even the woman he loves is Rosalind, Cleopatra, never The Dark Lady. He is part of his own phantasmagoria and we adore him because nature has grown intelligible, and by so doing a part of our creative power. 'When mind is lost in the light of the Self', says the Prashna Upanishad, 'it dreams no more; still in the body it is lost in happiness.' 'A wise man seeks in Self', says the Chāndôgya Upanishad, 'those that are alive and those that are dead and gets what the world cannot give.' The world knows nothing because it has made nothing, we know everything because we have made everything.

II

SUBJECT-MATTER

It was through the old Fenian leader John O'Leary I found my theme. His long imprisonment, his longer banishment, his magnificent head, his scholarship, his pride, his integrity, all that aristocratic dream nourished amid little shops and little farms, had drawn round him a group of young men; I was but eighteen or nineteen and I had already under the influence of *The Faerie Queene* and *The Sad Shepherd* written a pastoral play, and under that of Shelley's *Prometheus Unbound* two plays, one staged somewhere in the Caucasus, the other in a crater of the moon; and I knew myself to be vague and incoherent. He gave me the poems of Thomas Davis, said they were not good poetry but had changed his life when a young man, spoke of other poets associated with Davis and *The Nation* newspaper, probably lent me their books. I saw even more clearly than O'Leary that they were not good poetry; I read nothing but romantic literature, hated that dry eighteenth-century rhetoric; but they had one quality I admired and admire. They were not separated individual men, they spoke or tried to speak out of a people to a people, behind them stretched the generations. I knew, though but now and then as young men know things, that I must turn from that modern literature Jonathan Swift compared to the web a spider draws out of its bowels; I hated and still hate with an ever growing hatred the literature of the point of view; I wanted, if my ignorance permitted, to get back to Homer, to those that fed at his table. I wanted to cry as all men cried, to laugh as all men laughed, and the Young Ireland poets when not writing mere politics had the same want, but they did not know that the common and its befitting language is the research of a lifetime and when found may lack popular recognition. Then somebody, not O'Leary, told me of Standish O'Grady and his interpretation of Irish legends. O'Leary had sent me to O'Curry but his unarranged and uninterpreted history defeated my boyish indolence.

A generation before *The Nation* newspaper was founded the Royal Irish Academy had begun the study of ancient Irish literature.

That study was as much a gift from that Protestant aristocracy which had created the Parliament as *The Nation* and its school, though Davis and Mitchel were Protestants, was a gift from the Catholic middle classes who were to create the Irish Free State. The Academy persuaded the English government to finance an ordnance survey on a large scale; scholars, including that great scholar O'Donovan, were sent from village to village recording names and their legends. Perhaps it was the last moment when such work could be well done, the memory of the people was still intact, the collectors themselves had perhaps heard or seen the banshee; the Royal Irish Academy and its public with equal enthusiasm welcomed pagan and Christian—thought the Round Towers a commemoration of Persian fire-worship. There was little orthodoxy to take alarm; the Catholics were crushed and cowed; an honoured great-uncle of mine, his portrait by some forgotten master hangs upon my bedroom wall, a Church of Ireland rector, would upon occasion boast that you could not ask a question he could not answer with a perfectly appropriate blasphemy or indecency. When several counties had been surveyed but nothing published, the government, afraid of rousing dangerous patriotic emotion, withdrew support; large manuscript volumes remain containing much picturesque correspondence between scholars.

When modern Irish literature began, O'Grady's influence predominated. He could delight us with an extravagance we were too critical to share; a day will come, he said, when Slievenamon will be more important than Olympus; yet he was no Nationalist as we understood the word, but in rebellion, as he was fond of explaining, against the House of Commons, not against the King. His cousin, that great scholar Hayes O'Grady, would not join our non-political Irish Literary Society because he considered it a Fenian body, but boasted that although he had lived in England for forty years he had never made an English friend. He worked at the British Museum compiling their Gaelic catalogue and translating our heroic tales in an eighteenth-century frenzy; his heroine 'fractured her heart', his hero 'ascended to the apex of the eminence' and there 'vibrated his javelin', and afterwards took ship upon 'colossal ocean's superficies'. Both O'Gradys considered themselves as representing the old Irish land-owning aristocracy; both probably, Standish O'Grady certainly, thought that England, because decadent and democratic, had betrayed their order. It was another member of that order, Lady Gregory, who was to do for the heroic legends in *Gods and Fighting Men* and in *Cuchulain of Muirthemne* what Lady Charlotte Guest's *Mabinogion* had done with less beauty and style for those of Wales. Standish O'Grady had much modern sentiment, his style, like that of John Mitchel forty years before, shaped by Carlyle; she formed her style upon the Anglo-Irish dialect of her neighbourhood, an old vivid speech with a partly Tudor vocabulary, a syntax partly moulded by men who still thought in Gaelic.

I had heard in Sligo cottages or from pilots at Rosses Point endless stories of apparitions, whether of the recent dead, or of the people of history and legend, of that Queen Maeve whose reputed cairn stands on the mountain over the bay. Then at the British Museum I read stories Irish writers of the forties and fifties had written of such apparitions, but they enraged me more than pleased because they turned the country visions into a joke. But when I went from cottage to cottage with Lady Gregory and watched her hand recording that great collection she has called *Visions and Beliefs* I escaped disfiguring humour.

Behind all Irish history hangs a great tapestry, even Christianity had to accept it and be itself pictured there. Nobody looking at its dim folds can say where Christianity begins and Druidism ends; 'There is one perfect among the birds, one perfect among the fish and one among men that is perfect.' I can only explain by that suggestion of recent scholars—Professor Burkitt of Cambridge commended it to my attention—that St Patrick came to Ireland not in the fifth century but towards the end of the second. The great controversies had not begun; Easter was still the first full moon after the Equinox. Upon that day the world had been created, the Ark rested upon Ararat, Moses led the Israelites out of Egypt; the umbilical cord which united Christianity to the ancient world had not yet been cut, Christ was still the half-brother of Dionysus. A man just tonsured by the Druids could learn from the nearest Christian neighbour to sign himself with the Cross without sense of incongruity, nor would his children acquire that sense. The organised clans weakened Church organisation, they could accept the monk but not the bishop.

A modern man, *The Golden Bough* and *Human Personality* in his head, finds much that is congenial in St Patrick's Creed as recorded in his Confessions, and nothing to reject except the word 'soon' in the statement that Christ will soon judge the quick and the dead. He can repeat it, believe it even, without a thought of the historic Christ, or ancient Judea, or of anything subject to historical conjecture and shifting evidence; I repeat it, I think of 'the Self' in the Upanishads. Into this tradition, oral and written, went in later years fragments of Neo-Platonism, Cabbalistic words—I have heard the words Tetragrammaton Agla in Doneraile,—the floating debris of mediaeval thought, but nothing that did not please the solitary mind, even the religious equivalent for Baroque and Rococo could not come to us as thought, perhaps because Gaelic is incapable of abstraction—it came as cruelty. That tapestry filled the scene at the birth of modern Irish literature, it is there in the Synge of *The Well of the Saints,* in James Stephens, and in Lady Gregory throughout, in all of George Russell that did not come from the Upanishads, and in all but my later poetry.

Sometimes I am told in commendation, if the newspaper is Irish, in condemnation if English, that my movement perished under the firing squads of 1916; sometimes that those firing squads made our realistic movement possible. If that statement is true, and it is only so in part, for romance was everywhere receding, it is because in the imagination of Pearse and his fellow soldiers the Sacrifice of the Mass had found the Red Branch in the tapestry; they went out to die calling upon Cuchulain:

> Fall, Hercules, from Heaven in tempests hurled
> To cleanse the beastly stable of this world.

In one sense the poets of 1916 were not of what the newspapers call my school. The Gaelic League, made timid by a modern popularisation of Catholicism sprung from the aspidistra and not from the root of Jesse, dreaded intellectual daring and stuck to dictionary and grammar. Pearse and MacDonagh and others among the executed men would have done, or attempted, in Gaelic what we did, or attempted, in English.

Our mythology, our legends, differ from those of other European countries because down to the end of the seventeenth century they had the attention, perhaps the unquestioned belief, of peasant and noble alike; Homer belongs to sedentary men, even today our ancient queens, our mediaeval soldiers and lovers, can make a pedlar shudder. I can put my own thought, despair perhaps from the study of present circumstance in the light of ancient philosophy, into the mouth of rambling poets of the seventeenth century, or even of some imagined ballad singer of today, and the deeper my thought the more credible, the more peasant-like, are ballad singer and rambling poet. Some modern poets contend that jazz and music hall songs are the folk art of our time, that we should mould our art upon them; we Irish poets, modern men also, reject every folk art that does not go back to Olympus. Give me time and a little youth and I will prove that even 'Johnny I hardly knew ye' goes back.

Mr Arnold Toynbee in an appendix to the second volume of *The Study of History* describes the birth and decay of what he calls the Far Western Christian culture; it lost at the Council of Whitby its chance of mastering Europe, suffered 'final ecclesiastical defeat' in the twelfth century with 'the thorough-going incorporation of the Irish Christendom into the Roman Church, in the political and literary spheres it lasted unbroken till the seventeenth century'. He then insists that if 'Jewish Zionism and Irish Nationalism succeed in achieving their aims, then Jewry and Irishry will each fit into its own tiny niche . . . among sixty or seventy national communities', find life somewhat easier, but cease to be 'the relic of an independent society . . . the romance of ancient Ireland has at last come to an end . . . modern Ireland has made up its mind in our generation to find her level as a willing inmate in a work-a-day modern world.'

If Irish literature goes on as my generation planned it, it may do something to keep the 'Irishry' living, nor will the work of the realists hinder, nor the figures they imagine, nor those described in memoirs of the revolution. These last especially, like certain great political predecessors, Parnell, Swift, Lord Edward, have stepped back into the tapestry. It may be indeed that certain characteristics of the 'Irishry' must grow in importance. When Lady Gregory asked me to annotate her *Visions and Beliefs* I began, that I might understand what she had taken down in Galway, an investigation of contemporary spiritualism. For several years I frequented those mediums who in various poor parts of London instruct artisans or their wives for a few pence upon their relations to their dead, to their employers and their children; then I compared what we had heard in Galway, or I in London, with the visions of Swedenborg, and, after my inadequate notes had been published, with Indian belief. If Lady Gregory had not said when we passed an old man in the woods, 'That man may know the secret of the ages,' I might never have talked with Shree Purohit Swāmi nor made him translate his Master's travels in Tibet, nor helped him translate the Upanishads. I think I now know why the gamekeeper at Coole heard the footsteps of a deer on the edge of the lake where no deer had passed for a hundred years, and why a certain cracked old priest said that nobody had been to hell or Heaven in his time, meaning thereby that the rath had got them all; that the dead stayed where they had lived, or near it, sought no abstract region of blessing or punishment but retreated, as it were, into the hidden character of their neighbourhood. I am convinced that in two or three generations it will become generally known that the mechanical theory has no reality, that the natural and supernatural are knit together, that to escape a dangerous fanaticism we must study a new science; at that moment Europeans may find something attractive in a Christ posed against a background not of Judaism but of Druidism, not shut off in dead history, but flowing, concrete, phenomenal.

I was born into this faith, have lived in it, and shall die in it; my Christ, a legitimate deduction from the Creed of St Patrick as I think, is that Unity of Being Dante compared to a perfectly proportioned human body, Blake's 'Imagination', what the Upanishads have named 'Self': nor is this unity distant and therefore intellectually understandable, but imminent, differing from man to man and age to age, taking upon itself pain and ugliness, 'eye of newt, and leg of frog'.

Subconscious preoccupation with this theme brought me *A Vision*, its harsh geometry an incomplete interpretation. The 'Irishry' have preserved their ancient 'deposit' through wars which, during the sixteenth and seventeenth centuries, became wars of extermination; no people, Lecky said at the opening of his *Ireland in the Eighteenth Century*, have undergone greater persecution, nor did that persecution altogether cease up to our own day. No people hate as we do in whom that past is always alive; there are moments when hatred poisons my life and I accuse myself of effeminacy because I have not given it adequate expression. It is not enough to have put it into the mouth of a rambling peasant poet. Then I remind myself that, though mine is the first English marriage I know of in the direct line, all my family names are English and that

I owe my soul to Shakespeare, to Spenser and to Blake, perhaps to William Morris, and to the English language in which I think, speak and write, that everything I love has come to me through English; my hatred tortures me with love, my love with hate. I am like the Tibetan monk who dreams at his initiation that he is eaten by a wild beast and learns on waking that he himself is eater and eaten. This is Irish hatred and solitude, the hatred of human life that made Swift write *Gulliver* and the epitaph upon his tomb, that can still make us wag between extremes and doubt our sanity.

Again and again I am asked why I do not write in Gaelic; some four or five years ago I was invited to dinner by a London society and found myself among London journalists, Indian students and foreign political refugees. An Indian paper says it was a dinner in my honour, I hope not; I have forgotten though I have a clear memory of my own angry mind. I should have spoken as men are expected to speak at public dinners; I should have paid and been paid conventional compliments; then they would speak of the refugees, from that on all would be lively and topical, foreign tyranny would be arraigned, England seem even to those confused Indians the protector of liberty; I grew angrier and angrier; Wordsworth, that typical Englishman, had published his famous sonnet to François Dominique Toussaint, a Santo Domingo negro:

> There's not a breathing of the common wind
> That will forget thee

in the year when Emmet conspired and died, and he remembered that rebellion as little as the half hanging and the pitch cap that preceded it by half a dozen years. That there might be no topical speeches I denounced the oppression of the people of India; being a man of letters, not a politician, I told how they had been forced to learn everything, even their own Sanscrit, through the vehicle of English till the first discoverers of wisdom had become bywords for vague abstract facility. I begged the Indian writers present to remember that no man can think or write with music and vigour except in his mother tongue. I turned a friendly audience hostile, yet when I think of that scene I am unrepentant and angry.

I could no more have written in Gaelic than can those Indians write in English; Gaelic is my national language, but it is not my mother tongue.

III

STYLE AND ATTITUDE

Style is almost unconscious. I know what I have tried to do, little what I have done. Contemporary lyric poems, even those that moved me—'The Stream's Secret', 'Dolores'—seemed too long, but an Irish preference for a swift current might be mere indolence, yet Burns may have felt the same when he read Thomson and Cowper. The English mind is meditative, rich, deliberate; it may remember the Thames valley. I planned to write short lyrics or poetic drama where every speech [would] be short and concentrated, knit by dramatic tension, and I did so with more confidence because young English poets were at that time writing out of emotion at the moment of crisis, though their old slow-moving meditation returned almost at once. Then, and in this English poetry has followed my lead, I tried to make the language of poetry coincide with that of passionate, normal speech. I wanted to write in whatever language comes most naturally when we soliloquise, as I do all day long, upon the events of our own lives or of any life where we can see ourselves for the moment. I sometimes compare myself with the mad old slum women I hear denouncing and remembering; 'how dare you,' I heard one say of some imaginary suitor, 'and you without health or a home'. If I spoke my thoughts aloud they might be as angry and as wild. It was a long time before I had made a language to my liking; I began to make it when I discovered some twenty years ago that I must seek, not as Wordsworth thought words in common use, but a powerful and passionate syntax, and a complete coincidence between period and stanza. Because I need a passionate syntax for passionate subject-matter I compel myself to accept those traditional metres that have developed with the language. Ezra Pound, Turner, Lawrence, wrote admirable free verse, I could not. I would lose myself, become joyless like those mad old women. The translators of the Bible, Sir Thomas Browne, certain translators from the Greek when translators still bothered about rhythm, created a form midway between prose and verse that seems natural to impersonal meditation; but all that is personal soon rots; it must be packed in ice or salt. Once when I was in delirium from pneumonia I dictated a letter to George Moore telling him to eat salt because it was a symbol of eternity; the delirium passed, I had no memory of that letter, but I must have meant what I now mean. If I wrote of personal love or sorrow in free verse, or in any rhythm that left it unchanged, amid all its accident, I would be full of self-contempt because of my egotism and indiscretion, and I foresee the boredom of my reader. I must choose a traditional stanza, even what I alter must seem traditional. I commit my emotion to shepherds, herdsmen, camel-drivers, learned men, Milton's or Shelley's Platonist, that tower Palmer drew. Talk to me of originality and I will turn on you with rage. I am a crowd, I am a lonely man, I am nothing. Ancient salt is best packing. The heroes of Shakespeare convey to us through their looks, or through the metaphorical patterns of their speech, the sudden enlargement of their vision, their ecstasy at the approach of death, 'She should have died hereafter', 'Of many million kisses, the poor last', 'Absent thee from felicity awhile'; they have become God or Mother Goddess, the pelican, 'My baby at my breast', but all must be cold; no actress has ever sobbed when she played Cleopatra, even the shallow brain of a producer has never thought of such a thing. The supernatural is present, cold winds blow across our hands, upon our faces, the thermometer falls, and because of that cold we are hated by journalists and groundlings. There may be in this or that detail painful tragedy, but in the whole work none. I have heard Lady Gregory say, rejecting some play in the modern manner sent to the Abbey Theatre, 'Tragedy must be a joy to the man who dies.' Nor is it any different with lyrics, songs, narrative poems; neither scholars nor the populace have sung or read anything generation after generation because of its pain. The maid of honour whose tragedy they sing must be lifted out of history with timeless pattern, she is one of the four Maries, the rhythm is old and familiar, imagination must dance, must be carried beyond feeling into the aboriginal ice. Is ice the correct word? I once boasted, copying the phrase from a letter of my father's, that I would write a poem 'cold and passionate as the dawn'.

When I wrote in blank verse I was dissatisfied; my vaguely mediaeval *Countess Cathleen* fitted the measure, but our Heroic Age went better, or so I fancied, in the ballad metre of *The Green Helmet*. There was something in what I felt about Deirdre, about Cuchulain, that rejected the Renaissance and its characteristic metres, and this was a principal reason why I created in dance plays the form that varies blank verse with lyric metres. When I speak blank verse and analyse my feelings I stand at a moment of history when instinct, its traditional songs and dances, its general agreement, is of the past. I have been cast up out of the whale's belly though I still remember the sound and sway that came from beyond its ribs, and, like the Queen in Paul Fort's ballad, I smell of the fish of the sea. The contrapuntal structure of the verse, to employ a term adopted by Robert Bridges, combines the past and present. If I repeat the first line of *Paradise Lost* so as to emphasise its five feet I am among the folk singers, 'Of mán's fírst dísobédience ánd the frúit', but speak it as I should I cross it with another emphasis, that of passionate prose, 'Of mán's fírst disobédience and the frúit', or 'Of mán's fírst dísobedi-ence and the frúit', the folk song is still there, but a ghostly voice, an unvariable possibility, an unconscious norm. What moves me and my hearer is a vivid speech that has no laws except that it must not exor-cise the ghostly voice. I am awake and asleep, at my moment of rev-elation, self-possessed in self-surrender; there is no rhyme, no echo of the beaten drum, the dancing foot, that would overset my balance. When I was a boy I wrote a poem upon dancing that had one good line: 'They snatch with their hands at the sleep of the skies.' If I sat down and thought for a year I would discover that but for certain syllabic limitations, a rejection or acceptance of certain elisions, I must wake or sleep.

The Countess Cathleen could speak a blank verse which I had loosened, almost put out of joint, for her need, because I thought of her as mediaeval and thereby connected her with the general Euro-pean movement. For Deirdre and Cuchulain and all the other fig-ures of Irish legend are still in the whale's belly.

IV

WHITHER?

The young English poets reject dream and personal emotion; they have thought out opinions that join them to this or that polit-ical party; they employ an intricate psychology, action in character, not as in the ballads character in action, and all consider that they have a right to the same close attention that men pay to the mathe-matician and the metaphysician. One of the more distinguished has just explained that man has hitherto slept but must now awake. They are determined to express the factory, the metropolis, that they may be modern. Young men teaching school in some picturesque cathedral town, or settled for life in Capri or in Sicily, defend their type of metaphor by saying that it comes naturally to a man who travels to his work by Tube. I am indebted to a man of this school who went through my work at my request, crossing out all conventional metaphors, but they seem to me to have rejected also those dream associations which were the whole art of Mallarmé. He had topped a previous wave. As they express not what the Upanishads call 'that ancient Self' but individual intellect, they have the right to choose the man in the Tube because of his objective importance. They attempt to kill the whale, push the Renaissance higher yet, out-think Leonardo; their verse kills the folk ghost and yet would remain verse. I am joined to the 'Irishry' and I expect a counter-Renaissance. No doubt it is part of the game to push that Renaissance; I make no complaint; I am accustomed to the geometrical arrangement of history in *A Vision,* but I go deeper than 'custom' for my convictions. When I stand upon O'Connell Bridge in the half-light and notice that discordant architecture, all those electric signs, where modern heterogeneity has taken physical form, a vague hatred comes up out of my own dark and I am certain that wherever in Europe there are minds strong enough to lead others the same vague hatred rises; in four or five or in less generations this hatred will have issued in violence and imposed some kind of rule of kindred. I cannot know the nature of that rule, for its opposite fills the light; all I can do to bring it nearer is to intensify my hatred. I am no Nationalist, except in Ireland for passing reasons; State and Nation are the work of intellect, and when you consider what comes before and after them they are, as Victor Hugo said of something or other, not worth the blade of grass God gives for the nest of the linnet.

Introduction to Essays

WHEN I WAS thirty I thought the best of modern pictures were four or five portraits by Watts (I disliked his allegorical pictures—had not allegory spoiled Edmund Spenser); four or five pictures by Madox Brown; four or five early Millaises; four or five Rossettis where there are several figures engaged in some dramatic action; and an indefinite number of engravings by William Blake, who was my particular study. When I was thirty-five or so a woman of genius asked me to defend her against a German connoisseur. She had made her beautiful house a shrine for certain late Burne-Joneses—'that faun's head'

> The Burne-Jones Cartons
> Have preserved her eyes.

When I arrived he had firmly planted on a drawing-room chair a picture by Renoir perhaps or an imitator, of a fat naked woman lying on a Turkey carpet and had begun to call Burne-Jones empty and obsolete. She took me to another room and reproached me for keeping silent, but excused me as I must be upset by the connoisseur's 'over-dressed wife'. I could not excuse myself because I admired that slight, elegant, pale lady.

A little later poets younger than myself, especially the one I knew best, began to curse that romantic subject-matter which English literature seemed to share with all great literature, those traditional metres which seemed to have grown up with the language, and still, though getting much angrier, I was silent. I was silent because I am a timid man except before a piece of paper or rioters at the Abbey Theatre, and even there my courage is limited to certain topics. Perhaps I am a better man than I think, perhaps some part of my timidity is a dread of speaking ill-chosen words, of reproving Mr Wells, let us say, with the voice of Bulwer-Lytton; or perhaps there is some censorship like that of the psycho-analysts—yes, there must be a censorship. Now that I have all my critical prose before me, much seems an evasion, a deliberate turning away. Can I do better now that I am almost beyond caring?

I have never said clearly that I condemn all that is not tradition, that there is a subject-matter which has descended like that 'deposit' certain philosophers speak of. At the end of his essay upon 'Style' Pater says that a book written according to the principles he has laid down will be well written, but whether it is a great book or not depends upon subject-matter. This subject-matter is something I have received from the generations, part of that compact with my fellow-men made in my name before I was born; I cannot break from it without breaking from some part of my own nature; and sometimes it has come to me in supernormal experience; I have met with ancient myths in my dreams, brightly lit; and I think it allied to the wisdom or instinct that guides a migratory bird.

A table of values, heroic joy always, intellectual curiosity and so on—and a public theme: in Japan the mountain scenery of China, in Greece its cyclic tales, in Europe the Christian mythology, this or that national theme. I speak of poets and imaginative writers; the great realistic novelists almost without exception describe familiar scenes and people; realism is always topical, it has for public theme the public itself. Flaubert excused the failure of the principal character in his *Salammbô* in the words 'I could not visit her'. I think of the German actress who said to a reporter, 'To know a man you must talk with him, eat with him, sleep with him. That is how I know Mr Bernard Shaw.' Then too I would have all the arts draw together; recover their ancient association, the painter painting what the poet has written, the musician setting the poet's words to simple airs, that the horseman and the engine-driver may sing them at their work. Nor am I for a changeless tradition. I would rejoice if a rich betrothed man asked Mr T. S. Eliot and the dancer Ninette de Valois to pick a musician and compose a new marriage service, for such a service might restore a lost subject-matter to the imaginative arts and be good for the clergy. I admit other themes, even those that have no tradition; I have never blamed the brothers Carracci for painting the butcher's shop they came from, and why should not that fat naked woman look like pork? But those themes we share and inherit so long as they engage our emotions come first.

When that is no longer possible we are broken off and separate, some sort of dry faggot, and the time has come to read criticism and talk of our point of view. I thought when I was young—Walt Whitman had something to do with it—that the poet, painter and musician should do nothing but express themselves. When the laboratories, pulpits and newspapers had imposed themselves in the place of tradition the thought was our protection. It may be so still in the provinces, but sometimes when the provinces are out of earshot I may speak the truth. A poet is justified [not] by the expression of himself, but by the public he finds or creates, a public made by others ready to his hand if he is a mere popular poet, but a new public, a new form of life, if he is a man of genius. Somebody saw a woman of exuberant beauty coming from a public house with a pot of beer and commended her to Rossetti; twenty years later Mrs Langtry called upon Watts and delighted him with her simplicity. Lady Gregory had the story from Watts himself. Two painters created their public; two types of beauty decided what strains of blood would most prevail.

I say against all the faggots that it is our first business to paint, or describe, desirable people, places, states of mind. Rimbaud showed in a famous poem that the picking of lice was a good lawful theme for the Silver Age; the radical critics encourage our painters to decorate the walls with those cubes, triangles, ovoids, that are all stiff under the touch, or with gods and goddesses, distorted by Rubensesque exaggeration, dulled by hard doll-like faces that they may chill desire. We have arrived at that point where in every civilisation Caesar is killed, Alexander catches some complaint and dies; personality is exhausted, that conscious desirous shaping fate rules. But a relative of mine wears silver, many rings, and turns from gold with indifference; there are poetry societies that understand what I never could, books of prosody, and the art schools are more intelligent every day. (I have written of all these things in A Vision, but that book is intended, to use a phrase of Jacob Boehme's, for my 'schoolmates only'.)

Introduction to Plays

The theatre for which these plays were written was the creation of seven people: four players, Sara Allgood, her sister Maire O'Neill, girls in a blind factory who joined a patriotic society; William Fay, Frank Fay, an electric light fitter and an accountant's clerk who got up plays at a coffee-house; three writers, Lady Gregory, John Synge, and I. If we all told the story we would all tell it differently. Somewhere among my printed diaries is a note describing how on the same night my two sisters and their servant dreamt the same dream in three different grotesque forms. Once I was in meditation with three students of the supernormal faculties; our instructor had given us the same theme, what, I have forgotten; one saw a ripe fruit, one an unripe, one a lit torch, one an unlit. Science has never thought about the subject and so has no explanation of those parallel streams that make up a great part of history. When I follow back my stream to its source I find two dominant desires: I wanted to get rid of irrelevant movement—the stage must become still that words might keep all their vividness—and I wanted vivid words. When I saw a London play, I saw actors crossing the stage not because the play compelled them, but because a producer said they must do so to keep the attention of the audience; and I heard words that had no vividness except what they borrowed from the situation. It seems that I was confirmed in this idea or I found it when I first saw Sarah Bernhardt play in *Phèdre,* and that it was I who converted the players, but I am old, I must have many false memories; perhaps I was Synge's convert. It was certainly a day of triumph when the first act of *The Well of the Saints* held its audience, though the two chief persons sat side by side under a stone cross from start to finish. This rejection of all needless movement first drew the attention of critics. The players still try to preserve it, though audiences accustomed to the cinema expect constant change; perhaps it was most necessary in that first period when the comedies of Lady Gregory, the tragi-comedies of Synge, my own blank-verse plays, made up our repertory, all needing whether in verse or prose an ear attentive to every rhythm.

I hated the existing conventions of the theatre, not because conventions are wrong but because soliloquies and players who must always face the audience and stand far apart when they speak— 'dressing the stage' it was called—had been mixed up with too many bad plays to be endurable. Frank Fay agreed, yet he knew the history of all the conventions and sometimes loved them. I would put into his hands a spear instead of a sword because I knew that he would flourish a sword in imitation of an actor in an eighteenth-century engraving. He knew everything, even that Racine at rehearsal made his leading lady speak on musical notes and that Ireland had preserved longer than England the rhythmical utterance of the Shakespearean stage. He was openly, dogmatically, of that school of Talma which permits an actor, as Gordon Craig has said, to throw up an arm calling down the thunderbolts of Heaven, instead of seeming to pick up pins from the floor. Were he living now and both of us young, I would ask his help to elaborate new conventions in writing and representation; for Synge, Lady Gregory, and I were all instinctively of the school of Talma. Do not those tragic sentences, 'shivering into seventy winters,' 'a starved ass braying in the yard,' require convention as much as a blank-verse line? And there are scenes in *The Well of the Saints* which seem to me over-rich in words because the realistic action does not permit that stilling and slowing which turns the imagination in upon itself.

II

I wanted all my poetry to be spoken on a stage or sung and, because I did not understand my own instincts, gave half a dozen wrong or secondary reasons; but a month ago I understood my reasons. I have spent my life in clearing out of poetry every phrase written for the eye, and bringing all back to syntax that is for ear alone. Let the eye take delight in the form of the singer and in the panorama of the stage and be content with that. Charles Ricketts once designed for me a black jester costume for the singer, and both he and Craig helped with the panorama, but my audience was for comedy—for Synge, for Lady Gregory, for O'Casey—not for me. I was content, for I knew that comedy was the modern art.

As I altered my syntax I altered my intellect. Browning said that he could not write a successful play because interested not in character in action but in action in character. I had begun to get rid of everything that is not, whether in lyric or dramatic poetry, in some sense character in action; a pause in the midst of action perhaps, but action always its end and theme. 'Write for the ear,' I thought, so that you may be instantly understood as when actor or folk singer stands before an audience. I delight in active men, taking the same delight in soldier and craftsman; I would have poetry turn its back upon all that modish curiosity, psychology—the poetic theme has always been present. I recall an Indian tale: certain men said to the greatest of the sages, 'Who are your Masters?' And he replied, 'The wind and the harlot, the virgin and the child, the lion and the eagle.'

FROM On the Boiler

(1939)

FROM Preliminaries

IV

As I write these words the Abbey Players are finishing a successful American tour. These tours, and Irish songs and novels, when they come from a deeper life than their nineteenth-century predecessors, are taking the place of political speakers, political organisations, in holding together the twenty scattered millions conscious of their Irish blood. The attitude towards life of Irish writers and dramatists at this moment will have historical importance. The success of the Abbey Theatre has grown out of a single conviction of its founders: I was the spokesman because I was born arrogant and had learnt an artist's arrogance—'Not what you want but what we want'—and we were the first modern theatre that said it. I did not speak for John Synge, Augusta Gregory and myself alone, but for all the dramatists of the theatre. Again and again somebody speaking for our audience, for an influential newspaper or political organisation, has demanded more of this kind of play or less, or none, of that. They have not understood that we cannot, and if we could would not comply; the moment any dramatist has some dramatic sense and applies it to our Irish theme he is played. We may help him with his technique or to clear his mind of the second-hand or the second-rate in their cruder forms, but beyond that we can do nothing. He must find himself and mould his dramatic form to his nature after his own fashion, and that is why we have produced some of the best plays of modern times, and a far greater number of the worst. And what I have said of the dramatists is true of the actors, though there the bad comedians do not reach our principal company. I have seen English producers turn their players into

440

mimics; but all our producers do for theirs, or so it was in my day and I suppose it is still the same, is to help them to understand the play and their own natures.

Yet the theatre has not, apart from this one quality, gone my way or in any way I wanted it to go, and often looking back I have wondered if I did right in giving so much of my life to the expression of other men's genius. According to the Indians a man may do much good yet lose his own soul. Then I say to myself, I have had greater luck than any other modern English-speaking dramatist; I have aimed at tragic ecstasy, and here and there in my own work and in the work of my friends I have seen it greatly played. What does it matter that it belongs to a dead art and to a time when a man spoke out of an experience and a culture that were not of his time alone, but held his time, as it were, at arm's length, that he might be a spectator of the ages. I am haunted by certain moments: Miss O'Neill in the last act of Synge's *Deirdre* 'Stand a little further off with the quarrelling of fools'; Kerrigan and Miss O'Neill playing in a private house that scene in Augusta Gregory's *Full Moon* where the young mad people in their helpless joy sing 'The Boys of Queen Anne'; Frank Fay's entrance in the last act of *The Well of the Saints*; William Fay at the end of *On Baile's Strand*; Mrs Patrick Campbell in my *Deirdre*, passionate and solitary; and in later years that great artist Ninette de Valois in *Fighting the Waves*. These things will, it may be, haunt me on my deathbed; what matter if the people prefer another art, I have had my fill.

Prose Fiction

FROM The Celtic Twilight

(1893, 1902)

'Dust Hath Closed Helen's Eye'
(1899)

I

I have been lately to a little group of houses, not many enough to be called a village, in the barony of Kiltartan in County Galway, whose name, Ballylee, is known through all the west of Ireland. There is the old square castle,[1] Ballylee, inhabited by a farmer and his wife, and a cottage where their daughter and their son-in-law live, and a little mill with an old miller, and old ash-trees throwing green shadows upon a little river and great stepping-stones. I went there two or three times last year to talk to the miller about Biddy Early, a wise woman that lived in Clare some years ago, and about her saying, 'There is a cure for all evil between the two mill-wheels of Ballylee,' and to find out from him or another whether she meant the moss between the running waters or some other herb. I have been there this summer, and I shall be there again before it is autumn, because Mary Hynes, a beautiful woman whose name is still a wonder by turf fires, died there sixty years ago; for our feet would linger where beauty has lived its life of sorrow to make us understand that it is not of the world. An old man brought me a little way from the mill and the castle, and down a long, narrow boreen that was nearly lost in brambles and sloe-bushes, and he said, 'That is the little old foundation of the house, but the most of it is taken for building walls, and the goats have ate those bushes that are growing over it till they've got cranky, and they won't grow

---

[1] Ballylee Castle, or Thoor Ballylee, as I have named it to escape from the too magnificent word 'castle,' is now my property, and I spend my summers or some part of them there. (1924.)

445

any more. They say she was the handsomest girl in Ireland, her skin was like dribbled snow'—he meant driven snow, perhaps,—'and she had blushes in her cheeks. She had five handsome brothers, but all are gone now!' I talked to him about a poem in Irish, Raftery, a famous poet, made about her, and how it said, 'There is a strong cellar in Ballylee.' He said the strong cellar was the great hole where the river sank underground, and he brought me to a deep pool, where an otter hurried away under a grey boulder, and told me that many fish came up out of the dark water at early morning 'to taste the fresh water coming down from the hills.'

I first heard of the poem from an old woman who lives about two miles farther up the river, and who remembers Raftery and Mary Hynes. She says, 'I never saw anybody so handsome as she was, and I never will till I die,' and that he was nearly blind, and had 'no way of living but to go round and to mark some house to go to, and then all the neighbours would gather to hear. If you treated him well he'd praise you, but if you did not, he'd fault you in Irish. He was the great-est poet in Ireland, and he'd make a song about that bush if he chanced to stand under it. There was a bush he stood under from the rain, and he made verses praising it, and then when the water came through he made verses dispraising it.' She sang the poem to a friend and to myself in Irish, and every word was audible and expressive, as the words in a song were always, as I think, before music grew too proud to be the garment of words, flowing and changing with the flowing and changing of their energies. The poem is not as natural as the best Irish poetry of the last century, for the thoughts are arranged in a too obviously traditional form, so the old poor half-blind man who made it has to speak as if he were a rich farmer offer-ing the best of everything to the woman he loves, but it has naïve and tender phrases. The friend that was with me has made some of the translation, but some of it has been made by the countrypeople themselves. I think it has more of the simplicity of the Irish verses than one finds in most translations.

> Going to Mass by the will of God,
> The day came wet and the wind rose;
> I met Mary Hynes at the cross of Kiltartan,
> And I fell in love with her then and there.

I spoke to her kind and mannerly,
As by report was her own way;
And she said, 'Raftery, my mind is easy,
You may come to-day to Ballylee.'

When I heard her offer I did not linger,
When her talk went to my heart my heart rose.
We had only to go across the three fields,
We had daylight with us to Ballylee.

The table was laid with glasses and a quart measure,
She had fair hair, and she sitting beside me;
And she said, 'Drink, Raftery, and a hundred welcomes,
There is a strong cellar in Ballylee.'

O star of light and O sun in harvest,
O amber hair, O my share of the world,
Will you come with me upon Sunday
Till we agree together before all the people?

I would not grudge you a song every Sunday evening,
Punch on the table, or wine if you would drink it,
But, O King of Glory, dry the roads before me
Till I find the way to Ballylee.

There is sweet air on the side of the hill
When you are looking down upon Ballylee;
When you are walking in the valley picking nuts and black-
    berries,
There is music of the birds in it and music of the Sidhe.

What is the worth of greatness till you have the light
Of the flower of the branch that is by your side?
There is no god to deny it or to try and hide it,
She is the sun in the heavens who wounded my heart.

There was no part of Ireland I did not travel,
From the rivers to the tops of the mountains,
To the edge of Lough Greine whose mouth is hidden,
And I saw no beauty but was behind hers.

Her hair was shining, and her brows were shining too;
Her face was like herself, her mouth pleasant and sweet.

She is the pride, and I give her the branch,
She is the shining flower of Ballylee.

It is Mary Hynes, the calm and easy woman,
Has beauty in her mind and in her face.
If a hundred clerks were gathered together,
They could not write down a half of her ways.

An old weaver, whose son is supposed to go away among the Sidhe (the faeries) at night, says, 'Mary Hynes was the most beautiful thing ever made. My mother used to tell me about her, for she'd be at every hurling, and wherever she was she was dressed in white. As many as eleven men asked her in marriage in one day, but she wouldn't have any of them. There was a lot of men up beyond Kilbecanty one night sitting together drinking, and talking of her, and one of them got up and set out to go to Ballylee and see her; but Cloone Bog was open then, and when he came to it he fell into the water, and they found him dead there in the morning. She died of the fever that was before the famine.' Another old man says he was only a child when he saw her, but he remembered that 'the strongest man that was among us, one John Madden, got his death of the head of her, cold he got crossing rivers in the nighttime to get to Ballylee.' This is perhaps the man the other remembered, for tradition gives the one thing many shapes. There is an old woman who remembers her, at Derrybrien among the Echtge hills, a vast desolate place, which has changed little since the old poem said, 'the stag upon the cold summit of Echtge hears the cry of the wolves,' but still mindful of many poems and of the dignity of ancient speech. She says, 'The sun and the moon never shone on anybody so handsome, and her skin was so white that it looked blue, and she had two little blushes on her cheeks.' And an old wrinkled woman who lives close by Ballylee, and has told me many tales of the Sidhe, says, 'I often saw Mary Hynes, she was handsome indeed. She had two bunches of curls beside her cheeks, and they were the colour of silver. I saw Mary Molloy that was drowned in the river beyond, and Mary Guthrie that was in Ardrahan, but she took the sway of them both, a very comely creature. I was at her wake too—she had seen too much of the world. She was a kind creature. One day I was coming home through that field beyond, and I was tired, and who should come out but the Poisin Glegeal (the shining flower), and she gave me a glass of new milk.'

This old woman meant no more than some beautiful bright colour by the colour of silver, for though I knew an old man—he is dead now—who thought she might know 'the cure for all the evils in the world,' that the Sidhe knew, she has seen too little gold to know its colour. But a man by the shore at Kinvara, who is too young to remember Mary Hynes, says, 'Everybody says there is no one at all to be seen now so handsome; it is said she had beautiful hair, the colour of gold. She was poor, but her clothes every day were the same as Sunday, she had such neatness. And if she went to any kind of a meeting, they would all be killing one another for a sight of her, and there was a great many in love with her, but she died young. It is said that no one that has a song made about them will ever live long.'

Those who are much admired are, it is held, taken by the Sidhe, who can use ungoverned feeling for their own ends, so that a father, as an old herb-doctor told me once, may give his child into their hands, or a husband his wife. The admired and desired are only safe if one says 'God bless them' when one's eyes are upon them. The old woman that sang the song thinks, too, that Mary Hynes was 'taken,' as the phrase is, 'for they have taken many that are not handsome, and why would they not take her? And people came from all parts to look at her, and maybe there were some that did not say "God bless her." ' An old man who lives by the sea at Duras has as little doubt that she was taken, 'for there are some living yet can remember her coming to the pattern[1] there beyond, and she was said to be the handsomest girl in Ireland.' She died young because the gods loved her, for the Sidhe are the gods, and it may be that the old saying, which we forget to understand literally, meant her manner of death in old times. These poor countrymen and countrywomen in their beliefs, and in their emotions, are many years nearer to that old Greek world, that set beauty beside the fountain of things, than are our men of learning. She 'had seen too much of the world'; but these old men and women, when they tell of her, blame another and not her, and though they can be hard, they grow gentle as the old men of Troy grew gentle when Helen passed by on the walls.

The poet who helped her to so much fame has himself a great fame throughout the west of Ireland. Some think that Raftery was half blind, and say, 'I saw Raftery, a dark man, but he had sight enough to see

---

[1] A 'pattern,' or 'patron,' is a festival in honour of a saint.

her,' or the like, but some think he was wholly blind, as he may have been at the end of his life. Fable makes all things perfect in their kind, and her blind people must never look on the world and the sun. I asked a man I met one day, when I was looking for a pool *na mna Sidhe* where women of Faery have been seen, how Raftery could have admired Mary Hynes so much if he had been altogether blind. He said, 'I think Raftery was altogether blind, but those that are blind have a way of seeing things, and have the power to know more, and to feel more, and to do more, and to guess more than those that have their sight, and a certain wit and a certain wisdom is given to them.' Everybody, indeed, will tell you that he was very wise, for was he not not only blind but a poet? The weaver, whose words about Mary Hynes I have already given, says, 'His poetry was the gift of the Almighty, for there are three things that are the gift of the Almighty—poetry and dancing and principles. That is why in the old times an ignorant man coming down from the hillside would be better behaved and have better learning than a man with education you'd meet now, for they got it from God'; and a man at Coole says, 'When he put his finger to one part of his head, everything would come to him as if it was written in a book'; and an old pensioner at Kiltartan says, 'He was standing under a bush one time, and he talked to it, and it answered him back in Irish. Some say it was the bush that spoke, but it must have been an enchanted voice in it, and it gave him the knowledge of all the things of the world. The bush withered up afterwards, and it is to be seen on the roadside now between this and Rahasine.' There is a poem of his about a bush, which I have never seen, and it may have come out of the cauldron of Fable in this shape.

A friend of mine met a man once who had been with him when he died, but the people say that he died alone, and one Maurteen Gillane told Dr. Hyde that all night long a light was seen streaming up to heaven from the roof of the house where he lay, and 'that was the angels who were with him'; and all night long there was a great light in the hovel, 'and that was the angels who were waking him. They gave that honour to him because he was so good a poet, and sang such religious songs.' It may be that in a few years Fable, who changes mortalities to immortalities in her cauldron, will have changed Mary Hynes and Raftery to perfect symbols of the sorrow of beauty and of the magnificence and penury of dreams.

1900

II

When I was in a northern town a while ago I had a long talk with a man who had lived in a neighbouring country district when he was a boy. He told me that when a very beautiful girl was born in a family that had not been noted for good looks, her beauty was thought to have come from the Sidhe, and to bring misfortune with it. He went over the names of several beautiful girls that he had known, and said that beauty had never brought happiness to anybody. It was a thing, he said, to be proud of and afraid of. I wish I had written out his words at the time, for they were more picturesque than my memory of them.

1902

Regina, Regina Pigmeorum, Veni[1]
(1893)

ONE NIGHT a middle-aged man, who had lived all his life far from the noise of cab-wheels, a young girl, a relation of his, who was reported to be enough of a seeress to catch a glimpse of unaccountable lights moving over the fields among the cattle, and myself, were walking along a far western sandy shore. We talked of the Forgetful People, as the faery people are sometimes called, and came in the midst of our talk to a notable haunt of theirs, a shallow cave amidst black rocks, with its reflection under it in the wet sea sand. I asked the young girl if she could see anything, for I had quite a number of things to ask the Forgetful People. She stood still for a few minutes, and I saw that she was passing into a kind of waking trance, in which the cold sea breeze no longer troubled her, nor the dull boom of the sea distracted her attention. I then called aloud the names of the great faeries, and in a moment or two she said that she could hear music far inside the rocks, and then a sound of confused talking, and of people stamping their feet as if to applaud some unseen performer. Up to this my other friend had been walking to and fro some yards off, but now he passed close to us, and as he did so said suddenly that we were going to be interrupted, for he heard the laughter of chil-

---

[1] These words were used as an evocation in Windsor Forest by Lilly, the astrologer. (1924.)

dren somewhere beyond the rocks. We were, however, quite alone. The spirits of the place had begun to cast their influence over him also. In a moment he was corroborated by the girl, who said that bursts of laughter had begun to mingle with the music, the confused talking, and the noise of feet. She next saw a bright light streaming out of the cave, which seemed to have grown much deeper, and a quantity of little people,[1] in various coloured dresses, red predominating, dancing to a tune which she did not recognise.

I then bade her call out to the queen of the little people to come and talk with us. There was, however, no answer to her command. I therefore repeated the words aloud myself, and in a moment she described a very beautiful tall woman, who came out of the cave. I too had by this time fallen into a kind of trance,[2] in which what we call the unreal had begun to take upon itself a masterful reality, and I had an impression, not anything I could call an actual vision, of gold ornaments and dark hair. I then bade the girl tell this tall queen to marshal her followers according to their natural divisions, that we might see them. I found as before that I had to repeat the command myself. The beings then came out of the cave, and drew themselves up, if I remember rightly, in four bands. One of these bands, according to her description, carried boughs of mountain-ash in their hands, and another had necklaces made apparently of serpents' scales, but their dress I cannot remember. I asked their queen to tell the seeress whether these caves were the greatest faery haunts in the neighbourhood. Her lips moved, but the answer was inaudible. I bade the seeress lay her hand upon the breast of the queen, and after that she heard every word quite distinctly. No, this was not the greatest faery haunt, for there was a greater one a little farther ahead. I then asked her whether it was true that she and her people carried away mortals, and if so, whether they put another soul in the place of the one they had taken. 'We change the bodies,' was her answer. 'Are any of you ever born into mortal life?' 'Yes.'

[1] The people and faeries in Ireland are sometimes as big as we are, sometimes bigger, and sometimes, as I have been told, about three feet high. The old Mayo woman I so often quote thinks that it is something in our eyes that makes them seem big or little.
[2] The word 'trance' gives the wrong impression. I had learned from MacGregor Mathers and his pupils to so suspend the will that the imagination moved of itself. The girl was, however, fully entranced, and the man so affected by her that he heard the children's voices as if with his physical ears. On two occasions, later on, her trance so affected me that I also heard or saw some part of what she did as if with physical eyes and ears (1924).

'Do I know any who were among your people before birth?' 'You
do.' 'Who are they?' 'It would not be lawful for you to know.' I then
asked whether she and her people were not 'dramatisations of our
moods'? 'She does not understand,' said my friend, 'but says that
her people are much like human beings, and do most of the things
human beings do.' I asked her other questions, as to her nature, and
her purpose in the universe, but only seemed to puzzle her. At last
she appeared to lose patience, for she wrote this message for me
upon the sands—the sands of vision—'Be careful, and do not seek
to know too much about us.' Seeing that I had offended her, I
thanked her for what she had shown and told, and let her depart
again into her cave. In a little while the young girl awoke out of her
trance, and felt the cold wind from the sea, and began to shiver.

The Adoration
of the Magi
(1897)

I WAS SITTING reading late into the night a little after my last meet-
ing with Aherne, when I heard a light knocking on my front door;
and found upon the doorstep three very old men with stout sticks in
their hands, who said they had been told I would be up and about, and
that they were to tell me important things. I brought them into my study,
and when the peacock curtains had closed behind us, I set their chairs
for them close to the fire, for I saw that the frost was on their great-
coats of frieze and upon the long beards that flowed almost to their
waists. They took off their great-coats, and leaned over the fire warm-
ing their hands, and I saw that their clothes had much of the country
of our time, but a little also, as it seemed to me, of the town life of a
more courtly time. When they had warmed themselves—and they
warmed themselves, I thought, less because of the cold of the night than
because of a pleasure in warmth for the sake of warmth—they turned
towards me, so that the light of the lamp fell full upon their weather-
beaten faces, and told the story I am about to tell. Now one talked and
now another, and they often interrupted one another, with a desire, like
that of countrymen, when they tell a story, to leave no detail untold.
When they had finished they made me take notes of whatever conver-
sation they had quoted, so that I might have the exact words, and got
up to go, and when I asked them where they were going, and what they
were doing, and by what names I should call them, they would tell me
nothing, except that they had been commanded to travel over Ireland
continually, and upon foot and at night, that they might live close to
the stones and the trees and at the hours when the immortals are awake.

I have let some years go by before writing out this story, for I am
always in dread of the illusions which come of that inquietude of

the veil of the temple, which M. Mallarmé considers a characteristic of our times; and only write it now because I have grown to believe that there is no dangerous idea which does not become less dangerous when written out in sincere and careful English.

The three old men were three brothers, who had lived in one of the western islands from their early manhood, and had cared all their lives for nothing except for those classical writers and old Gaelic writers who expounded an heroic and simple life. Night after night in winter, Gaelic story-tellers would chant old poems to them over the poteen; and night after night in summer, when the Gaelic story-tellers were at work in the fields or away at the fishing, they would read to one another Virgil and Homer, for they would not enjoy in solitude, but as the ancients enjoyed. At last a man, who told them he was Michael Robartes, came to them in a fishing-boat, like S. Brendan drawn by some vision and called by some voice; and told them of the coming again of the gods and the ancient things; and their hearts, which had never endured the body and pressure of our time, but only of distant times, found nothing unlikely in anything he told them, but accepted all simply and were happy. Years passed, and one day, when the oldest of the old men, who had travelled in his youth and thought sometimes of other lands, looked out on the grey waters, on which the people see the dim outline of the Islands of the Young—the Happy Islands where the Gaelic heroes live the lives of Homer's Phaeacians—a voice came out of the air over the waters and told him of the death of Michael Robartes. While they were still mourning, the next oldest of the old men fell asleep whilst he was reading out the Fifth Eclogue of Virgil, and a strange voice spoke through him, and bid them set out for Paris, where a dying woman would give them secret names and thereby so transform the world that another Leda would open her knees to the swan, another Achilles beleaguer Troy.

They left their island, and were at first troubled at all they saw in the world, and came to Paris, and there the youngest met a person in a dream, who told him they were to wander about at hazard until those who had been guiding their footsteps had brought them to a street and a house, whose likeness was shown him in the dream. They wandered hither and thither for many days, until one morning they came into some narrow and shabby streets, on the south of the Seine, where women with pale faces and untidy hair looked at them out of the windows; and just as they were about to turn back because Wisdom could not have alighted in so foolish a neighbourhood, they came to the street and the house of the dream. The oldest of the old men, who still remembered some of the modern languages he had known in his youth, went up to the door and knocked, and when he had knocked, the next in age to him said it was not a good house, and could not be the house they were looking for, and urged him to ask for somebody who could not be there and go away. The door was opened by an old over-dressed woman, who said, 'O you are her three kinsmen from Ireland. She has been expecting you all day.' The old men looked at one another and followed her upstairs, passing doors from which pale and untidy women thrust out their heads, and into a room where a beautiful woman lay asleep, another woman sitting by her.

The old woman said: 'Yes, they have come at last; now she will be able to die in peace,' and went out.

'We have been deceived by devils,' said one of the old men, 'for the Immortals would not speak through a woman like this.'

'Yes,' said another, 'we have been deceived by devils, and we must go away quickly.'

'Yes,' said the third, 'we have been deceived by devils, but let us kneel down for a little, for we are by the deathbed of one that has been beautiful.' They knelt down, and the woman sitting by the bed whispered, and as though overcome with fear, and with lowered head, 'At the moment when you knocked she was suddenly convulsed and cried out as I have heard a woman in childbirth and fell backward as though in a swoon.' Then they watched for a little the face upon the pillow and wondered at its look, as of unquenchable desire, and at the porcelain-like refinement of the vessel in which so malevolent a flame had burned.

Suddenly the second oldest of them crowed like a cock, till the room seemed to shake with the crowing. The woman in the bed still slept on in her death-like sleep, but the woman who sat by her head crossed herself and grew pale, and the youngest of the old men cried out: 'A devil has gone into him, and we must begone or it will go into us also.' Before they could rise from their knees, a resonant chanting voice came from the lips that had crowed and said:

'I am not a devil, but I am Hermes the Shepherd of the Dead, I run upon the errands of the gods, and you have heard my sign. The woman who lies there has given birth, and that which she bore has the likeness of a unicorn and is most unlike man of all living things, being cold, hard and virginal. It seemed to be born dancing; and was gone from the room wellnigh upon the instant, for it is of the nature of the unicorn to understand the shortness of life. She does not know it has gone, for she fell into a stupor while it danced, but bend down your ears that you may learn the names that it must obey.' Neither of the other two old men spoke, but doubtless looked at the speaker with perplexity, for the voice began again: 'When the Immortals would over-throw the things that are to-day and bring the things that were yes-terday, they have no one to help them, but one whom the things that are to-day have cast out. Bow down and very low, for they have cho-sen this woman in whose heart all follies have gathered, and in whose body all desires have awaked; this woman who has been dri-ven out of Time and has lain upon the bosom of Eternity.'

The voice ended with a sigh, and immediately the old man awoke out of sleep, and said, 'Has a voice spoken through me, as it did when I fell asleep over my Virgil, or have I only been asleep?'

The oldest of them said, 'A voice has spoken through you. Where has your soul been while the voice was speaking through you?'

'I do not know where my soul has been, but I dreamed I was under the roof of a manger, and I looked down and I saw an ox and an ass; and I saw a red cock perching on the hay-rack; and a woman hug-ging a child; and three old men in chain armour kneeling with their heads bowed very low in front of the woman and the child. While I was looking the cock crowed and a man with wings on his heels swept up through the air, and as he passed me, cried out, "Foolish old men, you had once all the wisdom of the stars." I do not understand my dream or what it would have us do, but you who have heard the voice out of the wisdom of my sleep know what we have to do.'

Then the oldest of the old men told him they were to take the parchments they had brought with them out of their pockets and spread them on the ground. When they had spread them on the ground, they took out of their pockets their pens, made of three feathers, which had fallen from the wing of the old eagle that is believed to have talked of wisdom with S. Patrick.

'He meant, I think,' said the youngest, as he put their ink-bottles by the side of the rolls of parchment, 'that when people are good the world likes them and takes possession of them, and so eternity comes through people who are not good or who have been forgotten. Perhaps Christianity was good and the world liked it, so now it is going away and the Immortals are beginning to awake.'

'What you say has no wisdom,' said the oldest, 'because if there are many Immortals, there cannot be only one Immortal.'

'Yet it seems,' said the youngest, 'that the names we are to take down are the names of one, so it must be that he can take many forms.'

Then the woman on the bed moved as in a dream, and held out her arms as though to clasp the being that had left her, and murmured names of endearment, and yet strange names, 'Harsh sweetness', 'Dear bitterness', 'O solitude', 'O terror', and after lay still for awhile. Then her voice changed, and she, no longer afraid and happy but seeming like any dying woman, murmured a name so faintly that the woman who sat by the bed bent down and put her ear close to her mouth.

The oldest of the old men said in French, 'There must have been yet one name which she had not given us, for she murmured a name while the spirit was going out of the body,' and the woman said, 'She was merely murmuring over the name of a symbolist painter she was fond of. He used to go to something he called the Black Mass, and it was he who taught her to see visions and to hear voices.'

This is all the old men told me, and when I think of their speech and of their silence, of their coming and of their going, I am almost persuaded that had I followed them out of the house, I would have found no footsteps on the snow. They may, for all I or any man can say, have been themselves Immortals: immortal demons, come to put an untrue story into my mind for some purpose I do not understand. Whatever they were, I have turned into a pathway which will lead me from them and from the Order of the Alchemical Rose. I no longer live an elaborate and haughty life, but seek to lose myself among the prayers and the sorrows of the multitude. I pray best in poor chapels, where frieze coats brush against me as I kneel, and when I pray against the demons I repeat a prayer which was made I know not how many centuries ago to help some poor Gaelic man or woman who had suffered with a suffering like mine.

> *Seacht b-páidreacha fó seacht*
> *Chuir Muire faoi n-a Mac,*
> *Chuir Brighid faoi n-a brat,*
> *Chuir Dia faoi n-a neart,*
> *Eidir sinn 'san Sluagh Sidhe,*
> *Eidir sinn 'san Sluagh Gaoith.*

Seven paters seven times,
Send Mary by her Son,
Send Bridget by her mantle,
Send God by His strength,
Between us and the faery host,
Between us and the demons of the air.

Stories of
Red Hanrahan

(1905)

Red Hanrahan
(1903)

Hanrahan, the hedge schoolmaster, a tall, strong, red-haired young man, came into the barn where some of the men of the village were sitting on Samhain Eve. It had been a dwelling-house, and when the man that owned it had built a better one, he had put the two rooms together, and kept it for a place to store one thing or another. There was a fire on the old hearth, and there were dip candles stuck in bottles, and there was a black quart bottle upon some boards that had been put across two barrels to make a table. Most of the men were sitting beside the fire, and one of them was singing a long wandering song, about a Munster man and a Connaught man that were quarrelling about their two provinces.

Hanrahan went to the man of the house and said, 'I got your message'; but when he had said that, he stopped, for an old mountainy man that had a shirt and trousers of unbleached flannel, and that was sitting by himself near the door, was looking at him, and moving an old pack of cards about in his hands and muttering. 'Don't mind him,' said the man of the house; 'he is only some stranger came in a while ago, and we bade him welcome, it being Samhain night, but I think he is not in his right wits. Listen to him now and you will hear what he is saying.'

They listened then, and they could hear the old man muttering to himself as he turned the cards, 'Spades and Diamonds, Courage and Power; Clubs and Hearts, Knowledge and Pleasure.'

'That is the kind of talk he has been going on with for the last hour,' said the man of the house, and Hanrahan turned his eyes from the old man as if he did not like to be looking at him.

'I got your message,' Hanrahan said then; ' "He is in the barn with his three first cousins from Kilchriest," the messenger said, "and there are some of the neighbours with them." '

'It is my cousin over there is wanting to see you,' said the man of the house, and he called over a young frieze-coated man, who was listening to the song, and said, 'This is Red Hanrahan you have the message for.'

'It is a kind message, indeed,' said the young man, 'for it comes from your sweetheart, Mary Lavelle.'

'How would you get a message from her, and what do you know of her?'

'I don't know her, indeed, but I was in Loughrea yesterday, and a neighbour of hers that had some dealings with me was saying that she bade him send you word, if he met any one from this side in the market, that her mother has died from her, and if you have a mind yet to join with herself, she is willing to keep her word to you.'

'I will go to her indeed,' said Hanrahan.

'And she bade you make no delay, for if she has not a man in the house before the month is out, it is likely the little bit of land will be given to another.'

When Hanrahan heard that, he rose up from the bench he had sat down on. 'I will make no delay indeed,' he said; 'there is a full moon, and if I get as far as Kilchriest to-night, I will reach to her before the setting of the sun to-morrow.'

When the others heard that, they began to laugh at him for being in such haste to go to his sweetheart, and one asked him if he would leave his school in the old lime-kiln, where he was giving the children such good learning. But he said the children would be glad enough in the morning to find the place empty, and no one to keep them at their task; and as for his school he could set it up again in any place, having as he had his little inkpot hanging from his neck by a chain, and his big Virgil and his primer in the skirt of his coat.

Some of them asked him to drink a glass before he went, and a young man caught hold of his coat, and said he must not leave them without singing the song he had made in praise of Venus and of

Mary Lavelle. He drank a glass of whisky, but he said he would not stop but would set out on his journey.

'There's time enough, Red Hanrahan,' said the man of the house. 'It will be time enough for you to give up sport when you are after your marriage, and it might be a long time before we will see you again.'

'I will not stop,' said Hanrahan; 'my mind would be on the roads all the time, bringing me to the woman that sent for me, and she lonesome and watching till I come.'

Some of the others came about him, pressing him that had been such a pleasant comrade, so full of songs and every kind of trick and fun, not to leave them till the night would be over, but he refused them all, and shook them off, and went to the door. But as he put his foot over the threshold, the strange old man stood up and put his hand that was thin and withered like a bird's claw on Hanrahan's hand, and said, 'It is not Hanrahan, the learned man and the great songmaker, that should go out from a gathering like this, on a Samhain night. And stop here, now,' he said, 'and play a hand with me; and here is an old pack of cards has done its work many a night before this, and old as it is, there has been much of the riches of the world lost and won over it.'

One of the young men said, 'It isn't much of the riches of the world has stopped with yourself, old man,' and he looked at the old man's bare feet, and they all laughed. But Hanrahan did not laugh, but he sat down very quietly, without a word. Then one of them said, 'So you will stop with us after all, Hanrahan'; and the old man said, 'He will stop indeed, did you not hear me asking him?'

They all looked at the old man then as if wondering where he came from. 'It is far I am come,' he said; 'through France I have come, and through Spain, and by Lough Greine of the hidden mouth, and none has refused me anything.' And then he was silent and nobody liked to question him, and they began to play. There were six men at the boards playing, and the others were looking on behind. They played two or three games for nothing, and then the old man took a fourpenny bit, worn very thin and smooth, out from his pocket, and he called to the rest to put something on the game. Then they all put down something on the boards, and little as it was it looked much, from the way it was shoved from one to another, first one man winning it and then his neighbour. And sometimes the luck would go against a man and he would have nothing left, and then one or another would lend him something, and he would pay it again out of his winnings, for neither good nor bad luck stopped long with any one.

And once Hanrahan said as a man would say in a dream, 'It is time for me to be going the road'; but just then a good card came to him, and he played it out, and all the money began to come to him. And once he thought of Mary Lavelle, and he sighed; and that time his luck went from him, and he forgot her again.

But at last the luck went to the old man and it stayed with him, and all they had flowed into him, and he began to laugh little laughs to himself, and to sing over and over to himself, 'Spades and Diamonds, Courage and Power,' and so on, as if it was a verse of a song.

And after a while any one looking at the men, and seeing the way their bodies were rocking to and fro, and the way they kept their eyes on the old man's hands, would think they had drink taken, or that the whole store they had in the world was put on the cards; but that was not so, for the quart bottle had not been disturbed since the game began, and was nearly full yet, and all that was on the game was a few sixpenny bits and shillings, and maybe a handful of coppers.

'You are good men to win and good men to lose,' said the old man; 'you have play in your hearts.' He began then to shuffle the cards and to mix them, very quick and fast, till at last they could not see them to be cards at all, but you would think him to be making rings of fire in the air, as little lads would make them with whirling a lighted stick; and after that it seemed to them that all the room was dark, and they could see nothing but his hands and the cards.

And all in a minute a hare made a leap out from between his hands, and whether it was one of the cards that took that shape, or whether it was made out of nothing in the palms of his hands, nobody knew, but there it was running on the floor of the barn, as quick as any hare that ever lived.

Some looked at the hare, but more kept their eyes on the old man, and while they were looking at him a hound made a leap out between his hands, the same way as the hare did, and after that another hound and another, till there was a whole pack of them following the hare round and round the barn.

The players were all standing up now, with their backs to the boards, shrinking from the hounds, and nearly deafened with the noise of their yelping, but as quick as the hounds were they could not overtake the hare, but it went round, till at the last it seemed as if a blast of wind burst open the barn door, and the hare doubled and made a leap over the boards where the men had been playing, and went out of the door and away through the night, and the hounds over the boards and through the door after it.

Then the old man called out, 'Follow the hounds, follow the hounds, and it is a great hunt you will see to-night,' and he went out after them. But used as the men were to go hunting after hares, and ready as they were for any sport, they were in dread to go out into the night, and it was only Hanrahan that rose up and that said, 'I will follow, I will follow on.'

'You had best stop here, Hanrahan,' the young man that was nearest him said, 'for you might be going into some great danger.' But Hanrahan said, 'I will see fair play, I will see fair play,' and he went stumbling out of the door like a man in a dream, and the door shut after him as he went.

He thought he saw the old man in front of him, but it was only his own shadow that the full moon cast on the road before him, but he could hear the hounds crying after the hare over the wide green fields of Granagh, and he followed them very fast, for there was nothing to stop him; and after a while he came to smaller fields that had little walls of loose stones around them, and he threw the stones down as he crossed them, and did not wait to put them up again; and he passed by the place where the river goes underground at Ballylee, and he could hear the hounds going before him up towards the head of the river. Soon he found it harder to run, for it was uphill he was going, and clouds came over the moon, and it was hard for him to see his way, and once he left the path to take a short cut, but his foot slipped into a bog-hole and he had to come back to it. And how long he was going he did not know, or what way he went, but at last he was up on the bare mountain, with nothing but the rough heather about him, and he could neither hear the hounds nor any other thing. But their cry began to come to him again, at first far off and then very near, and when it came quite close to him, it went up all of a sudden into the air, and there was the sound of hunting over his head; then it went away northward till he could hear nothing at all. 'That's not fair,' he said, 'that's not fair.' And he could walk no longer, but sat down on the heather where he was, in the heart of Slieve Echtge, for all the strength had gone from him, with the dint of the long journey he had made.

And after a while he took notice that there was a door close to him, and a light coming from it, and he wondered that being so close to him he had not seen it before. And he rose up, and tired as he was he went in at the door, and although it was night time outside, it was daylight he found within. And presently he met with an old man that had been gathering summer thyme and yellow flag-flowers, and it seemed as if all the sweet smells of the summer were with them. And the old man said: 'It is a long time you have been coming to us, Hanrahan the learned man and the great songmaker.'

And with that he brought him into a very big shining house, and every grand thing Hanrahan had ever heard of, and every colour he had ever seen, was in it. There was a high place at the end of the house, and on it there was sitting in a high chair a woman, the most beautiful the world ever saw, having a long pale face and flowers about it, but she had the tired look of one that had been long waiting. And there were sitting on the step below her chair four grey old women, and the one of them was holding a great cauldron in her lap; and another a great stone on her knees, and heavy as it was it seemed light to her; and another of them had a very long spear that was made of pointed wood; and the last of them had a sword that was without a scabbard.

Hanrahan stood looking at them for a long time, but none of them spoke any word to him or looked at him at all. And he had it in his mind to ask who that woman in the chair was, that was like a queen, and what she was waiting for; but ready as he was with his tongue and afraid of no person, he was in dread now to speak to so beautiful a woman, and in so grand a place. And then he thought to ask what were the four things the four grey old women were holding like great treasures, but he could not think of the right words to bring out.

Then the first of the old women rose up, holding the cauldron between her two hands, and she said, 'Pleasure,' and Hanrahan said no word. Then the second old woman rose up with the stone in her hands, and she said 'Power'; and the third old woman rose up with a spear in her hand, and she said 'Courage'; and the last of the old women rose up having the sword in her hands, and she said 'Knowledge.' And every one, after she had spoken, waited as if for Hanrahan to question her, but he said nothing at all. And then the four old women went out of the door, bringing their four treasures with them, and as they went out one of them said, 'He has no wish for us'; and another said, 'He is weak, he is weak'; and another said, 'He is afraid'; and the last said, 'His wits are gone from him.' And then they all said, 'Echtge, daughter of the Silver Hand, must stay in her sleep. It is a pity, it is a great pity.'

And then the woman that was like a queen gave a very sad sigh, and it seemed to Hanrahan as if the sigh had the sound in it of hidden streams; and if the place he was in had been ten times grander and more shining than it was, he could not have hindered sleep from coming on him; and he staggered like a drunken man and lay down there and then.

When Hanrahan awoke, the sun was shining on his face, but there was white frost on the grass around him, and there was ice on the edge of the stream he was lying by, and that goes running on through Dairecaol and Druim-da-rod. He knew by the shape of the hills and by the shining of Lough Greine in the distance that he was upon one of the hills of Slieve Echtge, but he was not sure how he came there; for all that had happened in the barn had gone from him, and all of his journey but the soreness of his feet and the stiffness in his bones.

It was a year after that, there were men of the village of Cappaghtagle sitting by the fire in a house on the roadside, and Red Hanrahan that was now very thin and worn and his hair very long and wild, came to the half-door and asked leave to come in and rest himself; and they bid him welcome because it was Samhain night. He sat down with them, and they gave him a glass of whisky out of a quart bottle; and they saw the little inkpot hanging about his neck, and knew he was a scholar, and asked for stories about the Greeks.

He took the Virgil out of the big pocket of his coat, but the cover was very black and swollen with the wet, and the page when he opened it was very yellow, but that was no great matter, for he looked at it like a man that had never learned to read. Some young man that was there began to laugh at him then, and to ask why did he carry so heavy a book with him when he was not able to read it.

It vexed Hanrahan to hear that, and he put the Virgil back in his pocket and asked if they had a pack of cards among them, for cards were better than books. When they brought out the cards he took them and began to shuffle them, and while he was shuffling them something seemed to come into his mind, and he put his hand to his face like one that is trying to remember, and he said, 'Was I ever here before, or where was I on a night like this?' and then of a sudden he stood up and let the cards fall to the floor, and he said, 'Who was it brought me a message from Mary Lavelle?'

'We never saw you before now, and we never heard of Mary Lavelle,' said the man of the house. 'And who is she,' he said, 'and what is it you are talking about?'

'It was this night a year ago, I was in a barn, and there were men playing cards, and there was money on the table, they were pushing it from one to another here and there—and I got a message, and I was going out of the door to look for my sweetheart that wanted me, Mary Lavelle.' And then Hanrahan called out very loud, 'Where have I been since then? Where was I for the whole year?'

'It is hard to say where you might have been in that time,' said the oldest of the men, 'or what part of the world you may have travelled; and it is like enough you have the dust of many roads on your feet; for there are many go wandering and forgetting like that,' he said, 'when once they have been given the touch.'

'That is true,' said another of the men. 'I knew a woman went wandering like that through the length of seven years; she came back after, and she told her friends she had often been glad enough to eat the food that was put in the pig's trough. And it is best for you to go to the priest now,' he said, 'and let him take off you whatever may have been put upon you.'

'It is to my sweetheart I will go, to Mary Lavelle,' said Hanrahan; 'it is too long I have delayed, how do I know what might have happened her in the length of a year?'

He was going out of the door then, but they all told him it was best for him to stop the night, and to get strength for the journey; and indeed he wanted that, for he was very weak, and when they gave him food he ate it like a man that had never seen food before, and one of them said, 'He is eating as if he had trodden on the hungry grass.' It was in the white light of the morning he set out, and the time seemed long to him till he could get to Mary Lavelle's house. But when he came to it, he found the door broken, and the thatch dropping from the roof, and no living person to be seen. And when he asked the neighbours what had happened her, all they could say was that she had been put out of the house, and had married some labouring man, and they had gone looking for work to London or Liverpool or some big place. And whether she found a

worse place or a better he never knew, but anyway he never met
with her or with news of her again.

The Death of Hanrahan
(1896, 1905)

HANRAHAN, that was never long in one place, was back again
among the villages that are at the foot of Slieve Echtge, Illeton
and Scalp and Ballylee, stopping sometimes in one house and some-
times in another, and finding a welcome in every place for the sake
of the old times and of his poetry and his learning. There was some
silver and some copper money in the little leather bag under his
coat, but it was seldom he needed to take anything from it, for it
was little he used, and there was not one of the people that would
have taken payment from him. His hand had grown heavy on the
blackthorn he leaned on, and his cheeks were hollow and worn, but
so far as food went, potatoes and milk and a bit of oaten cake, he
had what he wanted of it; and it is not on the edge of so wild and
boggy a place as Echtge a mug of spirits would be wanting, with the
taste of the turf smoke on it. He would wander about the big wood
at Kinadife, or he would sit through many hours of the day among
the rushes about Lake Belshragh, listening to the streams from the
hills, or watching the shadows in the brown bog pools; sitting so
quiet as not to startle the deer that came down from the heather to
the grass and the tilled fields at the fall of night. As the days went
by it seemed as if he was beginning to belong to some world out of
sight and misty, that has for its mearing the colours that are beyond
all other colours and the silences that are beyond all silences of this
world. And sometimes he would hear coming and going in the
wood music that when it stopped went from his memory like a
dream; and once in the stillness of midday he heard a sound like the
clashing of many swords, that went on for a long time without any
break. And at the fall of night and at moonrise the lake would grow
to be like a gateway of silver and shining stones, and there would
come from its silence the faint sound of keening and of frightened
laughter broken by the wind, and many pale beckoning hands.

He was sitting looking into the water one evening in harvest time, thinking of all the secrets that were shut into the lakes and the mountains, when he heard a cry coming from the south, very faint at first, but getting louder and clearer as the shadow of the rushes grew longer, till he could hear the words, 'I am beautiful, I am beautiful. The birds in the air, the moths under the leaves, the flies over the water look at me, for they never saw any one so beautiful as myself. I am young; I am young: look upon me, mountains; look upon me, perishing woods, for my body will shine like the white waters when you have been hurried away. You and the whole race of men, and the race of the beasts, and the race of the fish, and the winged race, are dropping like a candle that is nearly burned out, but I laugh aloud because I am in my youth.' The voice would break off from time to time, as if tired, and then it would begin again, calling out always the same words, 'I am beautiful, I am beautiful.' Presently the bushes at the edge of the little lake trembled for a moment, and a very old woman forced her way among them, and passed by Hanrahan, walking with very slow steps. Her face was of the colour of earth, and more wrinkled than the face of any old hag that was ever seen, and her grey hair was hanging in wisps, and the rags she was wearing did not hide her dark skin that was roughened by all weathers. She passed by him with her eyes wide open, and her head high, and her arms hanging straight beside her, and she went into the shadow of the hills towards the west.

A sort of dread came over Hanrahan when he saw her, for he knew her to be one Winny Byrne of the Cross Roads, that went begging from place to place crying always the same cry, and he had often heard that she had once such wisdom that all the women of the neighbours used to go looking for advice from her, and that she had a voice so beautiful that men and women would come from every part to hear her sing at a wake or a wedding; and that the Others, the great Sidhe, had stolen her wits one Samhain night many years ago, when she had fallen asleep on the edge of a rath, and had seen in her dreams the servants of Echtge of the hills.

And as she vanished away up the hillside, it seemed as if her cry, 'I am beautiful, I am beautiful,' was coming from among the stars in the heavens.

There was a cold wind creeping among the rushes, and Hanrahan began to shiver, and he rose up to go to some house where there would be a fire on the hearth. But instead of turning down the hill as he was used, he went on up the hill, along the little track that was maybe a road and maybe the dry bed of a stream. It was the same way Winny had gone, and it led to the little cabin where she stopped when she stopped in any place at all. He walked very slowly up the hill as if he had a great load on his back, and at last he saw a light a little to the left, and he thought it likely it was from Winny's house it was shining, and he turned from the path to go to it. But clouds had come over the sky, and he could not well see his way, and after he had gone a few steps his foot slipped and he fell into a bog drain, and though he dragged himself out of it, holding on to the roots of the heather, the fall had given him a great shake, and he felt better fit to lie down than to go travelling. But he had always great courage, and he made his way on, step by step, till at last he came to Winny's cabin, that had no window, but the light was shining from the door. He thought to go into it and to rest for a while, but when he came to the door he did not see Winny inside it, but what he saw was four old gray-haired women playing cards, but Winny herself was not among them. Hanrahan sat down on a heap of turf beside the door, for he was tired out and out, and had no wish for talking or for card-playing, and his bones and his joints aching the way they were. He could hear the four women talking as they played, and calling out their hands. And it seemed to him that they were saying, like the strange man in the barn long ago, 'Spades and Diamonds, Courage and Power. Clubs and Hearts, Knowledge and Pleasure.' And he went on saying those words over and over to himself; and whether or not he was in his dreams, the pain that was in his shoulder never left him. And after a while the four women in the cabin began to quarrel, and each one to say the other had not played fair, and their voices grew from loud to louder, and their screams and their curses, till at last the whole air was filled with the noise of them around and above the house, and Hanrahan, hearing it between sleep and waking, said, 'That is the sound of the fighting between the friends and the ill-wishers of a man that is near his death. And I wonder,' he said, 'who is the man in this lonely place that is near his death.'

It seemed as if he had been asleep a long time, and he opened his eyes, and the face he saw over him was the old wrinkled face of Winny of the Cross Roads. She was looking hard at him, as if to make sure he was not dead, and she wiped away the blood that had grown dry on his face with a wet cloth, and after a while she partly helped him and partly lifted him into the cabin, and laid him down on what served her for a bed. She gave him a couple of potatoes from a pot on the fire, and, what served him better, a mug of spring water. He slept a little now and again, and sometimes he heard her singing to herself as she moved about the house, and so the night wore away. When the sky began to brighten with the dawn he felt for the bag where his little store of money was, and held it out to her, and she took out a bit of copper and a bit of silver money, but she let it drop again as if it was nothing to her, maybe because it was not money she was used to beg for, but food and rags; or maybe because the rising of the dawn was filling her with pride and a new belief in her own great beauty. She went out and cut a few armfuls of heather, and brought it in and heaped it over Hanrahan, saying something about the cold of the morning, and while she did that he took notice of the wrinkles in her face, and the greyness of her hair, and the broken teeth that were black and full of gaps. And when he was well covered with the heather she went out of the door and away down the side of the mountain, and he could hear the cry, 'I am beautiful, I am beautiful,' getting less and less as she went, till at last it died away altogether.

Hanrahan lay there through the length of the day, in his pains and his weakness, and when the shadows of the evening were falling he heard her voice again coming up the hillside, and she came in and boiled the potatoes and shared them with him the same way as before. And one day after another passed like that, and the weight of his flesh was heavy about him. But little by little as he grew weaker he knew there were some greater than himself in the room with him, and that the house began to be filled with them; and it seemed to him they had all power in their hands, and that they might with one touch of the hand break down the wall the hardness of pain had built about him, and take him into their own world. And sometimes he could hear voices, very faint and joyful, crying from the rafters or out of the flame on the hearth, and other times the whole house was filled with music that went through it like a wind. And after a while his weakness left no place for pain, and there grew up about him a great silence like the silence in the heart of a lake, and there came through it, like the flame of a rush-light, the faint joyful voices ever and always.

One morning he heard music somewhere outside the door, and as the day passed it grew louder and louder until it drowned the faint joyful voices, and even Winny's cry upon the hillside at the fall of evening. About midnight and in a moment, the walls seemed to melt away and to leave his bed floating on a pale misty light that shone on every side as far as the eye could see; and after the first blinding of his eyes he saw that it was full of great shadowy figures rushing here and there.

At the same time the music came very clearly to him, and he knew that it was but the continual clashing of swords.

'I am after my death,' he said, 'and in the very heart of the music of Heaven. O Cherubim and Seraphim, receive my soul!'

At his cry the light where it was nearest to him filled with sparks of yet brighter light, and he saw that these were the points of swords turned towards his heart; and then a sudden flame, bright and burning like God's love or God's hate, swept over the light and went out and he was in darkness. At first he could see nothing, for all was as dark as if there was black bog earth about him, but all of a sudden the fire blazed up as if a wisp of straw had been thrown upon it. And as he looked at it, the light was shining on the big pot that was hanging from a hook, and on the flat stone where Winny used to bake a cake now and again, and on the long rusty knife she used to be cutting the roots of the heather with, and on the long blackthorn stick he had brought into the house himself. And when he saw those four things, some memory came into Hanrahan's mind, and strength came back to him, and he rose sitting up in the bed, and he said very loud and clear, 'The Cauldron, the Stone, the Sword, the Spear. What are they? Who do they belong to? And I have asked the question this time.'

And then he fell back again, weak, and the breath going from him.

Winny Byrne, that had been tending the fire, came over then, having her eyes fixed on the bed; and the faint laughing voices began crying out again, and a pale light, grey like a wave, came creeping over the room, and he did not know from what secret world it came. He saw Winny's withered face and her withered arms that were grey like crumbled earth, and weak as he was he shrank back farther towards the wall. And then there came out of the mud-stiffened rags arms as white and as shadowy as the foam on a river, and they were put about his body, and a voice that he

could hear well but that seemed to come from a long way off said
to him in a whisper, 'You will go looking for me no more upon the
breasts of women.'

'Who are you?' he said then.

'I am one of the lasting people, of the lasting unwearied Voices,
that make my dwelling in the broken and the dying, and those that
have lost their wits; and I came looking for you, and you are mine
until the whole world is burned out like a candle that is spent. And
look up now,' she said, 'for the wisps that are for our wedding are
lighted.'

He saw then that the house was crowded with pale shadowy
hands, and that every hand was holding what was sometimes like a
wisp lighted for a marriage, and sometimes like a tall white candle
for the dead.

When the sun rose on the morning of the morrow Winny of the
Cross Roads rose up from where she was sitting beside the body,
and began her begging from townland to townland, singing the
same song as she walked, 'I am beautiful, I am beautiful. The birds
in the air, the moths under the leaves, the flies over the water look
at me. I am young: look upon me, mountains; look upon me, per-
ishing woods, for my body will be shining like the white waters
when you have been hurried away. You and the whole race of men,
and the race of the beasts, and the race of the fish, and the winged
race, are dropping like a candle that is nearly burned out. But I
laugh aloud, because I am in my youth.'

She did not come back that night or any night to the cabin, and
it was not till the end of two days that the turf-cutters going to the
bog found the body of Red Owen Hanrahan, and gathered men to
wake him and women to keen him, and gave him a burying worthy
of so great a poet.

Appendix

First Published Texts of Six Poems

Ephemera: An Autumn Idyl

'Your eyes that once were never weary of mine
Lie now half hidden under pendulous lids,
Veiled in a dreamy sorrow for their love
That wanes.' 'Ah, wistful voice,' replied the other,
'Though our sad love is fading, let us yet
Stand by the border of the lake once more,
Together in that hour of gentleness
When the poor tired child, passion, falls asleep.
How far away the stars seem, and how far
Is our first kiss, and ah, how old my heart!'   10
Pensive they paced along the faded leaves,
While slowly answered he whose hand held hers—
'Often has passion worn our wandering hearts,
Earth's aliens. Why so sorrowful? Our souls
Shall warm their lives at many a rustling flame.'

The woods were round them, and the yellow leaves
Fell like faint meteors in the gloom, and once
A rabbit old and lame limped down the path—
Autumn was over him—and now they stood
On the lone border of the sullen lake.   20
Turning, he saw that she had thrust dead leaves,
Gathered in silence, dewy as her eyes,
In bosom and hair.
          Then he: 'Let us not mourn
That we are tired, for other loves await us.
Hate on and love through unrepining hours;
Before us lies eternity; our souls
Are love, and a continual farewell.'

He spake once more and fondled with his lips
That word of the soul's peace—'Eternity.'

30   The little waves that walked in evening whiteness,
Glimmering in her drooped eyes, saw her lips move
And whisper, 'The innumerable reeds
I know the word they cry, "Eternity!"
And sing from shore to shore, and every year
They pine away and yellow and wear out,
And ah, they know not, as they pine and cease,
Not they are the eternal—'tis the cry.'

> [Text from *The Wanderings of Oisin and Other
> Poems* (1889). Major revisions, including the
> shortened title, done for *Poems* (1895).]

The Sorrow of Love

The quarrel of the sparrows in the eaves,
   The full round moon and the star-laden sky,
And the loud song of the ever-singing leaves
   Had hid away earth's old and weary cry.

And then you came with those red mournful lips,
   And with you came the whole of the world's tears,
And all the sorrows of her labouring ships,
   And all burden of her myriad years.

And now the sparrows warring in the eaves,
10   The crumbling moon, the white stars in the sky,
And the loud chanting of the unquiet leaves,
   Are shaken with earth's old and weary cry.

> [Text from *The Countess Kathleen and Various
> Legends and Lyrics* (1892). Major revisions done
> for *Early Poems and Stories* (1925).]

Dedication

I

There was a green branch hung with many a bell
    When her own people ruled in wave-worn Eri,
    And from its murmuring greenness, calm of faery
—A Druid kindness—on all hearers fell.

2

It charmed away the merchant from his guile,
    And turned the farmer's memory from his cattle,
    And hushed in sleep the roaring ranks of battle,
For all who heard it dreamed a little while.

3

Ah, Exiles, wandering over many seas,
    Spinning at all times Eri's good to-morrow,   10
    Ah, world-wide Nation, always growing Sorrow,
I also bear a bell branch full of ease.

4

I tore it from the green boughs winds tossed and hurled,
    Green boughs of tossing always, weary, weary,
    I tore it from the green boughs of old Eri,
The willow of the many-sorrowed world.

5

Ah, Exiles, wandering over many lands,
    My bell branch murmurs: the gay bells bring laughter,
    Leaping to shake a cobweb from the rafter;
The sad bells bow the forehead on the hands.   20

6

A honied ringing! under the new skies
    They bring you memories of old village faces,

Cabins gone now, old well-sides, old dear places,
And men who loved the cause that never dies.

> [Text from *Representative Irish Tales* (1891).
> Major revisions done for *Irish Statesman*, 8
> November 1924, and collected in *Early Poems
> and Stories* (1925).]

The Old Pensioner

I had a chair at every hearth,
    When no one turned to see
With 'Look at that old fellow there;
    And who may he be?'
And therefore do I wander on,
    And the fret is on me.

The road-side trees keep murmuring—
    Ah, wherefore murmur ye
As in the old days long gone by,
    Green oak and poplar tree!
The well-known faces are all gone,
    And the fret is on me.

> [Text from *Scots Observer,* 15 November 1890.
> Title revised for the next printing, *Poems* (1895),
> but the major revisions done for *Early Poems
> and Stories* (1925).]

The Scholars

Bald heads forgetful of their sins,
Old, learned, respectable bald heads
Edit and annotate the lines
That young men, tossing on their beds,
Rhymed out in love's despair
To flatter beauty's ignorant ear.

They'll cough in ink to the world's end;
Wear out the carpet with their shoes
Earning respect; have no strange friend;
If they have sinned nobody knows: 10
Lord, what would they say
Should their Catullus walk that way!

> [Text from *Catholic Anthology, 1914–1915*
> (1915), in which the lines were italicized. Major
> revisions done for *Selected Poems* (1929).]

Leda and the Swan

A rush, a sudden wheel, and hovering still
The bird descends, and her frail thighs are pressed
By the webbed toes, and that all-powerful bill
Has laid her helpless face upon his breast.
How can those terrified vague fingers push
The feathered glory from her loosening thighs!
All the stretched body's laid on the white rush
And feels the strange heart beating where it lies;
A shudder in the loins engenders there
The broken wall, the burning roof and tower   10
And Agamemnon dead.
                            Being so caught up,
So mastered by the brute blood of the air,
Did she put on his knowledge with his power
Before the indifferent beak could let her drop?

> [Text from *The Dial,* June 1924. Major revisions
> done for *A Vision* (1925).]

Notes

A NOTE ON THE NOTES

THESE NOTES attempt to annotate all direct references, such as names of persons, places, monuments, buildings, and so forth, as well as quotations from other writers. Most of Yeats's quotations are in fact slight misquotations, but this phenomenon has for the most part been ignored. Yeats's own commentary and annotations have been quoted only sparingly. References for verse are cited by line numbers in bold; for prose, the material being annotated is printed in bold. Rather than constantly using "see note to," information has been repeated across but not within discrete units. Thus, for example, the second reference to Robert Gregory in *The Wild Swans at Coole* is not annotated, but the allusion in *New Poems* is. Insofar as possible, these notes eschew interpretation, although the very decision to annotate a particular reference is often an interpretive act.

In that regard, *The Yeats Reader* occasionally engages in the kind of biographical annotation of unnamed individuals (e.g., "you" or "she") absent from my edition of the *Collected Poems* (1996) or the *Poems* (1997). Much can be said on either side of this issue. Indeed, what would have been the very first sentence encountered by a reader of the unpublished Scribner Dublin Edition of 1937 sets the terms of the debate: the poet writes always "out of his personal life," but there is always a "phantasmagoria," in which the personal is, if not transcended, subsumed. Various other comments on both sides of the question by Yeats himself could be cited. In the end, individual readers will have to decide whether the understanding that a particular poem is somehow "about" or "derived from" Yeats's relationship with, say, Maud Gonne assists or encumbers their experience of the lyric.

At the same time, all readers should be aware that many of the biographical glosses offered here (and the greater number put forth by other commentators) have less than a firm foundation. A classic example is "After Long Silence." Most critics have argued that the poem must describe a reunion between Yeats and the English novelist Olivia Shakespear (1863–1938), who had been his mistress in 1896–97 (his first sexual encounter) and, after a relatively brief estrangement, a close friend for the rest of his life (the sexual encounter may have been renewed on one or two later occasions, but the evidence is far from clear); indeed, Yeats sent a draft of the poem to her in a letter of 16 December 1929 and alluded to it in a letter of 24 October 1933. The first problem with this reading, however, is that if "long silence" is understood to mean weeks or months, if not longer, there is no evidence of such a gap in the relationship in the years preceding the composition of the poem. One can argue that "long silence" refers simply to an extended pause in their conversation, but we still have a second problem, the reference to "All other lovers being estranged or dead." Leaving aside the other women in Yeats's life (known or unknown to his biographers), his wife was certainly quite alive at the time; and again there is no evidence of any serious conflict in their relationship. As a final complication, the distinguished Yeats scholar David R. Clark has offered a detailed argument, based on the manuscript materials of the poem, that the lyric derives from Yeats's reencounter with Moina Mathers, wife of the English occultist Samuel Liddell Mathers, later MacGregor Mathers (1854–1918), one of the founders of the Order of the Golden Dawn. Yeats had been close to the Matherses in the 1890s but grew apart after a schism in the Order in 1900–1901. Yeats met with Moina Mathers for the first time in many years in London, probably in 1923. She was soon to object to Yeats's depiction of MacGregor Mathers in *The Trembling of the Veil* (1922) and wrote to protest; Yeats indeed made some revisions when *The Trembling of the Veil* was republished in 1926, in the interval dedicating the 1925 edition of *A Vision* to her: "You with your beauty and your learning and your mysterious gifts were held by all in affection, and though, when the first draft of this dedication was written, I had not seen you for more than thirty years, nor knew what you were doing, . . . it was plain that I must dedicate my book to you." The problem with this reading, though, is that there is no other evidence in Yeats's writings to suggest that Yeats and Moina Mathers were ever "lovers" in any usual sense of the word.

So: is "After Long Silence" about Yeats and Olivia Shakespear? Or Yeats and Moina Mathers? Or is it, whatever its biographical derivation (if any), a poem about a reunion of two aged lovers, recalling their youthful interlude together, and both regretting and, in one sense, celebrating the inescapable fact that "Bodily decrepitude is wisdom"? Placing these notes at the back of the volume and not signaling their existence in the text gives readers a choice of Yeats annotated or Yeats unadorned.

A NOTE ON THE TEXT

WHEN AVAILABLE, the texts have been taken from volumes in the Scribner/Palgrave Collected Edition of the Works of W. B. Yeats (Richard J. Finneran and George Mills Harper, General Editors): *Autobiographies,* ed. William H. O'Donnell and Douglas N. Archibald (1999); *Later Essays,* ed. William H. O'Donnell (1994); *The Plays,* ed. David R. Clark and Rosalind E. Clark (2001); and *The Poems,* second ed., ed. Richard J. Finneran (1997). For works not presently available in the Collected Edition, the following texts have been used, with some minor changes: *Essays and Introductions* (1961); *Explorations,* sel. Mrs. W. B. Yeats (1962); *Memoirs,* ed. Denis Donoghue (1972); *Mythologies* (1959); *The Secret Rose, Stories by W. B. Yeats: A Variorum Edition,* ed. Warwick Gould, Phillip L. Marcus, and Michael J. Sidnell (1992); and *A Vision* (1962).

In the Poems section, a stanza break coincides with the end of pages 5, 6, 9, 13, 16, 19, 22, 23, 25, 26, 32, 46, 56, 79, 81, 82, 87, 91, 94, 96, 97, 107, 111, 112, 113, 118, 127, 134, 144, 477, and 480.

NOTES TO THE POEMS

Crossways

A title first used in 1895 for poems selected from *The Wanderings of Oisin and Other Poems* (1889) and *The Countess Kathleen and Various Legends and Lyrics* (1892).

"The Song of the Happy Shepherd": first published *Dublin University Review*, October 1885. **1**: a region in southern Greece, depicted in ancient Greek poetry as a land of pastoral happiness. **9**: Chronos is Greek for "time"; personified by the Greek poet Pindar (518–438 B.C.) as "the father of all." **12**: in Christianity, the Rood is the cross on which Christ was crucified. **32**: star-bane, the poison of the stars. **47**: in Roman mythology, a faun has the body of a man but the horns, pointed ears, tail, and hind legs of a goat. **56**: as the source of opium, poppies are connected with dreams.

"The Sad Shepherd": first published *Dublin University Review*, October 1885.

"The Cloak, the Boat, and the Shoes": first published *Dublin University Review*, October 1886.

"The Indian to his Love": first published *Dublin University Review*, December 1886.

"The Falling of the Leaves": first published *The Wanderings of Oisin and Other Poems* (1889). **3**: rowan, a European mountain ash.

"Ephemera": first published *The Wanderings of Oisin and Other Poems* (1889); see Appendix.

"The Stolen Child": first published *Irish Monthly*, December 1886. **2**: "Sloped Wood," on the shore of Lough Gill, County Sligo. **15**: Rosses Point, a seaside village near Sligo. **29**: *Gleann an Chairte* ("Valley of the Monumental Stone"), a lake near Sligo.

"To an Isle in the Water": first published *The Wanderings of Oisin and Other Poems* (1889).

"Down by the Salley Gardens": first published *The Wanderings of Oisin and Other Poems* (1889). Although described by Yeats as "an attempt to reconstruct an old song from three lines imperfectly remembered by an old woman in the village of Ballysodare, Sligo, who often sings them to herself," in fact an adaptation of part of a nineteenth-century ballad. Yeats glossed "salley" as "willow." **7**: weir, a low dam, or a fence (e.g., of brushwood) built in a river for catching fish.

"The Meditation of the Old Fisherman": first published *Irish Monthly,* October 1886. Yeats claimed that "This poem is founded upon some things a fisherman said to me when out fishing in Sligo Bay."

The Rose

A title first used in 1895 for poems selected from *The Countess Kathleen and Various Legends and Lyrics* (1892) and one later poem; "Who goes with Fergus?" added in 1912; "To Some I have Talked with by the Fire" in 1933.

"To the Rose upon the Rood of Time": first published *The Countess Kathleen and Various Legends and Lyrics* (1892). Yeats explained that "the Rose is a favourite symbol with the Irish poets, both Gaelic and English, and is used, not merely in love poems, but in addresses to Ireland. . . ." A rose at the center of the cross is the central Rosicrucian symbol and is important in the Order of the Golden Dawn, an occult society Yeats joined on 7 March 1890. In Christianity, the Rood is the cross on which Christ was crucified. **3**: the most important warrior in the Ulster, or Red Branch, cycle of Irish mythology. As Yeats explains in the poem "Cuchulain's Fight with the Sea" (1892) and the play *On Baile's Strand* (1903), Cuchulain fights the waves after unknowingly killing his son in a duel. **4–5**: a Druid was an ancient Celtic priest and medicine man; Fergus was a king in the Ulster cycle. Yeats recounts this story in the poem "Fergus and the Druid" (1892). **23**: *Éire,* Ireland.

"Fergus and the Druid": first published *National Observer,* 21 May 1892. Fergus is king of Ulster in the Ulster, or Red Branch, cycle of Irish tales; Yeats follows the adaptation of the story by the Irish poet and antiquary Sir Samuel Ferguson (1810–66), in which Fergus voluntarily relinquishes his throne in favor of becoming a poet. Druids were ancient Celtic priests and medicine men. **10**: Conchubar was Fergus's stepson and successor.

"The Rose of the World": first published *National Observer,* 2 January 1892. **4**: in Greek mythology, Troy is destroyed by the Greeks during the Trojan War, fought over the abduction of Helen by Paris. **5**: in Irish mythology, Usna is the father of Naoise, Ainnle, and Ardan. Accompanied by his brothers, Naoise elopes with Deirdre, whom Conchubar had selected to become his queen; the three brothers are eventually killed by Conchubar's forces.

"The Lake Isle of Innisfree": first published *National Observer,* 13 December 1890. *Inis Fraoigh* ("Heather Island"), a small island in Lough Gill, County Sligo.

"The Pity of Love": first published *The Countess Kathleen and Various Legends and Lyrics* (1892).

"The Sorrow of Love": first published *The Countess Kathleen and Various Legends and Lyrics* (1892); see Appendix. **7**: the central figure of the

Odyssey, by the Greek poet Homer (ca. eighth century B.C.) and one of the leaders of the Greeks in the Trojan War; all of his men are lost during the return voyage to Greece. **8:** king of Troy, killed in the Trojan War.

"When You are Old": first published *The Countess Kathleen and Various Legends and Lyrics* (1892). The poem is based on "Quand vous serez bien vieille" ("When you will be very old") by the French poet Pierre de Ronsard (1524–85) and is addressed to Maud Gonne (1866–1953), Irish nationalist and Yeats's beloved, being among the lyrics in an 1891 vellum manuscript book entitled *The Flame of the Spirit* and inscribed for her.

"The White Birds": first published *National Observer,* 7 May 1892. Presumably addressed to Maud Gonne (1866–1953), Irish nationalist and Yeats's beloved. Yeats explained that "The birds of fairyland are white as snow. The 'Danaan Shore' is . . . fairyland."

"Who goes with Fergus?": first published *The Countess Kathleen and Various Legends and Lyrics* (1892), as a lyric in the play *The Countess Kathleen.*

"The Man who dreamed of Faeryland": first published *National Observer,* 7 February 1891. **1:** a village in County Leitrim. **13:** a barony in County Sligo. **25:** in County Sligo. **37:** *Lug na nGall* ("the Hollow of the Foreigners"), a townland in Glencar valley, County Sligo.

"The Dedication to a Book of Stories selected from the Irish Novelists": first published *Representative Irish Tales* (1891); see Appendix. **1:** Yeats explained that the bell-branch was "A legendary branch whose shaking cast all men into a gentle sleep." **2:** *Éire,* the normal Irish word for Ireland. **24:** Munster is one of the four provinces of Ireland, Connemara a district in County Galway.

"The Lamentation of the Old Pensioner": first published *Scots Observer,* 15 November 1890; see Appendix. Yeats described it as "little more than a translation into verse of the very words of an old Wicklow peasant," Wicklow being a county south of Dublin.

"The Two Trees": first published *The Countess Kathleen and Various Legends and Lyrics* (1892). In the Cabala, an esoteric theosophy developed in thirteenth-century Spain and France, the Tree of Life can have two sides, one good and the other evil. In an essay on Blake, Yeats also commented that "the kingdom that was passing was, he held, the kingdom of the Tree of Knowledge; the kingdom that was coming was the kingdom of the Tree of Life: men who ate from the Tree of Knowledge wasted their days in anger against one another, and in taking one another captive in great nets; men who sought their food among the green leaves of the Tree of Life condemned none but the unimaginative and the idle, and those who forget that even love and death and old age are an imaginative art." **15:** "gyring" is movement in a spiral.

The term does not appear in the text until *Selected Poems* (1929), by which time Yeats had developed the symbol of the gyres in *A Vision,* explained in a note to "The Second Coming" as "a double cone, the narrow end of each cone being in the centre of the broad end of the other": "the end of an age, which always receives the revelation of the character of the next age, is represented by the coming of one gyre to its place of greatest expansion and of the other to that of its greatest contraction."

"To Ireland in the Coming Times": first published *The Countess Kathleen and Various Legends and Lyrics* (1892). **4:** *rann,* a quatrain, verse, or stanza. **18:** Thomas Davis (1814–45), Irish political leader and writer; James Clarence Mangan (1803–49), Irish poet; Sir Samuel Ferguson (1810–66), Irish poet and antiquary.

The Wind Among the Reeds

First published 1899.

"The Hosting of the Sidhe": first published *National Observer,* 7 October 1893. Yeats explained that "the gods of ancient Ireland, the Tuatha de Danann, or the Tribes of the goddess Danu, or the Sidhe, from Aes Sidhe, or Sluagh Sidhe, the people of the Faery Hills, as those words are usually explained, still ride the country as of old. Sidhe is also Gaelic for wind, and certainly the Sidhe have much to do with the wind." *Tuatha Dé Danann,* "the people of the goddess Danu/Dana," was the name assigned to the Irish pagan gods by learned Christians to reduce their status by including them among earlier settlers of Ireland. Danu/Dana was the mother of the gods. Despite the euhemerization, the *Tuatha* were well known to be immortal beings—dwelling in islands and lakes, inside mountains, and especially inside the megalithic burial tumuli that abound in Ireland. The word for a supernaturally inhabited mound is *síd* (Old Irish), *síodh, sí* (Modern Irish). *Aes Síde* (Old Irish), *Aos Sídhe/Sí* (Modern Irish) means "mound folk." *Slóg/Slaug Síde* (Old Irish), *Slaugh/Slua Sídhe/Sí* (Modern Irish) means "mound armies." Both terms denote the supernatural beings miscalled "fairies." Old Irish *side, sithe,* Modern Irish *sidhe, sí,* means "a blast, puff, gust," not wind per se. The word is unrelated to the word for mound. **1:** a mountain in County Sligo, reputed to be the burial site of Maeve (Medb), queen of Connacht in the Ulster, or Red Branch, cycle of Irish mythology. **2:** Yeats explains that Clooth-na-Bare "went all over the world, seeking a lake deep enough to drown her faery life, of which she had grown weary, leaping from hill to hill, and setting up a cairn of stones wherever her feet lighted, until, at last, she found the deepest water in the world in little Lough Ia, on the top of the bird mountain, in Sligo." Clooth-na-Bare is derived from *Cailleach Bhéarra,* "The Hag of Beare" (a region in County Cork), the name of the speaker of a long ninth-century Gaelic poem. The figure of the old woman entered the popular imagination and became fused with "hag" folktales. Lough Dagea ("Two-Goose Lake") is on top of Slieve Daeane ("Two-Bird Mountain") in

County Sligo. **3:** Caoilte mac Rónáin, a close companion of Finn, the central figure in the Fenian cycle of Irish mythology. Yeats noted that "years after his death he appeared to a king in the forest, and was a flaming man, that he might lead him in the darkness," an episode recounted by the Irish novelist and historian Standish James O'Grady (1846–1928) in his *History of Ireland: Critical and Philosophical* (1881). **4:** Yeats explained that "Niam was a beautiful woman of the Tribes of Danu that led Oisin to the Country of the Young," a story he recounted in "The Wanderings of Oisin" (1889), Oisin being an important hero in the Fenian cycle.

"The Lover tells of the Rose in his Heart": first published *National Observer,* 12 November 1892. Presumably addressed to Maud Gonne (1866–1953), Irish nationalist and Yeats's beloved.

"The Fish": first published *Cornish Magazine,* December 1898. Presumably addressed to Maud Gonne.

"The Song of Wandering Aengus": first published *The Sketch,* 4 August 1897. Yeats describes Aengus as "the god of youth, beauty, and poetry. He reigned in Tir-nan-Oge, the country of the young." **1:** Yeats explained that "the hazel tree was the Irish tree of Life or Knowledge, and in Ireland it was doubtless, as elsewhere, the tree of the heavens." **9–14:** Yeats noted that "the Tribes of the Goddess Danu can take all shapes, and those that are in the waters often take the shape of fish." **14:** Yeats always associated apple blossom with his first meeting on 30 January 1889 with Maud Gonne.

"The Lover mourns for the Loss of Love": first published *The Dome,* May 1898. Presumably addressed to Maud Gonne. **2:** the "beautiful friend" presumably the English novelist Olivia Shakespear (1863–1938), Yeats's mistress in 1896–97.

"He reproves the Curlew": first published *The Savoy,* November 1896.

"He remembers Forgotten Beauty": first published *The Savoy,* July 1896. Presumably addressed to Olivia Shakespear.

"A Poet to his Beloved": first published *The Senate,* March 1896. Probably addressed to the English novelist Olivia Shakespear (1863–1938), Yeats's mistress in 1896–97.

"He gives his Beloved certain Rhymes": first published *The Savoy,* January 1896. Probably addressed to Olivia Shakespear.

"To his Heart, bidding it have no fear": first published *The Savoy,* November 1896.

"**The Cap and Bells**": first published *National Observer,* 17 March 1894. Yeats explained that "I dreamed this story exactly as I have written it, and dreamed another long dream after it, trying to make out its meaning. The first dream was more a vision than a dream, for it was beautiful and coherent, and gave me the sense of illumination and exaltation that one gets from visions, while the second dream was confused and meaningless. The poem has always meant a great deal to me, though, as is the way with symbolic poems, it has not always meant quite the same thing. Blake would have said, 'The authors are in eternity,' and I am quite sure they can only be questioned in dreams."

"**He hears the Cry of the Sedge**": first published *The Dome,* May 1898. Sedge is a grasslike plant found in watery places. **4–5**: an axle-tree is an imaginary line around which the heavens are supposed to revolve. Yeats explains that he made the "ancient Tree of Life" an axle-tree in this poem "for this was another way of representing it."

"**He thinks of Those who have spoken Evil of his Beloved**": first published *The Dome,* May 1898. Presumably addressed to Maud Gonne.

"**The Lover pleads with his Friend for Old Friends**": first published *Saturday Review,* 24 July 1897. Presumably addressed to Maud Gonne.

"**He wishes his Beloved were Dead**": first published *The Sketch,* 9 February 1898. Presumably addressed to Maud Gonne.

"**He wishes for the Cloths of Heaven**": first published *The Wind Among the Reeds* (1899). Probably addressed to Maud Gonne.

In the Seven Woods

First published 1903, including the play *On Baile's Strand* and the narrative poems "The Old Age of Queen Maeve" and "Baile and Aillinn"; three poems added in 1906 (one later removed) and two added in 1908. The seven woods are at Coole, the estate in County Galway of the Irish writer Lady Gregory (1852–1932).

"**In the Seven Woods**": first published *In the Seven Woods* (1903). The Seven Woods are part of Coole Park, the estate of Lady Gregory (1852–1932), an Irish writer and a close friend of Yeats. **6**: Tara, in County Meath, inaugural place of kings of the Uí Néill dynasty, then being excavated. The "new commonness" presumably refers to Edward VII (1841–1910), who assumed the throne on 22 January 1901, with his coronation on 9 August 1901. **12**: sometimes glossed as the constellation Sagittarius. **14**: *Páirc na Laoi,* "the fields of the calves," one of the Seven Woods.

"The Arrow": first published *In the Seven Woods* (1903). Presumably addressed to Maud Gonne (1866–1953), Irish nationalist and Yeats's beloved.

"The Folly of being Comforted": first published *The Speaker,* 11 January 1902. 1: possibly Lady Gregory. 2: well-belovèd: Maud Gonne.

"Never give all the Heart": first published *McClure's Magazine,* December 1905. 14: Maud Gonne had married the Irish nationalist Major John McBride (1865–1916) on 21 February 1903.

"Adam's Curse": first published *The Monthly Review,* December 1902. Adam, the first man in the Bible, is expelled from the Garden of Eden because of disobedience, God telling him "in the sweat of thy face shalt thou eat bread, till thou return unto the ground" (Genesis 3:19). In a larger sense the "curse" is the introduction of time and thus death into the world. 2: Kathleen Pilcher (1868–1919), Maud Gonne's sister. 3: you: Maud Gonne.

"Red Hanrahan's Song about Ireland": first published *The National Observer,* 4 August 1894, in the story "Kathleen-ny-Hoolihan." Red Hanrahan is an invented character, largely based on the Gaelic poet Eoghan Ruadh Ó Súilleabháin (Owen Roe O'Sullivan, 1748–84), and depicted in *Stories of Red Hanrahan* (1905). 1: in County Sligo, on the road from Sligo to Strandhill. 5: Cathleen the daughter of Houlihan, a traditional personification of Ireland. 6–7: Maeve (Medb), queen of Connacht in the Ulster cycle of Irish mythology, is said to be buried on Knocknarea, a mountain in County Sligo. 11: presumably used as the name of a mountain, although derived from *Cailleach Bhéarra,* "The Hag of Beare" (a region in County Cork), the name of the speaker of a long ninth-century Gaelic poem. The figure of the old woman entered the popular imagination and became fused with "hag" folktales. Lough Dagea ("Two-Goose Lake") is on top of Slieve Daeane ("Two-Bird Mountain") in County Sligo. Yeats's note, added to the 1902 edition of *The Celtic Twilight,* draws on information in *The Flight of the Eagle* (1897) by the Irish novelist and historian Standish James O'Grady (1846–1928); Lough Liath ("Gray Lake") is O'Grady's name for the lake on Slieve Fuadh in County Armagh, which is the traditional home of the *Cailleach Bhéarra.*

"The Old Men admiring Themselves in the Water": first published *Pall Mall Magazine,* September 1903.

"O do not Love Too Long": first published *The Acorn,* October 1905. 2: presumably a reference to Yeats's courtship of Maud Gonne.

The Green Helmet and Other Poems

First published 1910, including the play *The Green Helmet;* expanded by six poems in 1912 (four later removed).

"His Dream": first published *The Nation* (London), 11 July 1908. Yeats explained that "A few days ago I dreamed that I was steering a very gay and elaborate ship upon some narrow water with many people upon its banks, and that there was a figure upon a bed in the middle of the ship. The people were pointing to the figure and questioning, and in my dream I sang verses which faded as I awoke, all but this fragmentary thought, 'We call it, it has such dignity of limb, by the sweet name of Death.' I have made my poem out of my dream, and can almost say, as Blake did, 'The Authors are in Eternity.'"

"A Woman Homer sung": first published *The Green Helmet and Other Poems* (1910). The woman is Helen, whose abduction by Paris caused the Trojan War, depicted by the Greek poet Homer (ca. eighth century B.C.) in the *Iliad*. 3: Maud Gonne (1866–1953), Irish nationalist and Yeats's beloved.

"Words": first published *The Green Helmet and Other Poems* (1910). 2: Maud Gonne. 4: Ireland.

"No Second Troy": first published *The Green Helmet and Other Poems* (1910). Troy was destroyed at the end of the Trojan War. 1: Maud Gonne.

"Reconciliation": first published *The Green Helmet and Other Poems* (1910). 1: Maud Gonne. 2: on 21 February 1903, Maud Gonne married the Irish nationalist Major John McBride (1865–1916). 5–6: the play *The Green Helmet*. 10: a pun on the theater pit, the area in front of the stage.

"The Fascination of What's Difficult": first published *The Green Helmet and Other Poems* (1910). 4: Pegasus, in Greek mythology a winged horse associated with poetry. 6: home of the gods in Greek mythology. 11: Yeats was one of the three founding directors of the Abbey Theatre, Dublin.

"A Drinking Song": first published *The Green Helmet and Other Poems* (1910); written for *Mirandolina* (1910), an adaptation by the Irish writer Lady Gregory (1852–1932) of a comedy by the Italian playwright Carlo Goldoni (1707–93).

"The Coming of Wisdom with Time": first published *McClure's Magazine*, December 1910.

"On hearing that the Students of our New University have joined the Agitation against Immoral Literature": first published *The Green Helmet and Other Poems* (1912). The "new University" is University College Dublin, founded in 1845 as the Catholic University of Ireland.

"To a Poet, who would have me Praise certain Bad Poets, Imitators of His and Mine": first published *The Green Helmet and Other Poems* (1910). Addressed to the Irish writer A.E. (George W. Russell, 1867–1935).

"The Mask": first published *The Green Helmet and Other Poems* (1910) and described as "A Lyric from an Unpublished Play"; incorporated in *The Player Queen* (1922), where the first speaker is a man, the second a woman.

"Upon a House shaken by the Land Agitation": first published *McClure's Magazine*, December 1910. The house is Coole Park, the home of Lady Gregory. Fifteen tenants on her estate had successfully applied to the Land Court for a reduction in their rents. **4**: "lidless eye" refers to the folklore belief that only an eagle can stare directly into the sun.

"All things can tempt me": first published *English Review,* February 1909.

"Brown Penny": first published *The Green Helmet and Other Poems* (1910).

Responsibilities

First published 1914, including the play *The Hour-Glass* and the narrative poem "The Two Kings"; one poem added in 1916 but later removed.

"[Introductory Rhymes]": first published *Responsibilities: Poems and a Play* (1914). **3**: Benjamin Yeats (1750–95), Yeats's great-great-grandfather, a wholesale linen merchant. Yeats noted that "'Free of the ten and four' is an error I cannot now correct, without more rewriting than I have a mind for. Some merchant in Villon, I forget the reference, was 'free of the ten and four.' Irish merchants exempted from certain duties by the Irish Parliament were, unless memory deceives me again—I cannot remember my authority—'free of the eight and six.'" The Villon passage is mistranslated (correctly "free of the quarter and the tenth"), and the Irish exemption was "free of the six and ten per cent." **5**: John Yeats (1774–1846), Yeats's great-grandfather, rector of Drumcliff Church in County Sligo and friend of the Irish patriot Robert Emmet (1778–1803). **10**: in 1773 Benjamin Yeats married Mary Butler (1751–1834), who was connected with the Irish Ormondes, the Butler family of great wealth and power that had settled in Ireland in the twelfth century. In 1835, William Butler Yeats (1806–62), Yeats's grandfather, married Jane Grace Corbet (1811–76), daughter of William Corbet (1757–1824) and Grace Armstrong Corbet (1774–1864). Both the Corbets and especially the Armstrongs had a long history of military service. **11–12**: at the Battle of the Boyne in 1690, William III (1650–1702), who was Dutch, defeated James II (1633–1701). **13–14**: William Middleton (ca. 1770–1832), Yeats's maternal grandfather, a shipowner, merchant, and possibly smuggler. Biscay Bay is between Spain and France. **20**: Yeats would become forty-nine on 13 June 1914.

"To a Wealthy Man . . .": first published *Irish Times,* 11 January 1913. In 1907, the Irish art collector Sir Hugh Lane (1875–1915) offered the Dublin Municipal Gallery his important collection of paintings as a gift, on the condition that a suitable gallery be erected. Controversy developed over the choice of an architect, the site for the gallery, and indeed about the relative value of art. Lane decided to give the collection to the National Gallery in London instead, but on 3 February 1915 he added an unwitnessed codicil to his will restoring the paintings to Dublin. After Lane's death on the *Lusitania* on 7 May 1915, a dispute arose between the two galleries over the paintings, one not resolved until long after Yeats's death. Although Yeats told Lane that the poem was addressed to "an imaginary person," he described it to Lady Gregory as "about Lane's Gallery and Lord Ardilaun," referring to Sir Arthur Edward Guinness (1840–1915), an Irish philanthropist. **2–3:** generic names for the people, especially the poor (*Paídín*, "Paddy"). Pence is technically two or more pennies, but the term is also used for one. **4:** presumably from what Yeats called "the argument in Lady Ardilaun's letter to somebody." **5:** a coin worth one pound and one shilling, or 252 pence. **9:** Ercole d'Este I (1431–1505), duke of Ferrara, depicted in *The Book of the Courtier* (1528) by Baldassare Castiglione (1478–1529) as a patron of the arts. **12:** Titus Maccius Plautus (ca. 254–184 B.C.), Roman playwright, much favored by the duke of Ferrara. **14:** Guidobaldo de Montefeltro (1472–1508), Duke of Urbino, also highly praised in *The Book of the Courtier.* **20:** Cosimo de Medici (1389–1464), first of the Medici family to rule Florence and a patron of the arts; exiled to Venice in 1433 but returned in triumph a year later. **22–23:** Michelozzo de Bartolommeo (1396–1472), Italian architect, accompanied Cosimo de Medici into exile and designed for him the Library in St. Mark's, Florence. **26:** from "Peace in Life and Art" by the English poet Coventry Patmore (1823–96). **32:** eagles were thought to be able to look directly into the sun.

"September 1913": first published *Irish Times,* 8 September 1913, entitled "Romance in Ireland / (On reading much of the correspondence against the Art Gallery)." **1–2:** the image of the cash register ("till") suggests that "you" is the mercantile middle class. **8:** John O'Leary (1830–1907), Irish nationalist and an important influence on the early Yeats. **17:** Irishmen who emigrated to the continent after the Treaty of Limerick (1691) and during the times of the Penal Laws (1695–1727), which restricted the activities of Catholics. **20:** Lord Edward Fitzgerald (1763–98), a leader of the 1798 Rising, died of his wounds while in prison. **21:** Robert Emmet (1778–1803), executed for leadership of an abortive revolution; Wolfe Tone (1763–98), a leader of the 1798 Rising, committed suicide while in prison awaiting execution.

"To a Friend whose Work has come to Nothing": first published *Poems Written in Discouragement* (1913). Addressed to Lady Gregory (1852–1932), an Irish writer and a close friend of Yeats.

"Paudeen": first published *Poems Written in Discouragement* (1913).

"When Helen lived": first published *Poetry* (Chicago), May 1914. In Greek mythology, the abduction of Helen by Paris ("her boy") causes the Trojan

War. **8**: from *The Tragical History of Dr. Faustus* (1604) by the English playwright Christopher Marlowe (1564–93): "Was this the face that launched a thousand ships / And burnt the topless towers of Ilium?"

"On Those that hated 'The Playboy of the Western World,' 1907": first published *Irish Review,* December 1911. *The Playboy of the Western World* by the Irish playwright John Millington Synge (1871–1909) opened at the Abbey Theatre, Dublin, on 26 January 1907. Although there were some disturbances on the first night, the play caused rioting in the theater beginning with the second performance on 28 January, much of the audience finding the play a slander upon the Irish people. The poem is based on a painting by the English artist Charles Ricketts (1866–1931). **2**: castrated men. **4**: Don Juan, legendary hero of numerous literary and musical works, sentenced to hell for his libertine activities.

"The Three Beggars": first published *Harper's Weekly,* 15 November 1913. **5**: *libín-lón,* apparently a calque on "minnow-fare." **6**: a small town in Galway. **8**: Guaire Aidne (d. 663), king of Connacht, celebrated for his generosity.

"Beggar to Beggar cried": first published *Poetry* (Chicago), May 1914.

"The Witch": first published *Poetry* (Chicago), May 1914.

"The Peacock": first published *Poetry* (Chicago), May 1914. **5**: Three Rock Mountain is in County Dublin.

"To a Child Dancing in the Wind": first published *Poetry* (Chicago), December 1912. Presumably addressed to Iseult Gonne (1895–1954), Maud Gonne's daughter. **9**: perhaps the Irish playwright John Millington Synge (1871–1909).

"Two Years Later": first published *Poetry* (Chicago), May 1914. Presumably addressed to Iseult Gonne.

"A Memory of Youth": first published *Poetry* (Chicago), December 1912. **5**: Maud Gonne (1866–1953), Irish nationalist and Yeats's beloved.

"Fallen Majesty": first published *Poetry* (Chicago), December 1912. **1**: Maud Gonne.

"Friends": first published *The Green Helmet and Other Poems* (1912). **4**: probably Lady Gregory. **6**: Yeats began to spend his summers at Coole Park, the estate of Lady Gregory, in 1897. **10**: probably the English novelist Olivia Shakespear (1863–1938), Yeats's mistress in 1896–97 (his first sexual affair) and later a close friend. **17**: Maud Gonne.

"The Cold Heaven": first published *The Green Helmet and Other Poems* (1912).

"That the Night come": first published *The Green Helmet and Other Poems* (1912). 1: Maud Gonne.

"The Magi": first published *Poetry* (Chicago), May 1914. Yeats explained that after writing "The Dolls," "I looked up one day into the blue of the sky, and suddenly imagined, as if lost in the blue of the sky, stiff figures in procession. I remembered that they were the habitual image suggested by blue sky, and looking for a second fable called them 'The Magi'. . . , complementary forms of those enraged dolls." In Christian tradition, the Magi (wise men from the East) journey to Bethlehem to worship the infant Christ. 7: a hill in Jerusalem, site of Christ's crucifixion.

"The Dolls": first published *Responsibilities: Poems and a Play* (1914). Yeats explained that "the fable for this poem came into my head while I was giving some lectures in Dublin. I had noticed once again how all thought among us is frozen into 'something other than human life.' " The phrase derives from the *Public Address* (1810), by the English poet and engraver William Blake (1757–1827).

"A Coat": first published *Poetry* (Chicago), May 1914.

"[Closing Rhyme]": first published *New Statesman*, 7 February 1914. 5–6: from the Epilogue to *Poetaster* (1602) by the English playwright Ben Jonson (1572–1637); also printed as "An Ode to Himself" in *Underwoods* (1640). 7: *Coill na gCnó*, "The Wood of Nuts," one of the Seven Woods of Coole Park.

The Wild Swans at Coole

First published 1917, including the play *At the Hawk's Well;* seventeen poems added in 1919. Coole is the estate of the Irish playwright Lady Gregory (1852–1932).

"The Wild Swans at Coole": first published *The Sphere*, 23 June 1917. 7: Yeats began to spend his summers at Coole in 1897, often staying into the autumn.

"In Memory of Major Robert Gregory": first published *English Review,* August 1918. Robert Gregory (1881–1918) was Lady Gregory's only child; a pilot in the Royal Flying Corps, he was killed in action during World War I, in Italy on 23 January 1918. 1: Yeats and his wife, George (1892–1968), at Thoor Ballylee, a Norman tower in County Galway, near Coole Park; Yeats purchased and restored the tower and its two attached cottages in 1917, and spent many of his summers there. **17:** English poet (1867–1902). **25:** John Millington Synge (1871–1909), Irish playwright. **33:** (1839–1910), a maternal uncle of Yeats; a student of astrology and the occult, he lived at Ballina in County Mayo. **39:** astrological terms for heavenly bodies that are separated by 180, 90, and 120 degrees, respectively. **47:** Sir Philip Sidney (1554–86), English writer, statesman, and soldier. **57–60:** Castle Taylor, in County Galway, home of the Taylor family; Roxborough, in County Galway, the childhood home of Lady Gregory; Esserkelly, a village near Ardrahan, County Galway; Moneen, a village in County Galway, adjoining Esserkelly. **65:** Yeats wrote that although Robert Gregory "had so many sides: painter, classical scholar, scholar in painting and in modern literature, boxer, horseman, airman," "to me he will always remain a great painter in the immaturity of his youth, he himself the personification of handsome youth." **66:** Clare, a county in the west of Ireland.

"An Irish Airman foresees his Death": first published *The Wild Swans at Coole* (1919). The airman is Robert Gregory. **5:** the crossroads in Kiltartan, a barony in County Galway, near Coole Park.

"Men improve with the Years": first published *Little Review,* June 1917. **2:** in Greek mythology the Tritons are mermen.

"The Living Beauty": first published *Little Review,* October 1918.

"A Song": first published *Little Review,* October 1918.

"The Scholars": first published *Catholic Anthology, 1914–1915* (1916); see Appendix. **12:** Gaius Valerius Catullus (84?–54? B.C.), Roman poet.

"Lines written in Dejection": first published *The Wild Swans at Coole* (1917). **7:** in Greek mythology the Centaurs are usually depicted as having the upper part of a human body and the four-legged body of a horse.

"On Woman": first published *Poetry* (Chicago), February 1916. **10 ff:** several books of the Old Testament are traditionally ascribed to Solomon (ca. 972–ca. 932 B.C.), king of the Hebrews. The visit of the queen of Sheba (an area of Arabia) to Solomon is described in I Kings 10:1–13. Yeats may also draw on Arabic traditions about Solomon and Sheba. **30:** the pestle is a traditional symbol of fertility and birth; among its associations is with the Hindu goddess Soma, a deity of the moon.

"The Fisherman": first published *Poetry* (Chicago), February 1916. **4:** an area in County Galway; Connemara cloth is a rough tweed.

"Memory": first published *Poetry* (Chicago), February 1916. **6:** possibly a reference to Maud Gonne (1866–1953), Irish nationalist and Yeats's beloved.

"The People": first published *Poetry* (Chicago), February 1916. 9: Ercole d'Este I (1431–1505), duke of Ferrara, depicted in *The Book of the Courtier* (1528) by Baldassare Castiglione (1478–1529) as a patron of the arts. 13: Elisabetta Gonzaga (1471–1526), duchess of Urbino. 22: the "phoenix" is presumably Maud Gonne.

"Broken Dreams": first published *Little Review,* June 1917. Presumably addressed to Maud Gonne.

"A Deep-sworn Vow": first published *Little Review,* June 1917. 1: Maud Gonne. Yeats recalls her telling him that "she would never marry," but on 21 February 1903 she wed the Irish nationalist Major John McBride (1865–1916).

"The Balloon of the Mind": first published *New Statesman,* 29 September 1917.

"On being asked for a War Poem": first published *The Book of the Homeless* (1916), edited by the American novelist Edith Wharton (1862–1937). The war was World War I.

"Ego Dominus Tuus": first published *Poetry* (Chicago), October 1917. In *La Vita Nuova* (ca. 1292–93), the Italian poet Dante Alighieri (1265–1321) describes a dream-vision of a "lord of terrible aspect": "Speaking he said many things, among which I could understand but few; and of these, this: *Ego dominus tuus*" ("I am thy master"). *Hic* and *Ille* are Latin for "this one" and "that one." 4: an invented character who appears in a short story, "Rosa Alchemica" (1896), described as "something between a debauchee, a saint, and a peasant." 22: son of God in the Christian religion. 26: Guido Cavalcanti (ca. 1230–1300) and probably Lapo Gainni (ca. 1270–ca. 1330), poets and friends of Dante. 29: "tent-dwellers," nomad peoples of interior Arabia. 37: Beatrice, Dante's beloved, probably Beatrice Portinari (1266–90). 52: John Keats (1795–1821), English poet.

"The Double Vision of Michael Robartes": first published *The Wild Swans at Coole* (1919). Yeats explained that "Years ago I wrote three stories in which occur the names of Michael Robartes and Owen Aherne. I now consider that I used the actual names of two friends, and that one of these friends, Michael Robartes, has but lately returned from Mesopotamia, where he has partly found and partly thought out much philosophy. I consider that Aherne and Robartes, men to whose namesakes I had attributed a turbulent life or death, have quarrelled with me. They take their place in a phantasmagoria in which I endeavour to explain my philosophy of life and death. To some extent I wrote these poems as a text for exposition." The stories were Yeats's "Rosa Alchemica" (1896), "The Tables of the Law" (1896), and "The Adoration of the Magi" (1897). The poems are "The Phases of the Moon," "The Double Vision of Michael Robartes," and "Michael Robartes and the Dancer." 1:

Rock of Cashel, County Tipperary, ancient site of the kings of Munster; noted for its ecclesiastical ruins, especially the chapel constructed 1127–34 by Cormac Mac Carrthaig (d. 1138). **18**: in Greek mythology a sphinx has typically the body of a lion, wings, and the head and bust of a woman. Originally a monster, in later Greek art the sphinx becomes an enigmatic messenger of the gods. **19**: Guatama Siddhartha, known as the Buddha, "the enlightened one" (ca. 563–ca. 483 B.C.); Indian philosopher and the founder of Buddhism. **56–57**: Helen of Troy, depicted in the *Iliad* by Homer, the most important poet of ancient Greek literature.

Michael Robartes and the Dancer

First published in 1921. Michael Robartes is an invented character who first appears in a short story, "Rosa Alchemica" (1896).

"Michael Robartes and the Dancer": first published *The Dial*, November 1920. **19**: in Greek mythology the Olympian goddess of wisdom, patron of the arts, ruler of storms, and a guardian of cities; usually understood as a virgin goddess. **26**: Paolo Veronese (1528–88), Italian painter. **32–33**: the Italian artist Michelangelo Buonarroti (1475–1564) painted the ceiling of the Sistine Chapel in Rome in 1508–12; his *Morning* (more usually *The Dawn*) and *Night* are statues in the Medici Chapel in Florence. **39–40**: presumably an allusion to Christ's Last Supper, as in Luke 22:14–20. **43**: possibly the *Enneads* of the Neoplatonic philosopher Plotinus (205–69/70) in the Latin translation by Marsilio Ficino (1433–99).

"Easter, 1916": on 24 April 1916, the day after Easter Sunday, an Irish Republic was proclaimed, and a force of approximately 700 Irish Volunteers occupied parts of Dublin. The rebellion was suppressed by the British forces, with the final surrender occurring on 29 April 1916. **17**: Constance Gore-Booth (1868–1927), whom Yeats had known since the 1890s; in 1900 she had married Count Casimir Joseph Dunin-Markiewicz (1874–1932). **24**: Padraic Pearse (1879–1916), Irish poet and founder of St. Edna's School in County Dublin, the leader of the rebellion. **25**: Pegasus, in Greek mythology a horse sacred to the Muses. **26**: Thomas MacDonagh (1878–1916), Irish writer. **32**: Major John MacBride (1865–1916), Irish nationalist, the estranged husband of Yeats's beloved, the Irish nationalist Maud Gonne (1866–1953). **34**: Maud Gonne and her daughter, Iseult (1895–1954). **68–69**: a bill granting Home Rule to Ireland had passed into law in 1914 but had been simultaneously suspended for the duration of World War I, the English government promising to implement it thereafter. **76**: James Connolly (1868–1916), a trade union leader and military commander of the Irish forces during the rebellion.

"Sixteen Dead Men": first published *The Dial*, November 1920. Fifteen of the leaders of the Easter Rebellion were executed by the British 3–12 May 1916; Yeats has added to their number Sir Roger Casement (1864–1916), executed on 3 August 1916 for attempting to bring arms to Ireland from Germany. **16:** Lord Edward Fitzgerald (1763–98) and Wolfe Tone (1763–98), two of the leaders of the 1798 Rising.

"The Rose Tree": first published *The Dial,* November 1920. Yeats explained that "the Rose is a favourite symbol with the Irish poets" and that it is used "not merely in love poems, but in addresses to Ireland," citing "The little black rose shall be red at last" by the Irish poet Aubrey De Vere (1788–1846) and "Dark Rosaleen" by the Irish poet James Clarence Mangan (1803–49).

"On a Political Prisoner": first published *The Dial,* November 1920. The prisoner is Con Markiewicz. Although she was sentenced to death for her role in the Easter Rebellion, the sentence was commuted, and she was released from prison on 18 June 1917. **14:** a mountain near Sligo, the principal town of County Sligo in northwestern Ireland, the home of Yeats's maternal grandparents. Yeats spent a good portion of his early years in Sligo.

"The Second Coming": first published *The Dial,* November 1920. In Christian tradition, the Second Coming is the return of Christ at the apocalypse. Yeats's note explains the figure of the gyres as "a double cone, the narrow end of each cone being in the centre of the broad end of the other": "the end of an age, which always receives the revelation of the character of the next age, is represented by the coming of one gyre to its place of greatest expansion and of the other to that of its greatest contraction. At the present moment the life gyre is sweeping outward, unlike that before the birth of Christ which was narrowing, and has almost reached its greatest expansion. The revelation which approaches will however take its character from the contrary movement of the interior gyre. All our scientific, democratic, fact-accumulating, heterogeneous civilization belongs to the outward gyre and prepares not the continuance of itself but the revelation as in a lightning flash, though in a flash that will not strike only in one place, and will for a time be constantly repeated, of the civilization that must slowly take its place." **12:** Yeats describes *Spiritus Mundi* ("Spirit of the World") as "a general storehouse of images which have ceased to be the property of any personality or spirit." **14:** reminiscent of the Egyptian sphinx, which often has the body of a lion and the head of a man. **19:** "stony sleep" is the Christian era; the phrase is from *Urizen* (1794) by the English poet and engraver William Blake (1757–1827). **20:** the cradle of Christ. **22:** the birthplace of Christ, near Jerusalem.

"A Prayer for my Daughter": first published *Poetry,* November 1919. Anne Yeats was born 26 February 1919. **4:** the poem is set at Thoor Ballylee, a Norman tower near the estate of the Irish writer Lady Gregory (1852–1932). Yeats purchased and restored it in 1917, and spent many of his summers there. **27:** Aphrodite, goddess of love, beauty, and fertility in Greek mythology, in some accounts born from the foam of the sea. **29:** in some accounts, Aphrodite is married to Hephaestus, the lame god of fire and metalwork. **32:**

in Greek mythology, the horns of Amalthea, the goat that nursed Zeus, the ruler of the Olympian gods, flowed with nectar and ambrosia; one of them broke off and was given to Zeus. The cornucopia thus became a symbol of plenty. **42**: a songbird. **59**: Maud Gonne.

"To be Carved on a Stone at Thoor Ballylee": first published *Michael Robartes and the Dancer* (1921). **3**: a village in Galway, near Thoor Ballylee.

The Tower

First published 1928; one poem added and another replaced in 1933. In 1917 Yeats purchased a Norman tower and two attached cottages in County Galway, near Coole Park, the estate of the Irish writer Lady Gregory (1852–1932); he restored the property and spent many of his summers there.

"Sailing to Byzantium": first published *October Blast* (1927). In *A Vision* (1925), Yeats describes Byzantium ca. 560 as an ideal city. **19**: to perne is to move in a circular, spinning motion; a gyre is one half of the interlocked cones which Yeats uses in *A Vision* and elsewhere to image the rise and fall of civilizations, as in his note to "The Second Coming." The essential meaning of "perne in a gyre" is thus to reenter the world of time and conflict. **27–29**: Yeats's note explained that "I have read somewhere that in the Emperor's palace at Byzantium was a tree made of gold and silver, and artificial birds that sang," the probable source being *The History of the Decline and Fall of the Roman Empire* by the English historian Edward Gibbon (1737–94); the emperor was Theophilus, who ruled from 829 until his death in 842.

"The Tower": first published *The Criterion*, June 1927. **9**: a mountain near Sligo, the principal town of County Sligo in northwestern Ireland, the home of Yeats's maternal grandparents. Yeats spent a good portion of his early years in Sligo. **11**: in Greek mythology, the nine Muses are the patrons of the arts. **12**: Plato (ca. 428–ca. 347 B.C.), Greek philosopher, and Plotinus (205–70), Roman philosopher, the founder of Neoplatonism. **25–32**: a story from the chapter "Irish Gentry and Their Retainers" in *Personal Sketches of His Own Times* (1827–32) by the Irish writer Sir Jonah Barrington (1760–1834). The event occurred in 1778. **33–48**: the peasant girl was Mary Hynes, a celebrated beauty who died in the early 1840s. Cloone Bog is in County Galway, near Gort. **49**: Antony Raftery (1784–1835), a blind Gaelic poet, "Mary Hynes, or The Posy Bright." **52**: the Greek poet Homer (ca. eighth century B.C.) is traditionally thought to have been blind. **53**: the abduction of Helen by Paris caused the Trojan War. **57–72**: Red Hanrahan, an invented character, largely based on the Gaelic poet Eoghan Ruadh Ó Súilleabháin (Owen Roe O'Sullivan, 1748–84), and depicted in *Stories of Red Hanrahan* (1905). A bawn (*bán*) is a pasture or yard, sometimes fortified; but in the story the event described occurs in a barn. **80**: Yeats's note indicates that "the old bankrupt man lived about a hundred years ago. According to one legend he could only leave the Castle upon a Sunday because of his creditors, and according to another he hid in the secret passage." **85:** Yeats discusses the "Great Memory passing on from generation to generation," essentially a repository of archetypal images, in the "Anima Mundi" section of *Per Amica Silentia Lunae* (1918). **114:** Hanrahan's life is dominated by his vain search to recover his vision of a fairy goddess, Echtge. **132:** Edmund Burke (1729–97), Irish writer and orator; Henry Grattan (1746–1820), Irish political leader. **136:** in Greek mythology, the horns of Amalthea, the goat that nursed Zeus, the ruler of the Olympian gods, flowed with nectar and ambrosia; one of them broke off and was given to Zeus. The cornucopia thus became a symbol of plenty. **144:** traditionally, a swan sings only in the moments before its death. **156:** a paradise beyond the moon and thus timeless. **181:** compose one's soul, particularly in preparation for death.

"Meditations in Time of Civil War": first published *London Mercury,* January 1923. An Anglo-Irish Treaty was signed in London on 6 December 1921 and accepted by the Irish parliament on 7 January 1922, creating the Irish Free State. The terms of the treaty, especially the partition of the country, were unacceptable to the Republicans, who engaged in a civil war which continued into 1923.

I. Ancestral Houses. 25: peacocks were a feature of the gardens of Lady Ottoline Morrell (1873–1938) at Garsington, near Oxford in England. **27:** in Roman mythology, Juno is queen of the gods and a protector of women.

II. My House: Thoor Ballylee. **14:** John Milton (1608–74), English poet, "Il Penseroso" (1632). **21:** the tower was constructed by the de Burgo family in the thirteenth or fourteenth century. **28:** Anne Yeats, born 26 February 1919, and Michael Yeats, born 22 August 1921.

III. My Table. 2: in March 1920, a Japanese admirer, Junzo Sato, presented Yeats with a ceremonial sword. **8–11:** Geoffrey Chaucer, English poet (1343?–1400). Yeats understood the sword to date from ca. 1370 (mathematics was not one of his strengths). **32:** as a symbol of immortality; the peacock was sacred to Juno; in *A Vision* (1925), Yeats refers to a peacock's scream symbolizing the end of a civilization.

IV. My Descendants. 17: in Ptolemaic astronomy, the outermost concentric sphere, carrying the spheres of the fixed stars and the planets in its daily revolution. **21:** Lady Gregory. **22:** Yeats's wife, George (1892–1968), whom he married on 20 October 1917.

V. The Road at My Door. 1: a member of the Irish Republican Army. **2:** Falstaff is a character in several plays by the English dramatist William Shakespeare (1564–1616). **6–7:** members of the army of the Irish Free State.

VI. The Stare's Nest by My Window. 5: Yeats's note explains that "in the west of Ireland we call a starling a stare." **13–14:** in a letter to T. Sturge Moore on 15 August 1922, Yeats notes that "a motor has just passed with a National soldier and a coffin up on one end. . . ."

VII. I see . . . Emptiness. 9–10: Jacques Molay (1244–1314) was a Grand Master of the Knights Templar, a military-monastic order formed in 1118 to defend the Christian kingdom and protect pilgrims visiting the Holy Land; it was dissolved by Pope Clement V in 1312, and Molay was burned at the stake. Yeats's note argues that "a cry for vengeance because of the murder of the Grand Master of the Templars seems to me fit symbol for those who labour from hatred, and so for sterility in various kinds. It is said to have been incorporated in the ritual of certain Masonic societies of the eighteenth century, and to have fed class hatred." Freemason societies, which began in the seventeenth century, are often understood as anti-Catholic associations. **17–19:** a description of the painting *Ladies and Unicorns* by the French artist Gustave Moreau (1826–98). **20:** Yeats associates the rise of astrology in Babylon, an ancient city in Mesopotamia, with the development of exact science and a corresponding reduction in man's status in relation to the universe. **29:** Yeats's note explains that "I suppose that I must have put hawks into the fourth stanza because I have a ring with a hawk and a butterfly upon it, to symbolize the straight road of logic, and so of mechanism, and the crooked road of intuition: 'For wisdom is a butterfly and not a bird of prey.' " The quotation is from his poem "Tom O'Roughley"; the ring was designed for Yeats by the English artist Edmund Dulac (1882–1953).

"Nineteen Hundred and Nineteen": first published *The Dial,* September 1921, as "Thoughts upon the Present State of the World." During 1919, conflicts between the English-controlled government forces and the Irish Republican Army fighting for independence increased in number and intensity. **6:** probably the olive-wood statue of Athena Polias in the Erechtheum, one of the central buildings (constructed 421–407 B.C.) on the Acropolis in Athens. **7:** Phidias (ca. 490–ca. 432 B.C.), Greek sculptor, best known for his chryselephantine statues of Athena and Zeus. **8:** in the *History of the Peloponnesian War,* the Greek historian Thucydides (ca. 460–ca. 400 B.C.) mentions Athenian women "fastening up their hair in a knot held by a golden grasshopper as a brooch." The bees (ascribed to Phidias in early printings of the poem) may derive from a reference in *Greek Studies: A Series of Essays* (1895) by the English writer Walter Pater (1839–94) to "the golden honeycomb of Dedalus." **19–20:** "And they shall beat their swords into plowshares and their spears into pruninghooks; nation shall not lift up sword against nation, neither shall they learn war any more" (Isaiah 2:4). **20:** the English Parliament and monarch. **26–28:** Ellen Quinn, murdered at Gort, County Galway, in early November 1920. **46:** the olive tree, after the Persians had burned Athens in 480 B.C. **49:** Loïe Fuller (1862–1928), American dancer, best known for her serpentine dance; her troupe of dancers were Japanese, not Chinese. **54:** in ancient cosmology usually understood as 36,000 years, the time needed for the constellations to return to their original positions. **59–60:** probably the English poet Percy Bysshe Shelley (1792–1822) in *Prometheus Unbound* (1820): "My soul is like an enchanted boat / Which, like a sleeping swan, doth float / Upon the waves of thy sweet singing." **72:** perhaps the English mathematician and Platonist Thomas Taylor (1758–1835), in his "Concerning the Cave of the Nymphs," a paraphrase translation *of De Antro Nympharum* by Porphyry (232/33–ca. 305), a Greek Neoplatonic philosopher. **114–16:** Yeats explained that "the country people see at times certain apparitions whom they name now 'fallen angels,' now 'ancient inhabitants of the country,' and describe as riding at whiles 'with flowers upon the heads of their horses.' I have assumed in the sixth poem that these horsemen, now that times worsen, give way to worse." **118:** In a note on the Sidhe, or fairies, Yeats explained that "they journey in whirling wind, the winds that were called the dance of the daughters of Herodias in the Middle Ages, Herodias doubtless taking the place of some old goddess." In the Bible, John the Baptist denounced the marriage of Herod Antipas to Herodias, the divorced wife of his half brother Herod Philip and daughter of his half brother Aristobulus. During his birthday celebration Herod Antipas is so impressed by the dancing of Herodias' daughter by Herod Philip (called variously Herodias or Salome) that he swears to give her anything she asks; prompted by her mother, she asks for the head of John the Baptist, who is then killed. Herodias is also a witch-goddess in Germanic mythology, Jacob Grimm explaining in *Teutonic Mythology* (1883–88) that "quite early in the Mid. Ages the christian mythus of *Herodias* got mixed up with our native heathen fables: those notions about dame *Holda* and the 'furious host' and the nightly jaunts of sorceresses were grafted on it, the Jewish king's daughter had the part of a *heathen goddess* assigned her. . . ." Further, "Herodias was dragged into the circle of night-women . . . because she *played* and *danced,* and since her death goes booming through the air as the 'wind's bride.' " **128–29:** Yeats explained that "my last symbol, Robert Artisson, was an evil spirit much run after in Kilkenny at the start of the fourteenth century." Artisson appears in *The Historie of Ireland* (1577) by the English chronicler Raphael Holinshed (ca. 1515–ca. 1580) as the incubus of Dame Alice Kyteler, who was condemned as a witch on 2 July 1324. Holinshed notes that "she was charged to have nightly conference with a spirit called Robert Artisson, to whom she sacrificed in the high way nine red cocks, and nine peacock eyes."

"A Prayer for my Son": first published *Seven Poems and a Fragment* (1922). Michael Butler Yeats, b. 22 August 1921. **17 ff:** "You" is God, seen later in the stanza as Christ. In Christian tradition Christ is taken to Egypt by the Virgin Mary and her husband, Joseph, to escape the wrath of King Herod, who was afraid of the prophecy that Christ would supplant him (Matt. 2:1–18).

"Fragments": part I first published *Dublin Magazine,* October–December 1931, as part of an essay; part II first published *Collected Poems* (1933). **1:** John Locke (1632–1704), English philosopher, the founder of British empiricism. **2–4:** a parody of the creation of Eve from a rib of Adam in the Garden of Eden (Genesis 2:18–23). The spinning-jenny, a device capable of spinning many threads at once, was invented in 1764 by an Englishman, James Hargreaves (1720–78). 10: ancient capital of the Assyrian Empire, fell in 612 B.C.

"Leda and the Swan": first published *The Dial,* June 1924; see Appendix. In Greek mythology, the god Zeus comes to the mortal Leda in the form of a swan; in the version of the story which Yeats follows in *A Vision* (1925), the offspring are Helen, Clytemnestra, and the Dioscuri (Castor and Pollux). The abduction of Helen by Paris caused the Trojan War. The Greek forces were commanded by Agamemnon, brother of Helen's first husband, Menelaus. On his return from the war, Agamemnon is murdered by Aegisthus, lover of his wife, Clytemnestra. 10: Troy was destroyed by the Greeks at the end of the Trojan War.

"Among School Children": first published *The Dial,* August 1927. In his capacity as a member of the Irish Senate, Yeats had visited St. Otteran's School in Waterford, County Waterford, in November 1926. The school was run according to the principles of the Italian physician and educator Maria Montessori (1870–1952), which stressed the development of initiative and self-reliance by the students. 2: Rev. Mother Philomela, the Mistress of Schools. 9: Maud Gonne, associated with Helen of Troy in several earlier poems. 15–16: in the *Symposium* by the Greek philosopher Plato (ca. 428–ca. 347 B.C.), the Greek playwright Aristophanes (ca. 450–ca. 385 B.C.) argues that primal man was double, in a nearly spherical shape, until Zeus divided him in two, creating man and woman, as a hair divides a cooked egg; love is seen as an attempt to restore the lost unity. 26: an artist of fifteenth-century Italy. 34–36: Yeats explains that "I have taken the 'honey of generation' from Porphyry's essay on 'The Cave of the Nymphs,' but find no warrant in Porphyry for considering it the 'drug' that destroys the recollection of pre-natal freedom. He blamed a cup of oblivion given in the zodiacal sign of Cancer." In Thomas Taylor's translation, Porphyry notes that honey "aptly represents the pleasure and delight of descending into the fascinating realms of generation." Taylor also quotes the fifth-century Neoplatonist Ambrosius Theodosius Macrobius as arguing that "the starry *cup,* placed between Cancer and Lion, is a symbol of this mystic truth, signifying that descending souls first experience intoxication in that part of the heavens, through the influx of matter." 43: Greek philosopher (384–323 B.C.), depicted here as tutor to Alexander the Great (356–323 B.C.), king of Macedonia. 45: Greek philosopher and mathematician (582?–500? B.C.), discovered the mathematical basis of musical intervals; his golden thigh is described by Iamblichus (ca. 250–ca. 330), a Syrian Neoplatonist, in his *On the Pythagorean Life.* 47: in Greek mythology, the nine Muses are the patrons of the arts.

"From 'Oedipus at Colonus' ": first published *October Blast* (1927); a chorus from Yeats's translation of *Oedipus at Colonus* by the Greek dramatist Sophocles (496?–406? B.C.); the concluding poem (XI) of the sequence "A Man Young and Old." 6: Oedipus and his daughters, Antigone and Ismene.

"All Souls' Night": first published *London Mercury*, March 1921; included in *A Vision* (1925). In the Catholic church, All Souls' Day (usually November 2) is the feast in which prayers are offered for the souls of the faithful departed still suffering in purgatory. **1**: Christ Church, a college at Oxford University in England. **21**: William Thomas Horton (1864–1919), English mystical painter and illustrator. **25**: Amy Audrey Locke (1881–1916), Horton's beloved. **41**: Florence Farr Emery (1869–1917), English actress; in September 1912 she moved to India to become the principal of a girls' school. **53**: probably Sir Ponnambalam Ramanathan (1851–1930), founder of the school where Farr taught. **61**: Samuel Liddell Mathers, later MacGregor Mathers (1854–1918), English occultist and one of the founders of the Order of the Golden Dawn.

The Winding Stair and Other Poems

First published 1933.

"In Memory of Eva Gore-Booth and Con Markiewicz": first published *The Winding Stair* (1929). Yeats had known the Gore-Booth sisters since 1894. Eva (1870–1926) was a poet who became active in trade union associations for women in Manchester in England. Constance (1868–1927) married Count Casimir Joseph Dunin-Markiewicz (1874–1932) in 1910; she took part in the 1916 Easter Rebellion and was sentenced to death; the sentence was commuted, and she was released from prison on 18 June 1917; she remained active in Irish politics, supporting the Republican side in the Civil War. **1**: the Gore-Booth family home in County Sligo. **4**: the gazelle is Eva Gore-Booth. **11**: an ideal state. **16**: the neoclassical Georgian style of architecture dates from 1714 to 1820; Lissadell was constructed in 1832.

"A Dialogue of Self and Soul": first published *The Winding Stair* (1929). **1**: of Yeats's tower, Thoor Ballylee. **5**: in an 1899 note Yeats referred to the "pole of the heavens, the ancient Tree of Life in many countries" and indicated that the star was the North Star. **7**: in *A Vision* (1925), the last quarter of the Phases of the Moon is dominated by abstraction and movement toward the dark of the moon. **10**: in March 1920, a Japanese admirer, Junzo Sato, presented Yeats with a ceremonial sword. **25**: Bishū Osafuné Motoshigé, or Motoshigé of the later generation, flourished in the Era of Ōei (1394–1428). **64**: such as Maud Gonne (1865–1953), Irish nationalist and Yeats's beloved.

"Coole Park, 1929": first published in Lady Gregory, *Coole* (1931). Coole Park was the estate of the Irish writer Lady Gregory (1852–1932) in County Galway. **9**: Douglas Hyde (1860–1949), Irish scholar and translator, founder of the Gaelic League in 1893. **10**: in Greek mythology, the nine Muses are the patrons of the arts. **11**: "one" is Yeats. **13**: John Millington Synge (1871–1909), Irish playwright. **14**: John Shawe-Taylor (1866–1911), a Galway landlord and nephew of Lady Gregory, on 2 September 1902 called for a conference to discuss the acquisition by tenants of land at fair prices, which resulted in the Land Bill of 1903; Sir Hugh Lane (1875–1915), a nephew of Lady Gregory, offered his important collection of paintings to the Dublin Municipal Gallery as a gift, on the condition that a suitable gallery be erected. Controversy developed over the choice of an architect, the site for the gallery, and indeed about the relative value of art. Lane decided to give the collection to the National Gallery in London instead, but on 3 February 1915 he added an unwitnessed codicil to his will restoring the paintings to Dublin. After Lane's death on the *Lusitania* on 7 May 1915, a dispute arose between the two galleries over the paintings, one not resolved until long after Yeats's death.

"Coole and Ballylee, 1931": first published *Words for Music Perhaps and other Poems* (1932). **4:** Yeats mistakenly suggests that the river which runs past his tower, Thoor Ballylee, flows into Coole Lake. The Irish poet Antony Raftery (1784–1835) was blind, thus "dark"; in "Mary Hynes, or The Posy Bright," Raftery writes, "The cellar is strong in Ballylee," explained by Douglas Hyde in his edition of *Songs Ascribed to Raftery* (1903): "Said to allude to a great deep pool in the river, near where the house was." **26:** Lady Gregory. **46:** Pegasus, in Greek mythology a winged horse associated with poetry. **47:** Greek poet (ca. eighth century B.C.).

"The Choice": first published *Words for Music Perhaps and other Poems* (1932), as the sixth stanza of what was then called "Coole Park and Ballylee, 1931."

"Mohini Chatterjee": first published *A Packet for Ezra Pound* (1929). Mohini Chatterjee (1858–1936) was an Indian Brahman, or sage, whom Yeats met in Dublin in 1885 or 1886 when he lectured at the Dublin Hermetic Society.

"Byzantium": first published *Words for Music Perhaps and other Poems* (1932). In *A Vision* (1925), Yeats describes sixth-century Byzantium as an ideal city. However, it is possible that this poem describes a later Byzantium, in decline, as a note in Yeats's 1930 diary reads "Describe Byzantium as it is in the system [of *A Vision*] towards the end of the first Christian millennium. A walking mummy. Flames at the street corners where the soul is purified, birds of hammered gold singing in the golden trees, in the harbour [dolphins] offering their backs to the wailing dead that they may carry them to Paradise." **4:** Hagia Sophia ("Holy Wisdom"), church constructed 532–37 by the emperor Justinian I (483–565). **11:** in Greek mythology, Hades, a son of Kronos, is lord of the underworld, the abode of the dead. The "bobbin" is perhaps analogous to what Yeats calls "Plato's spindle": the "spindle of Necessity, on which all revolutions turn" in Book X of the *Republic* by the Greek philosopher Plato (ca. 428–ca. 347 B.C.). **25:** in *The Age of Justinian and Theodora: A History of the Sixth Century A.D.*, second edition (1912), William Gordon Holmes describes the "Forum of Constantinople [Byzantium], which presents itself as an extension of the Mese [the main street of the city]. This open space, the most signal ornament of Constantinople, is called prescriptively the Forum; and sometimes, from its finished marble floor, 'The Pavement.' " **33:** in *Apotheosis and After Life: Three Lectures on Certain Phases of Art and Religion in the Roman Empire* (1915), Mrs. Arthur Strong notes that dolphins "form a mystic escort of the dead to the Islands of the Blest."

"Vacillation": first published *Words for Music Perhaps and other Poems* (1932). **11–15:** *The Mabinogion,* a collection of Welsh romances of the eleventh to thirteenth centuries, describes a "tall tree by the side of the river, one half of which was in flames from the root to the top, and the other half was green and in full leaf." **16:** in Greek mythology, Attis is a vegetation god; Cybele, an earth-goddess, causes him to castrate himself, to prevent his marriage to another. As James G. Frazer explains in *The Golden Bough: A Study in Comparative Religion* (1890), during Attis' festival (March 22–27), "the effigy of a young man was attached to the middle" of a ceremonial tree as "a representation of his coming to life again in tree-form." The high priest of Cybele, called Attis, was traditionally a eunuch. **27:** in Greek mythology Lethe is a river in Hades; drinking its waters causes forgetfulness of the past. **35:** Yeats's "fiftieth year" was 13 June 1914 to 12 June 1915, when he was forty-nine. **59:** Châu-kung (d. 1105 B.C.), Chinese author and statesman, known as the duke of Chou. **63:** Babylon, ancient city in Mesopotamia, captured by Cyrus the Great in 539 B.C.; Nineveh, ancient capital of the Assyrian Empire, fell in 612 B.C. **74:** in the Bible, the prophet Isaiah is purified by an angel who touches a live coal to his lips (Isaiah 6:6–7). **77:** Homer, Greek poet (ca. eighth century B.C.); in Christian theology, original sin is the universal sinfulness of mankind, traditionally viewed as originating in the first sin committed by Adam and Eve in the Garden of Eden. **78:** Baron Friedrich von Hügel (1852–1925), Catholic religious philosopher. **80–82:** Saint Teresa of Avila (1515–82), Spanish Carmelite nun and one of the principal saints of the Catholic church; her body was said not to have decayed in her coffin. **84:** the Pharaohs, ancient kings of Egypt, were mummified after death. **88:** in the Bible, Samson kills a lion and later extracts honey from its carcass; from this experience he forms a riddle, "Out of the eater came what is eaten, and out of the strong came what is sweet." Samson later tells his wife the answer and thereby discovers her infidelity (Judges 14:5–20).

The next twenty-five poems in *The Winding Stair and Other Poems* are placed after the heading *Words for Music Perhaps,* a relic of the 1932 Cuala Press *Words for Music Perhaps and other Poems.*

"Crazy Jane and the Bishop": first published *London Mercury,* November 1930; I in the *Words for Music Perhaps* section. Crazy Jane is an invented character, based on "Cracked Mary," an old woman who lived near Lady Gregory and whom Yeats described as "the local satirist and a really terrible one." Yeats would have found the name Crazy Jane in a ballad of that title by the English writer Matthew Gregory Lewis (1775–1818). **1:** "blasted," struck by lightning. **5:** Jack the Journeyman is found in Lady Gregory's play *The Losing Game* (1902) and reappears in a lyric in Yeats's play *The Pot of Broth* (1903).

"Crazy Jane Talks with the Bishop": first published *The Winding Stair and Other Poems* (1933); VI in the *Words for Music Perhaps* section.

"Her Anxiety": first published *New Republic,* 22 October 1930; X in the *Words for Music Perhaps* section.

"Lullaby": first published *The New Keepsake* (1931); XVI in the *Words for Music Perhaps* section. **1–6:** in Greek mythology the abduction of Helen by Paris caused the Trojan War. **7–12:** in the medieval romance of Tristram and Iseult, Tristram is sent to Ireland to bring Iseult back to Cornwall to be the bride of King Mark; a potion which they unknowingly drink makes their love for each other irresistible. **13–18:** in Greek mythology, the god Zeus comes to the mortal Leda in the form of a swan; in the version of the story which Yeats follows in *A Vision* (1925), the offspring are Helen, Clytemnestra, and the Dioscuri (Castor and Pollux). Leda was the wife of the king of Sparta, on the west bank of the Eurotas River.

"After Long Silence": first published *Words for Music Perhaps and other Poems* (1932); XVII in the *Words for Music Perhaps* section. The poem is generally thought to be about Yeats and the English novelist Olivia Shakespear (1863–1938), his mistress in 1896–97 and later close friend.

The remaining eleven poems in *The Winding Stair and Other Poems* are part of the sequence "A Woman Young and Old."

"Father and Child": first published *The Winding Stair* (1929). Apparently derived from a remark by Yeats's daughter, Anne Butler Yeats (1919–2001), about a friend, Fergus Fitzgerald.

"Parting": first published *The Winding Stair* (1929); VII of "A Woman Young and Old." In a note to this and two other poems, Yeats indicates that "I have symbolized a woman's love as the struggle of the darkness to keep the sun from rising from its earthly bed."

"Her Vision in the Wood": first published *The Winding Stair* (1929); VIII of "A Woman Young and Old." **2:** "wine-dark" is a famous epithet for the sea in the work of the Greek poet Homer (ca. eighth century B.C.). **16:** cf. the Greek myth of Adonis and Aphrodite and the Irish myth of Diarmuid and Gráinne, in both of which a male lover is slain by a boar. **19:** an artist of fifteenth-century Italy. **20:** Andrea Mantegna (1431–1506), Italian painter.

"A Last Confession": first published *The Winding Stair* (1929); IX of "A Woman Young and Old."

"From the 'Antigone' ": first published *The Winding Stair;* Yeats's translation of a chorus from *Antigone* by the Greek dramatist Sophocles (496?–406? B.C.); XI of "A Woman Young and Old." **2:** the girl is Antigone. **6:** in Greek mythology, a mountain sacred to Apollo, Dionysus, and the Muses. **7:** in ancient cosmology the highest heaven, a sphere of fire. **10:** Antigone's brothers, Eteocles and Polynices, die at each other's hand. **15:** Oedipus is Antigone's father; at the end of the play, she commits suicide after being entombed in a vault by Creon.

Parnell's Funeral and Other Poems

First published as a section of *A Full Moon in March* (1935); the titular work is a play.

"Parnell's Funeral": third stanza first published *Dublin Magazine*, April–June 1932, as part of an essay; entire poem first published *The Spectator*, 19 October 1934. The Irish political leader Charles Stewart Parnell (1846–91) died in Brighton, England, on 6 October 1891 and was buried in Glasnevin Cemetery in Dublin on 11 October. In November 1890 he had lost his leadership of the Irish Parliamentary Party because of the scandal surrounding his long-term affair with Katharine O'Shea (1845–1921), wife of Captain William Henry O'Shea (1840–1905).

I. 1: Daniel O'Connell (1775–1847), the most important Irish politician of the first part of the nineteenth century, as Parnell was of the second. **4:** Yeats did not attend the funeral (a "sensitive and timid youth, I hated crowds"), but the phenomenon of the shooting star was widely reported. In his "Commentary" on the poem, Yeats quotes the account by the Irish historian and novelist Standish James O'Grady (1846–1928) in *The Story of Ireland:* "I state a fact—it was witnessed by thousands. While his followers were committing Charles Parnell's remains to the earth, the sky was bright with strange lights and flames." **6–15:** in his "Commentary" Yeats noted, "I think of the symbolism of the star shot with an arrow, described in the appendix to my book *Autobiographies*. I ask if the fall of a star may not upon occasion, symbolize an accepted sacrifice." In *Autobiographies* (1926), Yeats had included a new opening to part VI of "The Stirring of the Bones." First published in 1923, the addition describes a vision Yeats had in 1896 of "a galloping centaur, and a moment later a naked woman of incredible beauty, standing upon a pedestal and shooting an arrow at a star." In his "Notes," Yeats discusses the archetypal significance of the vision, drawing on information supplied by Vacher Burch, later lecturer at Liverpool Cathedral and the author of several studies of religion. Essentially, the vision is interpreted as analogous to "the Mother-Goddess whose representative priestess shot the arrow at the child whose sacrificial death symbolized the death and resurrection of the Tree-spirit, or Apollo." Burch told Yeats that "she is pictured upon certain Cretan coins of the fifth century B.C. as a slightly draped, beautiful woman sitting in the heart of a branching tree." Crete is an island southeast of Greece, Sicily an island south of Italy. Yeats's "Sicilian coin" has not been traced, although Burch drew his attention to George Francis Hill's *A Handbook of Greek and Roman Coins* (1899), which includes a coin showing "the Cretan goddess seated in her tree." **17**: Robert Emmet (1778–1803), Lord Edward Fitzgerald (1763–98), Wolfe Tone (1763–98), Irish nationalists. Emmet was executed by the English ("the strangers"); Fitzgerald died of his wounds; Tone took his own life on the morning of his execution. **20**: hysteria, causing suffocation or choking. **28**: in "The Proceedings of the Great Bardic Institution," ed. Professor [Owen] Connellan, *Transactions of the Ossianic Society* (1860), the poet Senchan causes ten mice to die by his satire. Connellan cites an 1853 paper by James H. Todd "on the subject of the power once believed to be possessed by the Irish bards of rhyming rats to death, or causing them to migrate by the power of rhyme."

II. 2: Eamon de Valera (1882–1975), President of the Executive Council of the Irish Free State since February 1932. **5**: William Cosgrave (1880–1965), first President of the Executive Council of the Irish Free State, 1922–32. **8**: Kevin O'Higgins (1892–1927), Minister for Justice and External Affairs in the Irish Free State, assassinated 10 July 1927; described by Yeats as "the finest intellect in Irish public life, and, I think I may add, to some extent, my friend." **9**: Eoin O'Duffy (1892–1944), first Commander of the Civic Guard; dismissed by de Valera early in 1933, he formed the "Blueshirts" movement and eventually became President of the Fine Gael party, before suddenly resigning from politics (although not permanently) on 22 September 1934. **11**: Anglo-Irish writer (1667–1745).

"A Prayer for Old Age": first published *The Spectator,* 2 November 1934.

The remaining twelve poems in *Parnell's Funeral and Other Poems* appear under the heading "Supernatural Songs."

"Ribh at the Tomb of Baile and Aillinn": first published *London Mercury,* December 1934; I of "Supernatural Songs." Ribh is an invented character, described by Yeats as "an imaginary critic of St. Patrick. His Christianity, come perhaps from Egypt like much early Irish Christianity, echoes pre-Christian thought," referring to St. Patrick (389?–461?), the Apostle of Ireland. Yeats also indicated that "I would consider Ribh, were it not for his ideas about the Trinity, an orthodox man." The Christian Trinity consists of the Father, the Son, and the Holy Ghost; in the poem "Ribh denounces Patrick," Ribh argues it should be "Man, woman, child (daughter or son) / That's how all natural or supernatural stories run." As described in the "Argument" to Yeats's narrative poem "Baile and Aillinn" (1902), "Baile and Aillinn were lovers, but Aengus, the Master of Love, wishing them to be happy in his own land among the dead, told to each a story of the other's death, so that their hearts were broken and they died." **16–17**: describing the dead in *Per Amica Silentia Lunae* (1918), Yeats commented "I do not doubt that they make love in that union which Swedenborg has said is of the whole body and seems from far off an incandescence," a reference to *The Delights of Wisdom Pertaining to Conjugal Love; After which follow the Pleasures of Insanity relating to Scortatory Love* (1768) and *Heaven and its Wonders and Hell: from Things Heard and Seen* (1758) by Emanuel Swedenborg (1688–1772), Swedish scientist, philosopher, and theologian.

"The Four Ages of Man": first published *London Mercury* and *Poetry* (Chicago), December 1934. Yeats commented in a letter that "They are the four ages of individual man, but they are also the four ages of civilisation. First age, *earth*, negative functions. Second age, *water*, blood, sex. Third age, *air*, breath, intellect. Fourth age, *fire*, soul etc."

"Meru": first published *London Mercury*, December 1934; XII of "Supernatural Songs." Mount Kailasa in Tibet is the twin of Mount Meru, in Hindu mythology located in the center of paradise; Mount Everest is in the Himalayas, on the border of Tibet and Nepal.

New Poems

First published 1938.

"The Gyres": first published *New Poems* (1938). The gyres are an important symbol in *A Vision* (1925). Yeats explains in a note to "The Second Coming" that the gyres are "a double cone, the narrow end of each cone being in the centre of the broad end of the other" and that "the end of an age, which always receives the revelation of the character of the next age, is represented by the coming of one gyre to its place of greatest expansion and of the other to that of its greatest contraction. At the present moment the life gyre is sweeping outward, unlike that before the birth of Christ which was narrowing, and has almost reached its greatest expansion. The revelation which approaches will however take its character from the contrary movement of the interior gyre. All our scientific, democratic, fact-accumulating, heterogeneous civilization belongs to the outward gyre and prepares not the continuance of itself but the revelation as in a lightning flash, though in a flash that will not strike only in one place, and will for a time be constantly repeated, of the civilization that must slowly take its place." **1**: a number of suggestions have been made for the identity of Old Rocky Face, including the Delphic Oracle and Ahasuerus, the cavern-dwelling Jew in *Hellas* (1822), by the English poet Percy Bysshe Shelley (1792–1822); whether Yeats intended a specific allusion is problematic. **6**: Greek philosopher (490?–430 B.C.). **7**: Hector, the oldest son of King Priam and Queen Hecuba of Troy, killed by Achilles during the Trojan War.

"**Lapis Lazuli**": first published *London Mercury,* March 1938. On 4 July 1935, Yeats received a lapis lazuli carving dating from the Ch'ien Lung period (1739–95) as a seventieth-birthday present from Henry (Harry) Talbot de Vere Clifton (1908–78), who was then the author of two volumes of poetry. **6**: zeppelins, rigid airships designed by Ferdinand, Graf von Zeppelin (1838–1917), a German military officer, were used to bomb London in World War I, the first war to involve the military use of airplanes as well. **7**: a pun on Kaiser Wilhelm (1859–1941), German emperor and king of Prussia during World War I; and William III (1650–1702), the Protestant king of England 1689–1702, who on 12 July 1690 defeated the forces of James II (1633–1701), the former Catholic king of England 1685–88, in a battle fought on the banks of the Boyne River. An anonymous ballad in *Irish Minstrelsy* (1888) describes how "King James he pitched his tents between / The lines for to retire; / But King William threw his bomb-balls in, / And set them all on fire." **10–11**: Hamlet and Ophelia are characters in *Hamlet* (1603) by the English playwright William Shakespeare (1564–1616); Lear and Cordelia in his *King Lear* (1608). **29**: the Greek sculptor Callimachus (late fifth century B.C.) refined the employment of the running drill; for the Erechtheum in Athens he made a golden lamp with a long chimney that reached to the roof.

"**Imitated from the Japanese**": first published *New Poems* (1938). Yeats noted in a letter that "I made this poem out of a prose translation of a Japanese Hokku in praise of Spring," a hokku being a poem of seventeen syllables, divided into lines of five, seven, and five syllables. The likely source is "My Longing After Departed Spring" by Gekkyo (1745–1824) and the accompanying commentary in *An Anthology of Haiku Ancient and Modern,* trans. Asatarō Miyamori (1931).

"**An Acre of Grass**": first published *London Mercury,* April 1938. **5**: in July 1932 Yeats moved to his last home, Riversdale, in Rathfarnam, County Dublin. **15**: Timon is a character in Shakespeare's *Timon of Athens* (1623). **16**: English poet and engraver (1757–1827). **19**: Michelangelo Buonarroti (1475–1564), Italian artist.

"**What Then?**": first published *The Erasmian* (Dublin), April 1937. **5**: Greek philosopher (ca. 428–ca. 347 B.C.).

"**Beautiful Lofty Things**": first published *New Poems* (1938). **1**: John O'Leary (1830–1907), Irish nationalist, a major influence on the young Yeats. **2–4**: John Butler Yeats (1839–1922) defended *The Playboy of the Western World* (1907) by the Irish playwright John Millington Synge (1871–1909) during a public debate at the Abbey Theatre, Dublin, on 4 February 1907; the play had been attacked as a slander on the Irish people. **5–6**: Standish James O'Grady (1846–1928), Irish novelist and historian, presumably at a dinner in Dublin given by T. P. Gill, editor of *The Daily Express,* in honor of the Irish Literary Theatre on 11 May 1899. **7–10**: in her journal for

11 April 1922, the Irish writer Lady Gregory (1852–1932) noted a threat by one of her tenants at Coole Park to take over land by violence if necessary: After referring the man to her brother, she "showed how easy it would be to shoot me through the unshuttered window if he wanted to use violence." **10–11:** Maud Gonne (1866–1953), Irish nationalist and Yeats's beloved, presumably on 4 August 1891, the day after she had rejected Yeats's first proposal of marriage. Howth is a fishing village on a promontory on the north side of Dublin Bay. In Greek mythology, Pallas Athena was the goddess of cities, of industry and the arts, of wisdom, and of war. **12:** in Greek mythology, the dynasty of gods headed by Zeus, the father of Athena.

"Come Gather Round Me Parnellites": first published *A Broadside,* January 1937. The Irish political leader Charles Stewart Parnell (1846–91) lost his leadership of the Irish Parliamentary Party in November 1890 because of the scandal surrounding his long-term affair with Katharine O'Shea (1845–1921), wife of Captain William Henry O'Shea (1840–1905). The Parnellites are those who remained loyal to him. **27–28:** in an essay Yeats claimed that *Parnell Vindicated: The Lifting of the Veil* (1931) by the Irish writer and nationalist Henry Harrison (1867–1954) "proved beyond controversy . . . that Captain O'Shea knew of their liaison from the first; that he sold his wife for money and other substantial advantages; that for £20,000, could Parnell have raised that sum, he was ready to let the divorce proceedings go, not against Parnell, but himself. . . ."

"The Great Day": first published *London Mercury,* March 1938.

"Parnell": first published *London Mercury,* March 1938. Charles Stewart Parnell.

"The Spur": first published *London Mercury,* March 1938.

"The Municipal Gallery Re-visited": first published *A Speech and Two Poems* (1937). The Municipal Gallery of Modern Art is in Dublin. At a speech at the Banquet of the Irish Academy of Letters on 17 August 1937, Yeats noted, "For a long time I had not visited the Municipal Gallery. I went there a week ago and was restored to many friends. I sat down, after a few minutes, overwhelmed with emotion. There were pictures painted by men, now dead, who were once my intimate friends. . . . Ireland not as she is displayed in guide book or history, but, Ireland seen because of the magnificent vitality of her painters, in the glory of her passions." **2:** *The Men of the West* by the Irish painter Seán Keating (1889–1977); *St. Patrick's Purgatory* by the Irish painter Sir John Lavery (1856–1941). **3–4:** *The Court of Criminal Appeal* by Lavery; Sir Roger Casement (1864–1916) was executed by the British for attempting to bring arms to Ireland from Germany. **4:** *Arthur Griffith* by Lavery; Griffith (1871–1922) was an Irish political leader and editor who often opposed Yeats. **5–7:** *Kevin O'Higgins* by Lavery; O'Higgins (1892–1927), Minister for

Justice and External Affairs in the Irish Free State, assassinated 10 July 1927, was described by Yeats as "the finest intellect in Irish public life, and, I think I may add, to some extent, my friend." **8–10:** *The Blessing of the Colours* by Lavery. **13–16:** perhaps *Lady Charles Beresford* by John Singer Sargent (1856–1925), an American artist who worked mainly in England; Lady Beresford (ca. 1853–1922) was the wife of William de la Poer, Baron Beresford of Metemmeh and Curraghmore, County Waterford. **21:** *Robert Gregory* by the English artist Charles Shannon (1863–1937); Robert Gregory (1881–1918), Lady Gregory's only child, was killed in World War I. **21–22:** *Sir Hugh Lane* by Sargent; Sir Hugh Lane (1875–1915) bequeathed his collection of modern art to the Municipal Gallery, leading to a dispute cited by Yeats in poems such as "To a Wealthy Man who promised a second Subscription to the Dublin Municipal Gallery if it were proved the People wanted Pictures." The dedication of the first edition of Shakespeare's *Sonnets* (1609) reads "To the onlie begetter of these insuing sonnets Mr. W. H. all happinesse and that eternite promised by our ever-living poet wisheth the well-wishing adventurer in setting forth." **23:** the "living" Hazel Lavery (d. 1935) is probably Lavery's *Portrait of Lady Lavery;* the "dying" is Lavery's *The Unfinished Harmony.* **25–26:** *Lady Gregory* by the Italian artist Antonio Mancini (1852–1930). Rembrandt Harmensz van Rijn (1606–69), Dutch painter and etcher; Yeats cited Synge's judgment in his Banquet speech. **34:** Coole Park. **39–40:** a passage from "The Ruins of Time" (1591) by the English poet Edmund Spenser (1552?–99), included by Yeats in his edition of *Poems of Spenser* (1906), reads, "He is gone now, the whiles the Foxe is crept / Into the hole, the which the badger swept." **44:** in Greek mythology, the giant Antaeus, son of Poseidon and Earth, grows stronger when in contact with the earth. **48:** *John M. Synge,* by John Butler Yeats. **49:** probably from Synge's poem "Prelude" (1909): "did but half remember human words."

"Are You Content": first published *London Mercury,* April 1938. **9:** the Reverend John Yeats (1774–1846), Yeats's great-grandfather, Rector of Drumcliff Church, County Sligo, 1811–46. **11–12:** the Reverend William Butler Yeats (1806–62), Yeats's grandfather, was rector of Tullyish, near Portadown. **12–13:** the Reverend William Butler Yeats married Jane Grace Corbet (1811–76) in 1835; her brother Robert Corbet (d. 1872) lived at Sandymount Castle on the outskirts of Dublin with his mother (Grace Armstrong Corbet, 1774–1864) and his aunt, Jane Armstrong Clendenin. **14:** William Pollexfen (1811–92), Yeats's maternal grandfather, a shipowner and merchant. **15:** William Middleton (ca. 1770–1832), Yeats's maternal great-grandfather, a shipowner, merchant, and possibly smuggler. In 1773 Benjamin Yeats (1750–95), Yeats's great-great-grandfather, married Mary Butler (1751–1834), who was connected with the Irish Ormondes, the Butler family of great wealth and power that had settled in Ireland in the twelfth century. **22–23:** in *Pauline* (1833), the English poet Robert Browning (1812–89) describes "an old hunter / Talking with gods."

[Last Poems]

Shortly before he died, Yeats had prepared an untitled table of contents for a volume of poems and two plays (*The Death of Cuchulain* and *Purgatory*). This material was published by the Cuala Press as *Last Poems and Two Plays* (1939); the title Yeats may have intended for the volume is unknown.

"**Under Ben Bulben**": first published *Irish Times* and *Irish Independent*, 3 February 1939. Ben Bulben is a mountain north of Sligo in County Sligo. **2**: the area around Lake Mareotis, south of Alexandria in Egypt, is associated with the rise of Christian monasticism in the fourth century. **3**: "The Witch of Atlas"(1824) by the English poet Percy Bysshe Shelley (1792–1822). **5–11**: in the *Hodos Chameliontos* section of *The Trembling of the Veil*, Yeats recalls Mary Battle, a servant of his uncle George Pollexfen (1839–1910), seeing visions of supernatural riders: "They are fine and dashing-looking, like the men one sees riding their horses in twos and threes on the slopes of the mountains with their swords swinging. There is no such race living now, none so finely proportioned." Ben Bulben is also associated with some events in the Fenian cycle of Irish mythology, particularly the death of Diarmuid. **25–26**: in his *Jail Journal* (1854), the Irish nationalist John Mitchel (1815–75) asked, "Give us war in our time, O Lord!" **43–44**: the Roman philosopher Plotinus (205–70), born in Egypt, the founder of Neoplatonism; Phidias (ca. 490–ca. 432 B.C.), Greek sculptor. In the *Fifth Ennead,* Plotinus argued that "the arts are not to be slighted on the ground that they create by imitation of natural objects; for, to begin with, these natural objects are themselves imitations; then, we must recognize that they give no bare reproduction of the thing seen but go back to the Ideas from which Nature itself derives, and, furthermore, that much of their work is all their own; they are holders of beauty and add where nature is lacking. Thus Pheidias wrought the Zeus upon no model of things of sense but by apprehending what form Zeus must take if he chose to become manifest to sight." **45–47**: Michelangelo Buonarroti (1475–1564), Italian artist; his painting on the ceiling of the Sistine Chapel in Rome includes a depiction of Adam about to be touched into life by God. **53**: an artist of fifteenth-century Italy. **62**: the gyres are an important symbol in *A Vision* (1925). Yeats explains in a note to "The Second Coming" that the gyres are "a double cone, the narrow end of each cone being in the centre of the broad end of the other" and that "the end of an age, which always receives the revelation of the character of the next age, is represented by the coming of one gyre to its place of greatest expansion and of the other to that of its greatest contraction. At the present moment the life gyre is sweeping outward, unlike that before the birth of Christ which was narrowing, and has almost reached its greatest expansion. The revelation which approaches will however take its character from the contrary movement of the interior gyre. All our scientific, democratic, fact-accumulating, heterogeneous civilization belongs to the outward gyre and prepares not the continuance of itself but the revelation as in a lightning flash, though in a flash that will not strike only in one place, and will for a time be constantly repeated, of the civilization that must slowly take its place." **64:** Edward Calvert (1799–1883) English artist; probably Richard Wilson (1714–82), English artist; William Blake (1757–1827), English poet and engraver; Claude Lorrain (1600–82), French artist. **65–66:** describing Blake's illustrations to Thornton's *Virgil* and alluding to Hebrews 4:9, the English artist Samuel Palmer (1805–81) said "they are like all that wonderful artist's work the drawing aside of the fleshly curtain, and the glimpse which all the most holy, studious saints and sages have enjoyed, of that rest which remaineth to the people of God." **80:** beginning with the Norman invasion of Ireland in 1169. **84–87:** the Reverend John Yeats (1774–1846) was Rector of Drumcliff Church, County Sligo, 1811–46. Yeats died in the South of France on 28 January 1939; his body was reinterred at Drumcliff on 17 September 1948, with the tombstone bearing the epitaph at the end of the poem.

"The Black Tower": first published *Last Poems and Two Plays* (1939). **7:** in *A Social History of Ireland* (1903), P. W. Joyce explains that "occasionally the bodies of kings and chieftains were buried in a standing posture, arrayed in full battle costume, with the face turned towards the territories of their enemies." Eógan Bél, a king of Connacht killed at the Battle of Sligo in 543 or 547, is said to have been so buried on Knocknarea, a mountain in County Sligo.

"Cuchulain Comforted": first published *Last Poems and Two Plays* (1939). Cuchulain is the major hero in the Ulster, or Red Branch, cycle of Irish mythology. **7–9:** cf. the Myth of Er in the *Republic* by the Greek philosopher Plato (ca. 428–ca. 347 B.C.), in which unborn souls have placed before them "lots and samples of life": "There he saw the soul which had once been Orpheus choosing the life of a swan out of enmity to the race of women, hating to be born of a woman because they had been his murderers; he also saw the soul of Thamyras choosing the life of a nightingale."

"The Statues": first published *London Mercury,* March 1939. **1–2:** the Greek philosopher Pythagoras (582?–500? B.C.) developed a theory of numbers. **14:** at the Battle of Salamis in 480 B.C. the Greeks defeated the Persians. **17–18:** writing to Ethel Mannin on 28 June 1938, Yeats suggested that "in reading the third stanza remember the influence on modern sculpture and on the great seated Buddha of the sculptors who followed Alexander." That is, the conquest of northwest India by Alexander the Great in 326 B.C. resulted in a Greek influence on the traditional representations of the Buddha (563?–483? B.C.), Indian philosopher and the founder of Buddhism. **19–20:** Hamlet is the main character of *Hamlet* (1603) by the English playwright William Shakespeare (1564–1616); in *The Trembling of the Veil* (1922) Yeats referred to "a mind that has no need of the intellect to remain sane, though it give itself to every fantasy: the dreamer of the Middle Ages. It is 'the fool of Faery . . . wide and wild as a hill,' the resolute European image that yet half remembers Buddha's motionless meditation, and has no trait in common with the wavering, lean image of hungry speculation, that cannot because of certain Hamlets of our stage fill the mind's eye. Shakespeare himself foreshadowed a symbolic change, that is, a change in the whole temperament of the world, for though he called his Hamlet 'fat' and even 'scant of breath', he thrust between his fingers agile rapier and dagger." 24: Grimalkin is a name for a cat, often with fiendish connotations, as in Shakespeare's *Macbeth* (1623). 25–26: Padraic Pearse (1879–1916), Irish poet, founder of St. Edna's School in County Dublin, and the leader of the 1916 Easter Rebellion; the General Post Office on O'Connell Street in Dublin was the headquarters of the Irish forces. Yeats told Ethel Mannin that "Cuchulain is in the last stanza because Pearse and some of his followers had a cult of him. The Government has put a statue of Cuchulain in the rebuilt post office to commemorate this," referring to *The Death of Cuchulain* (ca. 1911–12) by the Irish sculptor Oliver Sheppard (1865–1941).

"Long-legged Fly": first published *London Mercury*, March 1939. 5: Gaius Julius Caesar (100?–44 B.C.), Roman dictator and general, conqueror of the ancient western European territories of Gaul. 11: from a description of Helen of Troy, in Greek mythology the cause of the Trojan War, by the English playwright Christopher Marlowe (1564–93) in *The Tragical History of Dr. Faustus* (1604): "Was this the face that launched a thousand ships / And burnt the topless towers of Ilium?" 23: Pope Julius II (1443–1513), pope (Bishop of Rome and head of the Roman Catholic Church) 1503–13, commissioned Michelangelo's painting on the ceiling of the Sistine Chapel, 1508–12.

"High Talk": first published *London Mercury*, December 1938. 9: Malachi ("my messenger") is the supposed author of the last book of the Old Testament in the Bible; St. Malachy (1095–1148) is an Irish saint known for his reforms; Malachi Mulligan is the name applied to Yeats's friend Oliver St. John Gogarty (1878–1957), an Irish writer and physician, by the Irish writer James Joyce (1882–1941) in *Ulysses* (1922).

"Man and the Echo": first published *London Mercury*, January 1939. 1: a glen on the side of Knocknarea, a mountain in County Sligo. 11: *Cathleen ni Houlihan*, first produced by the Irish National Dramatic Company in Dublin on 2 April 1902. In *Irish Literature and Drama in the English Language: A Short History*, the Irish writer Stephen Gwynn (1864–1950) noted that "the effect of *Cathleen ni Houlihan* on me was that I went home asking myself if such plays should be produced unless one was prepared for people to go out to shoot and be shot." Yeats refers to the execution of the leaders of the 1916 Easter Rebellion. 13–14: probably the English actress and poet Margot Ruddock (1907–51). 15–16: probably Coole Park, the estate of Lady Gregory; after her death the house (owned by the Irish Forestry Department) fell into disrepair; it was sold to a contractor and demolished in 1942.

"The Circus Animals' Desertion": first published *London Mercury*, January 1939. 7: cf. the "brazen cars" of "Who goes with Fergus?" (1892). 10–16: in the Fenian cycle of Irish mythology, the mortal Oisin is enchanted by the goddess

Niamh and transported to three unsatisfactory paradises, as recounted in Yeats's "The Wanderings of Oisin" (1889). **17–24:** *The Countess Cathleen,* first produced by the Irish Literary Theatre in Dublin on 8 May 1899; the title role was played by Maud Gonne (1866–1953), Irish nationalist and Yeats's beloved. The Countess sells her soul to ransom the souls of her starving people but is saved at the end of the play. **25–32:** *On Baile's Strand,* first produced by the Irish National Theatre Society at the Abbey Theatre, Dublin, on 27 December 1904. At the end of the play, Cuchulain, having unknowingly killed his son, is fighting the waves while the Fool and the Blind Man go off to steal from the ovens.

"Politics": first published *London Mercury,* January 1939. Yeats found the epigraph by the German writer Thomas Mann (1875–1955) in "Public Speech and Private Speech in Poetry," an essay in the March 1938 *Yale Review* by the American writer Archibald MacLeish (1892–1982), which included some comments on Yeats's work.

NOTES TO THE PLAYS

Cathleen ni Houlihan

First published *Samhain* (October 1902), a periodical named after the Celtic festival for the start of winter on 31 October; first performed by the Irish National Dramatic Company, St. Teresa's Hall, Dublin, 2 April 1902. Cathleen ni Houlihan ("Cathleen the daughter of Houlihan") is a personification of Ireland.

Killala, in 1798: on 22 August 1798, a force of about 1,000 French soldiers landed at Killala in County Mayo in an unsuccessful attempt to aid in the 1798 Rebellion against the English.

hurling: an Irish game resembling field hockey. **Winny of the Cross-Roads:** a character who also appears in Yeats's story "Red Hanrahan." **Ballina:** a town in County Mayo. **Enniscrone:** a seaside village in County Sligo. **four . . . fields:** the four provinces of Ireland—Ulster, Munster, Leinster, and Connacht. **Kilglass:** a village near Killala. **Donough:** derived from a Gaelic folk song, translated as "Fair-haired Donough" by the Irish writer Lady Gregory (1852–1932) in the *Monthly Review* (October 1902). **red man of the O'Donnells:** Red Hugh O'Donnell (1571–1602), chief of the O'Donnells, fought against the English and died, probably by poison, while seeking aid from Spain. **man of the O'Sullivans:** Dónall O'Sullivan Beare (1560–1618), chief of the O'Sullivans of Beare, County Cork, fought against the English, eventually fleeing to Spain in 1603. **Brian:** Brian Ború ("Brian of the Tributes"), king of Ireland, killed by the Danes at the Battle of Clontarf. **Poor Old Woman:** the *Shan van vocht,* a personification of Ireland. **keening:** a wailing lamentation for the dead. **white-scarfed riders:** a white scarf tied across the breast was often worn by young men in rural Ireland at funerals, particularly of young men and of those who died tragically. **got the touch:** became enchanted.

On Baile's Strand

First published *In the Seven Woods* (1903); first performed Irish National Theatre Society, Abbey Theatre, Dublin, 27 December 1904. Baile's Strand is in County Louth, near Dundalk (Dundealgan).

Fay: William G. Fay (1872–1942), Irish actor and producer.

In the Ulster, or Red Branch, cycle of Irish mythology, Conchubar is king of Ulster, Cuchulain the most important warrior. While training as a youth with Queen Scáthach in Scotland, Cuchulain becomes involved in a war between her and her sister, Aoife; he defeats Aoife and leaves her pregnant with Connlaí. Cuchulain's fort was at Dundealgan.

Boann: "she of the white cattle," a water goddess. **Fand:** "Pearl of Beauty," the wife of Manannán mac Lir, god of the sea. **Banachas and Bonachas:** *Bananachs* and *Bocanachs,* female and male goblins. **Fomor:** the Fomorians, demons or evil gods in Irish mythology.

23: Maeve (Medb), queen of Connacht and wife of Ailill; Cruachan, in County Roscommon, was their capital; the northern pirates are the Norsemen. **24:** Sorcha, part of the Gaelic Otherworld. **25:** untraced. **44:** Fiachra. **85–87:** Cuchulain's father was the sun god, Lugh Lámhfada, his mother the mortal Dechtire. **97:** *Tír fo Thuinn,* "Land under the Wave," one of the names for the Celtic Otherworld. **193:** shape-changing is common in Irish mythology. **218:** a mythical beast with the shape of a horse and a long horn on its forehead, usually a symbol of holiness or chastity. **367:** Laoghaire Buadach ("Leary the Triumphant"), a warrior. **381:** the four provinces of Ireland—Ulster, Leinster, Munster, and Connacht. **413:** presumably identical with the Shape-Changers.

crubeen: pig's foot. **When you . . . eagle-cock:** described by Yeats as a "folk verse" and printed in the Anonymous section of his *A Book of Irish Verse* (1895). **Uathach:** daughter of Queen Scáthach and mistress of Cuchulain. **Alba:** Scotland.

11: Dubhthach Doéltenga ("Dubhthach the Backbiter"), a Red Branch warrior who deserted Conchubar and joined the forces of Maeve.

Deirdre

First published *Deirdre* (1907); first performed by the National Theatre Society, Molesworth Hall, Dublin, 24 November 1906. The story of Deirdre is part of the Ulster, or Red Branch, cycle of Irish mythology: Naoise, accompanied by his brothers Ainnle and Ardan, elopes to Scotland with Deirdre, whom Conchubar, king of Ulster, had selected to become his queen; eventually lured back to Ireland, the three brothers are killed by Conchubar's forces.

Mrs. Patrick Campbell: English actress (1865–1940), first played Deirdre in a revival at the Abbey Theatre, 9–14 November 1908; she also performed it in London and elsewhere in England in 1908–09. **Robert Gregory:** (1881–1918), the son of the Irish writer Lady Gregory (1852–1932), designed the set for the 1908 Dublin production.

Ulad: Ulster.

6: Conchubar's palace at Armagh, in Ulster. **13:** Lavarcam. **34 s.d.:** Fergus mac Roigh ("son of Roy"), previous king of Ulster, was tricked by his wife, Ness, into giving up the throne in favor of Conchubar, her son by another man. **119:** Lugaid

Redstripe is a warrior in the Fenian cycle. **121:** Edain was the second wife of Mid-hir, a king of the Sidhe; his jealous first wife transformed her into a fly; eventually she is reunited with Midhir. **154:** rouge. **161:** possibly Sorcha, the Gaelic otherworld. **175:** commenting on some lines about the death of the Earl of Leicester (1532?–88) by the English poet Edmund Spenser (1552?–99) included in *Poems of Spenser* (1906), Yeats noted that "at the end of a long beautiful passage he laments that unworthy men should be in the dead Earl's place, and compares them to the fox—an unclean feeder—hiding in the lair 'the badger swept.' " **269–70:** "Istian" and "Fanes" are unidentified. **409:** the "Dark-faced Messenger." **414:** the reaping hooks of the local farmers. **418:** a wicker snare for birds. **612:** *Leòdhas* is the Gaelic name for the Isle of Lewis, off Scotland.

At the Hawk's Well

First published *Harper's Bazaar,* March 1917; first performed in Lady Cunard's drawing room in London, 2 April 1916.

A Young Man: Cuchulain, the central hero of the Ulster, or Red Branch, cycle of Irish mythology. **Dulac:** Edmund Dulac (1882–1953), French-born English artist and illustrator.

66: the Sidhe are the fairies, understood as the descendants of the immortal gods of Ireland, the *Tuatha Dé Danann.* **Woman of the Sidhe:** identified in Yeats's play *The Only Jealousy of Emer* (1919) as Fand ("Pearl of Beauty"), wife of Manannán mac Lir, god of the sea. **239 s.d.:** while training in arms in Scotland with Queen Scáthach, Cuchulain becomes involved in a war between her and her sister, Aoife; he defeats Aoife and leaves her pregnant with Connlaí, whom he will later unknowingly kill.

The Words upon the Window-pane

First published *The Words upon the Window Pane: A Play in One Act, with Notes Upon the Play and Its Subject* (1934); first performed 17 November 1930 by the National Theatre Society at the Abbey Theatre, Dublin. Part of the play concerns the relationship between the Anglo-Irish writer Jonathan Swift (1667–1745) and Esther Johnson (1687–1728), "Stella," whom he had tutored in the late 1690s and to whom he wrote the letters (1710–13) in the *Journal to Stella;* and Esther Vanhomrigh (1690–1723), "Vanessa," whom he met in December 1707 and who fell in love with him.

The play was written at Coole Park, the estate in County Galway of the Irish writer Lady Gregory (1852–1932).

Dr. Trench: perhaps an allusion to Wilbraham F. Trench (1873–1939), Professor of English at Trinity College Dublin. **Corbets of Ballymoney:** Yeats had Corbet relatives, such as his great-uncle, Robert Corbet (?–1872); Ballymoney is a town in County Antrim. **Cambridge:** Cambridge University, in England. **Myers:** Frederic William Henry Myers (1843–1901), English psychical researcher, *Human Personality and its Survival of Bodily Death* (1903). **Conan Doyle:** Sir Arthur Conan Doyle (1859–1930), English physician and writer, creator of Sherlock Holmes; either *A New Revelation* (1918) or *History of Spiritualism* (1926). **Lord Dunraven:** Wyndham Thomas Wyndham-Quin (1841–1926), Irish steeplechaser and yachtsman. **David Home:** Daniel Dunglas Home (1833–86), Scottish spiritualist and medium. **Mrs. Piper:** Leonora E. Piper (1859–1950), American medium. **Blake:** William Blake (1757–1827), English poet and engraver; in his *Reminiscences* (1852), the English journalsit Henry Crabb Robinson (1775–1867) recalls Blake saying "I have never known a very bad man who had not something very good about him." **Swedenborg:** Emanuel Swedenborg (1688–1772), Swedish scientist and philosopher. **Harold's Cross:** a suburb of Dublin, a site of greyhound racing. **Grattan:** Henry Grattan (1746–1820), Irish political leader. **Curran:** John Philpot Curran (1750–1817), Irish lawyer and nationalist. **a poem:** "Stella to Dr. Swift on his birth-day November 30, 1721." **Donne:** John Donne (1572–1631), English poet. **Crashaw:** Richard Crashaw (1613?–49), English poet. **Bolingbroke . . . Ormonde:** Henry St. John Bolingbroke (1678–1751), English statesman; Robert Harley (1661–1724), English statesman; James Butler, duke of Ormonde (1665–1746), Irish statesman and soldier. **Brutus and Cato:** Marcus Junius Brutus (85–42 B.C.) and probably Cato the Younger, Marcus Porcius Cato (95–46 B.C.), Roman senators. **Rousseau:** Jean-Jacques Rousseau (1712–98), French philosopher and writer. **French Revolution:** 1789–99, overthrew the Bourbon monarchy and established the First Republic. *Gulliver: Gulliver's Travels* (1726). *Saeva indignatio:* "savage indignation." **Latin:** *"Ubi saeva Indignatio Ulterius Cor lacerare nequi."* **Belfast:** principal city in Northern Ireland. **Moody:** Dwight Lyman Moody (1837–99), American evangelist. **Sankey:** Ira David Sankey (1840–1908), American evangelist. **Folkestone:** a town in southeastern England. *Odyssey:* epic poem by the Greek poet Homer (ca. eighth century B.C.). **Purgatory:** a state after death in which souls are purified from venial sins or undergo the punishment necessary for salvation. *requiescat in pace:* "Rest in Peace." **Job . . . quotation:** "Then a spirit passed before my face; the hair of my flesh stood up" (Job 4:15). **a hymn:** by John Keble (1792–1866), English poet and clergyman. **Lord Treasurer:** Robert Harley. **Plutarch:** Greek biographer and essayist (46?–120). **questioned her:** Stella. **began to teach me:** 1708. **five years ago:** Vanessa moved to Ireland in autumn 1714. **Arbuthnot:** John Arbuthnot (1667–1735), English physician. **Dryden:** John Dryden (1631–1700), English writer; "great wits are sure to madness / Near allied," *Absalom and Achitophel* (1681). **Chrysostom:** St. John Chrysostom ("Golden-mouthed") (349–407), passage untraced. **pound note . . . ten shillings:** a pound was twenty shillings. **all the explanations:** as Yeats explained in his introduction to the play, these included a "physical defect," syphilis, and "dread of madness"; he concluded that "there is no satisfactory solution." **Perish . . . born:** "Let the day perish wherein I was born" (Job 3:3).

The Resurrection

First published *The Adelphi,* June 1927; first produced by the National Theatre Society, Abbey Theatre, Dublin, 30 July 1934.

Junzo Sato: a Japanese admirer who had presented Yeats with a ceremonial sword in March 1920.

In Christian tradition, the tomb of Christ is discovered empty on the third day after his crucifixion. He thereafter appears to several of his disciples.

Peacock Theatre: a smaller section of the Abbey Theatre, used for experimental plays.

I saw . . . a play: 1–8: this stanza recounts the death and, implicitly, the resurrection of Dionysus, god of wine and fertility in Greek mythology. Of the various accounts of his birth, Yeats draws on the one in which Dionysus is born of the god Zeus and a mortal woman. The jealousy of Hera, the wife of Zeus, leads to Dionysus being torn to pieces and devoured by the Titans; his heart is saved by Athena, the goddess of wisdom (the "staring virgin"), who carries it to Zeus. Zeus swallows the heart, leading to the rebirth of Dionysus by the mortal Semele. The nine Muses are the patrons of the arts in Greek mythology. Magnus Annus ("Great Year"), a Platonic Year, usually understood as 36,000 years, the time needed for the constellations to return to their original positions. Yeats noted that the astronomer Ptolemy (100?–170?) argued that a new Platonic Year commenced around the time of Christ.

Another Troy . . . called: 9–16: this stanza recounts the birth of Christ through reference to the *Fourth Eclogue* (40 B.C.) of the Roman poet Virgil (70–19 B.C.). At the end of the Golden Age, Astrea, daughter of Zeus and Themis and goddess of justice, withdraws from the earth and is transformed into the constellation Virgo. In a passage which Yeats quotes in *A Vision* (1925), Virgil prophesies the return of Astrea and the start of a new Golden Age. Beginning with the Council of Nicea (325), the *Fourth Eclogue* was interpreted as foretelling the birth of Christ, Astrea being equated with the Virgin Mary, and the star Spica (Alpha Virginis), the most prominent star in the constellation Virgo, with the Star of Bethlehem, which guided the Magi to the birthplace of Christ. Yeats also notes in *A Vision* that "the vernal equinox at the birth of Christ" falls between the signs Pisces and Aries in the zodiac and that the "sun's transition from Pisces to Aries had for generations been associated with the ceremonial death and resurrection of Dionysus." Thus the stanza implicitly parallels Virgin Mary/Christ not only with Virgo/Spica but also with Athena/Dionysus. In the *Fourth Eclogue* Virgil also prophesies another Trojan War and another journey by Jason and the Argonauts on the ship *Argo* in search of the Golden Fleece.

16: in *Select Passages Illustrating Neo-Platonism* (1923), E. R. Dodds notes that the Greek sophist Eunapius (ca. 347–ca. 420) quotes Antoninus (d. ca. 390) as describing the advance of Christianity as "a fabulous and formless darkness mastering the loveliness of the world."

Rabbi: Hebrew "my master," honorary title of the Jewish masters of the Law. **Alexandria:** the capital of ancient Egypt, which came under Roman rule in 30 B.C. **the Eleven:** the Twelve Apostles, the first disciples of Christ, except Judas, who betrayed him to the Jewish authorities. **last time:** The Last Supper, the final gathering of Christ and the Apostles, traditionally thought to have occurred on Holy Thursday, the day before the crucifixion. **he denied it:** Peter denied Christ three times. **Messiah:** "The Anointed One," the deliverer of mankind. **Calvary:** a hill outside Jerusalem, the site of the crucifixion. **goddess came to Achilles:** the goddess is Athena; Achilles is one of the greatest Greek warriors of the Trojan War. The incident is told by the Greek poet Homer (ca. eighth century B.C.) in the *Iliad*. **Lucretius:** (98–55 B.C.), Roman poet, *On the Nature of Things*. **Galilean women:** Galilee, the region in Israel associated with the life of Christ; the Virgin Mary, mother of Christ, and Mary the mother of James. **a man all shining:** "And all at once there was a violent earthquake, for the angel of the Lord, descending from heaven, came and rolled away the stone and sat on it. His face was like lightning, his robe as white as snow. . . . 'I know you are looking for Jesus, who was crucified. He is not here, for he has risen, as he said he would'" (Matthew 28:3–6). **Heraclitus:** Greek philosopher (540?–475 B.C.); Fragment 67: "Mortals are immortals and immortals are mortals, the one living the other's death and dying the other's life."

4–5: Yeats associates the rise of astrology in Babylon, an ancient city in Mesopotamia, with the development of exact science and a corresponding reduction in man's status in relation to the universe. **7–8:** the classical world epitomized by the Greek philosopher Plato (ca. 428–ca. 347 B.C.) and the Doric style of architecture, the oldest style of Greek architecture (seventh century B.C.).

Purgatory

First published posthumously in *Last Poems and Two Plays* (1939); first produced 10 August 1938 by the National Theatre Society, Abbey Theatre, Dublin.

In Catholic tradition, purgatory is a temporal state on the way to salvation in which souls after death either are purified from venial sins or undergo the temporal punishment that, after the guilt of mortal sin has been remitted, still remains to be endured by the sinner. In Book III of *A Vision* (1937), "The Soul in Judgment," Yeats describes at length the progress of the soul from death to rebirth. In one of the stages, called the *Dreaming Back,* the soul "is compelled to live over and over again the events that had most moved it; there can be nothing new, but the old events stand forth in a light which is dim or bright according to the intensity of the passion that accompanied them." In an interview in the *Irish Independent* (13 August 1938), Yeats explained that "My plot is my meaning. I think the dead suffer remorse and re-create their lives just as I have described. . . . In my play, a spirit suffers because of its share in the destruction of an honoured house; that destruction is taking place all over Ireland today. Sometimes it is the result of poverty, but more often because a new individualistic generation has lost interest in the ancient sanctities."

1: a divided door, so that the top can be left open for light and air. **49:** in County Kildare, the center of Irish horse racing and breeding. **63:** on 12 July 1690, William III (1650–1702), the Protestant king of England (1689–1702), defeated the forces of James II (1633–1701), the former Catholic king of England (1685–88), in a battle fought on the banks of the Boyne River. William's forces were victorious again the following year at the Battle of Aughrim, a village in County Galway, leading to the Treaty of Limerick (1691). **93:** held annually 9–11 August at Killorglin, County Kerry. **153:** Quintus Septimius Florens Tertullianus (160?–220?), Christian theologian, argued in *De Anima* that pleasure and remorse exist in the soul after death. **182:** "Eden Bower" (1870), by the English poet and painter Dante Gabriel Rossetti (1828–82): "Yea, where the bride-sleep fell upon Adam (*Alas the hour!*)."

The Death of Cuchulain

First published posthumously in *Last Poems and Two Plays* (1939); first produced 2 December 1945 by the Lyric Theatre Company, Abbey Theatre, Dublin.

Cuchulain is the central hero in the Ulster, or Red Branch, cycle of Irish mythology. While training as a youth with Queen Scáthach in Scotland, Cuchulain becomes involved in a war between her and her sister, Aoife; he defeats Aoife and leaves her pregnant with Connlaí, whom he unknowingly kills in the action depicted in *On Baile's Strand* (1903). Eithne Inguba is a mistress of Cuchulain, sent to him by his wife, Emer, to distract him from entering a battle with Maeve, queen of Connacht, in which legend says he will be killed; Yeats's play *The Only Jealousy of Emer* (1919) depicts the relationship among Cuchulain, Emer, and Eithne Inguba. The *Mórrígú (Mórrígán)* is the Irish goddess of war, who often takes the shape of a raven or crow; having attempted to seduce Cuchulain, she fights him and is wounded, thus becoming his mortal enemy.

series of plays: *On Baile's Strand* (1903); *The Green Helmet* (1908); *At the Hawk's Well* (1917); *The Only Jealousy of Emer* (1919). **Talma:** François-Joseph Talma (1763–1826), French actor. **Virgil:** Roman poet (70–19 B.C.). **Homer:** Greek poet (ca. eighth century B.C.). **Milton:** John Milton (1608–74),

English writer, *Comus*, first performed 29 September 1634 at Ludlow Castle. **sciolist:** a superficial pretender to knowledge. **Degas:** Hilaire-Germaine-Edgar Degas (1834–1917), French artist; the ballet was one of his favorite subjects. **Ramses the Great:** Ramses II, Pharaoh of Egypt (1279–1212 B.C.).

5: the seat of the kings of Ulster, near Navan in County Armagh. **6:** in County Louth. **21:** *Conall Cearnach,* "Conall of the Victories," foster brother to Cuchulain as well as a blood cousin. **86:** as the source of opium, poppies are connected with dreams or forgetfulness. **112:** one of Cuchulain's two great horses; mortally wounded by Erc, king of Leinster, it was able to kill eighty warriors before its death. **132:** the king of Ulster who in *On Baile's Strand* forbids the nascent friendship between Cuchulain and the unknown young warrior. **188:** Maeve was known for having a succession of lovers. **198:** the sons of Usna are Naoise, Ardan, and Ainnle, figures in the Deirdre legend. **214:** the General Post Office on O'Connell Street in Dublin, the headquarters of the 1916 Easter Rebellion. **215:** Padraic Henry Pearse (1879–1916), Irish poet and nationalist, and James Connolly (1870–1916), Irish trade union leader and nationalist, two of the leaders of the Easter Rebellion. **224–25:** *The Death of Cuchulain* (ca. 1911–12), by the Irish sculptor Oliver Sheppard (1865–1941), was placed in the General Post Office as a memorial to the Easter Rebellion.

NOTES TO
AUTOBIOGRAPHICAL WRITINGS

Reveries Over Childhood and Youth

First published 1916.

I. Seven Days: the Biblical account of creation in Genesis. **Fitzroy Road:** Yeats lived at 23 Fitzroy Road, Regent's Park, London, from July 1867 to July 1872. **Sligo:** principal town of County Sligo, in northwestern Ireland. **grandparents:** William Pollexfen (1811–92) and Elizabeth Middleton Pollexfen (1819–92), Yeats's maternal grandparents. **William Middleton:** (1820–82). **Spanish city:** unidentified. **Jordan:** in the Bible, Christ is baptized in the Jordan River. **Rosses Point:** a seaside village near Sligo. **Campbell of Islay:** John Francis Campbell (1822–85), Scottish folklorist; Islay is an island off western Scotland. **Captain Webb:** Matthew Webb (1848–83) swam the English Channel between France and England in 1875. The Niagara Rapids are a few miles north of Niagara Falls, on the border between New York State and Ontario, Canada. **Bath:** a resort city in southern England. **whose father:** William Middleton (1770?–1832). **great famine:** not the famines of the late 1840s but connected with a cholera epidemic in 1832. **an uncle:** probably Frederick Henry Pollexfen (1852–1929). *King Lear:* tragedy by the English playwright William Shakespeare (1564–1616), first published 1608. Falconer's *Shipwreck:* a poem (1762) by the English writer William Falconer (1732–69). **His father:** Anthony Pollexfen (1781?–1833). **old family place:** Kitley Manor, in Devon, England. **his mother:** Mary Stephens (1771–1830). **Galway:** principal town in County Galway. **Crimea:** site of the Crimean War in southeastern Russia, 1853–56. **youngest of my uncles:** Alfred Pollexfen (1854–1916). **another:** William Pollexfen (1847–1913). **six months ago:** in February 1913. **My sister:** Susan Mary ("Lily") Yeats (1866–1949). **George Pollexfen:** 1839–1910. **Ballina:** a town in County Mayo.

IX. my father: John Butler Yeats (1839–1922), Irish painter. *Lays of Ancient Rome:* book of poems by the English writer and historian Thomas Babington Macaulay (1800–59), published 1842. **Orange rhymes:** poems celebrating the victory at the Battle of the Boyne (1690) of William of Orange (1650–1702), king of England 1689–1702. *Ivanhoe . . . Minstrel:* a novel (1819) and poem (1805) by the Scottish writer Sir Walter Scott (1771–1832). *Iliad:* epic poem by the ancient Greek poet Homer (ca. eighth century B.C.). *Grimm's Fairy Tales:* tales collected by the German philologists and folklorists Jacob Ludwig Karl Grimm (1785–1863) and Wilhelm Karl Grimm (1786–1859), published 1812–15, expanded 1857. **Hans Andersen . . . *Duckling:*** Hans Christian Andersen (1805–75), Danish writer, "The Ugly Duckling" (1843). **Irving:** Sir Henry Irving, English actor (1838–1905). Shakespeare's *Hamlet,* published 1603. **Ellen Terry:** English actress (1847–1928) who joined Irving's company in 1878. **little boy . . . Sir Thopas:** in "The Prioress's Tale" and the "Tale of Sir Thopas," in the *Canterbury Tales* (ca. 1387–1400) by the English poet Geoffrey Chaucer (1343?–1400). **Balzac . . . *Comédie Humaine:*** Honoré de Balzac (1799–1850), French novelist; in 1834 he conceived of gathering all his fiction, completed and projected, into the collection *La comédie humaine*, "The Human Comedy." **Lucien de Rubempré:** character in Balzac's *Lost Illusions* (1837–43). **Richmond Park . . . Twyford Abbey:** Richmond Park is in Surrey; Coombe Wood at Kingston upon Thames; Twyford Abbey in Ealing, Middlesex.

XIV. close upon seventeen: Yeats turned seventeen on 13 June 1882. **Howth Castle:** dating from 1564, on Howth, a promontory on the north side of Dublin Bay; the Yeats family lived at Howth from the autumn of 1881 to the spring of 1884. **Solomon:** king of ancient Israel, 961–922 B.C., noted in the Bible for his wisdom: "He could talk about plants from the cedar in Lebanon to the hyssop growing on the wall; and he could talk of animals, and birds and reptiles and fish" (1 Kings 5). **Manfred:** main character of a dramatic poem (1817) by Lord Byron (1788–1824), English poet. **Prince Athanase . . . Alastor:** Percy Bysshe Shelley (1792–1822), English poet, "Prince Athanase" (1818), *Alastor, or The Spirit of Solitude* (1816), *The Revolt of Islam* (1818).

XV. *Prometheus Unbound:* lyrical drama by Shelley, published 1820. *Coriolanus:* play by Shakespeare, published 1623. **Benson:** Frank Robert Benson (1858–1939), English actor. **Keats:** John Keats (1795–1821), English poet. **"O sweet . . . voices":** *Manfred*, I.i: "I hear / Your voices, sweet and melancholy sounds." **Victorian:** of the age of Victoria (1819–1901), queen of England 1837–1901. **Wordsworth:** William Wordsworth (1770–1850), English poet. **Wordsworthian scholar:** the Reverend Stopford Augustus Brooke (1832–1916), divine and man of letters. **Raphael:** Italian painter (1483–1520). **Pre-Raphaelite:** the Pre-Raphaelite Brotherhood, a group of painters and poets who looked to the Middle Ages for inspiration, was established in 1848. **Academy:** Royal Academy of Arts, London, the principal British art organization.

XVI. a woman: untraced. **younger Ampère:** Jean-Jacques-Antoine Ampère (1800–64), French writer and philologist, son of the scientist André-Marie Ampère (1775–1836). **Spenser:** Edmund Spenser (1552?–99), English poet.

XXX. Young Ireland Society: a nationalist society in Dublin; Yeats attended some of their meetings in 1885–86. **verses:** probably "Dawn on the Irish Coast" (1877) by the Irish poet and nationalist John Locke (1847–89).

XXXIII. some months now: Yeats began *Reveries* in January 1914 and completed it on 25 December 1914.

The Trembling of the Veil

First published 1922. The opening section, "Four Years 1887–1891," published 1921 by the Cuala Press. "Ireland after the Fall of Parnell" and parts of "Hodos Chameliontos" and "The Tragic Generation" previously published in periodicals. Yeats took the title "The Trembling of the Veil" from "Poetry and Music in France" (*The National Observer*, 26 March 1892) by the French poet Stéphane Mallarmé (1842–98); see section IX of *The Tragic Generation*.

Book I: Four Years, 1887–1891

II. Pre-Raphaelite: the Pre-Raphaelite Brotherhood, a group of painters and poets who looked to the Middle Ages for inspiration, was established in 1848. **Rossetti:** Dante Gabriel Rossetti (1828–82), English poet and painter. **Blake:** William Blake (1757–1827), English poet and engraver. *Dante's Dream:* painting by Rossetti, 1871, in the Walker Art Gallery, Liverpool. **Carolus Duran:** Charles-Auguste-Émile Durand (1838–1917), French painter. **Bastien-Lepage:** Jules Bastien-Lepage (1848–84), French painter. **Huxley:** Thomas Henry Huxley (1825–95), English biologist, known for his support of the theory of evolution of Charles Darwin (1809–92). **Tyndall:** John Tyndall (1820–93), British physicist. **Titian's** *Ariosto:* there are two paintings of the Italian writer Ludovico Ariosto (1474–1533) traditionally ascribed to the Venetian painter Titian (1488?–1576); Yeats probably refers to the one in the National Gallery, London. **Madonna:** in Christianity, the Virgin Mary, mother of Christ.

V. Presently: 30 January 1889. **Bedford Park:** a section of London. **Gonne:** Maud Gonne (1866–1953), Irish nationalist. **my father:** John Butler Yeats (1839–1922), Irish painter. **John O'Leary:** Irish nationalist (1830–1907) and one of the leaders of the Fenian movement against English rule in Ireland. **Sibyl:** in Greek and Roman mythology, a woman with prophetic powers. **Florence Farr:** English actress (1860–1917). **Virgilian . . . goddess:** Virgil (70–19 B.C.), Roman poet, the *Aeneid*. **Donegal:** county in Ireland.

VIII. first meeting: September 1888. **Oscar Wilde:** Irish playwright, poet, and critic (1854–1900). **Henley:** William Ernest Henley (1849–1903), English writer and editor. *The Winter's Tale . . . King Lear:* two plays by the English playwright William Shakespeare (1564–1616), published 1623 and 1608. **Pater's . . .** *Renaissance:* Walter Pater (1839–94), English essayist and critic, *Studies in the History of the Renaissance* (1873). **father's friend . . . as editors:** the English artist Edwin Bale (1838–1923), art director for Cassell & Co., publisher of magazines edited by both Wilde and Henley. **Wilde's downfall:** Wilde was convicted of sodomy in 1895 and sentenced to two years in prison. **lads:** writers encouraged by Henley, described by Yeats as "Henley's young men."

XXI. Chaucer: Geoffrey Chaucer (1343?–1400), English poet.

XXII. Rhymers: the Rhymers' Club, a group of young writers who met on a regular basis in London during the early 1890s. **Johnson:** Lionel Johnson (1867–1902), English poet and critic. **Primrose League:** an Anglo-Irish conservative association, supporting "the maintenance of religions, of the estates of the realm and of the imperial ascendancy." **Fenian Brotherhood:** a nationalist association, also known as the Irish Republican Brotherhood. **"Unity of Being"** . . . *Convito:* Dante Alighieri (1265–1321), Italian poet, *Convivio* ("Banquet," ca. 1304–7); the concept but not the phrase is found in Dante. **Free Trader:** someone opposed to government restrictions on commerce. **"Call down . . . gone wild":** the first stanza of Yeats's "The Hawk," first published February 1916 in *Poetry* (Chicago). **Westminster:** Westminster Abbey in London, rebuilt in Gothic style starting in 1245. **Homer:** Greek poet (ca. eighth century B.C.). **Mausolus and Artemisia:** Mausolus (?–353 B.C.) was king of Caria 376?–353? B.C.; his tomb, erected by his widow, Artemisia (d. ca. 350 B.C.), was one of the Seven Wonders of the World. **Amazon:** in Greek mythology, the Amazons were a race of warlike women. **Centaur:** in Greek mythology, a centaur was human down to the waist, but had the legs and torso of a horse. *Divine Comedy:* begun by Dante ca. 1307, completed shortly before his death. **Don Quixote:** character in *Don Quixote,* 1605–15, by Miguel de Cervantes Saavedra (1547–1616), Spanish writer. **Morris:** William Morris (1834–96), English poet and designer. *Troilus and Criseyde:* Chaucer's *Troilus and Criseyde* (1385?). **Congreve . . . humour":** William Congreve (1670–1729), English dramatist, "Concerning Humour in Comedy" (1695). **Descartes:** René Descartes (1596–1650), French philosopher. **Tudor:** members of the Tudor dynasty occupied the throne of England 1485–1603. **"Turning . . . intensity":** the opening lines of Yeats's "The Second Coming," first published in *The Dial,* November 1920, and *The Nation* (London), 6 November 1920.

XXIII. Elizabethan: of the age of Elizabeth I (1533–1603), queen of England 1558–1603. **Tabard:** in Chaucer's *Canterbury Tales,* the pilgrims assemble at the Tabard Inn in Southwark. **Tolstoy . . . Karenina:** Leo Tolstoy (1828–1910), Russian novelist, *Anna Karenina* (1875–77). **Arthur Symons:** English poet and critic (1865–1945). **Verhaeren:** Émile Verhaeren (1855–1916), Belgian poet. **Maeterlinck:** Maurice Maeterlinck (1862–1949), Belgian dramatist. **Sufis:** Muslim mystics. *Prometheus Unbound:* lyrical drama (1820) by the English poet Percy Bysshe Shelley (1792–1822). **Patrick:** Saint Patrick (389?–461?), known as the Apostle of Ireland. **Columcille:** Saint Columcille (521–97), one of the three patron saints of Ireland. **Oisin . . . Finn:** figures in the Fenian cycle of Irish mythology. **Caucasus:** a mountain range in southern Russia. **Cro-Patrick:** a mountain in County Mayo, associated with the life of Saint Patrick. **Ben Bulben:** a mountain in County Sligo, associated with the story of Diarmuid and Grainne. **"the applied arts of literature":** untraced.

XXIV. O'Connell: Daniel O'Connell (1775–1847), Irish political leader. **Parnell:** Charles Stewart Parnell (1846–91), Irish political leader.

Book ii: Ireland After Parnell

X. Sligo: the principal town in County Sligo, in northwestern Ireland. **O'Leary:** John O'Leary (1830–1907), Irish nationalist. **Whitman:** Walt Whitman (1819–92), American poet. **Maud Gonne:** Irish nationalist (1866–1953) and Yeats's beloved. **Taylor:** John Francis Taylor (1850–1902), Irish barrister, journalist, and orator. **Carlyle:** Thomas Carlyle (1795–1881), Scottish essayist and historian. **Society:** National Literary Society, Dublin. **Stephen MacKenna:** 1872–1934, Irish journalist and translator. **Plotinus:** Roman philosopher (205–70), the founder of Neoplatonism.

Book III: Hodos Chameliontos

"Hodos Chameliontos": Yeats explains in section VII that during these years (the mid-1890s) he "was lost in that region a cabbalistic manuscript, shown me by MacGregor Mathers [Samuel Liddell Mathers, 1854–1918, English occultist] had warned me of; astray upon the Path of the Chameleon, upon Hodos Chameliontos."

IX. Juliet . . . Cleopatra: in *Romeo and Juliet* (1597) and *Antony and Cleopatra* (1623) by the English playwright William Shakespeare (1564–1616). **Dante's banishment:** the Italian poet Dante Alighieri (1265–1321) was banished from Florence in 1302. **Beatrice:** probably Beatrice Portinari (1266–90), Dante's beloved. **Villon:** François Villon (1431?–1461?), French poet. **Landor:** Walter Savage Landor (1775–1864), English writer. **Keats:** John Keats (1795–1821), English poet. **Andromeda . . . Perseus:** in Greek mythology, Perseus, a son of Zeus, rescues Andromeda, a princess of Ethiopia, as she is about to be sacrificed to a sea monster. **Devil:** the supreme spirit of evil. **"Ille . . . Hic . . . song":** lines 49–62 of Yeats's "Ego Dominus Tuus," first published in *Poetry* (Chicago), October 1917. The speakers' names are Latin for "this one" and "that one."

Book IV: The Tragic Generation

III. "a perfectly . . . body": Yeats elsewhere ascribes this phrase to the Italian poet Dante Alighieri (1265–1321), but although the concept occurs in Dante's work, the phrase does not. **Shakespeare:** William Shakespeare (1564–1616), English dramatist. **Titian:** Venetian painter (1488?–1576). **Jongsen:** Cornelius Janssen (1593–ca. 1664), Dutch painter. **Van Dyck:** Anthony van Dyck (1599–1641), Flemish painter. **Strozzi:** Bernardo Strozzi (1581–1644), Italian painter, *Portrait of a Gentleman*. **Sargent:** John Singer Sargent (1856–1925), American painter. **Wilson:** Woodrow Wilson (1856–1924), twenty-eighth President of the United States. **a certain poem:** Yeats's "The Phases of the Moon," first published in *The Wild Swans at Coole* (1919). **fatal face:** Charles I (1600–49), king of England from 1625 until his execution in 1649, painted by van Dyck in 1635. **Cromwell:** Oliver Cromwell (1599–1658), English sol-

dier and politician, played a leading role in the execution of Charles I.
Utopian: Utopia, an ideal society. **Wilde:** Oscar Wilde (1845–1900), Irish
writer. **Rhymers:** the Rhymers' Club, a group of young writers who met on a
regular basis in London during the early 1890s. **Shaw:** George Bernard Shaw
(1856–1950), Irish writer. **Narcissus . . . Pool:** in Greek mythology, Narcissus
is enchanted by the reflection of his own image in a pool. **Socialist:** a political
system favoring state ownership of the fundamental means of the production
and distribution of wealth. **"The cat . . . eyes":** lines 1–4 and 17–28 of Yeats's
"The Cat and the Moon," first published in *The Wild Swans at Coole* (1919).

IX. Lionel Johnson: English poet (1867–1902). **Synge:** John Millington Synge
(1871–1909), Irish playwright. **Dowson:** Ernest Dowson (1867–1900),
English poet. **"What portion . . . despair":** lines 49–51 of Yeats's "Ego Domi-
nus Tuus," first published in *Poetry* (Chicago), October 1917. **Edmund
Spenser . . . Acrasia:** Edmund Spenser (1552?–99), English poet, *The Faerie
Queene* (1590–96). **Lord Burleigh:** William Cecil (1520–98), English states-
man. **"rugged forehead":** an allusion to Burleigh in the Proem to Book IV of
The Faerie Queene. **Keats:** John Keats (1795–1821), English poet, *Endymion*
(1818). **Matthew Arnold:** English poet and critic (1822–88), "The Function
of Criticism at the Present Time" (1865). **Browning:** Robert Browning
(1812–89), English poet. **Tennyson:** Alfred Lord Tennyson (1809–92). **Shel-
ley:** Percy Bysshe Shelley (1792–1822), English poet. **Wordsworth:** William
Wordsworth (1770–1850), English poet. **Coleridge . . . *Khan*:** Samuel Taylor
Coleridge (1772–1834), English poet and critic, "The Rime of the Ancient
Mariner" (1798), "Kubla Khan" (1816). **Rossetti:** Dante Gabriel Rossetti
(1828–82), English poet and painter. **Commodus:** Lucius Aelius Aurelius
Commodus (161–92), Roman emperor (180–92). **Thebaid . . . Sea:** both the
Thebaid, the district of Thebes, ancient capital of Upper Egypt, and Lake
Mariotis, south of Alexandria, are associated with fourth-century Christian
monastic hermits. **dull brother:** William Michael Rossetti (1829–1919), En-
glish man of letters. **Stenbock:** Count Stanislaus Eric Stenbock (1860–95),
English poet. **Beardsley:** Aubrey Beardsley (1872–98), English artist. **Dow-
son:** Ernest Dowson (1867–1900), English poet. **Johnson:** Lionel Johnson
(1867–1902), English poet and critic. **Dark Angel . . . tears:** Lionel Johnson's
"The Dark Angel" (1895). **Pre-Raphaelitism:** the Pre-Raphaelite Brother-
hood, a group of painters and poets who looked to the Middle Ages for inspi-
ration, was established in 1848. **Impressionism:** a movement in art, especially
painting, begun in France in the early 1870s. **Mallarmé:** Stéphane Mallarmé
(1842–98), French poet, "Poetry and Music in France" (*The National
Observer,* 26 March 1892).

XIX. autumn of 1896: in fact, 21 December 1896. **Hôtel Corneille:** in Paris.
Synge's biographer: Maurice Bourgeois, *John Millington Synge and the Irish
Theatre* (1913). **Black Forest:** a mountainous region in southwest Germany.
Trinity College: in Dublin. **Aran Islands:** three islands off the west coast of
Ireland. **Inishmaan and Inishmore:** two of the Aran Islands. **Maud Gonne:**

Irish nationalist (1866–1953) and Yeats's beloved. **a year:** Synge first went to the Aran Islands in May 1898. **"from the squalor . . . the rich":** Synge, *The Aran Islands* (1907). **rioters:** both *In the Shadow of the Glen* (1903) and especially *The Playboy of the Western World* (1907) created disturbances in the theater. **Mathers:** Samuel Liddell Mathers, later MacGregor Mathers (1854–1918), English occultist. In the previous section of "The Tragic Generation," Yeats recalls Mathers saying that once "he met his Teachers in some great crowd, and only knew they were phantoms by a shock that was like an electric shock to his heart."

Book V: The Stirring of the Bones

VI. twenty-second year: when Yeats was twenty-one, 21 June 1886–20 June 1887. *The Wanderings of Oisin:* first published in *The Wanderings of Oisin and Other Poems* (1889). **Sligo . . . grandmother:** Sligo, on the northwestern coast of Ireland, the home of Yeats' s maternal grandparents, William Pollexfen (1811–92) and Elizabeth Middleton Pollexfen (1819–92). *Rosa . . . Savoy:* the story "Rosa Alchemica," *The Savoy* (April 1896). **a friend:** Olivia Shakespear (1863–1938), English novelist, at the time Yeats's mistress. **Mathers:** Samuel Liddell Mathers, later MacGregor Mathers (1854–1918), English occultist and one of the founders of the Order of the Golden Dawn. **Arthur Symons:** 1865–1945, English poet and critic. **Edward Martyn:** 1859–1923, Irish playwright. **Tulira Castle:** Martyn's home, in County Galway. **Fiona Macleod:** the pen name of the Scottish poet William Sharp (1855–1905). *The Archer:* rejected by *The Savoy,* the story was first published in Sharp's *Tragic Romances* (1897). **Greek . . . Daimons":** untraced. **London coroner:** William Wynn Wescott (1848–1925), one of the founders of the Order of the Golden Dawn. **Cabbala:** the esoteric theosophy developed in France and Spain in the thirteenth century. **a yachtsman:** unidentified. **Balzac's description:** Honoré de Balzac (1799–1850), French novelist, *Séraphita* (1834–35). **further light:** in *Autobiographies* (1926), Yeats attached a long note (first published in 1923) citing mythic analogues to his vision, provided by Vacher Burch, "a man learned in East Mediterranean antiquities." **Lady Gregory:** Lady Gregory (1852–1932), Irish writer. **once in London:** in May 1894. **her house:** Coole Park, County Galway. **a novel:** *The Speckled Bird,* never published by Yeats. **Hodos Chameliontos:** Yeats explains in section VII of "Hodos Chameliontos" that during these years (the mid-1890s) he "was lost in that region a cabbalistic manuscript, shown me by MacGregor Mathers [Samuel Liddell Mathers, 1854–1918, English occultist] had warned me of; astray upon the Path of the Chameleon, upon Hodos Chameliontos." **Flaubert's Saint Anthony:** Gustave Flaubert (1821–80), French novelist, *The Temptation of Saint Anthony* (1874). **Henry More:** 1614–87, English philosopher, *The Immortality of the Soul* (1659). **the next year:** 1897. **Dooney Rock:** on the shores of Lough Gill, County Sligo. **waterfall at Ben Bulben:** *Sruth-in-naghaidh-an-Aird* ("the Stream against the Cliff"), a waterfall on Ben Bulben, a mountain in County Sligo. **Inchy Wood:** one of the seven woods of Coole. **Emmanuel:** "God with us" (cf. Isaiah 7:14; Matthew 1:23). **Burkitt's** . . . *Christianity:* Francis Crawford Burkitt (1864–1935), professor of divinity, Cambridge University, *Early Eastern Christianity* (1904). **Gnostic Hymn:** the Gnostics were members of esoteric sects, for the most part derived from Christianity, of the second and third centuries. **Duras:** a promontory in County Clare. **French Count:** Count Florimond de Basterot (1836–1904), described by Yeats in *Memoirs* as "an old French count who had land on the seashore," Lady Gregory being "his principal Irish friend": "Paralyzed from the waist down through sexual excess in youth, he was spending his old age in the duties of religion and in attending chapel." **Synge:** John Millington Synge (1871–1909), Irish playwright. **Our theatre:** the Irish Literary Theatre, the forerunner of the Abbey Theatre, opened on 8 May 1899. **two volumes:** *Cuchulain of Muirthemne* (1902) and *Gods and Fighting Men* (1904). *Mabinogion:* a collection of Welsh tales from the eleventh to thirteenth centuries. *Morte d'Arthur:* published in 1485, a translation of old French poems about the legendary King Arthur of Britain (ca. sixth century) with adaptations from other sources, by the English writer Sir Thomas Malory (d. 1471). **John Shawe-Taylor:** (1866–1911), a Galway landlord and nephew of Lady Gregory; on 2 September 1902 called for a conference to discuss the acquisition by tenants of land at fair prices, which resulted in the Land Bill of 1903. **Hugh Lane:** 1875–1915, art collector and critic, another nephew of Lady Gregory; his offer to Dublin of his collection of modern paintings resulted in an extended controversy.

Dramatis Personae

First published *London Mercury,* November 1935–February 1936, and in book form by the Cuala Press, 9 December 1935.

VI. summer of 1897: Yeats went to Coole Park, the home of the Irish writer Lady Gregory (1852–1932) in County Galway, late in July 1897 and stayed until November. **miserable love affair:** with the Irish nationalist Maud Gonne (1866–1953). **Dowson:** Ernest Dowson (1867–1900), English poet. **girl in an Italian restaurant:** Adelaide Foltinowicz, the fifteen-year-old daughter of the restaurant keeper of the Poland restaurant in London. **"I have . . . fashion":** the refrain of Ernest Dowson's *"Non sum qualis eram bonae sub regno Cynarae"* (1896). *Visions and Beliefs: Visions and Beliefs in the West of Ireland, Collected and Arranged by Lady Gregory: With Two Essays and Notes by W. B. Yeats,* two volumes (1920). **Sligo:** the principal town of County Sligo, on the northwestern coast of Ireland. **mother's father:** William Pollexfen (1811–92). **father's grandfather:** John Yeats (1774–1846), rector of Drumcliff Church near Sligo. **witch-doctor:** unidentified. **Clare:** a county in Ireland. **Doneraile:** a village in County Cork. **Lord Castletown:** Bernard E. Castletown (1849–1937), Irish politician. **Biddy Early:** lived between Feakle and Tulla in County Clare, early to mid-nineteenth century. **her son:** Robert Gregory (1881–1918). **grandson:** Richard Gregory (1907–81).

XV. Moore: George Moore (1853–1933), Irish writer. *Diarmuid and Grania:* produced at the Abbey Theatre, 21 October 1901; not published until 1951. *Kubla Khan:* poem (1816) by the English writer Samuel Taylor Coleridge (1772–1834). *The Stream's Secret:* poem (1870) by the English poet and artist Dante Gabriel Rossetti (1828–82). *Deirdre:* a play by the Irish writer George W. Russell (pen name A.E.) (1867–1935), first produced 2 April 1902 by the Irish National Dramatic Society. **Fianna:** the warriors of the Fenian cycle of Irish mythology. *A Story-teller's Holiday:* published 1918. **last story:** *Aphrodite in Aulis* (1930). **Homeric:** of the age of the Greek poet Homer (ca. eighth century B.C.).

XXIII. her husband: Sir William Henry Gregory (1817–92). *Autobiography: Autobiography of Sir William Gregory* (1894). *Mr. Gregory's Letter-Box ... William Gregory:* published in 1898; letters to William Gregory (1762–1840), Under Secretary in Dublin, 1813–30. **Palmerston:** Henry John Temple, Lord Palmerston (1784–1865), Prime Minister of England 1855–58, 1859–65. **Wellesley:** Arthur Wellesley, Duke of Wellington (1769–1852), English general and Prime Minister, 1828–30, 1834. **Alfred Nutt:** Alfred T. Nutt (1856–1910), editor of the *Folk-lore Journal* and manager of the publishing firm of his father, David Nutt. **Malory:** Sir Thomas Malory (d. 1471), composed *Le Morte d'Arthur* (1485) from French poems and other sources. **eminent Trinity College professor:** Robert Atkinson (1839–1908), Professor of Romance Languages, Sanskrit, and Comparative Philology. Yeats is recalling Atkinson's testimony before a government committee studying the teaching of Irish in the schools, as reported in the *Daily Express* (Dublin), 23 February 1899: "asked if it was impossible to find an ancient Irish text book which was not silly or indecent, witness said . . . it would be difficult to find a book in which there was not some part in it of that sort." **Tudor English:** members of the Tudor dynasty occupied the throne of England 1485–1603. *Cuchulain . . . Men:* books by Lady Gregory, 1902 and 1904. **Roxborough:** an estate in County Galway, Lady Gregory's childhood home. **Percy's** *Reliques: Reliques of Ancient English Poetry* (1765), English and Scottish ballads collected by the English poet and antiquary Thomas Percy (1729–1811). **Kiltartan:** a barony in County Galway, near Coole Park. **"eternity . . . Carlyle:** Thomas Carlyle (1795–1881), Scottish essayist and historian, disliked the English essayist Charles Lamb (1775–1834), recalling in his *Reminiscences* (1881) that Lamb's talk was like "diluted insanity"; Yeats's "eternity glaring" is untraced. **Burial Service:** of the Irish Church. **"There one . . . heart":** lines 11–12 of "Coole Park, 1929," first published Lady Gregory's *Coole* (1931). **Synge:** John Millington Synge (1871–1909), Irish playwright. **"I saw . . . his people":** part of "Oisin's Laments" in *Gods and Fighting Men.* **Finn:** leader of the Fianna in the Fenian cycle of Irish mythology. **Grania . . . Diarmuid:** although betrothed to Finn, Grania elopes with Diarmuid. **" 'Sleep a little . . . the streams' ":** part of "The Wanderers" in *Gods and Fighting Men.*

The Bounty of Sweden

First published *The Bounty of Sweden: A Meditation, and a Lecture Delivered Before the Royal Swedish Academy and Certain Notes by William Butler Yeats* (1925).

II. **early in November:** 6 November 1923. **Nobel Prize:** for Literature, one of a series of prizes, awarded since 1901 and administered by the Swedish Academy of Science, at the bequest of the Swedish scientist and philanthropist Alfred Bernhard Nobel (1833–96). **Mann:** Thomas Mann (1875–1955), German novelist and critic, won the Nobel Prize for Literature in 1929. **Tagore:** Indian poet (1861–1941), won the Nobel Prize for Literature in 1913; in 1901 he had established a school to teach a blend of Eastern and Western philosophies. **Reuter:** Reuters, a news service founded by the German-born Paul Julius Reuter (1816–99). **quays:** docks.

III. **eight days later:** 14 November 1923. *Irish Times:* the most important newspaper in Ireland. **Gosse's . . . *Europe:* *Studies in the Literature of Northern Europe* (1879) by the English poet and critic Edmund William Gosse (1845–1928). **Life of Swedenborg:** Carl T. Odhner, *Emanuel Swedenborg, Servant of the Lord* (1901); Swedenborg (1688–1772) was a Swedish scientist, philosopher, and theologian. **ennoblement of his family:** Swedenborg was given a seat in the Swedish House of Peers in 1719, after he devised a method of transporting boats overland during the Siege of Fredrikshald (now Halden) in Norway.

XII. **Thursday:** 13 December 1923. **Academician:** a member of the Swedish Academy of Science. **King:** Gustav V (1858–1950), king of Sweden 1907–50. **Lady Gregory:** Irish writer (1852–1932). **Synge:** John Millington Synge (1871–1909), Irish playwright.

Memoirs

Having completed *Reveries Over Childhood and Youth* (1916), Yeats set to work on a continuation of his autobiography. In March 1921 he described the present manuscript as "Private. A first rough draft of Memoirs made in 1916–17 and containing much that is not for publication now if ever. Memoirs come down to 1896 or thereabouts." A considerable portion of the material appears in revised form in *The Trembling of the Veil* (1922). The full text of *Memoirs* was edited by Denis Donoghue and published in 1972.

X. **twenty-three:** Yeats dates this encounter with the Irish nationalist Maud Gonne (1866–1953) to 30 January 1889. **Miss O'Leary:** Ellen O'Leary (1831–89), Irish poet. **John O'Leary:** Irish nationalist (1830–1907). **Viceregal Court:** the English court in Dublin. **Bedford Park:** the Yeats family moved to Bedford Park in London on 24 March 1888. **father:** John Butler Yeats (1839–1922), Irish painter. **Blake:** William Blake (1757–1827), English poet and engraver; *Descriptive Catalogue* (1809): "The face and limbs that deviates or alters least, from infancy to old age, is the face and limbs of greatest Beauty and perfection." **the poet of antiquity:** Virgil (70–19 B.C.), Roman poet, the *Aeneid*. **Todhunter's ... *Troas:*** John Todhunter (1839–1916), Irish writer, *Helena in Troas* (1886). **Fairy ... *Peasantry:*** published in 1888. **The Countess Cathleen:** published in 1892. **Victor Hugo:** Victor-Marie Hugo (1802–85), French writer. **volume of ... translations:** *Translations from the Poems of Victor Hugo* (1885) by Henry Carrington. **Tristram of Lyonesse:** *Tristram and Lyonesse, and Other Poems* (1882), by the English poet Algernon Charles Swinburne (1837–1909), included "The Statue of Victor Hugo," one of his many tributes to the French writer. **Les Contemplations:** a volume of poems by Hugo, published in 1856. **Davis:** Thomas Davis (1814–45), Irish nationalist and writer. **O'Brien:** William O'Brien (1852–1928), Irish journalist and nationalist. **Boulangist:** Georges-Ernest-Jean-Marie Boulanger (1837–91), French soldier and politician, leader of a reform movement against the French Third Republic. *arrivistes:* ambitious and unscrupulous people. **"Animula Vagula" chapter:** in *Marius the Epicurean* (1885) by the English critic Walter Pater (1839–94). **young Brahmin:** Yeats met the Indian sage Mohini Chatterjee (1858–1936) in Dublin in 1885 or 1886. **"Blossom ... bosom":** from Yeats's "The Arrow," first published in *In the Seven Woods* (1903). **American ... novelists:** *Representative Irish Tales,* published in 1891 as part of the Knickerbocker Nuggets series by G. P. Putnam's Sons. **Victoria:** Victoria (1819–1901), queen of England 1837–1901.

XII: again in Ireland: Yeats traveled to Ireland in July 1891. **called:** on 22 July 1891. **she:** Maud Gonne. **little hotel:** the Nassau Hotel, South Frederick Street. **Orange Ulster ... Johnston:** the family home of Charles Johnston (1867–1931), a Theosophist and contemporary of Yeats at Erasmus Smith High School in Dublin, was at Ballykilbeg, County Down. **that evening:** 3 August 1891. **Howth ... Lighthouse:** Howth is a fishing village on a promontory on the north side of Dublin Bay. *The Countess Cathleen:* a play, first published 1892; "there is a kind of joy / In casting hope away, in losing joy, / In ceasing all resistance." **Sligo:** the principal town in County Sligo, in the northwest of Ireland. **George Pollexfen:** 1839–1910, brother of Yeats's mother, Susan Mary Pollexfen (1841–1900). **adopted a little child:** as Yeats learned several years later, on 11 January 1890 Maud Gonne had given birth to a son, Georges, by Lucien Millevoye (1850–1918), a French lawyer, journalist, and politician; Georges died on 31 August 1891.

XIII. Parnell's body: the Irish politician Charles Stewart Parnell (1846–91), died in Brighton in England on 6 October 1891 and was buried in Dublin on 11 October 1891. **Kingstown:** now Dun Laoghaire, County Dublin, the terminus of the ferry service between England and Ireland. **"Georgette":** little Georges, her son. **art school:** the Metropolitan School of Art, where Yeats studied 1884–86. **George Russell:** George W. Russell, pen name A.E. (1867–1935), Irish writer and painter. **draper's shop:** Pim's, in Dublin. **Theos-**

ophy: an occult philosophy developed by the Russian-born Helena Petrovna Blavatsky (1831–91), one of the founders of the Theosophical Society in New York in 1875. **Order:** Order of the Golden Dawn, an occult society into which Yeats was initiated on 7 March 1890. **Rahab ... Blake:** William Blake (1757–1827), English poet and engraver, *Jerusalem* (1804). **Esoteric ... Society:** from November 1888 until October 1890, in London. **initiated:** Maud Gonne was initiated into the Order of the Golden Dawn on 2 November 1891. **Nicholas . . . Pernella:** Nicholas Flamel (ca. 1330–1418), French alchemist; his wife, Pernelle (?–1397), assisted with his experiments. **sister:** Kathleen Pilcher (1868–1919). **her cousin:** May Gonne (1869–1929). **Young Ireland:** an Irish nationalist movement of the 1840s. **little patriotic society:** the Southwark Irish Literary Club in London, founded in 1883. **the most energetic of them:** unidentified. **T. W. Rolleston:** Thomas William Rolleston (1857–1920), Irish writer, editor of the *Dublin University Review,* 1885–86. **Jonson:** the phrase has not been traced in the work of the English dramatist Ben Jonson (1572–1637). In *Per Amica Silentia Lunae,* Yeats attributes "a hollow image of fulfilled desire" to the English writer Simeon Solomon (1840–1905), apparently misremembering *A Mystery of Love in Sleep* (1871): "a hollow image of unappeased desire." **his lyric:** "The Dead at Clonmacnoise." **Irish Literary Society:** founded in London on 28 December 1891. **Duffy:** Sir Charles Gavan Duffy (1816–1903), Irish nationalist and a cofounder of *The Nation* in 1842. **similar society:** the National Literary Society was founded in Dublin on 24 May 1892. **butter merchant:** unidentified.

XVI. plans: for furthering the "intellectual movement" in Ireland, particularly by establishing branches of the National Literary Society. **Land War . . . Plan of Campaign:** during the conflicts between landlords and tenants, a "plan of campaign" was urged by the Irish nationalists John Dillon (1851–1927) and William O'Brien (1852–1928): tenants should refuse to pay more than a fair rent; if the landlord did not accept that amount, they would pay nothing, and the funds would be used to aid evicted tenants. The plan was in effect from October 1886 to December 1890. **fall of Parnell:** the controversy over Parnell's relationship with Mrs. Katharine O'Shea (1845–1921) resulted in a split in the Parliamentary Party in November 1890, with the majority repudiating Parnell's leadership. **Home Rule:** Home Rule would have given the Irish Parliament the right to appoint the executive of Ireland, although taxing power would be retained by the British Parliament. The Home Rule Bill of 1886 failed to pass the British House of Commons; another bill in 1893 would fail to pass the House of Lords. **in Paris:** such as her speech to the Cercle Catholique des Étudiants du Luxembourg de Paris on 20 February 1892, described by Yeats in "The New 'Speranza' " (1892). **Michael Davitt:** (1846–1902), founder of the Irish National Land League in 1879. **Magnard:** Francis Magnard (1837–94), editor of the Paris newspaper *Le Figaro.* **"mysterious eye":** untraced. **quarrel . . . nine years:** the Parliamentary Party achieved a degree of unity in 1900 through the leadership of John Redmond (1856–1918). **Hyde:** Douglas Hyde (1860–1949), Irish scholar, founded the Gaelic League in 1893. **O'Leary:**

John O'Leary. **Purser:** Sarah Henrietta Purser (1848–1943), Irish artist. **Horse Show:** held each August in Dublin, a major social as well as equestrian event. **"fiery hand":** untraced.

XXIII. Third Rosses: Rosses Point, a seaside village near Sligo, County Sligo. **twenty-seventh year:** Yeats returned to London in late October 1891. **Henley:** William Ernest Henley (1849–1903), English writer and editor. **Hammersmith:** a district in London.

XXIV. literary dinner: in January or early February 1894. **woman of great beauty:** Olivia Shakespear (1863–1938), English novelist. **Eva Gore-Booth:** Irish poet and activist (1870–1926). **related to a member:** Lionel Johnson (1867–1902), English writer, her cousin. **Rhymers' Club:** a group of young writers who met on a regular basis in London during the early 1890s. *The Land of Heart's Desire:* first published 1894. **niece of a new friend:** Dorothy Paget (1885–1974), niece of the English actress Florence Farr (1860–1917). **went to Paris:** on 7 February 1894. **Mathers:** Samuel Liddell Mathers, later MacGregor Mathers (1854–1918), English occultist. **Bergson's sister:** in June 1890 Mathers married Moina Bergson (1865–1928), sister of the French philosopher Henri Bergson (1859–1941). **income . . . Order:** Annie E. F. Horniman (1861–1937), a fellow member of the Order of the Golden Dawn, provided Mathers an annual allowance of £449. **frater or soror:** male or female members of the Order of the Golden Dawn. **ill again:** Maud was pregnant with her daughter Iseult, born 6 August 1894. **soon to withdraw:** Maud Gonne resigned from the Order of the Golden Dawn in December 1894. **Horace:** Roman poet (65–8 B.C.). **Macpherson's Ossian:** the Ossian poems of the Scottish poet James Macpherson (1736–96) purported to be translations from a third-century Gaelic poet.

XXV. return from France: ca. 27 February 1904. **my play:** *The Land of Heart's Desire* was first performed at the Avenue Theatre, London, on 29 March 1894. **Diana Vernon:** the heroine of *Rob Roy* (1817) by the Scottish novelist Sir Walter Scott (1771–1832). **Her husband:** Henry Hope Shakespear (1849–1923).

XXX. my uncle's: George Pollexfen (1831–1910). **"Folly the comforter":** untraced. **Elizabethan:** of the age of Elizabeth I (1533–1603), queen of England 1558–1603. **Kew:** Kew Gardens, a botanical garden and park outside London. **her mother:** Harriet Maria Tucker (1821–1900). **each a woman friend:** Yeats's "sponsor" was perhaps Florence Farr; Olivia Shakespear's was probably Elizabeth Valentine Fox (1861–1931). **her house:** 18 Porchester Square, in London. **Dulwich Gallery:** in London. **Watteau:** Jean-Antoine Watteau (1684–1721), French painter. **National Gallery:** in London. **Mantegna:** Andrew Mantegna (1431–1506), Italian painter. **"The Shadowy Horses":** "He bids his Beloved be at Peace," first published in *The Savoy* (January 1896), begins "I hear the shadowy horses, their long manes a-shake." The other poems are probably "He gives his Beloved certain Rhymes," first pub-

lished in *The Savoy* (January 1896), and "A Poet to His Beloved," first pub-
lished in *The Senate* (March 1896). **flat . . . Temple:** Yeats moved into the
rooms of the English writer Arthur Symons (1865–1945) at 2 Fountain
Court, the Temple, London, in early October 1895. **Woburn Buildings:** Yeats
moved to his own rooms in 18 Woburn Buildings, London, in late February
or early March 1896. **Tottenham Court [Road]:** street in London. **January of
my thirtieth year:** in fact, his thirty-first, as he had completed his thirtieth year
on 13 June 1895. If January, the location would have been Fountain Court.
British Museum: then the site of the British Library as well. **da Vinci:**
Leonardo da Vinci (1452–1519), Italian artist, *The Notebooks*. **journey to
Italy:** possibly in early October 1896. **to Paris:** Yeats went to Paris in Decem-
ber 1896 and returned in January 1897. **in London:** in late February 1897.
many years: a letter from Yeats to Olivia Shakespear on 20 May 1900, about
the death of her mother, is the first evidence of renewed contact.

XL. Castle Rock . . . Lough Key: a fourteenth-century castle on Lough Key in
County Roscommon. **Hyde's father:** Reverend Arthur Hyde (?–1905). **Eleusis:**
a town in Greece, birthplace of the Eleusinian Mysteries, sacred rituals of
ancient Greece. **Samothrace:** island in the Aegean Sea, the center of the
ancient religious cult of the Cabiri. **Judea:** territory in Palestine, the setting of
most of the events in the Bible. **Slievenamon:** a mountain in County Tipper-
ary, associated with the *Tuatha Dé Danann,* the ancient gods of Ireland.
Knocknarea: a mountain in County Sligo, reputed to be the burial place of
Maeve, queen of Connacht in the Ulster cycle of Irish mythology. **Tarot:** a sym-
bolic set of cards, used to predict the future. **Unionist:** favoring the established
relationship between England and Ireland. **Coole:** the estate of the Irish writer
Lady Gregory (1852–1932) in County Galway. **Aengus:** god of love in Irish
mythology. **mistress:** Olivia Shakespear. **Lancelot:** lover of Guinevere, wife of
King Arthur, in Arthurian romance. **"I have . . . long":** untraced. **Emmanuel:**
"God with us" (cf. Isaiah 7:14; Matthew 1:23). **Eden:** in the Bible, the first
home of man. **Aedain:** usually Etain, in Irish mythology the second wife of Mid-
hir, a king of the sidhe. **woman I loved:** Maud Gonne. **some tale:** untraced.

XLIII: Belfast: the principal city in County Antrim in northern Ireland. **one
morning:** 7 December 1898. **Rutland Square:** in Dublin. **James Stephens:**
Irish nationalist (1825–1901), one of the leaders of the Fenian movement and
principal founder of the Irish Republican Brotherhood. **a relative:** Mary Ann
Cook, Comtesse de la Sizeranne. **command:** Thomas Gonne (1835–86) was
Assistant Adjutant-General in Dublin. **girl child:** Iseult Gonne (1894–1954).
Minerva: goddess of handicrafts in Roman mythology; identified with the
Greek goddess Athena.

Journal

The most important of the various journals and diaries of Yeats. The first entry
is dated December 1908; although most of the entries were made in 1909, Yeats

used the book as late as 30 October 1930. Many of the entries were published in *Estrangement: Being Some Fifty Thoughts from a Diary Kept by William Butler Yeats in the Year Nineteen Hundred and Nine* (1926) and *The Death of Synge, and Other Passages from an Old Diary* (1928). Denis Donoghue uses the title *Journal* in his edition of Yeats's *Memoirs* (1972).

10: PIAL: the initials of the motto in the Order of the Golden Dawn of Maud Gonne (1866–1953), Irish nationalist and Yeats's beloved: *Per Ignem ad Lucem,* "Through Fire to Light."

34: included in *Estrangement*. **Plutarch:** Greek biographer and essayist (46?–120), best known for his *Parallel Lives* of famous Greeks and Romans. **Wilde:** Oscar Wilde (1854–1900), Irish writer. **Whitman:** Walt Whitman (1819–92), American poet. **Wordsworth:** William Wordsworth (1770–1850), English poet. *Spectator:* an important London weekly.

35: included in *Estrangement*.

36: included in *Estrangement*. **Shakespeare:** William Shakespeare (1564–1616), English dramatist.

50: included in *Estrangement*. **Lady Gregory's:** Lady Gregory (1852–1932), Irish writer. **her son:** Robert Gregory (1881–1918). **my mother:** Susan Mary Yeats (1841–1900).

61: included in *Estrangement*. **Incarnation:** in Christianity, the union of the divine and the human in Christ. **thaumaturgy:** the working of wonders; miracle working; magic.

78: included in *Estrangement*. **Henderson:** W. A. Henderson, Secretary of the Abbey Theatre, 1906–12.

87: included in *Estrangement*.

107: included in *The Death of Synge*. **Saturnalia:** a weeklong Roman festival in honor of the god Saturn, who reigned during the Golden Age.

246: included in *The Death of Synge*.

Pages from a Diary Written in Nineteen Hundred and Thirty

Published posthumously in 1944.

XXI. *The Hosting . . . multitude":* Yeats's poems "The Hosting of the Sidhe" (1893), "The Everlasting Voices" (1896), and "To his Heart, bidding it have no Fear" (1896).

XL. Kant: Immanuel Kant (1724–1804), German philosopher. **Bacon:** Francis Bacon (1561–1626), English philosopher and statesman. **Newton:** Isaac Newton (1642–1727), English physicist and mathematician. **Locke:** John Locke (1632–1704), English philosopher. **Stendhal:** pseudonym of Marie-Henri Beyle (1783–1842), French novelist, *The Red and the Black* (1831). **Joyce:** James Joyce (1882–1941), Irish novelist. **Bennett:** Arnold Bennett (1867–1931), English novelist. **Galsworthy:** John Galsworthy (1867–1933), English novelist and playwright. **Synge:** John Millington Synge (1871–1909), Irish playwright. **O'Casey:** Sean O'Casey (1880–1964), Irish playwright, *The Silver Tassie* (1928). **A.E.:** pen name of George William Russell (1867–1935), Irish writer and painter. **Upanishads:** Hindu esoteric and mystical writings, ca. 400–200 B.C. *Celtic Twilight: The Celtic Twilight* (1893). **Blake:** William Blake (1757–1827), English poet and engraver. **Boehme:** Jacob Boehme (1575–1624), German theosophist and mystic. **Stephens:** James Stephens (1882?–1950), Irish novelist and poet. *Tain: Táin Bó Cuailgne,* "The Cattle Raid of Cooley" (seventh–eighth century), part of the Ulster cycle in Irish mythology. *Veda:* the oldest sacred literature of Hinduism. **Berkeley:** George Berkeley (1685–1753), Irish philosopher and clergyman. **Kilkenny:** county in Ireland. **secret society:** Berkeley founded the Philosophical Society on 10 January 1705/06. *Commonplace . . . this":* *Berkeley's Commonplace Book,* ed. G. A. Johnston (1930). **Salamis:** the Greeks defeated the Persians in the naval Battle of Salamis in 480 B.C. **Elizabeth:** Elizabeth I (1533–1603), queen of England 1558–1603.

NOTES TO CRITICAL WRITINGS

Ideas of Good and Evil

What is 'Popular Poetry'?

First published *Cornhill Magazine*, March 1902; included in *Ideas of Good and Evil* (1903).

Society: a nationalist society to which Yeats belonged in the mid-1880s. **Shelley:** Percy Bysshe Shelley (1792–1822), English poet. **Spenser:** Edmund Spenser (1552?–99), English poet. **pastoral play:** probably *The Island of Statues* (1885). **Allingham:** William Allingham (1824–89), Irish poet. **Ferguson:** Sir Samuel Ferguson (1810–86), Irish poet and antiquarian. **Connacht:** province in northwestern Ireland. **Adelphi:** a theater in London. **Italy:** Shelley left England for Italy in 1818. **"Yankee Doodle":** a popular eighteenth-century song of uncertain origin. **Victor Hugo's . . . Shakespeare:** Victor-Marie Hugo (1802–85), French poet and novelist, *William Shakespeare* (1864). **Shakespeare:** William Shakespeare (1564–1616), English dramatist. **Longfellow:** Henry Wadsworth Longfellow (1807–82), American poet. **Campbell:** Thomas Campbell (1777–1844), Scottish poet. **Hemans:** Felicia Dorothea Hemans (1793–1835), English poet. **Macaulay:** Thomas Babington Macaulay (1800–59), English writer and historian, *Lays of Ancient Rome* (1842). **Scott:** Sir Walter Scott (1771–1832), Scottish novelist and poet. **Burns:** Robert Burns (1759–96), Scottish poet. *Epipsychidion:* published 1821. **gardens of Adonis:** in *The Faerie Queene*; in Greek mythology, Adonis is connected with death and resurrection. **Tennyson:** Alfred, Lord Tennyson (1809–92), English poet, "Song—The Owl I." **Omar Khayyám:** *The Rubáiyát of Omár Khayyám*, a twelfth-century Persian poem translated in 1859 by the English writer Edward Fitzgerald (1809–83). **Jonson:** not in Ben Jonson (1572–1637), English playwright, but from "Of Beauty" (1625) by the English philosopher and statesman Francis Bacon (1561–1626): "There is no excellent beauty that hath not some strangeness in the proportion." **"Brightness . . . eye":** Thomas Nashe (1567–1601), English writer, "Adieu; Farewell Earth's Bliss" (1600); Helen, the legendary Greek beauty and cause of the Trojan War. **East . . . moon:** "The Land East of the Sun & West of the Moon" is a section of *The Earthly Paradise* (1868–70) by the English writer and designer William Morris (1834–96). **Whitman:** Walt Whitman (1819–92), American poet. **"ancestors . . . king":** *The Earthly Paradise.* **Aran:** an island off the west coast of Ireland. **"It . . . me":** a Gaelic poem translated as "The Grief of a Girl's Heart" by the Irish writer Lady Gregory (1852–1932) in *The Monthly Review* (October 1902). **Christ:** son of God in the Christian religion. **"I . . . earth":** a Gaelic poem translated as "The Invocation of the Graces" by Alexander Carmichael (1832–1912) in *Carmina Gadelica: Hymns and Incantations* (1900). **newer names:** Yeats helped organize the Irish Literary Society in London in 1891 and the National Literary Society in Dublin in 1892. **the prophet:** Enoch, in Jude 14–16. **"the imagination . . . himself":** derived from several comments by the English poet and engraver William Blake (1757–1827). **"His . . . government":** Blake's "The Everlasting Gospel" (1818).

Magic

First published *The Monthly Review,* September 1901; included in *Ideas of Good and Evil* (1903).

VIII. Aran Islands: three islands off the west coast of Ireland. **Faery:** in Irish mythology, the fairies are the descendants of the ancient gods of Ireland.

William Blake and the Imagination

First published *The Academy,* 19 June 1897; included in *Ideas of Good and Evil* (1903). William Blake (1757–1827), English poet and engraver.

Shelley: Percy Bysshe Shelley (1792–1822), English poet. **Wordsworth:** William Wordsworth (1770–1850), English poet. **Goethe:** Johann Wolfgang von Goethe (1749–1832), German writer. **Balzac:** Honoré de Balzac (1799–1850), French novelist. **Flaubert:** Gustave Flaubert (1821–80), French novelist. **Tolstoy:** Count Leo Nikolaevich Tolstoy (1828–1910), Russian novelist. **Whistler:** James Abbott McNeill Whistler (1834–1903), American painter. **Browning . . . hand":** Robert Browning (1812–89), English poet, Introduction to *Letters of Percy Bysshe Shelley* (1852). **Saracen:** in the Middle Ages, a Moslem. **Boehme:** Jacob Boehme (1575–1624), German theosophist and mystic. **"the body of God":** probably derived from Blake's *Jerusalem* (1804) or *Milton* (1804). **"the Divine Members":** *Milton.* **"every . . . holy":** *The Marriage of Heaven and Hell* (1790), *America: A Prophecy* (1793). *Vala:* 1797. **"foolish body":** letter to George Cumberland, 12 April 1827. **"phantom . . . water":** *Annotations to Lavater's "Aphorisms on Man"* (1789). **"vegetative . . . glory":** *A Vision of the Last Judgment* (1810). **Tennyson:** Alfred, Lord Tennyson (1809–92), English poet. *Songs of Innocence:* 1789. **"The Ideas . . . Evil":** "Ideas of Good and Evil," in Blake's Notebook. **"Prophetic Books":** the later long poems of Blake, including *Vala, Jerusalem,* and *Milton.* **correspondence . . . Israel:** in *Jerusalem.* **man's body:** as in *Milton.* **Axël:** a play (1886) by the French writer Villiers de l'Isle-Adam (1838–89). **Dante:** Dante Alighieri (1265–1321), Italian poet. **Mary:** mother of Christ. **Wagner:** Richard Wagner (1813–83), German composer: **Rhys:** John Rhys (1840–1915), Welsh philologist. **"Enitharmon":** in *Vala.* **Freia . . . Danu:** figures from Norse, Welsh, and Irish mythology, respectively. **"The joy . . . joy":** *Vala.*

The Symbolism of Poetry

First published *The Dome*, April 1900; included in *Ideas of Good and Evil*.

I. Symbolism ... *Literature:* Arthur Symons (1865–1945), English poet and critic, *The Symbolist Movement in Literature* (1899). **Shakespeare's talk:** William Shakespeare (1564–1616), English playwright, quoted by the English poet and playwright Ben Jonson (1572–1637) in *Timber, or Discoveries made upon Men and Matter* (1640); a "bull" in context means "empty talk, nonsense." **Wagner:** Richard Wagner (1813–83), German composer, between 1848–53 did not compose operas but worked in other genres and planned his tetralogy, *The Ring of the Nibelungen.* **Bardi:** Giovanni Bardi, Count of Vernio (1534–1612), gathered around him a group of scholars and musicians known as the *Camerata* ("salon") who began the development of modern opera. **Pléiade:** a group of seven sixteenth-century French poets. **pamphlet:** Joachim du Bellay (ca. 1522–60), French poet, *The Defense and Glorification of the French Language* (1549). **Goethe ... work":** Johann Wolfgang von Goethe (1749–1832), German writer; cf. *Conversations with Goethe* (1836–48) by the German writer Johann Peter Eckermann (1792–1854). **"to build ... a book":** Symons's introduction to *The Symbolist Movement in Literature.*

II. **"Symbolism in Painting":** first published as the introduction to *A Book of Images* (1898) by the English artist W. T. Horton (1864–1919). **Burns:** Robert Burns (1759–96), Scottish poet. **"The white ... me, O!":** "Open the Door to Me"; "white" should be "wan." **Blake ... dew":** William Blake (1757–1827), English poet and engraver, *Europe, a Prophecy* (1794). **Nash ... eye":** Thomas Nashe (1567–1601), English writer, "Adieu; Farewell Earth's Bliss" (1600). **"Timon ... cover":** *Timon of Athens* (1623). **O'Shaughnessy ... sighing:** Arthur O'Shaughnessy (1844–81), English poet, "Ode" ("We are the music makers") (1874); Nineveh, ancient capital of the Assyrian Empire. **Thessaly:** a region of ancient Greece. **Nine Hierarchies:** according to the *Celestial Hierarchy* of the mystical writer Dionysius the Areopagite (ca. 500), the lowest of the nine heavenly hierarchies are the angels. **"the eye ... all":** Blake, "The Mental Traveller" (1803). **"Our towns ... Babylonian heart":** Francis Thompson (1859–1907), English poet, "The Heart (ii)" (1897).

III. **symbolical and abstract poem:** perhaps *The Shadowy Waters* (1900).

IV. **"make a friend ... the air":** Blake, *A Vision of the Last Judgment* (1810). **Dante:** Dante Alighieri (1265–1321), Italian poet. **myth of Demeter:** in Greek mythology, Demeter was goddess of the corn and the harvest; her daughter, Persephone, was abducted by Hades, god of the underworld. Persephone's annual return from the underworld represents spring, her descent winter. **"I then ... difficulty":** Gérard de Nerval (1808–55), French writer, *The Dream and the Life* (1855). **Maeterlinck:** Maurice Maeterlinck (1862–1949), Belgian poet and playwright. **Villiers ... *Axël:*** play (1886) by the French writer

Villiers de l'Isle-Adam (1838–89). **somebody:** probably the French poet Stéphane Mallarmé (1842–98), as reported to Yeats by Symons.

V. Tennyson: Alfred, Lord Tennyson (1809–92), English poet. **beryl stone:** a magical stone used in scrying, or crystallomancy, as in "Rose Mary" (1881) by the English poet and painter Dante Gabriel Rossetti (1828–82). *Songs of . . . Experience:* Blake's *Songs of Innocence* (1789) and *Songs of Experience* (1794).

Ireland and the Arts

First published *The United Irishman,* 31 August 1901; included in *Ideas of Good and Evil* (1903).

William Morris: English poet and designer (1834–96). **Persephone:** in Greek mythology, the daughter of Demeter, carried off to the underworld by Hades. **burning . . . body:** the English poet Percy Bysshe Shelley (1792–1822) was cremated after his death in Italy. **Holy Family:** in the Christian religion, Joseph, his wife Mary, and her son, Christ. **Bearer of the Cross:** Simon of Cyrene carried the cross on which Christ was crucified. **art student:** Yeats studied at the Metropolitan School of Art, 1884–86. **Brown Bull:** in "The Cattle Raid of Cooley," part of the Ulster cycle of Irish mythology. **Patrick:** Saint Patrick (289?–461?), known as the Apostle of Ireland. **Young Ireland Societies:** Yeats belonged to one of these nationalist societies in the mid-1880s. **Davis:** Thomas Davis (1814–45), Irish nationalist and poet. **Brian Ború:** Brian of the Tributes (941?–1014), king of Ireland, slain at the Battle of Clontarf. **Whitman . . . own:** Walt Whitman (1819–92), American poet, "A Song of the Rolling Earth" (1881). **"excellent . . . strangeness":** from "Of Beauty" (1625) by the English philosopher and statesman Francis Bacon (1561–1626): "There is no excellent beauty that hath not some strangeness in the proportion." **Apostles:** the twelve disciples of Christ. **"The end . . . peace":** from "Peace in Life and Art" by the English poet Coventry Patmore (1823–96). ***Sero te . . . amavi!:*** "Too late have I loved thee, O Beauty so ancient and so new! Too late I have loved thee," from the *Confessions* (ca. 400) of the Christian theologian Saint Augustine (354–430). **Mass:** a ritual in celebration of Christ's sacrifice and his union with the faithful. **Ellis . . . authority":** Edwin John Ellis (1848–1916), English poet and co-editor with Yeats of the 1893 *Works* of the English poet and engraver William Blake (1757–1827), probably the "writer" mentioned. **Shelley's Italian light:** the English poet Percy Bysshe Shelley (1792–1822) traveled to Italy in 1818, where he remained until his death. **Highland:** the mountainous region of northern Scotland. **Burren Hills:** a rocky area in County Clare. **Robert Gregory:** Robert Gregory (1881–1918), the only child of Lady Gregory, was killed in World War I. **Cuchulain:** the main hero of the Ulster cycle in Irish mythology. **Baile and Aillinn:** figures in Irish mythology; Yeats explained that "Baile and Aillinn were lovers, but Aengus, the Master of Love, wishing them to be happy in his own land among the dead, told to each a story of the other's death, so that their hearts were broken and they died." **Hughes'** ... *Eurydice: Orpheus and Eurydice* (1897–1903) by the Irish sculptor John Hughes (1865–1941); in Greek mythology, Orpheus attempted to regain his bride, Eurydice, from the underworld. **Aengus and Etain:** in Irish mythology, Etain is the second wife of Midhir, a king of the *Sídhe*; Yeats understood them as lovers, writing that "Edain came out of Midhir's hill, and lay / Beside young Aengus in his tower of glass."

Samhain (1903)

The Reform of the Theatre

First published in *Samhain* (1903), a journal named after the Celtic festival for the start of winter on 31 October; included in "The Irish Dramatic Movement" section in volume IV of the *Collected Works in Verse and Prose* (1908).

Finn ... Lugaidh: Finn is the central character in the Fenian cycle of Irish mythology; as retold by the Irish writer Lady Gregory in *Gods and Fighting Men* (1904), Finn instructs the young Lugaidh's Son, "If you have a mind to be a good champion, be quiet in a great man's house." **Sainte-Beuve ... style:** Charles-Augustin Sainte-Beuve (1804–69), French writer and critic—although the remark appears to derive from the chapter "On the Writing of Essays" in *Dreamthorp*, by the English writer Alexander Smith (1830–67): "And style, after all, rather than thought, is the immortal thing in literature." **Falstaff:** a character in several plays by the English playwright William Shakespeare (1564–1616). **Hamlet:** character in Shakespeare's *Hamlet* (1603). *The Hour-Glass:* Yeats's *The Hour-Glass* (1903).

Samhain (1908)

First Principles

First published in *Samhain* (1908), a periodical named after the Celtic festival for the start of winter on 31 October; not included in "The Irish Dramatic Movement" section in volume IV of the *Collected Works in Verse and Prose* (1908); omitted, doubtless through oversight, from "The Irish Dramatic Movement" section of *Plays and Controversies* (1923); not restored until *Explorations* (1962).

I. Galway: county and city in Ireland. **Connacht:** province in northwestern Ireland. **French count:** Count Florimond de Basterot (1836–1904); his house was at Duras, a promontory in County Clare. *Un Grand Homme:* Honoré de Balzac (1799–1850), French novelist, *A Distinguished Provincial at Paris* (1839). **Arnold:** Matthew Arnold (1822–88), English poet and critic. **Ibsen:** Henrik Ibsen (1828–1906), Norwegian dramatist. **Macaulay:** Thomas Babington Macaulay (1800–59), English historian.

II. Young Ireland: a movement founded in 1842 to promote Irish culture and nationalism. **A.E.:** pen name of George W. Russell (1867–1935), Irish writer and painter. **Johnson:** Lionel Johnson (1867–1902), English poet; "Poetry and Patriotism," *Poetry and Ireland: Essays by W. B. Yeats and Lionel Johnson* (1908). **Tynan:** Katharine Tynan (1861–1931), Irish poet and novelist. **Mangan:** James Clarence Mangan (1803–49), Irish poet. **Burns:** Robert Burns (1759–96), Scottish poet. **Scott:** Sir Walter Scott (1771–1832), Scottish novelist and poet.

III. *Castle Rackrent:* novel (1800) by Maria Edgeworth (1767–1849), Irish novelist. *The Playboy: The Playboy of the Western World* (1907), by John Millington Synge (1871–1909), Irish playwright. **Kickham:** Charles Joseph Kickham (1828–1882), Irish novelist. **Banim:** Michael Banim (1796–1874), Irish novelist. **brother John:** John Banim (1798–1842), Irish novelist and playwright. **Radcliffe:** Anne Radcliffe (1764–1823), English novelist. **Griffin:** Gerald Griffin (1803–40), Irish novelist. **Carleton:** William Carleton (1794–1869), Irish novelist. **Lever:** Charles Lever (1806–72), Irish novelist. **Socratic:** refers to Socrates (470?–399? B.C.), Greek philosopher, who stressed the importance of self-knowledge. **Somebody:** untraced, although both the Scottish writer Thomas Carlyle (1795–1881) and the American writer Ralph Waldo Emerson (1803–82) argued that history is essentially biography. **French sense:** as *posé*, suggesting seriousness and gravity. **Goethe:** Johann Wolfgang von Goethe (1749–1832), German writer, *Wilhelm Meister's Apprenticeship* (1796).

IV. Elizabethan: of the age of Elizabeth I (1553–1603), queen of England 1558–1603. **Van Eycks:** the Flemish painters. Jan van Eyck (1390?–1441) and Hubert van Eyck (1370?–1426). **Corneille:** Pierre Corneille (1606–84), French dramatist. **Racine:** Jean-Baptiste Racine (1639–99), French dramatist. **Björnson:** Bjørnstjerne Martinius Bjørnson (1832–1910), Norwegian writer. **Boehme:** Jacob Boehme (1575–1624), German theosophist and mystic. **Mancini:** Antonio Mancini (1852–1931), Italian artist. **Lafayette:** a Dublin photographer who photographed Yeats in 1894 (and again in 1924). **certain pamphlet:** though in fact a short book, presumably *Das moderne Drama* (1852) by the German literary historian Herman Hettner (1821–82), a major influence on the Norwegian dramatist Henrik Ibsen (1828–1906).

V. *Les Comédiens . . . : The Unconscious Mummers* (1846). **Fourier:** Charles Fourier (1772–1837), French philosopher and socialist. **Savoy:** region in France. *The Hour-Glass:* Yeats's *The Hour-Glass* (1903). **principal actor . . . year:** presumably the Irish actor J. Dudley Digges (1874–1947), who played The Wise Man in *The Hour-Glass.* **Morris:** William Morris (1834–96), English writer and designer.

VI. *Cathleen ni Houlihan:* Yeats's *Cathleen ni Houlihan* (1902). *Gaol Gate . . . Moon:* Lady Gregory (1852–1932), Irish writer, *The Gaol Gate* (1909), *The*

Rising of the Moon (1903). **first played in the Abbey:** 27 December 1904, the opening night of the Abbey Theatre.

VII. preface to the *Comédie humaine:* Balzac's preface to "The Human Comedy," his extended series of novels and stories, was published in 1842. **Unionism:** the political position favoring the union of Ireland and England. **Michael Gillane . . . Cockade:** at the end of *Cathleen ni Houlihan,* Michael leaves to join the 1798 Rising against the English. Lady Gregory, *Dervorgilla* (1908); her love for Diarmuid results in the Norman invasion of Ireland. Lady Gregory, *The White Cockade* (1905); Patrick Sarsfield (d. 1693), Irish soldier who fought against the British. **Madame l'Épicière:** "Mrs. Grocer," i.e., the grocer's wife.

VII. my speech: 4 September 1908. **British Association:** the British Association for the Advancement of Science, which met in Dublin that year. **Adam . . . Eden:** in the Bible Adam is the first man, Eden the first residence of man.

The Cutting of an Agate

The Tragic Theatre

First published *The Mask* (Florence), October 1910; included in *The Cutting of an Agate* (1912).

Synge: John Millington Synge (1871–1909), Irish playwright; *Deirdre of the Sorrows* (1910), first produced at the Abbey Theatre 13 January 1910. **Ricard's portraits:** Louis-Gustave Ricard (1823–73), French painter. **Debussy:** Claude Debussy (1862–1918), French composer. **her lover:** Naoise. **unfinished work:** Synge died before completing the play. **him that had killed:** Conchubar. **Corneille:** Pierre Corneille (1606–84), French dramatist. **Racine:** Jean-Baptiste Racine (1639–99), French dramatist. **Shakespeare:** William Shakespeare (1564–1616), English dramatist. **Timon . . . last":** references to Shakespeare's *Timon of Athens* (1623), *Hamlet* (1603), and *Antony and Cleopatra* (1623). **"integrity of fire":** from the poem "Eros and Psyche" (1878) by the English writer Coventry Patmore (1823–96). **Falstaff:** character in several plays by Shakespeare. **Henry V:** Shakespeare's *Henry V* (1600). **translation . . . Dublin:** a translation by the Irish writer Lady Gregory (1852–1932) of *The Rogueries of Scapin* (1671) by the French dramatist Molière (1622–73), produced at the Abbey Theatre 4 April 1908. **Congreve's . . . course":** "Concerning Humor in Comedy" (1695), an essay in the form of a letter by the English dramatist William Congreve (1670–1729). **Thackeray's:** William Makepeace Thackeray (1811–63), English novelist. **big picture:** untraced. *Olympia* **of Manet:** Édouard Manet (1832–83), French painter, *Olympia* (1863). **Luxembourg:** a museum in Paris. **Sir Hugh Lane . . . Gonzales:** Sir Hugh Lane (1875–1915), art collector and critic (and nephew of Lady Gregory) owned Manet's 1869–70 portrait of his student Eva Gonzalès. **quarrel . . . window:** in *The Lame Devil* (1707) by the French writer Alain-René

Lesage (1668–1747) the "devil upon two sticks" explains a quarrel between a tragic poet and a comic author to the main character. **Titian . . . Bacchus:** there are two portraits of the Italian writer Ludovico Ariosto (1474–1533) traditionally ascribed to the Venetian painter Titian (1477?–1566); Yeats presumably refers to the one in the National Gallery, London. Titian's *Bacchus and Ariadne* dates from 1522.

Per Amica Silentia Lunae

First published 1918. The title, translated by Yeats as "Through the friendly silences of the moon," is from the *Aeneid* (II.255) by the Roman poet Virgil (70–19 B.C.).

"Anima Hominis": "Soul of Man"; Yeats dated this section "February 25, 1917."

I. marmorean Muse: in Greek mythology, the Muses are nine goddesses who inspire artists; Yeats described the poetry of the English poet Lionel Johnson (1867–1902) as "marmorean," resembling marble. **Dante . . . tuus":** in *La Vita Nuova* (ca. 1292–93), the Italian poet Dante Alighieri (1265–1321) describes a dream-vision of a "lord of terrible aspect": "Speaking he said many things, among which I could understand but few; and of these, this: *Ego dominus tuus*" ("I am thy master"). **Boehme . . . fruit":** Jacob Boehme (1575–1624), German theosophist and mystic, *The Forty Questions of the Soul* (1620).

V. Dowson: Ernest Dowson (1867–1900), English poet. **An old artist . . . ecstasy":** Yeats's father, John Butler Yeats (1839–1922); cf. his letter to Yeats of 2 July 1913. **wing-footed messenger:** in Greek mythology, Hermes, the messenger of the gods, wears winged sandals and hat and carries a magic wand; connected with Thoth, the Egyptian god of writing, and thus with the esoteric Hermetic writings of the first to fourth centuries. **ringers in the tower:** cf. "Julian and Maddalo" (1818) by the English poet Percy Bysshe Shelley (1792–1822). **Commons:** the House of Commons is one of the two houses of the British Parliament.

VIII. *Wilhelm* . . . destiny: Johann Wolfgang von Goethe (1749–1832), German writer, *Wilhelm Meister's Apprenticeship* (1796). **Heraclitus . . . destiny:** Heraclitus (540?–475? B.C.), Greek philosopher; Fragment 121, translated in Yeats's source as "Man's character is his fate." **"Doom eager":** "The Wanderer," an anonymous poem (ca. 975). **Seventh House:** in astrology, the seventh house governs marriage. **"sexual . . . hate":** untraced. **old Irish story:** untraced. **Slieve-na-mon:** a mountain in County Tipperary, a home of the gods in Irish mythology.

XI. Many years ago: August 1896. **Balzac . . . Man":** Honoré de Balzac (1799–1850), French novelist, *Séraphita* (1834–35). **Christ:** son of God in the Christian religion. **Buddha:** (583?–483? B.C.), Indian philosopher and founder of Buddhism. **Napoleon:** Napoleon Bonaparte (1769–1821), emperor of France. **Christian Cabbala . . . sun:** one of the central symbols in the Cabala, an esoteric theosophy first developed in the thirteenth century, is the Tree of Life, described by Yeats in *Autobiographies* as "a geometrical figure made up of ten circles or spheres called Sephiroth joined by straight lines. . . . The Sephiroth Tiphareth, attributed to the sun, is joined to the Sephiroth Yesod, attributed to the moon, by a straight line called the path Samekh, and this line is attributed to the constellation Sagittarius" (the Archer). Yeats also offers an interpretation of his vision by William Wynn Wescott (1848–1925), one of the founders of the Order of the Golden Dawn, an esoteric society to which he belonged: "The centaur is the elemental symbol and the woman the divine spirit of the path Samekh, and the golden heart is the central point upon the cabbalistic Tree of Life and corresponds to the Sephiroth Tiphareth." Yeats also notes that another occultist "reminded" him that "the cabbalistic tree has a green serpent winding through it which represents the winding path of nature or of instinct, and that the path Samekh is part of the long straight line that goes up through the center of the tree, and that it was interpreted as the path of 'deliberate effort,' " available only to those "who could attain to wisdom by the study of magic."

XIII. Landor . . . sing": Walter Savage Landor (1775–1864), English poet and prose writer, "Memory." **Ariosto . . . garden:** the Italian poet Lodovico Ariosto (1474–1533) retired to Ferrara in 1527 and devoted himself to his garden. **Wordsworth:** William Wordsworth (1770–1850), English poet, wrote little after 1835.

"Anima Mundi": "Soul of the World"; Yeats dated this section "May 9, 1917."

I. Connaught: province in northwestern Ireland. *A Tenedo . . . Lunae:* Virgil, *Aeneid* (II.255): "from Tenedos . . . by the friendly silence of the quiet moonshine." Tenedos is an island in the Aegean Sea. **Arab boy . . . antiquity":** "King Wird Khan, his Women and his Wazirs," in *A Plain and Literal Translation of the Arabian Nights Entertainment,* trans. Richard F. Burton (1885–86).

X. words written . . . Babylon: in Yeats's *The Hour-Glass* (1903): "There are two living countries, one visible and one invisible, and when it is summer there, it is winter here, and when it is November with us, it is lambing-time there." **"That . . . repentance":** *Nishikigi,* in *Certain Nobles Plays of Japan: From the Manuscripts of Ernest Fenollosa, Chosen and Finished by Ezra Pound, With an Introduction by William Butler Yeats* (1916). **"Time . . . away?":** Yeats's "The Moods" (1893).

XVI. pulsation of the artery: William Blake (1757–1827), English poet and engraver, *Milton.*

XXI. Shelley . . . thirst": Percy Bysshe Shelley (1792–1822), English poet, "Adonais." **Carlyle:** Thomas Carlyle (1795–1881), Scottish historian and essayist. **Swinburne:** Algernon Charles Swinburne (1837–1900), English poet. **Emmanuel:** "God with us."

A Vision

First published in 1925 (issued to subscribers on 15 January 1926); substantially revised for the 1937 edition. An earlier version of the introduction first published in *A Packet for Ezra Pound* (1929).

Introduction

XV. **Blake:** William Blake (1757–1827), English poet and engraver, *Milton* (1804–8). **Lewis:** Wyndham Lewis (1882–1957), English painter and novelist. **Brancusi:** Constantin Brancusi (1876–1957), Romanian-born French sculptor.

Book I: The Great Wheel

Part I: The Principal Symbol

II. **Simplicius:** a sixth-century scholar. **Aristotle:** Greek philosopher (384–322 B.C.). **Concord . . . Discord:** the Greek philosopher Empedocles (490?–430 B.C.) argued that all things are composed of four primal elements, combining and separating through the actions of two opposing forces. **Heraclitus . . . death":** Greek philosopher (540?–475? B.C.); Fragment 67, translated in Yeats's source as "Mortals are immortals and immortals are mortals, the one living the other's death and dying the other's life." **Pierre Duhem:** French philosopher (1861–1916), author of *Le Systeme du monde: Historie des doctrines cosmologiques de Platon à Copernic*, volume I (1913).

Part II: Examination of the Wheel

II. **Gentile:** Giovanni Gentile (1875–1944), Italian philosopher and educator. **Heraclitus . . . free":** Heraclitus, Fragment 25, "War is the father of all and the king of all; and some he has made gods and some men, some bound and some free." **Marxian:** of Karl Marx (1818–83), German political philosopher and revolutionary, the primary author of the *Communist Manifesto* (1848). **Plotinus:** Roman philosopher (205–70), the founder of Neoplatonism; cf. *Enneads* VI.9.6. **Dante . . . body":** Dante Alighieri (1265–1321), Italian poet, *Convito* (ca. 1304–7), exact phrase untraced. **Croce:** Benedetto Croce (1866–1952), Italian philosopher and historian.

Part III: The Twenty-eight Incarnations

Phase Fifteen. *Will . . . Body of Fate:* each of the twenty-eight phases is characterized by a certain balance among the Four Faculties of Will, Mask, Creative Mind, and Body of Fate. As explained in the 1925 edition, *Will* is "feeling that has not become desire because there is no object to desire; a bias by which the soul is classified and its phase fixed but which as yet is without result in action;

an energy as yet uninfluenced by thought, action, or emotion; the first matter of a certain personality—choice"; *Mask* is "the image of what we wish to become, or of that to which we give our reverence"; *Creative Mind* is "intellect, as intellect was understood before the close of the seventeenth century—all the mind that is consciously constructive"; and *Body of Fate* is "the physical and mental environment, the changing human body, the stream of Phenomena as this affects a particular individual, all that is forced upon us from without, Time as it affects sensation." **Christ:** son of God in the Christian religion.

Phase Seventeen. Shelley: Percy Bysshe Shelley (1792–1822), English poet. **Landor:** Walter Savage Landor (1775–1864), English writer. **Ahasuerus or Athanase:** Ahasuerus appears in Shelley's *Hellas* (1822) and *Queen Mab* (1813), Athanase in his "Prince Athanase" (1817). *Divine Comedy:* Dante's major work, begun ca. 1307 and completed shortly before his death. **Venus Urania:** Yeats knew from Mrs. Shelley's note to "Prince Athanase" that Shelley planned to show in the poem the progression from material to transcendent love, the latter symbolized in Greek mythology by Aphrodite (Venus in Roman mythology) Urania, the queen of the heavens. **Beatrice:** probably Beatrice Portinari (1266–90), Dante's beloved. **Great Yellow Rose:** an important symbol in the final section of the *Divine Comedy*. **"the groves . . . loves":** untraced, though "pale passion" occurs in "Descriptive Sketches" (1793) by the English poet William Wordsworth (1770–1850). **young man . . . thoughts:** in *Alastor* (1816). **old man . . . thou":** in *Hellas. The Cenci:* poetic drama, 1819. **Beatrice Cenci . . . father:** Beatrice Cenci (1577–99), Italian noblewoman, involved in the murder in 1598 of her incestuous father, Count Francesco Cenci. **a contemporary:** Giovanni Boccaccio (1313–75), Italian writer. **Byron:** Lord Byron (1788–1824), English poet. **first wife:** Harriet Westbrook (1795–1816). *Prometheus Bound:* lyrical drama by Shelley, 1820. *Per Amica Silentia Lunae:* prose work by Yeats, published in 1918.

Book V: Dove or Swan

IV. A.D. 1 to A.D. 1050. Byzantium: city founded by the Greeks ca. 660 B.C.; now Istanbul. **Justinian:** Justinian I (483–565), emperor of Byzantium 527–65. **St. Sophia:** Hagia Sophia ("Holy Wisdom"), the cathedral in Byzantium opened by Justinian in 537. **Academy of Plato:** in Athens, named after the Greek philosopher Plato (428?–347? B.C.), closed by Justinian in 529. **Gospel:** the Gospels are the four books of the New Testament describing the life of Christ. **Satan . . . Serpent:** the devil, depicted as a serpent in Genesis 3.

Essays for the Scribner Edition (1937)

Introduction

Written in 1937 for the unpublished Scribner "Dublin Edition"; first published 1961.

I. The First Principle. Dante: Dante Alighieri (1265–1321), Italian poet. **Milton:** John Milton (1608–74), English poet. **Shakespeare:** William Shakespeare (1564–1616), English playwright. **Raleigh . . . lie:** Sir Walter Raleigh (1552–1618), English courtier, navigator, and author, "The Lie" (1593–96?). **Shelley . . . mankind":** Percy Bysshe Shelley (1792–1822), English poet, "Julian and Maddalo" (1824). **Byron . . . sheath":** Lord Byron (1788–1824), English poet, "So, we'll go no more a roving" (1830). **Lear, Romeo:** characters in Shakespeare's *King Lear* (1608) and *Romeo and Juliet* (1597). **Oedipus:** in *Oedipus the King* and *Oedipus at Colonus* by the Greek dramatist Sophocles (496–406 B.C.). **Tiresias:** a blind prophet in Sophocles' *Antigone* and *Oedipus at Colonus*. **Rosalind:** in Shakespeare's *As You Like It* (1623). **Cleopatra:** character in Shakespeare's *Antony and Cleopatra* (1623). **Dark Lady:** figure in Shakespeare's *Sonnets* (1609). **"When mind . . . in happiness":** *Ten Principal Upanishads,* trans. Shree Purohit Swami and W. B. Yeats (1937), 45. The Upanishads are commentaries on the sacred scriptures of Hinduism. **"A wise . . . cannot give":** *Ten Principal Upanishads,* 109.

II. Subject-Matter. O'Leary: John O'Leary (1830–1907), Irish nationalist, spent five years in prison and fifteen years in exile for his role in the Fenian movement against British rule in Ireland. *The Faerie Queene:* poem (1590–96) by the English poet Edmund Spenser (1552?–99). *The Sad Shepherd:* pastoral play (1641) by the English playwright Ben Jonson (1572–1637). **pastoral play:** probably *The Island of Statues* (1885). *Prometheus Unbound:* poetic drama (1820). **one staged . . . the moon:** unpublished plays, identification uncertain. **Davis:** Thomas Davis (1814–45), Irish poet and nationalist. *The Nation:* the organ of the Young Ireland movement, which opposed British rule in Ireland. **Swift . . . bowels:** Jonathan Swift (1667–1745), English writer, *The Battle of the Books* (1704). **Homer:** Greek poet (ca. eighth century B.C.). **O'Grady:** Standish James O'Grady (1846–1928), Irish historian and novelist. **O'Curry:** Eugene O'Curry (1796–1862), Irish scholar. **Parliament:** the Irish Parliament, abolished in 1801, was dominated by the Anglo-Irish Protestant aristocracy. **Free State:** *Saorstát Eireann,* the Irish Free State, established in 1922. **Mitchel:** John Mitchel (1815–75), Irish writer and nationalist. **O'Donovan:** John O'Donovan (1809–61), Irish scholar, joined the Ordnance Survey in 1829. **banshee:** an attendant fairy that wails before a death. **Round Towers . . . fire-worship:** a view refuted by the Irish scholar George Petrie (1790–1866) in his *Essay on the Round Towers of Ireland* (1845). **rector:** unidentified; described in *Autobiographies* as "Uncle Beattie," though "no blood relation," and a "close friend" of Yeats's great-grandmother, Grace Armstrong Corbet (ca. 1768–1861). **withdrew support:** the Ordnance Survey was canceled in 1842. **Slievenamon:** a mountain in County Tipperary, a home of the gods in Irish mythology. **Olympus:** home of the gods in Greek mythology. **King:** Edward VII (1841–1910), king of England 1901–10. **Hayes O'Grady:** Standish Hayes O'Grady (1832–1915), Irish scholar. **Irish Literary Society:** Yeats and others founded the Irish Literary Society in London in 1891. **"fractured her . . . ocean's superficies":** cf. *Silva Gadelica: A Collection of Tales in Irish with Extracts Illus-*

trating Persons and Places (1892), though only the last quotation is exact. **Gregory ... Muirthemne:** Lady Gregory (1852–1932), Irish writer; *Cuchulain of Muirthemne* (1902), *Gods and Fighting Men* (1904). **Guest's Mabinogion:** a collection of Welsh heroic tales, translated by Lady Charlotte Guest (1812–95) in 1838–49. **Carlyle:** Thomas Carlyle (1795–1881), Scottish essayist and historian. **Sligo:** a town on the northwest coast of Ireland; home of Yeats's maternal grandparents. **Rosses Point:** a seaside village near Sligo. **Maeve ... mountain:** Maeve, a legendary queen of Connacht, is said to be buried on a cairn atop Knocknarea, near Sligo. *Visions and Beliefs: Visions and Beliefs in the West of Ireland* (1920), with contributions by Yeats. **Druidism:** the religious system of the ancient Celts. **"There is ... is perfect":** untraced; attributed elsewhere by Yeats to "some Irish saint, whose name I have forgotten." **Professor Burkitt ... the second:** Francis Crawford Burkitt (1864–1935), professor of divinity at Cambridge, sent Yeats a copy of his favorable review of Rev. John Roche Ardill, *St Patrick—A.D. 189* (1931). **The great ... Equinox:** the Irish method of calculating the date of Easter, the celebration of the resurrection of Christ, by the vernal equinox (ca. 21 March) had been discarded by the Roman Church in 343; the controversy was not resolved until the Synod of Whitby in 664. **Ark ... Egypt:** in the Bible, Noah's ark comes to rest on Mount Ararat in Turkey after the Flood; and Moses leads his people out of bondage in Egypt to the edge of Canaan. **Dionysus:** Greek god of wine and fertility. **tonsured:** the conflict between Irish and Roman styles of tonsure was another issue at the Synod of Whitby. **sign himself with the Cross:** a symbolic gesture indicating belief in the Christian Trinity of Father, Son, and Holy Spirit. **monk but not the bishop:** i.e., the local power of the monasteries rather than the power of the Church-appointed Bishop. *The Golden Bough:* James G. Frazer (1854–1941), English anthropologist and folklorist, *The Golden Bough: A Study of Magic and Religion,* first published in two volumes in 1890, expanded to fifteen by 1915. *Human Personality:* Frederic W. H. Myers (1843–1901), English poet and essayist, *Human Personality and its Survival of Bodily Death* (1903). **St. Patrick's Creed ... dead:** Saint Patrick (389?–461?), known as the Apostle of Ireland; "St. Patrick's Creed," included in his *Confessions,* states that Christ "is soon about to be the judge of the quick and the dead." **"the Self":** elsewhere Yeats quotes from the Chāndôgya Upanishad: "the wise man sees in Self those that are alive and those that are dead" (*Ten Principal Upanishads,* 109). **Neo-Platonism:** a system of philosophy derived from the work of the Greek philosopher Plato (ca. 428–ca. 347 B.C.), first developed in the third century A.D. **Cabbalistic ... Agla":** in the Cabala, an esoteric theosophy first developed in the thirteenth century, the Tetragrammaton consists of four Hebrew letters representing the name of God, and Agla is an acrostic of four Hebrew words meaning "thou art mighty, O Lord." **Doneraile:** village in County Cork. **Baroque and Rococo:** extravagant styles of the seventeenth and eighteenth centuries, respectively. **Synge:** John Millington Synge (1871–1909), Irish playwright, *The Well of the Saints* (1905). **Stephens:** James Stephens (1882?–1950), Irish novelist and poet. **Russell:** George W. Russell, pen name A.E. (1867–1935), Irish writer and painter. **firing ... 1916:** the execution of the leaders of the Easter

Rebellion in 1916. **Pearse:** Padraic Pearse (1879–1916), Irish writer and nationalist, one of the leaders of the Easter Rebellion. **Sacrifice of the Mass:** a ritual symbolizing the death and resurrection of Christ. **Red . . . Cuchulain:** Cuchulain is the main hero of the Red Branch, or Ulster, cycle of Irish mythology. **"Fall . . . world":** George Chapman (ca. 1559–1634), English dramatist, "Hymnus in Noctem." **Gaelic League:** founded in 1893 to preserve the Irish language. **aspidistra:** a small evergreen plant, associated with Victorian propriety. **Jesse:** in the Bible, father of King David. **MacDonagh:** Thomas MacDonagh (1878–1916), Irish writer and nationalist, one of the leaders of the Easter Rebellion. **"Johnny, I hardly knew ye":** an anonymous Irish street ballad, early nineteenth century. **Mr. Arnold . . . world":** Arnold Toynbee (1889–1975), English historian, *A Study of History* (1934). **Parnell:** Charles Stewart Parnell (1846–91), Irish political leader. **Swift:** Jonathan Swift (1667–1745), Anglo-Irish writer. **Lord Edward:** Lord Edward Fitzgerald (1763–98), Irish nationalist involved in the 1798 Rising. **Galway:** County Galway rather than the city. **Swedenborg:** Emanuel Swedenborg (1688–1772), Swedish scientist and mystic. **"That man . . . ages":** a favorite anecdote of Yeats. **Shree . . . Upanishads:** Shri Purohit Swami (1882–1941), trans. *The Holy Mountain: Being the Story of a Pilgrimage to Lake Amanas and of Initiation on Mount Kaila in Tibet* by Bhagwan Shri Hamsa (1934); *The Ten Principal Upanishads*. **Coole:** Lady Gregory's estate in County Galway. **rath:** raths are circular, prehistoric hill forts, believed to be inhabited by ancient gods in the form of fairies. **Judaism:** the religious culture of the Jews. **Unity . . . Dante:** the concept but not the phrase is found in Dante. **Blake's "Imagination":** Yeats elsewhere argued that to the English poet and engraver William Blake (1757–1827), "the historical Christ was indeed no more than the supreme symbol of the artist's imagination." **"eye . . . frog":** Shakespeare, *Macbeth* (1623). **A Vision:** first published 1925, revised 1937. **"deposit":** St. Paul uses the Greek word for "deposit" (*paratheke*) in the New Testament in reference to the spiritual heritage; interpreted as "tradition" by the English theologian John Henry Cardinal Newman (1801–90). **Lecky . . . day:** William E. H. Lecky (1837–1903), Irish historian, *A History of Ireland in the Eighteenth Century* (1892). **marriage:** to Bertha Georgie Hyde-Lees, 20 October 1917. **Morris:** William Morris (1834–96), English poet and designer. **Tibetan monk:** untraced. *Gulliver: Gulliver's Travels* (1726). **epitaph:** rendered by Yeats ("Swift's Epitaph") "Swift has sailed into his rest; / Savage indignation there / Cannot lacerate his breast. / Imitate him if you dare, / World-besotted traveller; he / Served human dignity," the first line and "world-besotted" being Yeats's additions. **dinner:** untraced; perhaps in 1931, in connection with the seventieth birthday of the Indian writer Rabindranath Tagore (1861–1941). **Wordsworth . . . thee":** William Wordsworth, English poet (1770–1850), "Poems dedicated to National Independence and Liberty: VII: To Toussaint L'Ouverture"; L'Ouverture (1743–1803) rebelled against French rule in Haiti and died in prison. **Emmet:** Robert Emmet (1778–1803), Irish nationalist, executed for leading an abortive rebellion against British rule in Ireland. **Sanscrit:** ancient language of India.

III. Style and Attitude. "**The Stream's Secret**": Dante Gabriel Rossetti (1828–82), English poet and painter, "The Stream's Secret" (234 lines). "**Dolores**": Algernon Charles Swinburne (1837–1909), English poet, "Dolores" (386 lines). **Burns:** Robert Burns (1759–96), Scottish poet. **Thomson:** James Thomson (1700–48), English poet. **Cowper:** William Cowper (1731–1800), English poet. **Thames valley:** the river valley above London. **Pound . . . Lawrence:** Ezra Pound (1885–1972), American poet; W. J. Turner (1889–1946), English poet; D. H. Lawrence (1885–1930), English novelist and poet. **Browne:** Sir Thomas Browne (1605–82), English physician; his *Religio Medici* (1642) uses an elaborate style. **delirium from pneumonia:** December 1929–January 1930, from Malta Fever. **Moore:** George Moore (1852–1933), Irish novelist. **salt . . . eternity:** in a note to *Visions and Beliefs*, Yeats attributes this idea to Jean Bodin, *De la Demonomanie des Sorciers* (1580). **Milton or Shelley's Platonist:** Milton, "Il Penseroso"; Shelley, "Prince Athanase." **tower Palmer drew:** "The Lonely Tower" (1879), an etching illustration of "Il Penseroso" by the English artist Samuel Palmer (1805–81), reprinted in *The Minor Poems of Milton* (1889). "**She should . . . awhile**": Shakespeare, *Macbeth* (1623), *Antony and Cleopatra* (1623), *Hamlet* (1603). **pelican:** thought to feed its young with its own blood and thus used in symbolic art to represent Christ. "**My baby . . . breast**": Shakespeare, *Antony and Cleopatra*. **some play:** untraced. **four Maries:** four companions since childhood of Mary, Queen of Scots (1542–87), queen of Scotland 1542–67. **letter of my father's:** this letter from John Butler Yeats (1839–1922) is untraced. "**cold . . . dawn**": Yeats's "The Fisherman" (1916). *Countess Cathleen:* Yeats's play *The Countess Cathleen* (1892), in blank verse. *The Green Helmet:* Yeats's play *The Green Helmet* (1910), in iambic heptameter (equivalent to ballad meter if the line is divided after the fourth stress). **Deirdre:** the lover of Naoise in Irish mythology and the main character in Yeats's play *Deirdre* (1907). **Cuchulain:** Yeats wrote five plays about Cuchulain: *On Baile's Strand* (1903); *The Green Helmet* (1910, revision of *The Golden Helmet*, 1908); *At the Hawk's Well* (1917); *The Only Jealousy of Emer* (1919); and *The Death of Cuchulain* (1939). The last three draw on the conventions of Japanese Noh drama, an elaborate form developed in the fourteenth century. **cast up . . . belly:** in the Bible, Jonah is swallowed by a "great fish" and stays in its belly for three days. **Queen . . . ballad:** Paul Fort (1872–1960), French poet, "The Queen in the Sea." **Bridges:** Robert Bridges (1844–1930), English poet. *Paradise Lost:* by Milton (1667). "**They snatch . . . skies**": untraced. **One of the more distinguished:** untraced.

IV. Whither? Young men . . . Sicily: probably C. Day Lewis (1904–72), English poet and novelist; and D. H. Lawrence, respectively. **Tube:** the London underground railway system. **Mallarmé:** Stéphane Mallarmé (1842–98), French poet. "**that ancient Self**": *Ten Principal Upanishads*, 30. **Leonardo:** Leonardo da Vinci (1452–1519), Italian artist. **O'Connell Bridge:** crosses the Liffey in the center of Dublin. **Victor Hugo . . . linnet:** Victor-Marie Hugo (1802–85), French poet, novelist, and playwright; remark untraced.

Introduction to *Essays*

Written in 1937 for *Essays* in the unpublished Scribner "Dublin Edition"; first published 1961.

Watts: George Frederic Watts (1817–1904), English painter. **Spenser:** Edmund Spenser (1552?–99), English poet. **Madox Brown:** Ford Madox Brown (1821–93), English painter. **Millaises:** paintings by John Everett Millais (1829–96), English painter. **Rossetti:** Dante Gabriel Rossetti (1828–82), English poet and painter. **Blake:** William Blake (1757–1827), English poet and engraver. **woman of genius:** Mrs. Patrick Campbell (1865–1940), English actress. **Burne-Jones:** Edward Burne-Jones (1833–98), English painter. **German connoisseur:** untraced. **"The Burne-Jones . . . eyes":** from "Hugh Selwyn Mauberly" (1920) by the American poet Ezra Pound (1885–1972). **Renoir:** Auguste Renoir (1841–1919), French painter. **one I knew best:** probably Pound. **rioters at the Abbey Theatre:** as at the production of John Millington Synge's *The Playboy of the Western World* in January 1907. **Wells:** H. G. Wells (1866–1946), English novelist. **Bulwer-Lytton:** Edward Bulwer-Lytton (1803–73), English novelist. **"deposit":** St. Paul uses the Greek word for "deposit" *(paratheke)* in the New Testament in reference to the spiritual heritage; interpreted as "tradition" by the English theologian John Henry Cardinal Newman (1801–90). **"Style" Pater:** "Style" (1888) by the English writer Walter Pater (1839–94). **Flaubert . . . *Salammbô*:** Gustave Flaubert (1821–80), French novelist, *Salammbô* (1862). **"I could . . . her":** cf. Flaubert's letter to Charles-Augustin Sainte-Beuve, 23–24 December 1862. **German actress:** probably Elisabeth Bergner (1900–86), Austrian-born English actress. **Shaw:** George Bernard Shaw (1856–1950), Irish playwright. **Eliot:** T. S. Eliot (1888–1965), poet and critic. **de Valois:** Ninette de Valois (1898–), Irish dancer and choreographer. **brothers Carracci:** Agostino (1557–1602) and Annibale (1560–1609) Carracci were brothers, Lodovico Carracci (1555–1619) their cousin; the painting *Butcher Shop* (ca. 1582–83), probably by Annibale Carracci, may depict the three of them as butchers. **Whitman:** Walt Whitman (1819–92), American poet. **a woman:** possibly a waitress discovered by Rossetti at the Bell Savage Inn in London. **Mrs. Langtry:** Lillie Langtry (1853–1929), English actress and famous beauty; Watts painted her portrait in 1880. **Lady Gregory:** Lady Gregory (1852–1932), Irish writer. **Rimbaud:** Arthur Rimbaud (1854–91), French poet, "The Ladies who Look for Lice" (1882–83). **Silver Age:** follows the Golden Age in Greek mythology; dominated by sensuality. **Rubensesque:** Peter Paul Rubens (1577–1640), Flemish painter. **Caesar:** Gaius Julius Caesar (ca. 100–44 B.C.), leader of Rome, was assassinated; Alexander the Great (356–323 B.C.), conqueror of much of the eastern world, died of a fever. *A Vision:* published 1925, revised 1937. **Boehme:** Jacob Boehme (1575–1624), German theosophist and mystic. **"schoolmates only":** untraced.

Introduction to *Plays*

Written in 1937 for *Plays* in the unpublished Scribner "Dublin Edition"; first published 1961.

I. The theatre: the Abbey Theatre, Dublin. **Sara . . . Synge:** Sara Allgood (1883–1950); Molly Allgood, "Marie O'Neill" (1885–1952); William G. Fay (1872–1947); Frank J. Fay (1870–1931); Lady Gregory (1852–1932); John Millington Synge (1871–1909). **patriotic society:** *Inghinidhe na hÉireann,* "Daughters of Ireland," founded 1900 by Maud Gonne, Irish nationalist and Yeats's beloved. **coffee-house:** Coffee Palace Hall, Dublin. **printed diaries:** *Estrangement,* section 52. **Sara Bernhardt . . .** *Phèdre:* Sarah Bernhardt (1844–1923), French actress; the lead in *Phèdre* (1677) by the French playwright Jean Racine (1639–99) was one of her most famous roles. *The Well of the Saints:* by Synge, first produced at the Abbey Theatre, 4 February 1905. **Talma:** François Joseph Talma (1762–1826), French actor. **Gordon Craig:** Edward Gordon Craig (1872–1966), English stage designer. **"shivering . . . yard":** cf. "shivering into seventy years," Lady Gregory, *The Workhouse Ward* (1908); cf. "an old braying jackass strayed upon the rocks," Synge, *The Playboy of the Western World* (1907).

II. Ricketts . . . costume: Charles Ricketts (1866–1931), English painter and stage designer, designed a costume in 1904 for a planned prologue to Yeats's *The Shadowy Waters* (1900). **O'Casey:** Sean O'Casey (1880–1964), Irish playwright. **Browning . . . character:** Robert Browning (1812–89), English poet, preface to his play *Strafford* (1837). **Indian tale:** untraced.

On the Boiler

First published posthumously in 1939.

Preliminaries

IV. American tour: from September 1937 to May 1938. **founders:** Lady Gregory (1852–1932), Irish writer; John Millington Synge (1871–1909), Irish playwright; and Yeats. **Miss O'Neill . . . fools":** Molly Allgood, "Marie O'Neill" (1885–1952), Irish actress, in *Deirdre of the Sorrows,* first performed 13 January 1910. **Kerrigan . . . Anne":** J. M. Kerrigan (1885–1964), Irish actor, and O'Neill in *The Full Moon,* first performed 10 November 1910. **Frank Fay's . . . Saints:** Frank J. Fay (1870–1931), Irish actor, in Synge's *The Well of the Saints,* first performed 4 January 1905. **William Fay . . . Strand:** W. G. Fay (1872–1947), Irish actor, in Yeats's *On Baile's Strand,* first performed 27 January 1904. **Mrs. Patrick Campbell . . .** *Deirdre:* Mrs. Patrick Campbell (1865–1940), English actress, first performed in *Deirdre* on 9 November 1908. **Ninette de Valois . . .** *Waves:* Ninette de Valois (1898–), Irish dancer and choreographer, in Yeats's *Fighting the Waves,* first performed 13 August 1929.

NOTES TO PROSE FICTION

The Celtic Twilight (1893, 1902)

'Dust Hath Closed Helen's Eye' (1899)

First published *The Dome* (October 1899); included in the revised edition of *The Celtic Twilight* (1902). **"Dust . . . Eye"**: from "Adieu; Farewell Earth's Bliss" (1600) by the English writer Thomas Nashe (1567–1601).

1. square castle, Ballylee: Yeats purchased the property, a Norman tower with two attached cottages, in 1917; renamed it Thoor Ballylee (Irish *Túr*); and spent several summers there. **Biddy Early**: (1798–1874), known as a healer and someone able to predict the future; discussed in Yeats's essay "Ireland Bewitched" (1899). **Mary Hynes**: a celebrated beauty who died in the early 1840s. **cranky**: gnarled, from Irish *creanncaí*. **Raftery . . . about her"**: Antony Raftery (1784–1835), Gaelic poet, "Mary Hynes, or The Posy Bright"; a translation by the Irish writer Lady Gregory (1852–1932) is found later in the story. **"verses . . . dispraising it"**: Raftery's "The Story-telling of the Bush." **a friend**: Lady Gregory. **Kilbecanty**: a village in County Galway. **Cloone Bog**: in County Galway. **Derrybrien . . . Echtge hills**: a village in a range of mountains in County Galway and County Clare; Echgthe is said to be of the *Tuatha Dé Danann*, the ancient gods of Ireland. **"the stag . . . wolves"**: from a Gaelic poem, translated by Lady Gregory in *Gods and Fighting Men* (1904). **Ardrahan**: a village in County Galway. **Poisin Glegeal**: *An Pósaidh Glégeal*, "The Bright Posy." **Kinvara**: a barony in County Galway. **Duras**: a village in County Galway. **Troy . . . Helen**: in Greek mythology, the abduction of Helen of Troy caused the Trojan War. *na mna Sidhe*: "of the fairy woman." **Coole**: Lady Gregory's estate in County Galway. **Kiltartan**: a village in County Galway. **Rahasine**: Rahasane Park, originally the name of an estate near Craughwell, County Galway. **Hyde**: Douglas Hyde (1860–1949), Irish folklorist and Gaelic scholar.

Regina, Regina Pigmeorum, Veni

First published in *The Celtic Twilight: Men and Women, Dhouls and Faeries* (1893). The title means "Queen, Queen of the Fairies, Come." **One night**: ca. 14 October 1892. **middle-aged man**: Yeats's uncle, George Pollexfen (1839–1910). **young girl**: Lucy Middleton, a cousin of Yeats. **Windsor Forest**: near London. **Lilly**: William Lilly (1602–81), English astrologer, *History of His Life and Times* (1715). **Mayo woman**: Mary Battle, a servant of Yeats's uncle; Mayo, a county in Ireland. **Mathers**: Samuel Liddell Mathers, later MacGregor Mathers (1854–1918), English occultist and one of the founders of the Order of the Golden Dawn.

The Adoration of the Magi (1897)

First published in *The Tables of the Law. The Adoration of the Magi* (1897); intended for *The Secret Rose* (1897) but excluded at the request of the publisher. **Magi:** in Christian tradition, the Magi, Wise Men from the East, journey to Bethlehem to worship the infant Christ. **Aherne:** Owen Aherne, an invented character who also appears in the companion story, "The Tables of the Law" (1896). **Inquietude . . . Mallarmé:** Stéphane Mallarmé (1842–98), French poet, "Poetry and Music in France" (*National Observer,* 26 March 1892). **poteen:** an alcoholic beverage made from potatoes. **Virgil:** Roman poet (70–19 B.C.). **Homer:** Greek poet (ca. eighth century B.C.). **Michael Robartes:** an invented character who also appears in the companion story "Rosa Alchemica" (1896). **Saint Brendan:** Irish monk (486?–578?), granted a vision of secret islands to which he attempted to travel. **Islands of the Young:** *Tír na nÓg,* "the Land of the Young," the Elysium of Irish mythology, home of the gods and of the dead. **Phaeacians:** as Yeats explained, in the *Odyssey* the Phaeacians "told Odysseus that they had set their hearts in nothing but 'in the dance and changes of raiment, and love and sleep.' " **Fifth Eclogue:** an error for the *Fourth Eclogue,* in which Virgil prophesies a repetition of the past, including a second Trojan War. **Leda:** in Greek mythology, Leda is impregnated by the god Zeus in the form of a swan. **Achilles:** one of the leaders of the Greeks in the Trojan War, caused by Paris' abduction of Helen, a daughter of Leda by Zeus. **Seine:** the river which flows through Paris. **Hermes:** in Greek mythology, Hermes is the messenger of the gods. **unicorn:** a mythical beast, pure white with the shape of a horse and a long horn on its forehead, often symbolic of chastity. **manger:** the birthplace of Christ in Christian tradition. **Saint Patrick:** (389?–461?), known as the Apostle of Ireland. **Black Mass:** an inversion of the Roman Catholic Mass, worshiping Satan rather than Christ. **Order . . . Rose:** the Rose was a major symbol in the Order of the Golden Dawn, an occult society to which Yeats belonged. **"Seacht . . . air":** an inaccurate text and translation of the first six lines of a Gaelic poem sent to Yeats on 2 November 1896 by the poet and translator G. A. Greene (1853–1921). **paters:** prayers. **Mary . . . Son:** in Christianity, the Virgin Mary is the mother of Christ. **Bridget:** Saint Bridget (453?–524?), one of the three patron saints of Ireland.

Stories of Red Hanrahan (1905)

Red Hanrahan (1903)

First published *The Independent Review,* December 1903; included in *Stories of Red Hanrahan* (1905). **Hanrahan:** an invented character, largely based on the Gaelic poet Eoghan Ruadh Ó Súilleabháin (Owen Roe O'Sullivan, 1748–84). **hedge schoolmaster:** Yeats explained that in the eighteenth century, "government had done its best to crush out education," and thus "Ireland was plentifully stored with hedge schoolmasters," "men who set up school behind the hedges." **Samhain Eve:** October 31, the Celtic festival to celebrate the start of winter. **Munster . . . Connacht:** two of the four provinces of Ireland. **Kilchriest:** village in County Galway. **Loughrea:** village in County Galway. **Virgil:** Roman poet (70–19 B.C.). **Mary Lavelle:** O'Sullivan's sweetheart was named Mary Casey. **Venus:** goddess of love and beauty in Roman mythology. **Lough Greine:** a lake in County Clare, fed by the river Graney. **coppers:** one-penny coins. **Granagh:** a townland in County Galway. **Ballylee:** a townland in County Galway. **Slieve Echtge:** Slieve Echgthe, a range of mountains in County Galway and County Clare; Echgthe is said to be of the *Tuatha Dé Danann,* the ancient gods of Ireland. **cauldron . . . sword:** cf. the Four Treasures of the *Tuatha Dé Danann:* the Cauldron of the Dagda, the Stone of Destiny, the Spear of Lugh, and the Sword of Nuada. **Silver Hand:** Nuada of the Silver Hand. **Daire-caol:** "the narrow oak wood," in Slieve Echgthe. **Druim-da-rod:** "the ridge of the two roads," in Slieve Echgthe. **Cappaghtagle:** "the plot of rye land," a townland in County Galway.

The Death of Hanrahan

First published as "The Death of O'Sullivan the Red" in *The New Review* (December 1896) and included in *The Secret Rose* (1897) as "The Death of Hanrahan the Red"; significantly revised for *Stories of Red Hanrahan* (1905). **Slieve Echtge:** Slieve Echgthe, a range of mountains in County Galway and County Clare; Echgthe is said to be of the *Tuatha Dé Danann,* the ancient gods of Ireland. **Illeton . . . Ballylee:** townlands in County Galway. **Kinadife:** *Coill na Daibchce,* "the Wood of the Cauldron," between Illeton and Scalp. **Lake Belshragh:** small lake on the top of Slieve Echgthe in County Galway. **Sidhe:** the fairies, understood as the immortal gods of ancient Ireland. **grey-haired women:** also in the story "Red Hanrahan." **Cherubim and Seraphim:** two classes of angels in the Old Testament. **keen:** a wailing lament for the dead.